LITERACY IN EARLY
MODERN EUROPE

To
Keith and Eva

LITERACY IN EARLY MODERN EUROPE

CULTURE AND EDUCATION 1500–1800

R. A. Houston

Second Edition

An imprint of **Pearson Education**

Harlow, England · London · New York · Reading, Massachusetts · San Francisco
Toronto · Don Mills, Ontario · Sydney · Tokyo · Singapore · Hong Kong · Seoul
Taipei · Cape Town · Madrid · Mexico City · Amsterdam · Munich · Paris · Milan

PEARSON EDUCATION LIMITED

Head Office:
Edinburgh Gate
Harlow CM20 2JE
Tel: +44 (0)1279 623623
Fax: +44 (0)1279 431059

London Office:
128 Long Acre
London WC2E 9AN
Tel: +44 (0)20 7447 2000
Fax: +44 (0)20 7240 5771
Website: www.history-minds.com

First published in Great Britain in 2002

© Pearson Education Limited 2002

The right of R. A. Houston to be identified as Author
of this Work has been asserted by him in accordance
with the Copyright, Designs and Patents Act 1988.

ISBN 0 582 36810 3

British Library Cataloguing in Publication Data
A CIP catalogue record for this book can be obtained from the British Library

Library of Congress Cataloging in Publication Data
A CIP catalog record for this book can be obtained from the Library of Congress

Transferred to digital print on demand, 2006

Typeset in 11.5/14pt Garamond MT by Graphicraft Limited, Hong Kong

The Publisher's policy is to use paper manufactured from sustainable forests.
Printed and bound by CPI Antony Rowe, Eastbourne

CONTENTS

of everyday communication than in an alien one, and easier if it uses phonetic spelling. Because of the diversity of social, political and economic structures across Europe, it would be unrealistic to expect that any single combination of these could be used to explain developments over the whole continent. Their relative significance varied over time and space.

The writings of educational theorists can be studied to determine prevailing attitudes to education among intellectuals, clerics and secular administrators who established the principles and guided the implementation of educational 'policy'. However, assessing the effect of education on pupils or the reasons why parents chose to educate their children is a good deal harder because of shortcomings in documentation. Direct evidence of attitudes and aspirations is rare and it is usually necessary to infer from prescription or casual allusion and from patterns of school attendance and literacy which fit the rest of the social context. Such inferences are, nevertheless, essential since 'an education incorporates three distinct things: a conscious cultural tradition, an educational ideology, and a curriculum' (Grafton and Jardine 1986: 219). Much of this book depends on quantitative material which, in the words of Dr Johnson, 'brings everything to a certainty which before floated in the mind indefinitely'. Yet statistical skeletons need to be fleshed out by more qualitative material when discussing meanings and understandings.

Much space could be used trying to define literacy. While the ability to sign one's name is a useful and much used indicator, it is best to think not of one literacy, but of several litera*cies*, of a variety of ways in which the products of a culture can be acquired and transmitted. *Reading* of print or writing was possible at two levels. Some people could decipher texts, read them aloud and memorise them in a mechanical or ritual way – though their personal understanding may have been questionable. The facility of those who possessed this intermediate or semi-literacy should not be exaggerated. Those with better education and a deeper immersion in printed and written culture could comprehend the text with greater precision, reading and thinking silently. They could understand new texts as well as familiar ones. However, reading was not restricted to written or printed words alone. People could gather information and ideas from *looking*: interpreting pictures and prints in broadsheets and pamphlets or watching and participating in plays and processions. Gesture remained a subtle and important form of non-verbal communication.

If they wanted to transmit their own thoughts other than through speech, people had to learn to *write*, or rather compose – an advanced skill which required considerable training and practice, and which effectively marked full literacy for most people. The other, more common, level of writing was in fact copying or writing without necessarily understanding. It was at this stage that people learned to sign their names on documents, and this ability is commonly used as an indicator that someone could read and understand printed and written texts in the vernacular: the language of everyday life. A small minority of men could also copy or compose in Latin, the international language of learning throughout the middle ages and the sixteenth century, or in another pan-European language like French which came to take its place in the eighteenth century. Even those who had none of these skills were not culturally isolated for they could *listen* – hear a priest's sermons or a friend reading aloud – and therefore participate actively or passively in discussions with their peers. Finally comes numeracy, which ranged from the fundamental and nearly ubiquitous skill of day-to-day counting through formal arithmetic to abstract and esoteric mathematical sciences. The way to understand literacy in early modern Europe is to assess the access which people had to the different bands in the spectrum and the ways they used them.

The imperfect nature of early modern sources generally makes it necessary to categorise people as literate or illiterate. However these are best seen not as discrete categories, but as steps in a hierarchy of skills. At the same time, seeing and listening could bridge the gap between literate and illiterate. What is more, literacy can be used for different purposes: to serve some practical or *functional* end such as economic need among tradesmen, in which case reading and writing would be advantageous; or to fulfil a religious need, where reading alone is all that is commonly required. In the words of Harvey Graff (1987: 4), literacy 'is above all a technology or set of techniques for communications and for decoding and reproducing written or printed materials'.

A negative definition is also possible. Illiteracy could mean inability to read and write Latin (the medieval *illitteratus*). The first known use of 'illiterate' in English was in 1556. The word *illettré* was scarcely used in north-east France or the southern Netherlands until the mid-eighteenth century, when it was included in Trévoux's *Dictionnaire Universel* to mean someone who did not know anything about literature; *non lettré* meant without Latin. The word *analphabète* did not come into use until the late nineteenth century (Ruwet and Wellemans 1978: 14).

Just as literacy can be defined in different ways, so can it be acquired by following a variety of paths. The most obvious was attending a formal school held by a professional schoolmaster. However not all schools were in dedicated buildings. Some teachers worked in the homes of the pupils they taught or in barns and outhouses; they moved to their pupils rather than the children coming to a building designated as a school. Children might learn in the home from parents or older children or kin. Schooling was more often an expression of social practices rather than a discrete phase of the life cycle lived out in the distinctive environment of a formal classroom. Furthermore, the school could be an expression of a desire for learning as much as it was an independent stimulator of literacy. Schooling must be seen in the context of social and economic life in early modern Europe as well as being regarded as an autonomous force. Education and literacy created certain opportunities, but they were themselves dependent on the societies in which they grew and can thus be treated both as agents of change and as indicators or even products of social developments.

The institutional frameworks, social norms and mental climate in which people lived between the Renaissance and the Industrial Revolution were very different from those of the modern world. Educational provision was, to modern eyes, fragmented and the scale of schools was small. The purposes of education may seem restrictive and the uses to which it could be put may appear limited. The family and the local community were far more significant to everyday life, communications were rudimentary, technology primitive, life expectancy at birth short (35 years on average), the role of magic and religion in everyday life pervasive – the latter was 'the idiom in which men thought' – concepts of 'liberty', 'democracy' and 'equality' as they are presently understood were almost unknown. The societies of early modern Europe were varied both in their internal makeup and when compared with each other. Anything more than the broadest similarities in patterns and development should not be expected since there are bound to be inconsistencies, anomalies and contradictions in the structures of education and literacy and the way they changed.

The first part of this book deals with the ways in which people became literate, both in and out of school, and analyses the educational hierarchy, teaching methods, teachers and the forces behind developments in schooling in the early modern period. Alternative pathways to literacy are set alongside the demand for learning. Developments in higher education are also summarised. A chapter on the extent of reading and writing follows one on sources for the study of early modern literacy. The uses of literacy are discussed, including substantial chapters on book production, distribution, ownership and reading. The mental world of early modern readers is considered at different points in Chapters 8 and 9. Language differences and their impact on literacy and communication are assessed. Finally, the significance of literate and oral communication to cultural stability and change is considered.

The early modern period witnessed substantial changes in political, religious, economic and social life. Yet alongside these developments there were also significant enduring characteristics which tempered their impact. The central themes of this book can be summarised under these two headings, beginning with continuities. The educational hierarchy comprised an anarchic and geographically uneven variety of overlapping and sometimes competing components. The standard of teaching too was far from uniform. Teaching methods and materials changed little until the eighteenth or even nineteenth century. At both elementary and more advanced levels the pedagogic regime was often rigidly traditional, designed to pass on an agreed body of knowledge and more or less fixed interpretations. Formal schooling was an important first stage in the learning process for many people, but it was usually brief and basic. Learning was a piecemeal affair that might last throughout a person's life, the pace and timing determined by their religious, cultural and economic needs. To call early schooling 'primary' implies a progression to 'secondary' which, for most people, did not exist. 'Post-elementary' education was very much the preserve of the middling and upper classes, for which it was an important way of preserving economic and social dominance. Order, stability and conformity were the watchwords of the authorities. The overriding aim was to offer an education appropriate to a person's established place in society.

This had profound implications not only for what was taught and how, but also to whom. One result was that women tended to be much less literate than men and the lower orders less educated than their social superiors. It was not until the eighteenth century that there began to be significant convergence in the basic literacy of males and females, and then only in north-western Europe. Sex and social class determined access to education, as did parental attitudes and cost in a world where children were expected to contribute to the family budget from an early age. University education was the preserve of the middling and upper classes. Oral culture remained central to the lives of ordinary people even though the printed word played an increasing role. The lower orders retained an interest in simple religious and recreational literature at a time when the middling and upper classes were broadening their reading tastes. Most people read religious works and popular ephemera rather than major volumes of current scholarship. The range of books available expanded enormously between 1500 and 1800, but censorship by ecclesiastical and secular authorities continued to restrict what could be read. What is more, the process by which ideas were transmitted remained a complex one. Language barriers existed within as well as between countries, denying access to ideas and information to those that did not speak or read the language in which literature was printed. The existence of multiple languages and dialects were one facet of the cultural variety of early modern Europe. The spread of new ideas depended not simply on what was read, but also on personal demonstration and on how literature was understood. The impact of literacy was contingent on the existing mental and material environment.

Ecclesiastical interest in and control of education grew in the age of Reformation and Counter-Reformation and remained strong throughout the early modern period. Religious emphases were central to curricula, especially at elementary level. Yet the power of the state and the significance of secular concerns were growing. From the late medieval period, the state began to play an increasing role in everyday life through its administrators, who collected taxes, recruited soldiers, dispensed justice and enforced order. Such intervention increased noticeably during the seventeenth and eighteenth centuries and had two implications for educational change. First, the state's demand for trained officials had a direct impact on the increase in post-elementary education and on the expansion of the universities that occurred at different times in the countries of early modern Europe. Second, those forced to deal with the state had similarly to seek out basic and advanced literacy. At the same time, the state's drive for control over its subjects involved an insistence on linguistic uniformity and, notably in the eighteenth century, national campaigns that sought to structure education under government control and to extend literacy. Some of these campaigns were highly successful by the standards of the day, but it is best to be wary of equating legislation with achievement. Nor should the spread of secularism be exaggerated, since many of the developments in post-elementary education were brought about by religious orders such as the Jesuits and even in the eighteenth century the church provided many of the teachers and much of the drive behind day-to-day schooling.

Indeed the state was not the only force for change. The struggle between the Reformed Faiths and the Roman Catholic Church from the time of Luther created a powerful incentive for both religions to provide education and to insist on basic literacy and religious knowledge for their adherents. Individual men and women also used reading and writing in their search for a satisfying relationship with God. Religious inspiration waned to some extent during the seventeenth century, but was revived towards its end when the Lutheran Pietist movement began to regenerate education in countries like Prussia and Denmark. Pietism was at its most successful when harnessed to the secular needs of the absolutist rulers of the eighteenth century. The third force behind change was economic. Population growth in the sixteenth and eighteenth centuries, urbanisation, nascent industrial developments and the expansion of both internal and overseas trade involved growing numbers of ordinary people in market transactions for which literacy and numeracy were useful. Most of the trends in education and literacy during this period, both positive and negative, were functions of political, religious and economic changes.

There were, however, certain largely autonomous developments of which the invention and spread of printing by movable type was the most significant. This technological innovation made books cheaper and more available. Hundreds of millions of copies were printed between the 1450s and 1800, thus creating a huge potential for intellectual exchange and advance as well as for broadening the cultural horizons of early modern men and women. The development of printing was episodic and its impact, as with any innovation, took time and favourable circumstances fully to be felt. Both the forms and the goals of censorship, always varied, changed in the seventeenth and eighteenth centuries. Changes took place in the intellectual climate too, notably in the age of the Enlightenment – which was in essence an educational 'movement'. The eighteenth century saw the extension of the humanist idea that education could be a good thing in itself coupled with the concept that schooling made a nation's subjects more useful, that is, education as a way of training bureaucrats (cameralism). Universities, which might seem the natural nurseries and beneficiaries of 'Enlightenment', saw their overall fortunes suffer in the eighteenth century.

The people of early modern Europe were the final force behind change. The push of institutions had to be complemented by the demand created by individuals and social groups. One example is the growing demand for vocational and vernacular education from the end of the seventeenth century to replace the classical, humanist curricula that had dominated post-elementary schooling from the fifteenth century. For education and literature, Latin began to be replaced by vernacular languages. Certain languages and dialects decayed as a result of proscription or a loss of faith in them on the part of certain social groups. Associated with this was a fundamental change in reading tastes away from the religious and practical towards secular, entertaining material and from slow, intensive reading to swift and extensive devouring of novels and periodical literature, notably in the eighteenth century. Education and literacy opened up a Pandora's box for some of the people of early modern Europe since it was not always possible to control the uses to which reading and writing were put. This became obvious in the years of the English Revolution (1640s and 1650s) or of the French Revolution. Throughout, change was slow, uneven and not irreversible. Even in 1800 the people of southern and eastern Europe remained largely illiterate, eschewing (or being excluded from) formal education and living in communities which apparently favoured oral forms.

Chapter 2

THE WORLD OF THE SCHOOL

Types of School

The diverse systems of schooling which exist in modern Europe share the characteristic of strict stratification according to age and curriculum. Access to a particular type of school or a certain class within a school depends on age and academic attainment. Over much of western Europe, education is funded by the state and complemented by a 'private sector' of fee-paying institutions and schools subsidised by secular or religious charities. By contrast, varieties of school were legion in the early modern period. There were, for example, petty schools, poorhouses or 'hospitals', work schools, evening classes, grammar schools, academies, colleges, and 'normal' schools (teacher-training establishments). The range of size, curriculum and prestige between the smallest village school and the grandest *collège* was enormous. At the lowest reaches were the tiny Spanish *amigas* or nursery schools run by women for children as young as three or four. Ranked among the most exalted were the state academies of eighteenth-century Russia, the Jesuit colleges, which were the closest thing in the seventeenth century to a 'national' (or even international) system, or the famous English grammar schools.

Most countries had a pyramid of schools. Seventeenth- and eighteenth-century Finland had its elementary *pedagogier*, post-elementary *trivialskolor* and élite *gymnasier*. At a more local level, the north German city of Braunschweig in the second half of the seventeenth century possessed some forty petty schools called *Winkelschulen*, two vernacular grammar schools and three Latin grammar schools (Luttinen 1985: 31; Friedrichs 1982: 372). However, except for the Jesuits, there was no planned, co-ordinated and unified 'educational system' in any European country until the eighteenth century. Instead there

was an anarchic jumble of different types of school whose functions sometimes complemented each other, sometimes rivalled or overlapped.

Educational establishments can, nevertheless, be classified according to
funding, curriculum or government. Under the last heading there were three
categories. First, independent schoolteachers working for fees and subject only
to market forces. These comprised a majority of all schools in, for example,
Renaissance Italy, schools that were attended almost exclusively by boys.
Some 89 per cent of Venetian pupils (almost all boys) attended its independent schools, 7 per cent church schools, and 4 per cent communal (*sestiere*)
schools. The distribution is similar for Florence, but Rome and Lucca had a
higher proportion in communal schools (Grendler 1989: 43, 105–6). Second,
were endowed schools based on a bequest towards a salary or a building.
Usually found in towns, they sometimes charged additional fees. They were
common in England, rare in Italy, France and Spain. Private education continued to dominate provision even during the years of Revolutionary government in France, and places for those unable to pay actually fell after 1789.
Third, were church schools, paid for, staffed and supervised by clerics. Of
limited importance in Renaissance England, Spain and Italy – in the latter
two the church only became important during the sixteenth century – these
provided the bulk of education in pre-eighteenth-century Russia and other
parts of eastern Europe. Bulgarian *kiliyni* or cell schools were found mostly
in monasteries and churches. Some were connected to centres for the production of manuscript books. In the west the licensing of teachers by lay
rulers and ecclesiastical authorities began in the age of the Reformation. For
example, in Catholic Bavaria the central bureaucracy took over supervision
of elementary education in 1569, but information flows depended on reports
by clergy to district fiscal officials and funding was left to local communities
(Hsia 1989: 115).

The other way to understand educational provision is to categorise the
level of learning provided. The most significant divide was between institutions that taught Latin and those that did not, but there were also differences
based, for example, on the availability of writing instruction, arithmetic, philosophy, rhetoric (oral and written techniques of presenting an argument),
theology or technical training (in, for example, navigation or ballistics). To a
considerable extent, the numbers in a school, the social composition of its
children and its standing depended on the sort of education it provided. The
Latin/vernacular divide was paralleled by distinctions between the sex and
social class of pupils. There were proprietary girls' schools in all countries,
but the upper reaches of the educational hierarchy were effectively the

preserves of males. Funding was not an important distinguishing feature in most countries since the bulk of schools were financed partly by fees paid by parents and partly from charitable or communal resources. Scotland's parish schools were principally funded by taxation of local landowners, Ukraine's by the church or religious confraternities, and some of England's by charitable endowment or civic coffers.

Early modern classifications can further facilitate understanding of education. During the eighteenth century, most continental states set about re-organising and formalising the structure of education, sometimes codifying and sometimes extending existing provision. Different types of school were designed to provide different skills for different social classes. Take the case of the *Allgemeine Schulordnung* promulgated for the Galician province of the Austrian Habsburg monarchy in 1774, shortly after it was annexed from Poland. A three-tier system was envisaged. At the lowest level, *trivial* or elementary schools were to teach reading, religious knowledge and arithmetic to boys from a peasant and artisan background. Next came the *haupt* (high) school, located in towns and providing the same education, plus writing, for bourgeois boys. Finally, the provincial capital was to contain a *normal* school for training teachers. By 1789, Galicia had 144 elementary schools, 19 principal schools and the Lvov normal school. However, even after the ordinance there were many other schools for Jews, girls and German speakers in the province, illustrating the enduring variety of educational provision (Adler 1974: 31–2; Krupa 1981). The Danish schools laws of 1814, building on eighteenth-century ordinances, envisaged a similar hierarchy: elementary rural *almueskoler*, urban *borgerskoler* along with vocational schools for craftsmen and tradesmen's children; post-elementary *real* schools, Latin schools and teacher-training colleges, all for middle-class boys (Gold 1977).

Elementary Schools

These categories are all approximate, but it is useful to think in terms of a hierarchy or pyramid of institutions when examining the huge variety of schooling available in early modern Europe. At the base came the tens of thousands of elementary schools that existed in cottages and tenements throughout the period. Many of these have left no trace in surviving documentation, making it impossible to judge their numbers accurately. They were probably small in size and often seasonal to suit the rhythms of the harvest year. Men and women alike ran them, teaching very simple 'academic' skills (usually religious knowledge and reading) and some practical ones like spinning to children aged roughly six (the age of discretion according to most thinkers) to ten. Some French, Italian, German and Spanish schools taught only religion at the most basic level. In sixteenth- and seventeenth-century Ukraine the simplest teaching came from parish schools run by the church or by religious confraternities. Pupils were few in number, less than a dozen on average in seventeenth-century Hungary, Germany and Poland. In some places these petty schools were frowned upon because they were hard to supervise and competed with officially sanctioned establishments. In seventeenth-century Scotland teachers were strictly enjoined to instruct only the very young or girls in reading, religion and practical skills which would help children of the lower classes to gain an honest living when they grew up. Polish school laws of the eighteenth century forbade the teaching of Latin in the elementary schools. Yet the failure of repeated attempts to eradicate them suggests that their low fees, local situation and humble ambitions suited the aspirations of numerous parents.

The lowest level of the educational hierarchy comprised schools with the humble goal of teaching basic literacy. Most aimed to serve the needs of the lower orders, though some could act as stepping-stones for boys from the lower and middling ranks to make their way into grammar schools. In the medieval period those with parents too humble in status and too straitened in circumstances to pay for tuition (and who were lucky enough to receive any education) did so along with the better off, provided for by charity. Increasingly in the early modern period, specialist schools for the poor were set up, such as the northern Italian Schools of Christian Doctrine. A voluntary teaching movement, begun in Italy in the late fifteenth century, was formalised by Castellino da Castello when he set up a confraternity to operate the schools in 1539. These Schools of Christian Doctrine taught religion and basic reading and writing for an hour or two on Sundays and holidays, using simple books such as the sixteen-page duodecimo *Summario della Vita Christiana*. Lay volunteers taught more than half the boys and girls aged 4–14 at Bologna in 1568; Rome in 1611 had 78 Schools of Christian Doctrine with 10,000 attendees; Milan in 1600 had 700 lay people teaching 20,000 children in Sunday schools. These schools were particularly important in Italy since outside the major towns free (endowed) schooling was much less common than in, say, England (Grendler 1989).

During the sixteenth century, the numbers of poor grew and they became a large and permanent class in all countries of Europe. Their betters saw them in a more menacing light and as a result there was growing social alienation between the middling and upper ranks in society and those who made up the rural and urban masses. Society was becoming more sharply divided and one reflection of this was the growing provision, notably in the larger towns from the 1520s, of poor hospitals and work schools. Their aim was to curb what some thought was the turbulence of lower-class youth and to turn them into useful members of an ordered society (Chartier *et al.* 1976: 48). The best-known examples of these specialist institutions for the poor are the hospitals or boarding-houses for orphans and the destitute, set up to take poor children off the streets, discipline them and train them to be productive and orderly members of society. For example, the rather grand-sounding '*colegios de niños de la doctrina*' in some sixteenth-century Spanish towns were actually orphanages designed to deal with the problems of poverty (Nalle 1992: 113), and as early as 1550 the poorhouse at Bruges in the Low Countries accommodated 230 children.

It was in French towns such as Paris and Lyon that there occurred an important landmark in growing specialist provision for the poor. This was the development of the *hôpitaux généraux* during the seventeenth century. Paris's first formal *école de charité* was founded in 1636 and was soon emulated. The *hôpital général* was a boarding school to which an elementary school was often attached, attended partly by its own inmates, partly by day pupils from the poor of the town. Commensurate with their purpose, the hospitals taught religion above all, followed by practical skills which would help the children to find employment at their allotted social level and, almost as an afterthought, reading and writing. Similarly, regulations for the Blue- and Grey-Coat charity schools in the English city of York specified that five hours of the day were devoted to spinning and weaving, with reading, writing and the rules of arithmetic thrown in only as a 'relief from more painful tasks'.

In Grenoble were the *petites écoles* run by a charitable body called Le Bureau des Ecoles Charitables. Founded in 1707 they lasted until 1789. Their aim was to instil a 'love of work' rather than 'perilous idleness', and to promote acceptance of circumstances rather than disorderly protest. 'Little schools form good Christians and therefore good citizens.' As it had in the seventeenth century, the religious imperative remained strong. The Christian Brothers, founded by Jean-Baptiste de la Salle, provided the teachers. The number of Brothers working in Grenoble grew between 1709 and 1730, at which date proper premises and a royal sanction were secured. There were four schools, each with 80 pupils. The Brothers aimed to create co-operative and obedient individuals. The role of the Bureau diminished over time. As in towns like Aix, charitable giving for religious purposes decreased steadily over the eighteenth century and in the 1770s they had to turn to the town for funds to rebuild the school after it fell down. In the late eighteenth century the emphasis shifted to work 'schools', such as one for girls from the *dépôt de mendicité* set up by a lace manufacturer in a nearby village in 1779 (Norberg 1985: 74–5, 159–68).

Indeed, schools for the poorest children increasingly included instruction in practical skills. For boys this meant some form of handicraft such as weaving or carpentry, for girls spinning and knitting. The merits of practical training as a way of reducing poverty and disorder among the lower orders were proclaimed from Seville in southern Spain to Stralsund in northern Germany during the sixteenth century, but it was the eighteenth century which witnessed the most marked proliferation of specialist 'work schools'. *Ecoles de filature*, begun in Normandy in the 1760s, were designed to fulfil the needs of both poor relief and education, but the poor were increasingly treated as workers rather than morally improvable beings. In Ireland, the 'charter schools' of the 1730s, 1740s and 1750s were state-funded (from 1746), but run by a private, Protestant society whose aim was to proselytise the children of the Catholic poor and teach them 'useful employments and regular habits of industry' (Cullen 1980: 199; Ó Ciosáin 1997: 63).

A growing number of work schools were attached to industrial enterprises. The English Lord Beaumont founded a school at his Coleorton mine in Leicestershire in the early eighteenth century, while in Finland some landowners chose to attach *ruukikoulu* or factory schools to logging plants or foundries on their estates (Hufton 1974: 167–8; Whittaker 1984: 13). Individual landlords might share the views of civic authorities about the uses of practical education. One member of the Russian Kurakin family wrote to an overseer on his Ukrainian estates in the middle of the eighteenth century: 'I am sending twelve young sons of my serfs to learn their letters so that they can be made suitable for my service' (Black 1979: 46–7).

These rather grand examples are not altogether typical of the sort of elementary education given to the poor. There were catechism schools, which existed for only a few weeks in the year to instruct children about to receive communion. Many were hole-in-the-wall institutions with casual funding and an exiguous existence. During the 1560s there was a school in the *Patio de los Naranjos* outside Seville cathedral to teach reading and writing to poor boys. A religious confraternity paid the teacher's salary and a local bookseller supplied primers free (Perry 1980: 177). All these types of school shared a limited curriculum of religious knowledge, work, reading and possibly the rudiments of writing and counting. They also demonstrate the importance of charitable giving in providing or subsidising education.

Given directly to a school or indirectly to a religious body or lay confraternity, charity was important to education in some countries. The bequest of Mr John Smarte of Romford in Essex to the town of Stratford-upon-Avon in 1676 is typical of the sort of provision made by testators concerned about education. Smarte recognised that there were a number of prestige grammar schools, but few schools for the poor teaching basic English reading and writing. Like most educational endowments in England at this period, his was for a vernacular school. His bequest included a provision for an old woman to teach 20 boys and girls reading and one to pay for a writing master. Basic books such as 20 each of primers, psalters, catechisms and Bibles were to be provided and all education for the needy boys and girls selected was to be free (Richardson and James 1983: 149). Endowing schools fulfilled religious and secular obligations. During the 1630s, Claire Rouille, widow of Jean Tronson, a Parisian tax administrator, left 200 livres to the confraternity of *Bon Secours* to provide basic religious and practical instruction to poor girls in St Eustache parish.

The sorts of schools helped by donors like Smarte or Rouille were humble and very cheap to attend; sometimes they were free because of endowments. For most children from the lower classes, boys and girls alike, this basic instruction in literacy and labour was as far as formal education went. This was true whether it took place in well-documented poorhouses or more characteristic local elementary schools. Some boys might go on to an apprenticeship or possibly to a grammar school on a scholarship, leading ultimately to a post as a clergyman or a minor official. That these individuals were rare is no accident. Attitudes to the education of the poor were stark and unambiguous. They should be trained as productive, godly and obedient members of society, and any education they received should not alter the social order or their place in it. The men who dominated society and government had clear and firm views on the goals of education. It should preserve the distinctions in society rather than blurring them and it should encourage the lower orders to accept their position rather than seeking to change it. There were, of course, subtleties in the exposition of these views and differences of opinion about whether educating ordinary people or keeping them ignorant was the best way of maintaining stability. Some thinkers began to advocate education as a good in itself during the eighteenth century (an idea which had existed even in the fifteenth century), yet the conservative consensus was overwhelming and so wholly different from the ostensible aims of schooling today as to require categorical statement.

Official attitudes to the education of the lower orders were remarkably homogeneous between countries and over time. Reports by bodies concerned with poor relief (such as the Italian *Carità dei Poveri* during the 1790s), deliberations of civic authorities, private correspondence among members of political and intellectual élites, debates in learned societies, articles in newspapers and periodicals, books and pamphlets: all contain evidence of a set of shared assumptions that education for any rank in society should be appropriate to the place of that stratum in the overall polity. Middling and upper classes should be taught to create wealth and to be faithful servants of church and state, lower classes to work and to obey. Eighteenth-century debates about those with political responsibility were mainly about the sort of curriculum best suited to training them. The masses were to be orderly, godly, diligent, tractable and content. Or, as the French thinker Charles Rollin put it in the early eighteenth century, education was to create '*bons chrétiens, bons fils, bons pères, et bons citoyens*' (Black 1979: 9).

The desirable ends of education for the poor fitted together into a coherent whole. However, different interest groups stressed different aspects. The church was primarily concerned with moulding a population that shared its precepts. After the Reformation there was the added stimulus of protecting and propagating a new faith or defending Catholicism and defeating what French authorities termed 'the so-called reformed faith' *(la religion prétendue reformée)*. The prime aim was, of course, to save souls. The approved method of doing so involved a rigid set of rules since the competing churches each tended to perceive only one path to godliness and salvation (though in countries as diverse as Russia and the Netherlands, Jews were allowed to keep their own schools). Religious emphases pervaded education throughout the period despite the growing power of the state and the development of more secular concerns. During the seventeenth and eighteenth centuries secular authorities began to take over the mantle of the church, while realising that the ecclesiastical emphasis on obedience to God's Word was integral to the creation of a disciplined population.

This connection between order and education was explicitly stated in an ordinance of 1652 issued by the city council of Nördlingen in southern Germany. The council 'had occasion to consider how remarkably much the common weal depends on well-conducted schools, and how one of the duties of rulers is to ensure that young people be diligently educated, with great circumspection and appropriate severity, and that they be habituated, aroused and encouraged to do what is good'. It therefore set out regulations to preserve the peace and prosperity of the city with the help of its schools.

Lack of schooling was perceived to be dangerous, leading, in the words of the States of Holland in 1596, to wanton idleness, improper behaviour and all sorts of foolishness. Proper education for the poor could, on the other hand, work wonders. The representatives from Seville to the Castilian Cortes (Estates) in 1548 argued that the creation of a House for the Instruction of Christian Doctrine there in 1546 meant that there were 'fewer thieves than before, less disease and contagious illness, and more doctrine and better example among the poor'. Religion, basic literacy and work training would preserve order, prevent mischief, acquaint the children of the poor with honest labour and make them strangers to the law courts and the poor hospital when they grew up (Friedrichs 1979: 224; van Deursen 1978: 58; Kagan 1974: 19; Strauss 1978).

In addition to political order, enhanced social stability could be expected from the right sort of educational provision. The 1775 Austrian education commission envisaged elementary schooling raising a breed of 'citizen who was enlightened in accordance with his role in society'. The Parlement of Aix agreed that what the poor needed was 'an education which would make them useful to the public without changing their status in society' (Becker-Cantarino 1977: 41; Fairchilds 1976: 88). Education for the masses was not a way of opening up avenues of social mobility, but of preserving rank and degree in society by offering training suited to an existing role predetermined by their social origins.

Attitudes towards the place of ordinary people in the social hierarchy did not alter. However, a lively debate began in the later seventeenth century about the best means of achieving a loyal, obedient, pious and industrious population. One camp asserted that the best way to ensure stability was to keep the masses in ignorance of anything except basic religious precepts. Their arguments hinged on the possibility that educating ordinary people could give them ideas above their station and could make them idle and discontented. The Englishman Bernard de Mandeville in his 1723 *Essay on charity and charity schools* sums up the viewpoint. 'Reading, writing, and arithmetic are', he opined, 'very pernicious to the Poor . . . Men who are to remain and end their days in a laborious, tiresome and painful station of life, the sooner they are put upon it at first, the more patiently they'll submit to it for ever after' (Watt 1972: 42). Similarly, Italian élites had a highly ambivalent attitude towards education in the eighteenth century (Roggero 1992: 113–35).

In the opposing camp were those who believed in the power of learning to elevate the minds of ordinary people to a level where they would share the attitudes of their betters. Scottish Enlightenment thinkers were almost unanimous in endorsing the improving power of education. On the continent too there were fervent optimists. In his *Über die Geschichte der Menschheit* (1764), the Swiss Isaak Iselin called education the greatest of man's endeavours. At the same time, the Polish intellectual Poplawski enthused:

> Let us lead the peasants out of the gross darkness of ignorance by giving them the learning that is proper for them; certainly, as we increase their willingness to work and make them more useful citizens of their country, so shall we make them better farmers when their reason, raised high as if awakened, will stimulate and whet their ability in every respect. (Seidler 1977: 343)

The liveliest debate took place in France. Like-minded individuals included Diderot in their ranks. Ranged against them was Voltaire, La Chalotais (a Breton magistrate who wrote extensively on the subject) and others like the Toulousain *intendant* who wrote in 1759: 'I believe it unnecessary to prove at great length the uselessness of school teachers in the villages. These are forms of knowledge that ought not to be given to the peasants . . . nothing is less necessary for the peasants than knowing how to read'. Importantly, nobody advocated an education that treated middling and lower classes alike or that aimed to do anything except conserve the existing social order (Trenard 1980; Chisick 1981).

Consensus about what was ultimately desirable for the masses was substantial. Even Utopian writers of the eighteenth century, able to depict their vision of a perfect society untempered by practical constraints, spoke of education controlled and funded by the state, geared to producing virtuous, upstanding individuals who would be loyal and useful members of society (Bridgman 1977: 570–71). Concrete proposals often shared these emphases. Abbé Baudeau's educational plans offer an example of physiocratic thinking in the eighteenth century. His five social groups were to be found in five separate schools doing five different curricula. Heading the hierarchy were the princes at their colleges learning the principles of natural law, the rights of nations, history, political economy, mathematics, military sciences and modern languages; at its foot came the peasantry in their parish catechism schools. In fact and fiction alike, the projected schemes included everyone from the poor to the princes, the unifying principle being the sense of what was *appropriate* to the different classes of society. Spanish intellectuals of the seventeenth century had urged that access to grammar schools should be restricted to the 'naturally superior' classes in order to fix the social order, and even the 'enlightened' leaders of eighteenth-century Spain tried to do the same (Grosperrin 1976: 158; Kagan 1974: 44, 47).

The concept of an appropriate training, which would not upset the social applecart, was thus not simply applied to the lower orders. It also informed attitudes towards the education of females throughout the early modern period. Women's literacy was inferior to that of males, a pattern created by prevailing attitudes to the nature of the female sex and to what girls should learn. Men conventionally described females as intellectually and morally inferior, endowed with less reason than men, easily influenced and thus in need of strong guidance. Women's place in society was as dutiful daughter, obedient wife and careful mother. If educated at all, girls received training for these roles. Early school regulations summarise the approach to female education. The 1593 ordinance regulating the girls' school of Lutheran Göttingen (drawn up by the clergy) stated that its purpose was:

> to initiate and hold girls in propriety and the fear of God. To fear God, they must learn their catechism, beautiful psalms, sayings, and other fine Christian and holy songs and little prayers, so that they can both read and recite them. For propriety, they must learn to love God's word, to honour their parents, to guard themselves against disobedience, improper talk and gestures, the temptation to steal and lie, and to turn indolence to work, reading, writing, sewing, in order they are kept busy and forget thereby other frivolities. (Hsia 1989: 114)

Two centuries later the same assumptions can still be found east of the Elbe. In the words of the Russian Commission for establishing public schools in 1783, 'the intent and the end of education for girls . . . is to make them good housekeepers, true wives and trustworthy mothers' (Black 1979: 163). Such attitudes did not simply apply to the lower orders. Russia had its *Smol'nyi* Institute from the 1760s, a finishing school for gentlewomen. Male aspirations for women of that social class, which attended it, are neatly summarised in the comments of Catherine the Great's adviser, Ivan Betskoi.

> We educate our daughters in reading, writing and diverse knowledge so that they can be useful citizens . . . As mothers they will raise their children well. As wives they will fulfil their duties better. As grandmothers they will not fill their grandchildren with ignorant and superstitious tales about the devil and such. On the contrary their conversations will encourage worth [and] control passions. (Nash 1981: 307)

These comments refer principally to women of the upper classes. In short, women's education should enhance their social role and moral influence, rather than their academic potential. Mothers needed to be instructed in religion so that they could bring up their children to fear God, while religious and moral attitudes had to be instilled in servant girls who might otherwise infect the children of their noble and bourgeois employers with improper ideas.

Attitudes towards girls' education were not universally restrictive. Religious reformers took an interest in ensuring that women could read the same works as their spiritual equals. Erasmus wanted 'the weakest woman' to read the Gospels, equating females with what contemporaries saw as backward and heathen races – 'Scots and Irishmen ... Turks and Saracens' (Millett 1976: 561; Grendler 1989: 87–9). With other humanists such as Vives, Erasmus pioneered a more sympathetic approach to female capacities for learning, albeit within a conservative conception of their place in society. The German Ambrosius Moibanus argued that girls were intellectually equipped to handle the same range of topics as boys, an idea which was followed up in the proposed 1574 *Jungfrauschulordnung* for the electorate of Brandenburg (Green 1979: 98, 103). This outlook gathered strength in an increasing number of writings from the later seventeenth century. Rather than concentrating on training a housekeeper, nanny or ornament, writers such as Daniel Defoe advocated a broader education and the concept of wives as companions. Early English 'feminists' like Mary Astell during the 1700s and Mary Woll-stonecraft in the 1790s pointed to the circularity of the argument that women were inferior, therefore should not receive a full education, then using their poor educational standards to justify an opinion about their intellectual inferiority. The voice of women is rarely heard on this (or any other) subject. Surviving writings show a conservative emphasis. The German Anna-Maria Schurman set out reasoned arguments for better educating women, couching them in terms of a better preparation for their traditional roles.

Attitudes such as these determined the type of schooling available to girls. Schools for girls were of two kinds. There were elementary ones similar to those for boys where work and basic literacy were the staple fare, and what might be called academies for girls, but which were really finishing schools for the daughters of the upper bourgeoisie, gentry and nobility. Numerically, the former predominated. Indeed, most education for girls was in the lowest echelons of the school hierarchy. Only here was provision made on equal terms for boys and girls. The *grand chantre* of the cathedral chapter of Notre Dame in Paris controlled 334 elementary schools in 1789 of which 167 (exactly half) were for girls. At Lyon in the 1790s there were actually more petty schools for females than males: 16 compared with 11 (Perrel 1980: 79; Gutton 1970: 471). Restricted education for females seems particularly to have characterised Catholic Europe. In Renaissance Venice boys were educated at formal day schools or in Schools of Christian Doctrine. Only 0.2 per cent of girls of school age attended, compared with 26 per cent of boys. A higher proportion of girls who received instruction did so in Schools of Christian Doctrine or in convents (of which there were about 25 in the city) or at home (Grendler 1989: 46). Those girls who received any formal education were all from noble and wealthy-commoner families. Female education existed only for the urban élites of Catholic Germany and school ordinances at, for example, Landsberg (1612) and Pfaffenhoffen (1656) contain no mentions of education for girls (Hsia 1989: 115–16). Across Catholic Europe elementary schools for boys were much more prevalent than for girls until late in the eighteenth century. There were 24 elementary schools for boys run by the Madrid guild of *maestros de primeras letras* at the end of the seventeenth century and more followed. However, it was not until 1783 that a decree allowed the establishment of free girls' schools in each of the city's 32 quarters (Soubeyroux 1987: 255–6). The first general survey of schools in Castile (1797) showed 305,000 boys at elementary schools and 89,000 girls learning religion and practical skills, making up just over a fifth of all children aged 6–13 years (Viñao 1999: 52–3).

The proportion of girls who received *any* education was indeed less than that of boys across much of southern and eastern Europe throughout this period. The total of boys' schools in the Spanish region of Navarra outnumbered girls' by two to one in 1807. Just north across the French border, 62 per cent of eligible boys attended school in the Pyrenean diocese of Tarbes in the later eighteenth century; of eligible girls, a mere 2 per cent went to school. Only 9 per cent of pupils in Russian public schools at the end of the eighteenth century were female (Kagan 1974: 29; Chartier *et al.* 1976: 43; Alston 1969: 19).

Boys and girls commonly sat together in the humblest schools. This was not altogether acceptable to authorities that demanded segregation in the interests of morality and proper spiritual development. Spanish authorities laid increasing stress on this during the seventeenth century, and at all periods the older the children the stronger the imperative to divide classes according to sex. In charity boarding establishments for the poor, segregation was pursued obsessively by administrators (Kagan 1974: 27, 29; Fairchilds 1976: 89). Nuns provided separate education for girls in Catholic countries. The only formally recognised girls' school prior to 1783 in Madrid was the *Colegio de las Salesas Reales*, founded on royal initiative in 1758. Run by nuns, it catered for girls of the Spanish nobility and administrative élites

(Rubio 1997). In rural parishes south of Lyon in France, the nuns of St Joseph set up groups comprising a handful of girls to teach them religion, housewifery and a little reading and writing. Female religious orders proliferated in seventeenth-century France and some, though not all, took a keen interest in the education of poor girls: Ursulines, Béates, Filles de Notre Dame, Visitandines, Clarisses, Filles de la Croix, Soeurs de Nevers and many more (Gutton 1970: 475; Perrel 1980: 75–9; Davis 1975: 73).

The curriculum for girls was much the same across Europe. Religion, sewing, knitting, spinning, housekeeping, some reading and writing were the extent of education for the vast majority of girls. Beyond elementary learning, few ever progressed. Social and economic pressures might curtail their education as it did for their brothers, but so too did cultural attitudes. Regulations for the English grammar school of Banbury (1594) forbade girls above the age of nine to attend, denying them any classical education, and girls were formally barred from the Latin and German grammar schools in seventeenth-century Braunschweig (Friedrichs 1982: 374–5; Kintzinger 1990).

Attitudes to the education of girls were symptomatic of those towards the bulk of the population and informed the training of those who attended the simplest schools of early modern Europe. There are prominent, if atypical examples of women who transcended the limits imposed on them. And it is true that a higher proportion of girls were going to school in the eighteenth century than ever before. Less than one pupil in ten was female in the Polish diocese of Cracow during the early decades, but by 1792 the figure was 26 per cent (Litak 1973: 65). There were almost no schools for girls in seventeenth-century Russia, but again the situation improved during the eighteenth century. Yet, there were few opportunities for girls outside élite social circles to participate in educational advances in the 'secondary' sector.

Post-elementary Schools

For the majority of children, schooling began and ended in the elementary schools that offered the basics of literacy. In north-western Europe boys and girls were given basic education in approximately equal numbers. The situation in schools that went beyond basic instruction in reading, religion and perhaps writing was different in important ways. This explains why girls' finishing schools were discussed in the previous section, since education for older girls was not really comparable with that for boys. The 'secondary' schools had more structured curricula and they were much more selective in terms of sex and social class. Girls were effectively, and sometimes explicitly, barred from the grammar schools and colleges of Europe. Boys from the middling ranks in society dominated places. Again, the social composition and curriculum of these schools were dictated by social assumptions about the importance of education to different sections of society.

For the average parent, learning beyond the basics of religion and literacy for a son (still less a daughter) was an unthinkable luxury. Boys who did attend a 'secondary' school probably went to one of the thousands of Latin or vernacular grammar schools dotted across Europe. In the fifteenth century in western Europe, Latin was taught principally in clerical schools. From the early sixteenth century new and more secular institutions modelled on Italian civic academies began to make their presence felt: the French municipal *collèges* and the German *Fürstenschulen* (Huppert 1984; Grafton and Jardine 1986). The core of their curriculum was instruction in Latin grammar, literature and rhetoric, along with vernacular grammar and arithmetic. These schools were divided according to curriculum. The full *trivium* of Latin grammar, dialectic (formal logic and reasoning) and rhetoric was only offered by élite institutions. Training was formal and literary.

In the countries of western Europe, Latin was the premier language of post-elementary education. In areas such as Muscovy higher learning was in Church Slavonic. In both cases the language was alien to everyday speech and was taught to a minority as an élite discipline. Examples from the Ukraine during the seventeenth century illustrate the sort of curricula that were offered. The church and urban religious confraternities principally funded grammar schools in this Polish dependency. Prominent among these was the Lvov school, set up in 1586 and offering, at various stages in its development, Latin and Polish grammar, philosophy, theology, drama, music, arithmetic, dialectics and geometry. Moscow grammar school taught 66 of its 232 pupils Greek and the remainder Church Slavonic grammar in 1686; a year later it was remodelled into the *Slaviano-Greko-Latinskoe Uchilishche* which offered more variety. Spanish grammar schools were known as *Colegios* or *Escuelas de Gramática*, teaching grammar based on a late fifteenth-century text by Nebrija, Latin literature, religion, history, geography, mathematics, philosophy and rhetoric (Kagan 1974: 31). In conception, the classical curriculum on offer across western Europe was homogeneous, though the precise range of topics within it depended on the availability of teachers.

The central importance of the grammar schools in early modern education and society lay in the classical curriculum they offered. Latin was *the* language of learning over all of Europe except for the eastern regions influenced by Muscovite, Byzantine traditions. It was used extensively in the law and the church, and it created a bond between those trained in its language and literature. In sixteenth-century Ireland it was used by clergy, scholars and nobility to correspond with each other and with their peers abroad. In Spain, Latin brought status and prestige to those with knowledge of it. It remained an important teaching and learning medium. In Renaissance Italy Latin primers could be used to teach vernacular lessons because Italian is closest to Latin in sound and pronunciation (Grendler 1989: 153). Latin texts were accepted by Scottish Presbyterians in the mid-seventeenth century, even if preaching and services had to be in the vernacular.

Latin continued to be a passport to culture and status, but its importance declined during the early modern period. Ferdinand I's administrative reforms of the mid-sixteenth century involved a replacement of Latin with German in the courts of justice of Inner Austria, a development which had already taken place in Francis I's France. Agricultural literature followed the same trend as developments in administration. Reprints of ancient writings by Vergil and Pliny were in Latin, but 84 per cent of all new publications on farming and gardening during the sixteenth century were in modern languages (Burian 1970–71: 84; Beutler 1973: 1298–1300). The timing of this change differed across Europe, but it was fastest between c.1650 and c.1750. Scottish and English post-elementary schools began to move away from a classical, religious curriculum from the end of the seventeenth century and towards practical, secular training. Parents began to demand more vocational training for their sons all over western Europe and, as in the southern Netherlands, to boycott guild schools with their archaic curricula. The Danish school law of 1739 formalised this development by abolishing more than half the existing Latin schools (Dixon 1958: 25).

Increasingly it was thought that 'the learning which is acquired at grammar schools is of little or no use to such as are set to ordinary trade, and consequently that time might have been better spent in attaining some useful knowledge, nay much more profitably in learning to write a good hand, arithmetic, and other things of that nature'. So wrote the English non-conformist Francis Brokesby in 1701. Yet, the rate of change should not be exaggerated. The decline of Latin grammar schools in England after 1660 was only relative, the result of a growing number of non-classical and dissenting academies from the 1690s. Non-conformists or dissenters such as Quakers, Baptists, Presbyterians and Methodists refused to accept the Anglican Church of England and set up their own schools. Nevertheless larger, more fashionable grammar schools survived and prospered as did those which adapted their curricula to new demands (O'Day 1982: 196–216). Some 80 new grammar schools were established in England 1660–85 and of those set up between 1660 and 1714, 147 were still operating in the 1860s.

Latin remained important to post-elementary education in France too. Efforts to remove it from the curriculum of *collèges* after the expulsion of the Jesuits in the third quarter of the eighteenth century had to be abandoned. Further attempts to focus exclusively on vernacular training during the Revolution also failed to endure. Under Bonaparte, new *lycées* replaced the *Ecoles Centrales*, teaching a curriculum of 'intellectual traditionalism and apolitical modernism' aimed at the sons of the bourgeoisie and using Latin (Higonnet 1980: 66). Methods of teaching Latin also remained wedded to Renaissance ideas. Classrooms continued to reverberate to the sound of Latin grammar drills for the rhetorical style of the Jesuits and their successors tested memorisation and delivery as much as understanding and the capacity for independent thought. Only in the eighteenth century did new practices enter into the deeply traditional teaching of Latin, including the greater use of the vernacular for explanation (Compère and Pralon-Julia 1990).

Use of Latin as a communications medium also persisted. Polish might have been a literary language as early as the sixteenth century, but Latin continued to be used for theological treatises until the eighteenth. People used French on funeral monuments in Germany, but until the second half of the eighteenth century the French élites preferred Latin (Higonnet 1980: 50). Latin was replaced temporarily by English in legal proceedings during the 1650s, but was restored in 1660 and not finally removed until 1733. Inventories of 100 Dutch theologians, scholars, lawyers and government officials who died in 1700 show that most learned books were still in Latin. It was only after the 1680s that the majority of books in the Frankfurt and Leipzig fair catalogues were in German. As an institutionalised medium of communication for education, law and politics, Latin survived in Hungary, Croatia and Slavonia until the nineteenth century (Thomas 1986: 101; Gibbs 1971: 333; Kamen 1984: 214; Kessler 1976). Even in the revamped universities of eighteenth-century Germany, where vernacular teaching was becoming more common, a formal dissertation in Latin remained a central part of the examination process (Evans 1981: 181–2). Those who lectured in the vernacular at a British university might be attacked for vulgarising a subject, including medical luminaries like the Scottish Dr William Cullen. Writing styles indicate that, while scholars like Edward Gibbon (*A History of the Decline and Fall of the Roman Empire*, published 1777–88) wrote in the vernacular, they continued to think in Latin.

With its stress on grammar, especially Latin, post-elementary education was funded by charity, civic treasuries, taxation of landowners, lay religious confraternities, the state and parental fees as well as by the various churches of early modern Europe. From their foundation in the middle of the sixteenth century to their forced dissolution in the 1760s and 1770s, the most powerful single force in post-elementary education was the Jesuit order. It is impossible to overestimate the importance of this dedicated order, for their methods, their schools and their example pervaded educational practice in Protestant as well as Catholic countries.

Jesuit grammar schools and colleges flourished in all the countries of Catholic Europe from the 1560s onwards. As early as 1559 they took over the 'liberal arts' university of Évora in Portugal. Seven new colleges were opened in Lithuania between 1580 and 1585, there were 20 in adjacent Ruthenia in 1620 and by 1630 somewhere in the region of 10,000 pupils had passed through Jesuit schools in the Polish kingdom. Between 10,000 and 15,000 boys a year went through Jesuit schools in Spain, and by the early eighteenth century one boy in every three who received any kind of Latin schooling there obtained it with the Society of Jesus. The Jesuits could boast more than a hundred academies in Italy by 1600 and the one at Padua taught nearly 1,000 students: five times the size of the arts faculty of the city's university. Just before their suppression in 1762 they had about 1,300 teachers across France. Their college at Lyon alone had 1,000 pupils (Martel 1938: 225–8; Kagan 1974: 51–8; 1986: 174).

When a school had to be revived, a 'backward' region enlightened or a 'lost' land like Bohemia recovered for the faith, the Jesuits were given the job. In the 1570s bishop Vilém Prusinovský called them in to found an academy at Olmütz in Moravia (central Europe), an establishment which quickly received the title of a university from the pope (Evans 1974: 3–5). The French municipal *collèges* set up in the sixteenth century resisted Jesuit infiltration and control until the seventeenth century, but in some areas of Europe the terms grammar school and Jesuit school were synonymous. The *comté* of Nice before the reforms of Victor Amadeus II in 1729 is an example (Huppert 1984; Féliciangéli 1980).

The system of classical education that prevailed in most continental grammar schools, colleges and academies originated in Renaissance Italy and was perfected by the Jesuits during the first century of their existence. Their *Ratio Educationis* had a classical core followed by training in philosophy for the older boys and then instruction in basic theology as a precursor to university entrance. Poland/Lithuania provides an example of the system in operation at its three main levels. The most basic schools offered five or six years of classes and were comparable with an English grammar school. Examples of such gymnasia included Lublin, Jarosław, Riga and Dorpat, though the last two had no rhetoric classes. Boys lived in a closed community under strict rules. The first six years of Jesuit education were spent in this fashion. 'Philosophy' – the formal, medieval, scholastic kind coupled with some mathematics and science – came only after this basic training and then only in some colleges. This marked the second level of college, the philosophy courses of which provided logic in the first year, mathematics and natural philosophy (physics) in the second, ethics and metaphysics (where available) in the third. Complete colleges such as Vilna (made into an academy in 1578) and Poznań additionally offered theology courses (Litak 1978; Grafton and Jardine 1986). Jesuit schools and colleges were usually free and the standard of teachers very high (Bailey 1977: 106–7; Perry 1980: 17). Jesuit methods were held in such esteem that Orthodox parents in Poland were happy to send their sons to the Catholic schools. The clandestine Jesuit Latin school at Gouda in the Dutch Republic was even attended by the sons of Calvinist clergymen (Martel 1938: 229–30; van der Laan 1977: 279).

The Jesuits were by no means the only religious order involved in education. In France, the second most important order was that of the Oratorians with some 400 teachers in 1762: one-third the Jesuit total. In Hungary the Dominicans, Benedictines, Franciscans, Minorites and Promontors played their part. Indeed, during the eighteenth century, other religious groups became increasingly important. The Jesuit curriculum was losing ground to new demands from parents and the state for practical, technical and secular training. Because of their supra-national loyalty to church and papacy rather than to national authority, the Jesuits were becoming increasingly out of place in the absolutist states of eighteenth-century Europe. They had often come under attack from Protestants in the past. In Transylvania the Unitarians pioneered a take-over of Jesuit schools (including the college at Kolozsvár) after the Order's early expulsion from the area in 1603. In the eighteenth century, elements of Catholic opinion too began to cast doubt on their place in the church.

New groups more suited to the changing intellectual climate flourished from the end of the seventeenth century, among them the Piarists. Already active in Italy, the Piarists did not open their first school in Spain until 1677 and only opened a further 12 there before 1800. They were opposed both by the Jesuits and by the secular schoolmasters' guild (Viñao 1990: 582–3). In Poland and the Austrian territories other religious orders stimulated Jesuit colleges, founded their own and, when the Jesuits were finally expelled, took over many of their institutions. However, the state campaigns of the eighteenth century were much more damaging to the Jesuits than competition from other orders. In some countries such as Italy the proscription of the Society of Jesus was a serious blow, albeit tempered both by the existence of other orders – the Summists and Barnabites took over in Parma, for example – and the drift of ousted Jesuit teachers back into their former posts under new guises. The university of Évora in Portugal was shut down in 1759 when the Jesuits left, though it was reopened with new statutes in 1772 (Evans 1979: 133; Litak 1978: 135–7; Marques 1972: 414).

Alongside the *collèges* at the top of the hierarchy of 'secondary' education came the academies. One example from Ukraine in the seventeenth century was the Mohyla academy at Kiev, modelled on that at Cracow, which had its own halls of residence and feeder schools. It offered a course of education lasting 8–12 years, beginning with grammar and working up through rhetoric, history and geography to philosophy and theology in stages of one to three years' study. Others offered more specific training, notably military schools. Venice had a training school for officers in the early seventeenth century, but the first large military academy was founded in Savoy in 1677, the next of importance being at Berlin (1717). Those in Russia taught foreign languages, geometry, history, geography along with the trappings of the gentleman soldier such as dancing, heraldry and fencing. Russian technical training under Peter the Great was directly related to the needs of war with the Ottoman empire and Sweden. Mathematics at the Moscow academy was taught from Leontii Magnitskii's *Arifmetika* (1703), a text central to the whole educational programme in the school. All education there was practical and specific rather than theoretical. For example, geography was in fact maps and surveying, astronomy was treated as the equivalent of celestial navigation. From 1731 the military academies were reserved for sons of the gentry and graduates could walk straight into a commission in the forces without any other experience (Alston 1969: 8; Okenfuss 1973).

Academies throughout Europe were explicitly designed to defend aristocratic privilege and perpetuate their dominance of society. Some, like the Prussian *Ritterakademien* (knights' academies) of the eighteenth century, boasted curricula which were the equal of full-blown universities. In France, students who wished to study arts subjects, notably philosophy, had, until the middle of the sixteenth century, to attend a university. Thereafter, humanist influence, a changing social environment and the competition between Catholic and Protestant stimulated the foundation in most major towns of local colleges where youths could follow a curriculum similar to that offered by university arts faculties (Brockliss 1978: 517; McClelland 1980; Huppert 1984).

Despite similarities in designation, not all academies and colleges were equal. The lesser municipal *collèges* of France, numbering about 100 on the eve of the French Revolution (and additional to approximately 250 Catholic and former Jesuit colleges) are an example. Under civic rather than ecclesiastical control, they taught Latin and French grammar (Bailey 1977). As well as offering different curricula and prestige, academies and colleges experienced differing fortunes over time. The more dynamic side of the academies represented in Germany contrasts forcefully with the stagnation of the Tuscan institutions during the seventeenth and much of the eighteenth centuries. However, terminological difficulties make comparison difficult. Tuscan 'academies' were not always teaching institutions. Described by one authority as 'clubs of upper-class dilettantes devoted to things cultural', Tuscan academies before the Enlightenment went out of their way to avoid involvement in current intellectual affairs. Instead they seem to have preferred to retain the 'flaccid obscurantism' of set intellectual forms which had survived from the fifteenth-century 'golden age' of thought (Chojnacki 1974: 537–40). Like the Portuguese *Academias*, including John V's 1720 Royal Academy of History, or the British Academy, these were élite clubs with funds and presses rather than colleges on the French or German model (Carrato 1977: 359). The term 'academy' could cover a wide range of institutions. In England, an academy was approximately equivalent to a grammar school, as in the phrase 'dissenting academy'.

The importance of the grammar schools and *collèges* lay in three areas. First, they provided training in skills that could be directly useful in obtaining a job as an official of church or state. Humanist education – the *studia humanitatis* of grammar, rhetoric, poetry, history, and moral philosophy – opened up careers in diplomacy, government service, the clergy and education. The ability to speak eloquently and without rehearsal in classical Latin, and to read, write and teach it were viewed with approval by employers looking for obedient and self-disciplined accumulators, classifiers and regurgitators of material. Classical education had few explicit employment goals, but it strongly presupposed certain destinations for its young men and thus it was vocational in important ways (Grafton and Jardine 1986: 23–4). The more practical and non-classical institutions of the late seventeenth century onwards equipped boys to enter commerce or the military or some of the developing professions. Second, by concentrating on the classics, traditional grammar schools enabled young men to participate in international scholarship and, by assimilating a uniform set of values and information, to become members of a social and cultural élite. In fifteenth-century Italy and sixteenth-century England advanced education for a minority of pupils was aimed at 'the production of a small, politically active minority who were heirs to a mature foreign culture, and who were thereby hallmarked as of the requisite moral and intellectual calibre to make substantial contributions to their own developing communities' (Grafton and Jardine 1986: 220). Classical education was a seal of cultural approval and could be an end in itself as well as a means to an end. In Muscovy, training in Church Slavonic grammar and literature performed a similar function. Third, the schools afforded qualifications for entry into establishments of higher education.

Academies and colleges can be seen as vocational training centres with specific careers in mind for their pupils in the church, the law, the army or civil service. More obviously vocational to modern readers were places that taught the skills of buying and selling. *Scuoli d'Abbaco* (abacus schools) in Renaissance Florence were in fact elementary commercial schools offering courses in exchange rates, interest calculations, contract and partnership law, and weights and measures. One Venetian school that taught arithmetic and double-entry book-keeping boasted 143 pupils in 1587. In the seventeenth century this powerful, independent city-state had schools for civil lawyers and notaries, courses in Greek and Turkish for merchants' sons, colleges of naval architecture and design (Goldthwaite 1972; Grendler 1990).

Linguistic skills were also valuable for international traders. Sailors, skippers, merchants and dockers at great ports such as Antwerp, Genoa and London must have picked up foreign languages from visitors. Boys could also receive formal instruction in the larger towns (Caravolas 1995). Francesco Scudieri of Cremona, son of a cloth merchant, gave his occupation as 'man of letters who teaches music and Italian language to Germans and other northerners' (MacKenney 1987: 183). Along the Baltic coast, enterprising Dutchmen set up specialist language schools to cash in on the growing demand for command of foreign tongues which had been generated by the expansion of international trade. Jan van Deelen ran a French school at Gdansk (Danzig) in the 1590s to teach boys practical skills in that language, such as how to count, prepare invoices, bargain, solve delivery problems, make out receipts and deal with the customs. He drew on a long tradition of such schools in the Low Countries, and during the seventeenth century many more were set up in the Baltic cities: Toruń and Elblag, for instance (Grobelak 1979: 176–80). Merchants needed arithmetic for accounts, currency transactions, weights and measures; geography to estimate distance and insurance; foreign languages to bypass the need for middle men; writing for orders and accounts.

The eighteenth century saw a proliferation of these vocational schools. Many eighteenth-century Dutch communities had 'evening-classes', running from 4pm to 7pm on winter evenings in the countryside, later in the towns, where working youths could attend when their duties as apprentice or servant were done. Boys were in the majority (de Booy 1980a: 267). In eastern Europe specialist technical education grew out of military needs. Peter the Great's garrison schools (*Garnizonnye Shkoly*) were part of his campaign for the modernisation of Russia, teaching officers' sons reading, writing and mathematics with a military slant. He set up mining schools at Olonets (1716) and Ekaterinburg (1721) to train men for state armaments and later private industries (Kahan 1985: 153; Keep 1985: 201–4).

In Italy the eighteenth century witnessed an expansion and formalisation of technical education. Except for Venice, technical instruction had been handled by individual guilds until the sixteenth and seventeenth century. When these began to decline some of the more enterprising states of the north started to provide vocational training in geography, geometry, mathematics, navigation and modern languages as an alternative to the traditional classical curriculum (Roggero 1992). Germany and the Austrian dominions were leaders in this field, notably in mining academies. Technical education spread more slowly in the francophone countries and in Italy before the nineteenth century, two notable exceptions being the French *Ecole des Ponts et Chaussées* (1744) and the *Ecole des Constructeurs de Navires* (1763). Most countries latched on to the idea of technical education from the later eighteenth century. Portugal's schools for nautical and commercial studies began to appear in earnest from the third quarter of the eighteenth century, though building on three centuries of practical experience (Marques 1972: 414). Denmark's school laws of 1814 included a provision for classes in vocational skills at the urban *borgerskoler*.

All these institutions had a practical purpose. In some senses they were the forerunners of the technical high schools (*polytechniques* and *technische Hochschulen*) of the nineteenth century. Not so the artistic school founded by the Lithuanian court treasurer Antonio Tyzenhauz, a philanthropist who took serf children aged eight to ten and employed foreign teachers to instruct them in dancing, music and the ballet. In the early 1780s, 16 girls and 18 boys spent half of the day in these endeavours, the rest of the time being devoted to more traditional scholastic areas such as needlework and French for the girls, writing and arithmetic for the boys (Mamontowicz-Łojek 1968).

Where were the Schools?

Across Europe the early modern period saw an important shift from restricted to widespread, if not universal, literacy. Population increase, economic growth, social change, the development of the nation state, Reformation and Counter-Reformation, the intellectual currents of the Renaissance and the Enlightenment: all served to stimulate the demand for reading, writing and counting. Associated with this change was a marked increase in educational facilities. New schools were created and existing ones enlarged, the pool of educational resources expanding so widely as to merit the title 'educational revolution' conferred on England for the century *c.*1540–1640 by Lawrence Stone (1964). Stone's work on England has been emulated and extended in other countries to reveal a remarkable rise in documented schooling. Developments in Stone's century built on an existing medieval tradition of schooling and were therefore an acceleration of a trend rather than a completely new departure. Schooling at all levels had been present in the late medieval period. Under the impact of the dynamic forces of the sixteenth century, educational provision expanded rapidly. The pace of change, glacial in some parts of Europe (such as Muscovy), approached a torrent in others. Württemberg had 512 communities with just 50 schools in 1534 and 270 by 1581. At least 410 new schools, mostly endowed grammar, were established in England between 1480 and 1660. In reality the figure is probably double this if fee-paying schools which taught Latin among their subjects are included (Stone 1964: 42–7). More than twenty new colleges were founded in Portugal's main towns in the 1530s and 1540s. Of 271 French *collèges* in existence in 1789, 53 per cent had been founded before 1600 and 74 per cent before 1650 (Marques 1972: 195; Chartier *et al.* 1976: 186). In some areas the trend began later or was continued longer. Bremen in 1638 had four parish schools and 26 *Winkelschulen*. By 1716 there were 39 'corner schools' and in 1788 about a hundred; the first *Armenschule* was founded in 1705 for poor children (Engelsing 1973: 48). English universities too doubled their intake between *c.*1550 and *c.*1640 and the London Inns of Court, legal training centres, also flourished.

Stone's arguments have proved influential in promoting research into early modern schooling. Nevertheless there are a number of qualifications as well as amplifications to be made. Estimates of the availability of schooling in different parts of Europe are fraught with difficulties. The official enquiries by church and state into the plantation of schools (which provide the most accessible statistical sources) used different criteria of a 'school'. Some investigations sought to identify the presence of a teacher, and might treat anyone at all qualified to instruct as such – minister or church assistant, for instance, in Norwegian dioceses – while others counted teachers licensed by ecclesiastical authorities. Concern might be with the provision of a salary or the presence of a building that could be designated a school. A final category of investigation was interested only in schools that taught certain subjects, usually Latin. Surviving records certainly underestimate the number of schools which existed in some form or another, and discriminate against areas where traditions of informal, seasonal and peripatetic teaching were strong: the Dauphiné of France, for example. The French diocese of Tarbes on the eve of the Revolution illustrates the potential for distortion, which can occur. In lowland parts, 69 per cent of parishes had a fixed school, 5 per cent a peripatetic school and 26 per cent none at all. For valleys the figures are 40 per cent, 24 per cent and 36 per cent respectively, while for mountain areas (the diocese was partly in the Pyrenees) they are 11 per cent, 5 per cent and 84 per cent (Chartier et al. 1976: 25; Furet and Ozouf 1982: 70). Mountain areas come out badly whichever criterion is adopted. The valley/lowland divide, substantial in terms of fixed schools, is much less obvious if travelling teachers are taken into account.

Great care is therefore needed when comparing figures on the number of schools in different areas. One authority asserts that England around 1600 had one school for every 10,000 people whereas the German duchy of Württemberg, with 401 folk schools in 512 communities, had a ratio of one per 1,100 (Green 1979: 93). This comparison is not valid since the English figures refer to grammar schools and the German ones to all types of (mainly vernacular) institution. What is more, the English figure is a substantial underestimate: 1:4,000 or better is closer to the truth (Stone 1964: 44). Despite problems of comparison, it is possible both to outline the relative availability of formal education in regions of Europe and to distinguish between the environments that helped and hindered schooling. Local and regional varia-tions were substantial. However towns were usually more favoured than rural areas and lowland more than upland zones; Protestant countries usually had more schools per head of population than Catholic; north-western Europe (except Scandinavia) was better endowed than the Mediterranean world and eastern Europe.

In all parts of Europe, urban environments boasted superior educational provision. Antwerp had 150 schools of all kinds in the mid-sixteenth century, Ghent had 40 (12 of them grammar schools), Flushing six and Veere (with a population of only 2,000) three. Breda could claim 14 teachers, Tournai 11 and Poperinghe seven (Parker 1979: 21). Venice at the end of the sixteenth century had 250 teachers in a population of 135,000 and Milan, which was much smaller, 120 schools of various sorts. The Venetian figure of one teacher for every 135 males aged 20 or younger is superior to that of Lyon in the 1550s and 1560s where the ratio is 1:400, though the figure of 38 masters at Lyon excludes those at the Latin *Collège de la Trinité* (Davis 1975: 209). The concentration of schools, especially post-elementary ones, in towns is illustrated by the case of Spain. By 1600 there were 4,000 grammar schools and most towns of more than 500 households had one. Rural areas languished in school provision and attendance. A census of Latin grammar schools in the 1760s revealed that villages of less than 100 residents (*vecinos*), in which half of Castile's population lived, contributed only 10 per cent of the pupils; 44 per cent came from towns of 1,000 *vecinos* or more (Kagan 1974: 42, 47–8). Schooling was more widely available in towns and cities than in the countryside. In three Polish dioceses during the mid-seventeenth century, two-thirds of urban parishes had schools, compared with half of rural communities. A century later the bishop of Cracow's visitation of 753 parishes in Little Poland revealed figures of 61 per cent and 27 per cent respectively (Olczak 1974: 325; Litak 1973: 47–8).

A more extreme profile exists for Scandinavian countries. Denmark's 1539 church ordinance on education makes no mention of rural schools, asking parents to instruct in the home instead (Dixon 1958: 13). In Finland, virtually all schools of any consequence were in towns. The same is true of Sweden, where an enquiry of 1768, prompted by the clergyman Schlüter's private scheme for parish schools, showed the imbalance. Sweden had 2,216 parishes at this time, almost all rural. Excluding Stockholm and the island of Gotland (on which all 92 parishes had schools), there were 165 settled rural schools (75 privately endowed, the rest parish-funded). A further 100 ambulatory schools existed where the master went from farm to farm and hamlet to hamlet, staying for two or three weeks in each. All 60 of the main towns had schools, some two, but only an eighth of rural parishes could claim one. By 1802 the proportion of parishes with fixed schools had risen from 7 per cent to 11 per cent (Barton 1977: 529, 536). In Norway ambulatory schools were the norm, with just 5 per cent of pupils in the diocese of Akershus attending a fixed school in 1775 and only 11 per cent in the 1830s (Guttormsson 1990: 21–2). Instead of fixed schools there were in much of rural Scandinavia peripatetic pedagogues teaching in barns or parlours: Danish *omganslærer*, for example. The most extreme example is Iceland. It had only two grammar schools, located at Hólar and Skálholt, transferred to Reykjavík (the largest town on the island with about 500 inhabitants) and amalgamated into one institution in 1801.

Differences also existed between rural areas, notably between upland and lowland regions. In 1814, 92 per cent of the 400 parishes in the densely settled diocese of Lund in southern Sweden had schools whereas there were hardly any in the thinly-peopled northern diocese of Härnösand (Barton 1977: 536). Just a half of villages in some western parts of Brandenburg (1801–3) had a sexton or other person who could act as a teacher – Arendsee and Salzwedel, for instance – while some central provinces reported that every parish had such a man (Neugebauer 1985: 270). The problems faced by upland communities are neatly summarised in James McParlan's 1802 *Statistical Survey of the County of Donegal* in Ireland.

> The state of education in the mountain regions is much more backward than in any other part of Ireland that I am acquainted with; in the remote and sequestered glens, the inhabitants, being only few and scattered, and unable to employ teachers, are indeed in a very degrading state of ignorance.

Poverty and dispersed population militated against the extensive provision of fixed schools. However, the example of the Hautes Alpes of south-eastern France shows that these drawbacks did not necessarily mean an ignorant population, since literacy there was higher than in neighbouring lowland zones. Vovelle has written of lowland Provence as '*riche et ignorante*', whereas the uplands were '*pauvrement savante*' (Granet-Abisset 1996: 115).

Spatial variations in schooling were not solely a function of economics and geography. A major theme in historical writing on education is that Protestantism and schooling are connected. Luther, Calvin and the other revolutionaries who broke the mould of medieval Christendom after 1517 shared the belief that the Bible was the sole source of truth and that each individual Christian should have access to the Word of God through the Scriptures. Luther changed his views on education during the 1520s. He ceased to believe that private Bible reading was the best way of spreading the Reformation to individual believers in the way he wanted. Instead he advocated the expert guidance which could be provided by pastors and the central role of the catechism in promoting religious understanding (Gawthrop and Strauss 1984: 34–5). However, for many reformers the way to a godly life and indeed salvation itself was by reading. Protestant communities might therefore be more likely to wish to educate their children than Catholic ones, and would create schools to do so. A correlation might be expected between the confessional leanings of a region, country or community and the availability of schooling – and the extent of literacy.

There is a considerable measure of truth in this argument. The Reformation's three generations each contributed to educational advances. In the German lands the sixteenth century saw the first, Lutheran-inspired drive. The advent of the Calvinist or Reformed faith had a direct (if delayed) impact on the expansion of education in countries such as Scotland and the United Provinces in the seventeenth century. The influence of the Lutheran Pietists coupled with state action catapulted Prussian society into mass literacy during the eighteenth century. In regions where Catholics and Protestants competed for the hearts and minds of the people, the dynamism of Protestant educational provision enervated Catholic schooling.

Examples of the stimulus provided by Protestantism in its various forms are not far to seek. Protestants provided education for a broader range of the population than Catholics in Reformation Germany. At Augsburg in 1623 there were 20 Protestant and four Catholic schoolmasters teaching 1,550 Protestants (826 boys and 724 girls) and 240 Catholic pupils (118 boys, 122 girls); the ratio of Protestants to Catholics (both sexes and all ages) in the town was 4:1, in schools 6:1 (Hsia 1989: 114). By the end of the seventeenth century, the largest concentration of Protestants in France was to be found in the south east: Rhône, Privas, Vernoux, Cévennes and Causses. In the upland parts of this region, Protestant communities almost always had a school whereas these were thinner on the ground in Catholic towns and villages. Protestants were apparently more successful than Catholics in overcoming constraints of distance and poverty. The lowland areas were uniformly better provided with schools, though in most parts of France Catholic communities adjacent to Protestant ones had better educational provision and higher literacy than their co-religionists in Catholic-dominated areas. A similar emulation or competition effect is evident in eastern Europe. The first Protestant school in Poland was established at Pincôw near Cracow in 1551, and most of the early foundations were Calvinist. Dioceses such as Poznań, which had a number of Protestant schools, enjoyed superior Catholic schooling thanks to the force of competition. Some Catholics were prepared to send their sons to Protestant schools, despite official opposition (Laget 1971: 1416–17; Vovelle 1975: 135; Martel 1938: 214–17; Litak 1973: 50, 57).

Before being carried away by the educational dynamism of the Protestants, it should be recognised that these developments were not irreversible and could be matched by the powerful forces that carried the Catholic or

Counter-Reformation to the states of Europe. Protestant schools in Poland and the Ukraine were commonly sited near the castles of their protectors rather than in the important centres of population where the Jesuits placed their colleges. Indeed, the Protestant schools suffered damaging competition from Jesuit foundations at Vilna, Polotsk, Niasviz, Orsa, Pinsk, Vitebsk and Brest after 1569. The dynamic Jesuits had 14 colleges in the province of Poland in 1608 and a further 11 in Lithuania; by 1756 these figures had risen to 39 and 28 respectively (Litak 1978: 126). Further east still, the challenge of Counter-Reformation Catholicism stimulated the reorganisation of Russian Orthodox education during the seventeenth century. Nor was the effect of the Reformation always immediate. In Prussia and Denmark it was not the Lutheran Reformation of the sixteenth century which brought about widespread literacy, but the Pietist campaign of the early eighteenth century (Dixon 1958: 14, 18; Gawthrop and Strauss 1984).

The crucial question is what would have happened if Protestantism had *not* been present? The answer to this is less simple than might at first be supposed. First of all, it is clear that the religious complexion of a region was only one factor influencing schooling. Educational provision in some Catholic parts of Europe was at least as good as Protestant, notably north-eastern France and the towns of northern Italy. In Protestant parts of south-eastern France, school provision and attendance were inferior to Catholic areas of mainly Protestant Baden in Germany (Maynes 1979: 614). Second, the Reformation did not suddenly create schools in places where none had existed before. In Scotland, England and Poland, a strong tradition of schooling had existed well before the Reformation. Most important towns had a grammar school by the fourteenth century at the latest. Third, the power of Protestantism could be a mixed blessing and competition between faiths could damage education. After the rising of 1641, Irish Catholic schools were persecuted by the English Protestant establishment. Catholic parents could only send their sons to Protestant schools, where they were treated as second-class citizens and evangelised by teachers who subscribed to an alien faith. As early as 1596 Bishop Lyon of Cork reported that while parents were happy to have their boys taught English, a Protestant education was not acceptable. He also recorded suspicious circumstances concerning grammar books, pages of which announcing the Elizabethan supremacy had been ripped out 'although they came new from the merchants' shops' (Moody *et al.* 1976: 137–40).

The ratio of school places to the numbers of eligible children varied enormously between different parts of Europe, between town and country, and according to the sex of the child. Eastern and southern Europe were less favoured than the north and west. Within these broad distinctions there were differences between, for example, the north and south of Spain, or between upland and lowland parts of Languedoc. England experienced two main phases of school creation. The first was during the reigns of Elizabeth I and James I and was principally a phenomenon of the southern and eastern counties, which at that time were the richest and most economically developed. The second period of expansion came at the end of the seventeenth century and beginning of the eighteenth. Between 1698 and 1723 some 1,329 charity schools were set up, and in the four decades before 1740 one third of all the schools not providing a classical education in 1818 were created (Tompson 1977: 74).

On Europe's eastern and northern fringes, major changes did not take place before the eighteenth century. Russian state initiatives during the 1780s produced the first significant increase in schooling: 8 public schools in 1782, 269 in 1790 and 315 by 1800, the number of teachers rising from 26 to 790 during the same period (Black 1979: 149). One community in ten had a school in late-seventeenth-century Moravia and even in 1781 less than 3 per cent of the total population were attending schools in this and neighbouring provinces of the Habsburg empire. In the province of Upper Austria were to be found 303 schools with 12,900 pupils in 1774, compared with 410 and 19,300 just a decade later. In Scandinavia too the plantation of rural schools did not take off until the later eighteenth century. In Sweden only 10–15 per cent of rural parishes had a school in 1768. By 1814 at least 45 per cent possessed one (O'Brien 1970: 561; Barton 1977: 536; Tóth 2000: 36–9).

Just as the timing and rate of expansion were uneven across Europe, so too were the fortunes of different types of school. Most obvious is that advances in education for boys had almost invariably to precede those for girls. The German duchy of Brandenburg is a case in point. From 1500–39 its 102 towns had 55 boys' schools in all, but only four for girls. Between 1540 and 1572 the number of boys' schools had risen to 78, the girls' to just nine. The steady expansion of educational provision for male children continued to the end of the century when there were 100 schools. It was between 1573 and 1600 that a huge leap in the number of girls' schools took place, up five-fold to 45 (Green 1979: 106). Yet expansion of education for girls was not usually accompanied by improvements in the quality and scope of their learning until the eighteenth century. For example, it was only in the second half of the eighteenth century that females were taught any arithmetic in the schools of north-west Germany (Norden 1980: 123–4).

The process of educational advance was cumulative in most cases. Halting, uneven and slow it might be, but one generation was usually able to build on the achievements of its predecessors. However, progress was not uniform, and it was not irreversible. Warfare and disease were the most common causes of short-term dislocation. Mostly the reverses were temporary, as was the case in the Netherlands during the duke of Alva's attempt to suppress the Dutch revolt between 1567 and 1573. During the Russian occupation of Finland in 1717 many buildings were burned down and one teacher resorted to carving an ABC book into the trunk of a tree so that he could continue lessons in the forest out of sight (Whittaker 1984: 16). Fighting between Russia, Poland and Sweden, raging through parts of Byelorussia in the years 1654 to 1667, seriously damaged the few schools which existed in the region, a setback from which they never recovered. Civil war and plague in Transylvania (1657–60) decimated schooling. Some buildings were destroyed, others had their libraries dispersed. One of the two Icelandic grammar schools, that at Skálholt, was destroyed by an earthquake in 1784.

Less spectacular, but potentially much more damaging, was a creeping erosion of educational advances by poverty and apathy. Ecclesiastical visitation records show that most Polish parishes had a school of some sort in the late sixteenth and early seventeenth centuries. However, by the third quarter of the eighteenth century clerical disinterest, wars and economic depression had produced deterioration in some areas, notably the outlying parts of Little Poland. Comparing the dioceses of Poznań, Pszczew and Srem in the mid-seventeenth century with the period of the national education commission (1777–84) shows that in Poznań the proportion of parishes with schools stagnated at 49 per cent, in Pszczew it fell from 70 to 62 per cent and in Srem there was a modest rise from 51 to 60 per cent (Wiśniowski and Litak 1974: 321–2; Olczak 1974: 325–6). Poland had enjoyed an expansion of education contemporaneous with much of England between c.1575 and c.1625, but had been unable to sustain it on a national level. Even the Jesuits' fortunes followed this chronology. Jesuit schools in Poland also saw their most dynamic phase between c.1560 and c.1648. After the peace of Westphalia, military, economic and social changes combined with the problems of recruitment to the order to usher in a period of stagnation. At their lowest point, in 1710 during the Great Northern War, the number of Jesuit teachers in Lithuania fell from the 1700 level of 126 to 91 (Litak 1978).

Advancing or retreating, developments in schooling tended to be episodic. Both the demand for and the supply of education increased in Spain in the sixteenth century, but fell in the seventeenth century as a result of economic contraction and political change. Some 59 Jesuit colleges were founded in four Spanish provinces during the sixteenth century, compared with 30 in the seventeenth century (Viñao 1999: 59). The seventeenth century saw consolidation of the teaching profession (including new professional associations and new regulations governing them) and a standardisation of the sorts of teaching materials used. Church interest in education also seems to have waned in the seventeenth century. Renewed educational impulses in the second half of the eighteenth century were checked when, in the early nineteenth century, the clerical network of schools was dismantled by liberals (at a time of political and economic crisis) in the name of 'Enlightenment' (Viñao 1999: 51, 70–71).

Paradoxically, certain types of economic success could also damage education and literacy in the short term. This was because industrial expansion, mostly of domestic industry, created employment for children. Industrial development and population increase in the towns of north-east France, England, Scotland and northern Germany from the end of the eighteenth century strained educational resources and in some cases caused them to contract. Around Bielefeld poor peasants had a constant need for child labour. The number of petty schools at Bremen fell from around 100 in 1788 to 60 in 1810 because children were working in tobacco processing and could not attend day schools. A rise in evening and Sunday classes could only partly compensate for the social and educational problems caused by early industrialisation (Hofmeister *et al.* 1998: 374–81; Engelsing 1973: 70).

National Literacy Campaigns

Co-ordinated initiatives to promote schools existed in the form of princely patronage of learning (and the arts), a long-established tradition given renewed impetus by Renaissance humanism. Examples include the elector of Saxony's patronage of prestigious schools at Grimma, Pforta, and Meissen during the 1540s, and the foundation of the Calvinist *Gymnasien* and academies of Herborn (1584) and Bremen (1585). The Dukes of Catholic Bavaria spent money on Jesuit schools and colleges to educate the élites in Latin rather than on ordinary German schools (Hsia 1989: 115). Royal patronage continued to play a role in educational expansion throughout the early modern period. In the 1720s several hundred *rytterskoler* or elementary schools were established on the royal estates of Denmark, and these 'crown schools' increased in number to provide perhaps one for every 30 rural children in favoured areas by the mid-eighteenth century.

For all that princely patronage was important, increases in schooling were attributable mainly to piecemeal measures. Princes tended to give money to high-profile individual establishments rather than wide-ranging projects. The early modern period saw much greater intervention by governments in the interests of regulation, systematisation and even provision. During the sixteenth century the principal drive to control, extend and structure the provision of education came from a desire for religious conformity whether in the bounds of a nation state or within a principality or even a single town. The seventeenth century was a period of comparative stagnation except in Scotland, parts of Germany and some of the Scandinavian countries. During the eighteenth century the overwhelming aim was to assert state control over education, provide resources for it and, in Catholic countries, to fill the gap created by the suppression of the Jesuits.

Early attempts to structure education and to extend its provision were initiated largely by the church. Ecclesiastical authorities envisaged that the parish clergy would educate boys and girls, and thus took a keen interest in what was being taught and by whom. Church constitutions of the Protestant principalities of Germany required each pastor to possess a Bible and to ensure that children were taught the elements of religious knowledge. The word *Børnaelærdom* (religious education for children) runs through all Danish educational regulations from 1539 onwards. The church always had a say in who was to be appointed as a schoolteacher, and in some cases had the right of nomination. Ecclesiastical authorities also kept a close watch on the content of education. Formal visitations were conducted on an annual basis in seventeenth-century Scotland, while Dutch clergy and parish elders in Waal and Holland were ordered to visit their schools quarterly during the 1620s. Visitations were less frequent at Amsterdam in the early seventeenth century, but might last up to two weeks (van Deursen 1978: 60).

The church's right to vet educators had long been established and was consolidated in the century of the Reformation. It did not, however, work alone. The backing of secular authorities was essential if ecclesiastical injunctions were to be obeyed, as Scottish and German reformers recognised. Indeed, reformers and governments worked together to draft educational regulations. More than 100 *Schulordnungen* were promulgated in the German principalities between 1518 and 1600, most of them religious in content though supported by the power of the civil magistrates (Strauss 1978). Day-to-day supervision of Danish schools after 1739 was left to parish clergy and officials though ultimate control rested with the bishop and county sheriff.

The reasons behind the interest of lay authorities are not far to seek. Some writers believed that the state had a positive duty to educate its people, following the Renaissance ideal that learning, progress and the overall quality of a nation were interdependent. The sixteenth-century Spanish jurist Diego de Simancas wrote: 'One of the most important functions of the state must be that children and youths are correctly educated and perfectly taught, since subjects who are poorly trained as children grow up to be the worst enemies of the homeland' (Kagan 1974: 12). To some extent, rulers felt that providing education, and grammar schools in particular, was a mark of their standing as enlightened, Christian monarchs. The efforts of Christian III of Denmark in his Icelandic territory in the 1540s offer one example. Some rulers were clearly committed to the Protestant faith, including the Calvinist duke of Zweibrücken and the Lutheran count of Sponheim, both with lands on the Rhine. Practical reasons also existed. Most sixteenth-century states suffered from a lack of literate administrators, and a commitment to extend education was often associated with a desire to select the most gifted children as possible trainees for official posts (Vogler 1976: 350–52; Dixon 1958: 10–11). A more destructive aim was the eradication of a faith, one of Louis XIV's goals being to extirpate Protestantism by insisting on education by Catholic teachers.

Co-operation between ecclesiastical and secular authorities in the creation of national educational systems and the fostering of literacy was central to the success of initiatives before the eighteenth century. The different approaches taken in Scotland and Sweden provide examples. Scotland had the first educational campaign that was truly national in its conception. At the time of the Calvinist Reformation in 1560, John Knox and his followers had set out their ambition for training a nation of believers in their manifesto, the *Book of Discipline* – a document that had more to say about education than any other topic. However, it was not until 1616 that the Scottish Parliament (independent from that of England until 1707) passed legislation. It specified that every parish was to have a school and a teacher whose salary was to be paid by the local landowners in rural areas, and by the town council in urban communities. Further legislation in 1633, 1646 and finally 1696 strengthened these provisions, making them enforceable at law. The results were impressive. By the beginning of the eighteenth century, virtually all parishes in the most densely settled and economically developed central lowlands of Scotland had a parish school, some more than one. These schools provided basic literacy for the youngest children and usually instruction in both English and Latin grammar. Scholastic education was to be supplemented by the learning of the catechisms and Creeds at home, an ambitious programme that produced a population with remarkable, if not total, literacy by the mid-eighteenth century (Houston 1985).

Sweden's experience was very different, though the goals of religious orthodoxy, social order and national development were much the same. Instead of Calvinism, it was the Lutheran church that provided the drive towards mass reading ability in Sweden. Poverty and dispersed settlement made the extensive creation of schools impossible except in some of the southern provinces. The church strove instead to ensure that men, women and children acquired a basic knowledge of religion and reading, to be taught by parish priests and by literates to illiterates in the home rather than in schools. One important figure, C. G. Nordin, who later became a bishop, argued against the establishment of schools in 1785 in terms which show what could be achieved without them.

> Through the attention of the authorities and the efforts of the clergy during the past forty years, the public has ... acquired the ability to read in a book in such numbers that in general parents can themselves, without expense, give their children necessary Christian instruction in their own homes. And if certain parents should not be capable of this or should lack time or opportunity, there are generally old soldiers, widows, maidservants, cripples or others in every village who can occupy themselves with giving instruction ... That instruction in such cases might be less than perfect ... is something that has to be accepted, especially since it makes little difference whether a manservant or maid spells badly. (Barton 1977: 539)

Compared with Scotland, this was a more limited campaign, but one which seems to have created universal reading ability by the mid-eighteenth century.

The long time scale involved in educational programmes is clear from German examples. A study of the Electoral District of Saxony between 1520 and 1675 has shown that few new schools came into existence before 1560. One positive reason is because there was a long tradition of town schools for boys dating back to the thirteenth century (Worms, Lübeck, Breslau and Wismar were among the first, founded in the 1260s). These focused on Latin training and were the resort of sons of the urban patriciates. German-language instruction was discouraged in the sixteenth century. A state initiative to promote education predated the 1580 *Schulordnung*, but attendance was no more than a few hundred across the Electorate at any time during the sixteenth century. In 1575 just 19 per cent of communities had boys' schools. However, 70 per cent of parishes had boys' schools in 1618 and 94 per cent had schools by 1675 (Karant-Nunn 1990: 131–7; Kintzinger 1990). The situation for Saxon girls was very different. Just 10 per cent of parishes had schools for girls in 1575 and one authority concludes that 'Until the 1570s, opportunities for girls to gain an education were probably fewer than they had been before the Reformation' (Karant-Nunn 1990: 138). 'Most Renaissance towns lacked the social unity and ideological consensus necessary for universal education' to be provided for both sexes and all social levels (Grendler 1990: 777).

School attendance was hard to enforce in Germany during the Thirty Years War (1618–48). By the early eighteenth century it seems to have become easier. The church court of Wildberg near Stuttgart punished both youths and parents for non-attendance and granted fees to subsidise schooling (Ogilvie 1986: 304–6). During the period 1706–25 attendance grew despite a declining birth rate, and schooling became a normal provision of apprentice contracts. The church and community seem to have been keen to widen participation in basic education, and by 1715 it was expected that parents would normally send their children to school for up to five years (Ogilvie 1986: 307–8).

Church registers in this part of Baden-Württemberg distinguish three levels of religious education or knowledge that can be used as a proxy measure of schooling: infant, catechist, communicant. The transition from infant generally happened at age 7 or 8 years, from catechist at 14 or 15. Seven was the minimum age for starting school and 14 or 15 the age when boys and girls started going into service (Ogilvie 1986: 311–13). However, education did not end then. Every year between 1706 and 1725 an average of five young people were fined by the church court of Wildberg for not attending the *Kinderlehr*, an advanced Sunday school for unmarried people up to age 24 (Ogilvie 1986: 320). These German examples show the slow progress of educational campaigns. Yet they also suggest growing successes in centralised control and enforcement from the end of the seventeenth century.

Extensive efforts to regulate education were instigated in the states of continental Europe during the eighteenth century: Poland, the Habsburg monarchy, Prussia, Denmark, Spain and Portugal. The essence of the eighteenth-century reforms was the provision of a national, secular educational programme suited to the needs of the state. Secular authorities implemented them for largely secular, utilitarian ends, in contrast with the earlier church-inspired programmes that stressed religious learning and orthodoxy. And most were the product of individuals or groups of intellectuals stimulated by the ideas of the Enlightenment and able to catch the ear of the government. In eighteenth-century Portugal the *estrangeirados* (literally 'imitative of foreigners'), an élite of widely travelled intellectuals, formed an important pressure group. In the Netherlands the *Maatschappij Tot Nut Van Het Algemeen* (Society for the Common Good) performed a similar function, presenting in the 1780s schemes for a national education system covering all classes, regulated by the government, offering a standardised curriculum and non-doctrinal religious instruction. Danish initiatives from 1784 (building on schemes first set out as early as 1539 and further developed in 1739) grew out of a change of government and arose from social reforms introduced by the nobility to improve their economic standing relative to that of the peasantry. The net effect was to reduce paternalist ties with tenants and to loosen the bonds of communal life. In order to fit the peasants to be good citizens in their newly independent condition, it was felt necessary to improve education and a commission was set up in 1789 (Gold 1977: 51–2).

Attempts at secularisation and state control began in the early eighteenth century – the Austrian authorities tried to curb the Jesuit domination of education as early as the 1710s and in 1723 the Hungarian Diet brought public education under the nominal control of the government. However, it was not until after the middle of the century that reforms were implemented in earnest (Carrato 1977: 361; van der Laan 1977: 294–6). Examples from the *comté* of Nice, Poland and the Austrian territories show what was afoot. Victor Amadeus II of Savoy mounted one of the first eighteenth-century state takeovers of education. Central to his efforts was state control over teaching. Formerly vested in municipalities, bishops and, principally, the Jesuit order, a law of 1729 transferred control by specifying that all masters were to possess a royal diploma from Turin university (a step partly aimed at reviving the flagging fortunes of that institution). Administration of the reforms was in the hands of the Reform Ministry based in Turin and was delegated to local officials or *riformatori*. They were in charge of licensing teachers, supervising exams and checking that education was directed at ensuring loyalty to the crown and the laws of the kingdom rather than to any supra-national religious ideal. These reforms epitomised the secular emphasis in eighteenth-century educational change. Victor Amadeus's measures were part of a programme of social, economic and governmental reorganisation transforming the Savoyard state from a duchy to an autonomous monarchy after the end of the War of Spanish Succession (Bordes 1979; Féliciangéli 1980). In areas of northern Italy under Habsburg control, further reforms of the 1760s and 1770s were designed to train bureaucrats and produce obedient subjects. University teachers were chosen for their political soundness and practical training rather than on intellectual merit, and government-vetted textbooks were substituted for lectures. Maria Theresa went as far as establishing a school of public administrators at Padua (Langeli and Toscani 1991; Roggero 1999).

The state initiative in Poland, begun after the expulsion of the Jesuits in 1773, was one of the most successful in Europe. Building on a long tradition of educational provision and on earlier reforms by individuals such as Stanislaw Konarski (who founded a noble college in 1741), the commissioners sought to reform teaching methods and to create a formal educational hierarchy staffed by trained teachers. Poland's National Education Commission even involved itself with the production of schoolbooks. By commissioning authors to produce texts of the appropriate level for different classes or selecting them by open competition, the Polish body was able to avail itself of the best pedagogic writers in Europe. The Elementary Book Society, founded in 1775 by the National Commission, produced 29 texts between 1777 and 1792. Reforms were not, however, implemented overnight and the Commission's main contribution during the eighteenth century was less to increase the number of schools than to outline new educational goals and fresh teaching methods (Majorek 1973; Bartnicka 1973; Seidler 1977; Litak 1973: 63).

The blueprint for change in Hungary was the *Ratio Educationis*. Part one of this programme covered the organisation and funding of schools, part two the syllabus and teaching methods, part three defined scholastic discipline. Other areas of the Austrian empire such as Transylvania had their own ordinances. The reform programme of Maria Theresa and Joseph II did help to expand education in their territories, as well as formalising control of schools and colleges by the secular authorities. As with other educational reorganisation programmes, the aim of the Austrian one was to demote the church to the status of an adviser on religious education, though in reality the church remained important for teaching and everyday administration of ordinary schools. The empress Maria Theresa spoke for all the rulers of contemporary Europe when she said that 'school affairs are and will forever remain a realm of politics' (Adler 1974; Bajkó 1977; O'Brien 1970).

On paper, the national literacy campaigns of the early modern period appear extremely impressive, especially those of the eighteenth century. Educational provision was expanded and subjected to an unprecedented measure of control. Funding was increased, curricula improved and more children than ever passed through schools. In 1717, Frederick William I ordered compulsory attendance for all children aged 5–12 in Prussia. Overall achievements in expanding and improving education were, for early modern states with limited funds and coercive powers, considerable, even if they were subject to compromise and therefore geographically patchy. In central Europe the reforms did expand schooling appreciably after 1774, and the new methods of teaching formulated by Maria Theresa's adviser, Johann Ignaz von Felbiger, were to become important during the nineteenth century (Melton 1988).

Over the rest of Europe, consolidation and codification of existing provision occurred. Yet some states made hardly any changes. Other than in the Habsburg territories and Nice/Savoy, only the church in Italy provided anything like a system of schools in the seventeenth century. Italian church schools (directed by and under the authority of a cathedral chapter, bishop or religious order) had become moribund in the late middle ages, but during the Counter-Reformation education was taken over by religious orders (Grendler 1989). In the seventeenth century orders like the Jesuits and Piarists, which established élite schools to mould the best and the brightest of the upper classes, captured school governance through more cost-effective financing. With a humbler clientele, the Somaschi and Scolopians offered subsidised elementary and vocational education.

Even relatively small and monolithic states did not go down the road of centralisation. England never had anything but the vaguest central government policy on education at any stage during the early modern period. In its satellite states of Scotland, Wales and Ireland the eighteenth century did not involve any significant developments in state control. Despite the ferment of writing on education and the national campaigns elsewhere, the eighteenth century similarly saw little activity in Sweden. Of the major continental states, France did not attempt a systematic reorganisation, though there were royal ordinances promulgated in 1698, 1700 and 1724 (the last before the Revolution) to establish teachers in all French parishes and to allow local taxation of inhabitants to pay for education. Schools of some kind were already present in most French communities by the end of the sixteenth century, and the main development in the seventeenth was the church hierarchy's systematic backing for educational provision (Chartier et al. 1976: 27; Croix 1981: 1202; Graff 1987: 149).

The principal problem faced by all European states, even in the later eighteenth century, was a lack of funds to pay for impressive schemes and of coercive power, without which it often proved impossible to implement even the most basic reforms. National educational programmes exemplified the weaknesses of early modern state power. The difficulties involved in realising schemes of educational provision envisioned by intellectuals and codified by legislatures is neatly illustrated in the case of Portugal. In 1772 the

School Board issued a report on education which formed the basis for a royal decree. The addendum to the decree, called the *Mapa dos professores e mestres das escolas menores*... ordered, among other things, that 479 elementary schools should be set up in the most densely populated communities. The problems of establishing this educational network were huge. Nothing like an adequate pool of qualified teachers existed to staff the new foundations. Furthermore, the proposed system of financing was difficult to operate. A new tax, the *subsídio literário*, was to be levied on the consumption of meat and alcohol in order to place education on a stronger and more independent financial footing. The 100 million *reales* that this tax was soon realising each year were supposed to pay for the public educational system. In reality the funds were siphoned off for the school of commerce, the noble college, the Lisbon academy of science and various other élite institutions. In Spain too the royal reforms of a decayed system did little more than halt further educational decline during the eighteenth century (Carrato 1977: 378–9).

Potential obstacles were endless. Authorities might insist on compulsory education for all children between certain ages, as Duke Ernest the Devout of Saxe-Gotha did in 1642. Yet they often lacked systematic means of ensuring attendance. Laws might be passed, but administrators omitted to institute formal means of control, a problem in early seventeenth-century Scotland and in many German principalities during the sixteenth and early seventeenth centuries. Town councils might find clandestine schools impossible to eradicate, as in eighteenth-century Cracow. Russian efforts to introduce the lessons learned from Prussia in the later eighteenth century foundered on the shortage of qualified teachers and the absence of a tradition of institutionalised learning in Muscovy. Implementation of the ambitious Danish–Norwegian school law of 1739 was delegated to local landowners, who were lukewarm about meeting the costs (Dixon 1958: 26). However, in the eastern parts of Denmark the provision of schools was probably good by the mid-eighteenth century and in the longer term the legislation seems to have had an effect. The number of permanent elementary schools grew from about 600 in 1739 to 1,700 by the 1780s.

Historians have tended to emphasise the significance of national literacy campaigns because they are, in some senses, the precursors of the regulated and integrated systems that developed in the nineteenth and twentieth centuries and because they mark one facet of the state's desire to tighten its control over its subjects. The immediate effect on literacy was usually slight since the laws tended either simply to codify existing practice or failed to provide adequate machinery to implement change. A good example is the state of

Brandenburg-Prussia, frequently held up by advocates of educational reorganisation in the early nineteenth century as an early and successful example
of what could be achieved by central control. Elementary education was
theoretically compulsory after 1717: children were to attend for two days a
week even in summer. Yet not every parish in the early eighteenth century
had a school or a teacher. Popular education continued to depend, as it had
done in the middle ages, on local clergy, town and village authorities and on
local landowners and their officials. Parents too were an important part of
the equation. Numerically, independent, fee-paying *Winkelschulen* were more
significant than official schools even at the end of the eighteenth century
and most impetus behind educational innovation came from the localities
(clergy, teachers, and urban authorities) rather than from central government
(Neugebauer 1985; Melton 1988). A similar pattern prevailed in Britain.
More than two-thirds of England's school children were educated in schools
wholly financed by fees in 1750, and even in Scotland, which had a much
more active campaign, the figure was still 43 per cent in 1818.

Who went to School?

Advances in schooling took place all the way across Europe during the early
modern period, from Iceland to Hungary and from Finland to Spain. More
school places were available than ever before both at the elementary and
the more advanced levels. Historians have waxed lyrical about the dramatic
effect of the 'educational revolution' in producing widespread literacy.
The enormous achievements of individuals, religious orders, town councils,
parish vestries, church and state cannot be denied. However, the creation
of schools did not necessarily make education available to all the children
of school age since opportunity was determined by cultural attitudes, economics and, to a lesser extent, geography. School age in modern societies
is usually fixed by legislation. Attempts were made to do this in the early
modern period, but the concept of an eligible population is still a difficult
one for historians to define. Roughly 6 to 12 years old is approximately correct for western Europe in the sixteenth and seventeenth centuries. Among
schoolchildren of known age at La Rochelle in 1689, 86 per cent were aged 7
to 14 (Chartier *et al.* 1976: 53).

The percentage of children who were able to attend school at some stage
during their youth varied considerably over time and space. During the
eighteenth century a fifth to a third represents an average achievement.

Areas where half or more of the school-age children received instruction at some stage during the year were educationally advanced. Less than 10 per cent can be seen as the bottom of the range, with figures close to 1 per cent by no means unknown even in 1800. Among the favoured zones was Brandenburg-Prussia, where attendance in the second half of the eighteenth century ran at 50 per cent or more. Investigations conducted in the 1830s showed that some communities could boast figures as high as 93 per cent (Gawthrop and Strauss 1984: 53–4). The northern provinces of the Low Countries, England, Lowland Scotland and much of north-eastern France enjoyed similar levels. A survey of the diocese of Reims in 1774 showed that virtually all parishes had a school and that 14 per cent of the total population were being schooled, roughly four-fifths of eligibles. Further to the south, the city of Lyon had approximately 24,000 children of school age during the eighteenth century, of whom roughly 7,000 attended school (Chartier *et al.* 1976: 42; Perrel 1980: 81). Southern Germany too could boast extensive school attendance. In the towns of Mannheim and Heidelberg at the end of the eighteenth century, enrolment levels exceeded 80 per cent (Graff 1987: 289). The number of schools increased in Bohemia between 1780 and 1809, but population growth kept the attendance level at about two-thirds (O'Brien 1970: 545–6, 562). Conceivably, some communities had reached these levels long before the eighteenth century. Renaissance Florence may have put nearly half of its children through elementary school, though only 13 per cent of boys were educated in Latin grammar (Graff 1987: 78).

These figures represent the best achievements in eighteenth-century Europe. In the vast tracts of eastern, central and southern Europe where attendance at school was not a normal part of growing up, attendance rates were minimal. Even after reforms had led to a major expansion of schools in the last two decades of the eighteenth century, Russia had less than half of 1 per cent of its school-age population under instruction in 1807. Around 53,000 Russians received elementary education and approximately 9,000 were taught beyond the most basic level. The Hungarian province of Galicia could claim a meagre 20,000 attendees out of roughly half a million eligibles in 1789. And the best estimate for Poland in the early eighteenth century, given the sparse facilities and small size of schools, is less than 1 per cent (Alston 1969: 19; Kahan 1985: 153–4; Adler 1974: 44; Krupa 1981: 82; Litak 1973: 53–5).

Many German states, north-eastern France, Holland and most of mainland Britain, along with certain (mainly urbanised) areas of Italy, were the most favoured from the point of view of educational provision. Rural eastern

Spain, southern and western France, rural northern and central Italy, the southern Netherlands and parts of the Habsburg monarchy form an inter-mediate group. Of Vienna's 19,314 eligibles in 1770, 4,665 attended public schools, 6,632 went to Sunday schools or were taught privately, leaving only 42 per cent who received no education at all (O'Brien 1970: 562). At the bottom come eastern Europe (including Poland and Galicia), much of Scandinavia, the west of Ireland, Highland Scotland and the deep south of Italy. However, even this outline does not cover all the dimensions of edu-cation, for the social distribution also varied. After all, the mere existence of school places does not necessarily mean that all ranks in society had an equal opportunity to use them.

Indeed, the most obvious fact about the social origins of pupils is that it was, in general, only in the most elementary schools that a representative cross-section of early modern communities was found. Only in the humblest classes of the educational hierarchy did the children of labourers and jour-neymen sit with those of merchants and artisans in numbers roughly pro-portional to their share in society as a whole. These were the classes that taught reading and religious knowledge, usually by rote. For many children they were the beginning and end of their educational career. At the more advanced levels, the grammar schools and the *collèges*, the imbalance in the social distribution of the boys was marked and the domination of places by the landed classes and the bourgeoisie was striking. There were only three pupils of peasant stock among 112 at the Jesuit *collège* at Nice in 1726; 24 were artisans, the rest the sons of nobles, merchants and professional men. The *école royale*, which replaced the Jesuit school after the secularisation of educa-tion by Victor Amadeus II in 1729, was only slightly more socially balanced: four peasants and 28 artisans among 90 pupils (Bordes 1979: 419–20). The *collège* at Avallon in southern France had 20 per cent artisans and 7 per cent farmers in its intake between 1711 and 1779. Among the élite who could afford to enter as *pensionnaires* to the *collège* of Grenoble, 1786–92, less than 1 per cent were farmers. Some of the smaller provincial *collèges* of France, which depended on the social and occupational make-up of their immediate hinterland for pupils, could claim a more even social spread. That of Auch, 1598–1607, could manage 44 per cent artisans and 35 per cent farmers (Chartier *et al.* 1976: 193; Frijhoff and Julia 1976: 117). However, most stu-dents at the important French schools were bourgeois in origin and the same was probably true of Spain (Kagan 1974: 53). Their parents could see the benefits of post-elementary education for their sons and could pay the living expenses and fees required. Artisans and peasants who did attend a *collège* went to one of the lesser ones which were little better than grammar schools, while the traditional nobility (the *noblesse d'épée* as opposed to the legal and administrative nobility or *noblesse de robe*) preferred to educate their sons at home.

A similar social profile existed in the better grammar schools of seventeenth-century England. More than half the boys at Bury St Edmunds school in 1656 were from gentry or aristocratic backgrounds. Some 17 per cent were the sons of clergy and professionals, 16 per cent tradesmen, 15 per cent yeomen and none at all from the ranks of husbandmen or labourers. The social bias is pronounced (O'Day 1982: 36). Some mixing did take place in the more elevated schools of England and elsewhere in Europe. In the public schools of Russia in 1801 a third of pupils were peasants. A survey of 38 major schools in the province of Novgorod meanwhile revealed that 11 per cent of children were from serf backgrounds (Black 1979: 148; Alston 1969: 19).

Institutions of 'secondary' and higher education were very much the preserve of the gentry and the bourgeoisie. Nor were the better-off classes above poaching places intended for the children of the poor. Well-off middle-class parents might feel it beneath them to send their offspring to public schools, as they did in the Habsburg monarchy under Maria Theresa. In contrast, they were usually assiduous in placing their sons in schools that had any reputation at all for excellence. Dublin's City School was supposed to be for the sons of impoverished freemen. Members of the prosperous middling and upper classes, including in the seventeenth century the future Duke of Marlborough, nevertheless took up many places. Charitable resources earmarked to educate children of the poor at the grammar school in Nördlingen were diverted for the use of boys whose parents appear from taxation records to have been far above the breadline (O'Brien 1970: 545; MacLysaght 1969: 206; Friedrichs 1979: 227).

Segregation might take many forms. Even when their contracts stipulated it, some teachers were reluctant to take poor children because they lowered the tone of the school and might drive away children of the better sort (Dixon 1958: 17). Furthermore, it was accepted that in practice children of the 'better sort' of parents, what one French educational manual called '*les personnes de condition*', sat apart from the poor, who were likely to be 'verminous and foul both in their clothes and speech' (Chartier *et al.* 1976: 119). Social priorities could be expressed by sending one's children to separate schools. The English landed classes objected to their sons being taught with 'mechanics' (artisans) and tradesmen – and the subjects that those classes wanted. Thus there developed élite and (by the standards of the day) very large schools. By the late 1720s Eton, Westminster and Winchester together had 1,000 boys under instruction.

Free schools were important because cost was the most serious obstacle to educating a child. In a sense there was no 'free' schooling because a poor family would have to forgo the contribution which even a youngster could make to its budget. However, if church, community or a charitable body could bear some or all of the money cost of an education, basic schooling might become available to poor boys and girls who would otherwise have been left ignorant. Most countries provided some sort of subsidy to the children of the poor. In this context, the word 'poor' meant needy or deserving rather than merely lacking money. The French *petites écoles*, a step above the simplest schools, usually had bursaries attached to them to enable lower-class boys to attend. Members of the teaching guilds in Spanish, German and French towns were supposed to take on a few poor children free of charge. A handful of Spanish boys were taken on charity, *de limosna*, in Madrid's schools, and religious bodies such as the Franciscans and the *Béates* provided very basic literacy for some poor children in Catholic countries. Few were lucky enough to get this far. If parents or guardians wanted to educate a child, they usually had to pay. Even then formal opportunities for access did not preclude informal constraints on attendance. Because children from all social groups might attend a *petite école*, lower-class parents might be reluctant to admit their poverty and claim free schooling, or to send their badly dressed, dirty and scrofulous children to sit with their betters (Poutet 1971: 94, 96).

The cost of schooling depended on length of attendance, whether a boy had to board (as was common at the prestige grammar schools) and curriculum. The teacher based payment on the selections which parents made from the pedagogic menu provided. The simpler the skill, the cheaper it was to learn. The charges set by the Madrid schoolmasters' guild in the seventeenth century were two *reals* a month for reading and four for reading with writing. In contemporary Rotterdam, three months' instruction in reading commanded a fee of 20 *stuivers*, reading and writing 30 *stuivers* (Larquié 1981: 156; van Deursen 1978: 61). These graded fees meant that for poorer families, only basic instruction in reading and the ubiquitous religious knowledge would be affordable, if that.

For the well-off middle and upper classes, the decision to educate was only partly related to cost; for the lower orders it was often the only consideration. Those who lived in abject poverty comprised between 10 and 20 per cent of the early modern population. They had no surplus income and could not hope to educate their children unless someone else paid. Many more, perhaps the majority of the population of most countries, lived on the margin of poverty, generating a modest surplus in good years then falling into debt in bad times. The categories are seen in the rather extreme case of southern Spain. A 1575 survey of New Castile counted 70 per cent of adult males as *jornaleros* (landless agricultural labourers) who were chronically poor. The peasantry was scarcely better off, needing half their gross annual produce to pay taxes and dues, and nearly all the rest for rent. Small wonder that the inhabitants of a village near Toledo complained in 1580 that 'after paying the rent, nothing was left to them' (Kamen 1984: 154).

The marginality of many families is shown by the marked contraction in the numbers attending elementary schools in France during years of bad harvest and high food prices such as 1589–94, 1693–95 and 1711–13. Children were taken away from school or never sent in order to save the few pennies that might make the difference between survival and starvation for a family. For these sorts of people, the cost of post-elementary education was an unthinkable burden. A good post-elementary education in early seventeenth-century Amsterdam could cost anything from 45 to 300 guilders a year. The latter sum was half as much again as the most that a wage earner could expect to make in a year (Kamen 1984: 154; Chartier *et al.* 1976: 52; Vogler 1976: 341; van Deursen 1978: 72–3).

The importance of the net cost of education to parents is evident from comparison of an area where the burden was largely borne by parents with one where schooling was heavily subsidised by the better-off or by the community. Communities in the Vaucluse region of southern France paid their teachers a small salary supplemented by fixed fees of five to ten *sous* a month which parents were required to contribute. Nearly 90 per cent of the teacher's income came from fees around 1800. In contrast, towns and villages in the Baden area of Germany, which possessed a similar, mainly agricultural, economy, were able to pay a much higher proportion of the teacher's income as a salary; the average master derived only 25 per cent of his earnings from fees. Baden communities could do this because they had substantial amounts of communal property and could thus earmark resources for the teacher's stipend or *Schulpfründe*. As a result, the real cost of educating a child was nine times as high in the Vaucluse as it was in Baden. In the former area, only 20–30 per cent of children aged 6–13 attended school *c.*1800 compared with Baden's 70–90 per cent (Maynes 1979).

Cost was an important determinant of the length of time a child might spend in a school. Education for most children was sporadic and discontinuous, especially among the lower orders. The majority of boys and girls who attended any school could expect to receive between one and three years of education. In the Serbian and Romanian provinces of the Habsburg monarchy, only boys destined for holy orders were educated for more than three years in the rural schools. Those lucky enough to attend any school in southern Norway in the eighteenth century spent five years there on average. Boys who reached grammar-school level could look forward to a longer and more intensive course: three to five years at the Latin school of Hornbach in the Rhineland, for instance. The Latin school at Lannepax, south of Condom in Gascony, was said to offer a six-year course as early as 1500 (Adler 1974: 25, 43; Vogler 1975: 287; Loubès 1983: 317). Significantly, a year at an elementary school meant in reality just a few months. Rural schools in the southern Norwegian diocese of Akershus ran for an average of ten weeks in the year during the 1740s. Even the 1827 school law laid down a very modest three-month 'year'. In the Low Countries during the seventeenth century, it was usual for children to spend between five and ten weeks a year in rural elementary school. Undemanding as these requirements sound, absenteeism of about one-third was the norm at any point in time (Tveit 1981; 1985; de Booy 1980a: 265).

School regulations might lay down minimum and maximum durations of schooling. Those governing St Etienne du Mont in 1730 prescribed two years for any pupil, and charity schools for the poor generally had few aspirations beyond a year or two of catechism and reading. However, authorities might also try to increase the duration of learning. Eighteenth-century ordinances for the Austrian provinces specified that learning should start at age six and last for six or seven years. Parents were obliged to send their offspring and local baptism records were to be consulted to make sure that all eligibles were dispatched to a school (O'Brien 1970: 557; Ogilvie 1986). Legislation from the German principality of Baden in the late eighteenth century said that education should begin at 6 or 7 and last until 13 or 14 (Graff 1987: 289). Danish regulations of 1539 envisaged attendance to age 12, after which time only boys of proven aptitude for learning were kept on until 16 (Dixon 1958: 11).

Secular and ecclesiastical regulations can indicate who went to school, at least on paper. Indeed, orders by church and/or state were often no more than aspirational. Laws of 1717 and 1763 in Brandenburg-Prussia required compulsory school attendance. A Hanoverian consistory decree of 1734 required schooling for three-quarters of the year, but this was relaxed to suit the economic needs of different classes in 1736 following protests from both parents and clergy. Such decrees were both more ambitious and ultimately more successful in Hanover than in Hildesheim, where schooling was much less accepted by rural communities (Melton 1988; Hofmeister *et al.* 1998: 355–9). Much further east, in western Pomerania, the notionally compulsory schooling of children had to be subordinated to a family's need to provide labour services to their lord (Lukasiewicz 1996).

In earlier times, initiatives came from the church more than the state. In 1484 the bishop of Cuenca in Spain ordered sacristans to teach reading, writing and doctrine to parish boys for four hours a day; parents were to send at least one son to the parish school. However, the curriculum was not specified and there were no sanctions on parents or priests who failed to comply. Mid-sixteenth-century orders were more realistic and precise, re- quiring pupils under 12 years to be able to cross and bless themselves, those over 12 to know four prayers, Ten Commandments and other basics of faith. Some bishops linked attempts to provide education with sanctions against those deemed ignorant. Communicants had to display basic religious knowl- edge before enjoying the rite, and at the 1601 synod headed by cardinal Rojas this also became a requirement for marriage. In 1566 the bishop of Cuenca ordered clergy not to marry people unless they could recite the prayers and in 1602 priests were to refuse absolution to penitents ignorant of the cate- chism (Nalle 1992: 106–7).

It was not until the eighteenth century that church requirements were enforced in a way that palpably influenced literacy in parts of Protestant Europe. In the Swedish kingdom, advances in reading had occurred without linking confirmation to literacy achievements, whereas in Denmark, Norway, Greenland and Iceland pietistical regulations introduced 1736–44 started the mass reading campaign. A Danish royal decree of 1736 required candi- dates for confirmation to be at least 14 or 15 years old and to be sufficiently well informed for a church examination. It was not until 1759 that confirma- tion became compulsory. The Swedish church law of 1686 enjoining reading for youths was not connected to confirmation, which was only adopted as a normal duty and then a requirement (it was not a sacrament of the Lutheran church) in the second half of the eighteenth century in that kingdom (as in Denmark). The link to confirmation was important because those who had not been confirmed could not obtain a marriage licence or land lease and could not enlist in the army (Guttormsson 1990: 19–20). In Denmark– Norway the introduction of confirmation as a routine obligation in the 1730s was followed by legislation which tried, among other things, to extend schooling beyond the usual two or three years from age six. However, further legislation over many decades (culminating in 1814) was required before an effective system was produced.

Indeed, it was in the second half of the eighteenth century that the richer and more powerful states of Europe were achieving speedier results. There were 1,272 elementary or 'trivial' schools in Bohemia in 1779 compared with 1,906 in 1781. When Maria Theresa's law obliging all children aged six and above to be sent to school was passed in 1774 only some 30,000 attended, perhaps a sixth of those of 'school age'. By 1784 the figure had risen to 119,000 – perhaps three-fifths of eligibles – and to nine-tenths by 1828 (Ducreux 1989: 213). Again, successes varied widely, even within regions. In the last third of the eighteenth century Hanover was committed on paper to a three-class teaching system, a long school year, and minimum reading and writing standards. Hildesheim aimed at teaching the catechism alone in a six-month year. A striking success story was the prosperous Halberstadt region. In 1589 41 per cent of villages had a school and all had one by 1710. Halberstadt cathedral chapter launched qualitative educational reforms to a system with excellent provision in 1776 following government and consistory legislation. They included a visitation system, close examination of teacher qualifications, and a sophisticated and extensive programme of education that included arithmetic for boys and girls. The resulting literacy rates for males and females were among the highest in Europe (Hofmeister *et al.* 1998: 359–64). This contrasts with another part of the German 'sphere', the villages around Szentgotthárd in Hungary, where just 6 per cent of boys from those too young to have attended their first communion (and therefore eligible to be educated) were at school in 1770 (Tóth 1989: 535). Across eastern Europe the incentives even to educate boys seems to have been lacking. Of 1,432 youths enrolled in post-elementary schools in the Russian province of Archangel between 1786 and 1803, only 52 received a graduation certificate (Alston 1969: 19).

The implications of a brief and basic education for the literacy of the early modern masses are clear and important. Optimists believed that a child could be taught to read, by which they meant read aloud from a set text, in the space of a year. In the province of Utrecht in the sixteenth century a more realistic three years was postulated (van Deursen 1978: 68). Given that most children spent three years or less in a school, formal education could only have produced a commonality possessed of the most rudimentary literacy. The level of facility in reading must have been low, that of writing less still. Quality of understanding cannot have been high either. Even if basic literacy was increasing, many were unable to participate in the scientific and literary advances of the early modern period.

Education depended principally on financial resources. Money made an education available and there is clear evidence from countries as diverse as Spain, Scotland and Germany that the children of parents who were paying the highest fees tended to receive more of the teacher's time. Masters in control of large classes of mixed age and ability had an inclination to neglect ordinary plodders in favour of the potential high-fliers who were learning Latin and who might progress to an academy or university. The poorer classes had limited access to all except the most basic schooling. Social conservatism and inequalities of wealth strictly tempered any democratising effect which schooling might have had.

Chapter 3

WAYS OF TEACHING

One of the most valued goals of modern education is to inculcate a capacity to think independently. The pupil should assimilate an existing body of information and then exercise critical understanding upon it. If such a thing happened in the early modern period, it came about largely by accident. Teaching methods in the sixteenth, seventeenth and much of the eighteenth centuries were explicitly designed to instil a fixed set of ideas and facts into the pupil. At both elementary and advanced educational levels, the emphasis was on the reception of a particular viewpoint, usually dictated by the dominant ecclesiastical and secular authorities. Orthodoxy was prized more than originality. As Lawrence Stone (1977: 166) wrote, the classical education of post-Renaissance Europe, seen by many as the jewel in the pedagogic crown, 'demanded effective repression of the will, the imagination, the emotions, and even intellectual curiosity'. Educators stressed the transmission of approved knowledge, an emphasis that only began to encompass understanding in the eighteenth century. The means by which pupils learned to read and write were central to the meaning their skills took on and had an important bearing on the uses to which they could be put.

Teaching Materials

This stress on order and conformity ensured that memorising or learning by rote played an enormous role in the educational process. In most elementary schools it was the only means of learning offered to the children. Writers on education argued that constant repetition instilled a habit of learning in pupils, a view extended by the sixteenth-century Strasbourg educationalist Jean Sturm who asserted that it helped develop the memory (Trenard 1977:

437). Religious education across Europe was founded on rote learning of the essentials of faith. The aspirations of Protestant and Catholic churches alike were humble, requiring little more from their flocks than an ability to memorise set forms of words which were regurgitated at intervals to teacher or priest. The Creed, the Lord's Prayer, the Ten Commandments, a basic catechism and perhaps some psalms: for many children this was as far as their education went. What passed for reading was often not what modern observers would understand by the word. For example, the literacy campaign in Scandinavia was based on known texts, the definition of understanding predicated on specific responses to particular questions (Luttinen 1985; Strauss 1978).

Two kinds of reading existed. One, phonetic literacy, involved recognising then pronouncing letters, syllables and words without necessarily understanding their full grammatical meaning. This was similar to rote learning. If readers had a sense of the text, it came principally from extraneous sources. A priest or teacher gave an authoritative explication to a group, the interpretation being guided if not controlled. Examples included Latin prayers or even reading the Bible, with meaning derived from sermons and priestly instruction. The other was reading with comprehension. This meant reading silently and with full understanding (Saenger 1989: 142). The Danish call the former type of reading *undenadslæsning*, the latter *indenadslæsning*. Silent reading first developed among the laity during the fifteenth century. Reading with understanding only became a priority in the mid-eighteenth century, and then only in north-western Europe. For example, the Danish school law of 1739 specified that pupils should not only learn by heart, but should also be equipped to read the Bible 'for their own edification and benefit'. Roger Chartier sums up the diverse nature of reading.

> All who can read texts do not read them in the same fashion, and there is an enormous gap between the virtuosi among readers and the least skilled at reading, who have to oralize what they are reading in order to comprehend it and who are at ease only with a limited range of textual or typographical forms. (Chartier 1994: 4)

The aspiration to produce uniformity, order and godliness by education could be realised most effectively through the medium of the catechism. A catechism was a list of questions about the central tenets of the Christian faith accompanied by set answers. Some catechisms were brief and featured one-word answers such as yes, no, God, Christ; others were more substantial and called for a fuller knowledge. The 'shorter' catechism (actually a substantial work), involved questions, answers, and a biblical reference to substantiate the latter. The 'proof' version, which could be up to three times longer, had the same information and also reproduced the full text of the reference. All were to be learned by heart.

Across Europe, from Greenland to Galicia, the catechism was the key to religious education. A Lutheran prayer book and catechism were available in Croat as early as 1601. Even the eastern Orthodox church, to which the catechitical form had been unknown in the medieval period, produced one in Polish and Church Slavonic in 1645 (Martel 1938: 109). Secular and ecclesiastical figures were united in their advocacy of this powerful pedagogic tool. It was, after all, ideal for their purpose of passing on simple knowledge and agreed concepts to a (hopefully) passive audience. Basic religious precepts were set out unambiguously for children to learn by frequent repetition, aided by the pastor. The catechitical form was central to all teaching and learning. Even arithmetic teaching texts resembled simple catechisms because they did not try to explain theory, relying instead on memorising rules and examples.

Catechism was at the leading edge of any early modern Christianisation or conversion campaign. From the 1470s in Spain the catechism was the main tool wielded by the church hierarchy in their drive to instruct the people in religion, an emphasis reinforced if not initiated by the Council of Trent (1545–63). A Dominican called Villanova set up catechism schools at Milan in 1536 as part of the early Catholic response to the challenge of the Protestant reformers. The catechism there was known as an *interrogatio*. Luther's shorter, small or lesser catechism was the main weapon in the hands of Hans Egede, an evangelical preacher who worked to convert and educate the Eskimo subjects of the Danish crown in Greenland after 1721 (Gawthrop and Strauss 1984: 35–9; Dedieu 1979: 263–5; Poutet 1971: 93; Gadd 1981: 84). Griffith Jones, the major figure in expanding Welsh education in the eighteenth century, called his creation 'Circulating and Catechizing Schools' (Jenkins 1997: 332).

In England and Germany the catechism would 'lay the foundations of religious knowledge, enable the faithful to understand more of the Scriptures and sermons they heard and the meaning of the sacraments and other ceremonies that took place in church, and it would both encourage virtue and discourage vice' (Green 1996: 558). German catechising was done in home, church and school, English principally in church. Memorising short forms achieved learning. In England there were probably two broad catechitical experiences. One was 'an elusive majority who were exposed to a limited amount of catechising in church and who for the most part probably did little more than master the staple formulae and a few basic answers built around them'. The other was 'a captive minority in schools who were exposed to more regular bouts of catechising and who were expected to learn more, retain it for longer, and achieve greater understanding as well' (Green 1996: 560). English scholars of the late seventeenth and early eighteenth centuries probably learned by a mixture of listening, speaking and reading.

Germany had two drives, one in the middle quarters of the sixteenth century, the other (pietistically inspired) in the late seventeenth and early eighteenth centuries. England (and perhaps some Catholic states) started later, but sustained the successes for a century and a half. English catechising was probably more successful than Strauss has claimed for Germany because of the greater degree of political and ecclesiastical stability after the 1560s, England's homogeneity of language, improving clerical standards, and a strong commitment to use new techniques of learning to replace visual aids (Green 1996: 558–9).

Most catechising before the late seventeenth century was based on rote learning of basic facts. From the early eighteenth century English catechists were increasingly concerned with understanding, and charity school regulations of 1701 emphasised this. Eighteenth-century English criticisms of religious training were not that people did not *know* the basics of religion, but did not *understand* them, suggesting that levels of expectation (and achievement) had risen. Yet, even then, catechists continued to assume learners whose reading skills were poor and with whom oral repetition was the best teaching method (Green 1996: 242, 263–4). In the German lands too it was not until the end of the seventeenth century that significant religious groups such as the Pietists began to advocate and practise the teaching of mass reading and critical understanding of catechism and the Bible. There was no comparable development in Catholic Spain. The use of catechisms was encouraged by the Counter-Reformation church in the sixteenth century and again by reforming, Jansenist bishops of the second half of the eighteenth century. However their use remained in the sphere of memorisation rather than reading, of orality rather than literacy (Viñao 1990: 582).

The whole point of the catechism was that it was *safe*. Repeating set phrases rooted the basic religious tenets in the minds of the masses and, by stressing the religious basis of civic obligation, its use strengthened the social order. The potentially disruptive influence of reading the Bible and of independent thought was substantially reduced. Small wonder that from Luther in the early sixteenth century to Condorcet in the late eighteenth century there was substantial agreement that the purpose of religious education should be to encourage submission to the dictates of the faith and that for this purpose the catechism was unequalled.

Catechism was about rote learning. The next stage was deciphering print and writing. Teaching reading began with an alphabet that the pupil learned by heart as a sequential whole. The next step was to recognise individual letters out of order, then to identify syllables, whole words and phrases. Pupils were asked to name single letters, spell out syllables and words, pronounce words and finally to read aloud in class. In France the pupil pronounced a flat vowel before consonants so that 'letters did not link together phonetically in combinations that could be recognised by the ear as syllables of a word' (Darnton 1986: 18). This mode of teaching changed hardly at all during three centuries and was used in all types of elementary school in slavish emulation of past practice. Printed ABCs were generally of pamphlet size, set out alphabetically and sometimes with verses to help memorisation. The official 1695 Swedish psalm book – which went through more than 250 editions and one and a half million copies before 1819 – had 413 psalms, number 260 of which was called 'The Golden ABC' since each of its 24 verses began with a different letter of the alphabet (Claeyssen 1980; Lucchi 1978; Johansson 1981: 162). The sixteenth-century Italian *Babuino* provided word practice for elementary classes in the form of lists of names and adjectives for regions, countries, cities and inhabitants (Schutte 1986: 10, 12).

More substantial were grammatical primers, ranging in content from the very simple to the fairly demanding. The Dutch *Trap der Jeugd* (Stages of Youth) was made up of a list of increasingly difficult words to test spelling and recognition, and only in chapter seven was the child introduced to reading through the medium of family trees from the Bible. *Spiegel der Jeugd* (Mirror of Youth), used as reading practice, contained a litany of the cruelties inflicted by the Spaniards and French on the Dutch Protestants (de Booy 1980a: 266–7).

Slightly more advanced than the Stages of Youth was the Russian *Bukvar* published by Ivan Fedorov in Lvov in 1574. It came in two parts. The first was an ABC (*Azbuka*) to give command of the alphabet and some of the basics of grammar and orthography, including guides to conjugation, declension and derivation. The second consisted of texts for reading and memorising, beginning with a set of prayers from the Book of Hours. This was a much simpler work than the Church Slavonic *Grammatiki Sflavénskiia Právilnoe Síntagma* published in Ev'ye in 1619. The first fully analytical Russian (as distinct from Church Slavonic) grammar was not produced until 1696 and then by a Dutchman in Oxford since most educated Russians studied Church

Slavonic rather than the vernacular. The religious and moral content of all school books was high. The 1770 Russian *Detskaia kniga* (Children's book) comprised 40 question and answer couplets, each with a moral, political or social lesson, making it 'a catechism of autocracy and service in the Russian Empire' (Jakobson 1955: 12–25; Black 1977: 445; Tompson 1977: 66–70; Marker 1990; Okenfuss 1980).

ABCs, primers, grammars and classical texts were all produced specifically as school books from the sixteenth century. This disproves the claim that there were no special books for children until the eighteenth century when the concept of childhood as a singular phase of life is said to have originated (Okenfuss 1980; Moore 1985). The press of the cathedral of Valladolid produced 55 million *cartillas* for the Kingdom of Castile and Spanish America between 1588 and 1781 (Viñao 1997). In the petty schools, however, teaching materials were commonly not standardised. *Le Répertoire des Ouvrages Pédagogiques au XVIe Siècle* lists nearly 3,000 separate books preserved in French libraries which were used in schools, though not all were 'school books' in the strict sense (Choppin 1980: 8). Teachers might make up their own teaching materials or use almost anything as a basis for instruction, and often had to in parts of Europe where texts were sparse or parents too poor to buy them. German catechisms of the sixteenth century were often manuscript, suggesting they were locally produced and learned orally, the teacher declaiming questions and answers. Most surviving English catechisms are in print, and the frequent new and reprint editions from the 1570s to the 1700s (the message and layout remained much the same throughout) suggest strong demand and wide distribution (Green 1996). A chronic shortage of texts hampered education in central Europe during the early eighteenth century since the few primers available were printed in a Russian version of Church Slavonic barely comprehensible to speakers of the local vernacular. In Iceland, children might learn their writing by copying out old manuscripts or the exercises of older boys as a way of easing the pressure on texts. Even at the prestige grammar schools on the island, boys might have to copy out their own version of a textbook from the sole example or take it down by dictation from the teacher (Adler 1974: 25; Hermannsson 1958: xxi).

Evidence from Italy and Germany in the sixteenth and seventeenth century suggests that the Bible was not extensively used except for teaching the more advanced classes. School regulations from the German duchy of Württemberg in 1559 make no mention of the use of the Bible until the fifth or sixth form. In Sweden too the full Bible was too expensive to figure extensively among household contents until the nineteenth century (Johansson

1981: 162). Some schools did use canonical Bibles at an early date and biblical texts such as psalters were extensively used throughout the early modern period. However, surviving children's Bibles were generally small, illustrated, and based around stories. The Old Testament outweighed the New in the sixteenth century, then the balance slowly shifted until the New Testament dominated these simple editions in the nineteenth century. Luther's collection of biblical stories (*Passional*) was replaced soon after his death by simpler, fictionalised versions. There is no indication that the *Passional* was used in sixteenth-century schools, supporting Gawthrop and Strauss's argument that Bible reading was not practised in the classroom (Bottigheimer 1993: 73). In the words of one authority: 'The lay Bible was not in itself a means of proclaiming the true Word, but a device to fix in the memory what had been preached and read of that Word . . . a "primer" to train the memory to retain initial or basic biblical knowledge which had already been communicated by other means' (Robinson-Hammerstein 1989: 31). Children's versions of the Bible in the sixteenth and seventeenth centuries were designed to caution against wrongdoing, while in the eighteenth century models of virtuous behaviour became more common.

Lutheran school ordinances did not prescribe Bible reading. Calvinist ones did. Similarly, Lutheran versions of the sixteenth and seventeenth century were invariably in edited or extracted form, including 'catechized, versified, hymnified and epitomized'. In contrast, Calvinist versions included canonical text. Calvinist children read from the Bible, Lutherans read about the Bible. Calvinist Germans, young and old, probably read Luther's Bible rather than another translation, and many more Calvinists than Lutherans read Luther's version. Patterns of Bible reading among Catholics and Lutherans may have been closer than among Lutherans and Calvinists. Thus, Bible instruction in schools began in the sixteenth and seventeenth century, but only in Calvinist communities. It became more widespread in affluent urban communities in the eighteenth century, even if reasons of cost kept Bibles from being used for mass education until the nineteenth century. As late as 1817 it was reported that at one village school near Bremen in northern Germany, four children at a time shared the sole Bible in rotation. Throughout the early modern period in Germany, canonical Bibles were less common than texts based on the Bible. The most popular school Bible of the eighteenth century was Johann Hübner's *Twice fifty-two selected Bible histories* (1714) (Engelsing 1973: 87–8; Bottigheimer 1993: 74–86). Figures for German book ownership reinforce the emphases in religious reading identified above. Bibles made up 14 per cent of religious books owned in the Lutheran Rhineland city of Speyer in the 1740s, compared with 20 per cent in the 1780s; the bulk of religious works were hymn books, devotionals (nearly 50 per cent) and confessionals (François 1982: 357).

A child who received any formal education probably stopped at reading, especially if that child was poor and female. Writing cost more and might be regarded as superfluous. Taking one school, that at Marbais in Brabant (Low Countries), at one particular time, 1730, 40 boys and 26 girls are recorded in receipt of reading instruction compared with just 17 boys and 4 girls taking writing lessons (Ruwet and Wellemans 1978: 71). One in ten of all pupils in the small towns of Larvik and Drammen near Oslo received writing instruction *c*.1800, though in the larger Scandinavian cities more than half were taught it (Tveit 1985). Writing was indeed a quite separate skill from reading, and was taught at a relatively advanced stage in the school career, usually starting in the third or fourth year. Teaching reading and writing simultaneously began in the eighteenth century, though this practice was not widely adopted until the nineteenth century.

Writing was a delicate task requiring the use of fragile quill pens and expensive materials unsuited, so some commentators believed, to the coarse hands of lower-class children. Writing materials were expensive, and in poor countries such as Finland children used a sandbox and either their fingers or a stick, then a slate and chalk or a wax tablet and stylus before graduating to a pen and paper (Luttinen 1985: 38). Blackboards did not come into general use in rural schools until the second half of the eighteenth century. Bulgarian cell schools used the *panakida*, a thin wooden board covered with a layer of wax which was marked with a sharp stick, or a *pesochnitsa* or wooden box filled with sand. In place of an abacus, children could use a tray of sand with counters (or even finger indentations) arranged in specific ways.

Learning to write initially meant copying rather than creating (Grendler 1989: 323–9). In the classroom, a board with printed examples of letters and writing styles, called a *cartelón, cartel* or *muestra de escritura* in Spain, was placed at the front of the class for copying by those pupils whose parents had paid for them to learn writing (Viñao 1997: 154). Finnish schools of the early modern period never taught composition to those children who were learning writing. Instead, they copied letters, accounts and memos of the kind which they might encounter in later life, or took dictated passages to show that they could write legibly and spell tolerably. Some Low Countries schools of the eighteenth century drew a distinction between copying classes and the more exalted Latin, arithmetic and composition classes (Luttinen 1985: 34–8; Ruwet and Wellemans 1978: 33).

Even professional scribes might never progress beyond passive copying to active composition. Many Russian manuscripts of the sixteenth century contain serious errors which can only have resulted from mechanical copying by clerks who treated the original document as a series of characters rather than as an integral and intelligible text, a familiar problem in copied documents throughout medieval Europe. Seventeenth-century Hungarian officials showed great problems with the official language, Latin. Even simple tasks like writing their Christian names in Latin were beyond many (Tóth 2000: 130–40). Phonetic spelling of book titles by Parisian appraisers' clerks at the same time suggests a lack of familiarity with the volume in question. Marot's *L'Adolescence* became *La Dolescence*, for example (Schutz 1955: 7). In fairness, spelling was not fixed until the eighteenth century. The first specific English grammar was published in 1586, but the most significant expansion in production of vernacular grammars came during the seventeenth century and of dictionaries from the 1730s.

Teaching Methods

It was traditionally thought that early modern childhood was difficult, brutal and short (de Mause 1976). Corporal punishment was an everyday part of growing up and integral to the educational process. This picture of childhood has recently undergone substantial revision (Pollock 1983). Yet it remains influential and indeed contains an element of truth. Early modern societies permitted the moderate physical correction of children – and indeed all dependent members of families, including servants – by parents and those in their place. Some educational theorists argued that beating was a way of curbing a child's independent urges and of regulating his or her socialisation. The pious San Antonio of Florence opined in the fifteenth century that children needed 'both bread and blows'. The Dominican friar Dominici pronounced that 'frequent yet not severe whippings do them good', and there was an English saying which ran: 'As a sharp spur makes a horse run, so a rod makes a child learn' (Ross 1976: 200, 214; Dunn 1976: 396–7; Tucker 1976: 246).

In practice, corporal punishment does not seem to have been a central feature of learning. Excessive correction, frowned upon by both parents and authorities, could result in the dismissal of a brutal teacher. Indeed, there was a more positive strain to educational writing, including the approach popularised by writers such as the Englishman John Brinsley in his *Ludus literarius or the grammar school* (1612). Brinsley treated learning as a competitive game and believed in advancement through emulation and competition among the peer group. Unusually, he also advocated the inculcation of more critical understanding into the pupil rather than stuffing him with memorised facts and responses (O'Day 1982: 49–53; Chartier *et al.* 1976: 121–3).

Even if the rod was not a normal pedagogic tool, early modern classrooms still bore little resemblance to the experience of readers of this book. A school normally consisted of just one room into which children of all ages were crammed, some as young as five years, others as old as 12. Most pupils sat on benches, though those who were learning to write might be placed at desks. The teacher sat at a desk which children approached individually in order to have their lessons heard, reading or reciting from memory. Regulations from the Dutch town of Haastrecht in 1723 specified that each pupil should be heard at least four times a day (van der Laan 1977: 309; Chartier *et al.* 1976: 114–26). The concept of teaching groups rather than individuals and in classes divided according to age and ability was an eighteenth-century departure, associated with educational reformers like Felbiger in the Austrian empire or the Brethren of the Christian Schools in France (O'Brien 1970: 558; Furet and Ozouf 1982: 78–80, 115). The only concession to differing ages and standards of attainment was to put those learning, say, arithmetic on different benches or on different sides of the room from those doing reading or writing. Jan Steen's lively painting, *A school for boys and girls* (*c.*1670), depicts controlled anarchy, those children not at the master's feet being left to work or play apparently as they wished. Elementary schools were probably crowded during the winter when attendance was highest. The Danish School Commission of 1789 assumed 50–60 children would fit into a room 25 metres square. Élite institutions had more than one master and several classrooms. Edinburgh's Royal High School had five teachers, compared with two at most grammar schools in lesser Scottish burghs (one teaching Latin, the other English) and just one in ordinary rural parishes during the early eighteenth century (Camic 1985: 144).

School hours varied. In the Dutch town of Haastrecht, class hours were 9–12am and 1–4pm with Saturday afternoon, the market day and all day Sunday off. At Dalkeith in Scotland, children arrived much earlier and were sent home at 9am for an hour to breakfast with their families. At the lower reaches of the educational hierarchy the hours in school were devoted to a mix of religion, reading and other literate skills, and practical training. During a five-hour day at a French cloister school in the seventeenth century, one hour was spent on religion, one and a half on sewing and weaving, two and a half on reading and writing (Chartier *et al.* 1976: 237). Religion was extremely important, but it rarely took up the majority of the day. During the eighteenth century it became less significant as parents began to demand a more secular emphasis in schooling.

Classes could vary considerably in size. Average attendance at 7 of the 39 *Winkelschulen* of the north German town of Braunschweig in 1673 was just 15. The vast majority of rural schools in the Polish diocese of Cracow around the middle of the eighteenth century had less than ten pupils, in towns less than 20. These numbers were low compared with the early seventeenth-century average for towns in southern Austria of 33 or the Dutch figure of 70 to 130. A survey of Madrid's schools in 1642 showed that they ranged in size from 38 to 140 pupils. At one elementary school in the German town of Mannheim (1755), 400 pupils were taught by two masters, though this unusual example may have been the result of rapid population growth (Kagan 1974: 13; Friedrichs 1982: 373; Litak 1973: 56–7).

Methods of teaching and the organisation of the classroom changed little between 1500 and 1800. Regulations ensured that every minute of the day was filled in an orderly and profitable way, though in practice even the strictest pedagogues recognised that young minds needed at least some variety and a little free time. Schools at all levels emphasised set forms and the transmission of a fixed body of knowledge through an established ped-agogic regime. For example, the programme of Latin grammar, rhetoric and literature was rigorous, methodical and precise, drilling the pupil in difficult literary and linguistic skills and drumming a large volume of facts into him. Even the famous schools such as that run by Guarino Guarini at Verona in the fifteenth century never bridged the gap between, on the one hand, the zealous and idealist rhetoric that literary studies would transform all men into paragons of virtue and, on the other, the plain reality that what they offered was a training in routine competence to a social élite. Creative achieve-ment, moral training and the formation of a 'Renaissance man' were quite different and incidental to the learning process (Grafton and Jardine 1986).

Nevertheless new ideas were circulating more widely in the eighteenth century. From the late seventeenth century in Lutheran Germany and Denmark, the Pietists began to promulgate an important message about learning. Originally a movement for purer Christianity and for moral reform among the clergy, Pietism in the eighteenth century became the purveyor of a state-supported campaign of education operating through schools. The Pietists argued that people should be taught to read the Bible critically, the teacher explaining and discussing meaning rather than simply handing it down. Fear of social instability diminished in the German lands after the

Thirty Years War, allowing the promotion of active, unsupervised individual reading. With its evangelical aspect tamed, the Pietist model of citizens as members of a godly congregation and an ordered corporate community, and therefore as obedient and useful servants of the state, appealed not only to Lutheran countries like Denmark–Norway (Gawthrop and Strauss 1984: 44–9). The influence of Pietism is also found in British educational revival movements such as the Welsh Society for the Promotion of Christian Knowledge, set up in 1699 (Jenkins 1997: 320–21).

Named after them, an important innovation in teaching was the 'pietistical inversion' of the eighteenth century, meaning that learning to read should precede memorisation and words were taught before their component parts were explored. This order of teaching had become firmly established in the Nordic countries by the late eighteenth century (Grendler 1989: 161). Mechanical spelling and rote learning were increasingly under fire in the late eighteenth century, notably by the German Samuel Heinicke, who was one of the pioneers of the phonetic method of teaching reading. Under Maria Theresa, Felbiger proposed teaching in groups organised by age and ability, and a Socratic or questioning method of instruction to replace rhetoric and repetition (O'Brien 1970: 558). Meanwhile in Denmark, Christian Cramer also spoke out against the prevalent one-class, one-teacher layout in schools (Engelsing 1973: 65–6, 77; Dixon 1958: 32). Yet it is questionable if these ideas made much headway across Europe as a whole before the nineteenth century. Instead, as Mary Wollstonecraft wrote of the best London boys' academies at the end of the eighteenth century, 'the memory is loaded with unintelligible words ... without the understanding's acquiring any distinct ideas', a comment as applicable to the most elevated *collèges* as it was to the humblest *Winkelschulen* (Houston 1985: 229).

Schoolmasters

In modern developed nations it is conventional to describe teaching as a profession, perhaps even a vocation. Men and women who become teachers are usually university graduates and/or undergo prolonged instruction in specialist training colleges. With variations, schoolmasters and schoolmistresses enjoy a respected status in the community, and concern over their morality, competence and remuneration is often deeply felt. In early modern Europe the situation was rather different. Few people entered teaching in the expectation that they would end their days in such an occupation, except perhaps at the top of the educational hierarchy. Except when grouped into guilds, it is unlikely that teachers saw themselves as a 'profession' or had any sense of group identity before the major national educational reorganisations of the second half of the eighteenth century. Teachers then became more of a profession as formal selection criteria and even examinations began to be put in place (Blanc 1988; Brüggemann 1988). The change influenced urban teaching more quickly than rural and indeed created a gulf between 'qualified' teachers and others (Roggero 1994a). It was only in the more advanced schools that significant numbers had either been to university or had experience of formal training in a seminary. Financial remuneration was frequently poor and the social standing of educators tended to be low. Differences in pay, qualifications and status were considerable and it is best to think in terms of a 'mixed-ability staff'. Some teachers were decent, capable and conscientious people who were respected by the parents of the children they taught; others were negligent, incompetent and disdained.

The standards demanded by communities when they hired elementary teachers varied. In some cases this amounted simply to an expectation that the candidate would be God-fearing and respectable, with some basic competence in the subjects he or she proposed to teach. The town council of Seville in southern Spain began paying the salaries of some teachers in the late 1540s and an ordinance of 1561 about licensing stressed above all the need for men 'of good life and custom' (Perry 1980: 178). Concerned by the spread of religious heterodoxy after the Reformation, secular and ecclesiastical authorities all over Spain displayed a keen interest in the strict orthodoxy of teachers.

Elsewhere in Europe, similar basic standards were set. A Piarist priest called Hueber appointed the local gravedigger to teach some poor children for free in the rapidly growing Viennese suburb of Lerchenfeld in 1737, because he had 'good handwriting and some knowledge of arithmetic' (O'Brien 1970: 546; Brüggemann 1988). For some central European church authorities, a good voice and the ability to read music were paramount considerations so that the teacher could lead religious services. Czech *kantoři* or cantors are an example. Dutch magistrates' procedures were more formal and more rigorous. The town council appointed the schoolmasters in Haastrecht after a public examination held in the church or, sometimes, in an inn. Candidates had to provide ample proof of their 'manner of living', and to display ability in reading, writing, arithmetic and singing (van der Laan 1977: 308–9). More formal tests and more demanding examinations were introduced in many parts of Europe during the eighteenth century under the influence of Enlightenment ideas and the growing desire of the state to control many areas of life. The Habsburg general school ordinance of 1774 (*Allgemeine Schulordnung*) specified that teachers should pass a state exam. The Danish law of 1739 set a minimum age of 22 for post-elementary teachers who should, in addition, have been either a student at a Latin school or already have taught in a vernacular school (Dixon 1958: 24).

Teachers' formal qualifications can be measured in the case of those who had graduated from a university – or simply been to one, since many who went into teaching had not completed their university courses. For graduates in theology, teaching could be a way of filling in time until a parish living and the attractive job of clergyman became available. The English parish clergy contained a majority of university graduates by 1600 and, between 1627 and 1641, 154 of 261 licensed schoolmasters in the diocese of London were graduates (Wide and Morris 1967: 397). Many more teachers were, of course, outside the licensing system. However, it has been suggested that the over-production of university-educated men from the mid-seventeenth century may have had positive implications for school teaching in England and Germany (Vierhaus 1988: 55–7; Brüggemann 1988).

Before the eighteenth century, the Jesuits and other regular clergy ran the majority of Catholic Europe's formal teacher-training colleges. Efforts to reform seminary education in France show what was being attempted and illustrate the limitations of centralised initiatives prior to the eighteenth century. The Council of Trent's rather general proposals were never formally adopted in France, though widely received. Its suggestion to establish new centres for 'poor' trainee adolescent clergy as young as 12 were viewed with scepticism by cathedral chapters with whose choir schools they seemed to compete. The few established in the sixteenth century seldom performed their envisioned functions. By the 1630s the seminary at Rouen had become a staging post for the clients of the powerful Guises and Orleans families, and later became known as 'the seminary of the rich'. Between 1642 and 1660, 42 new seminaries were established, some 56 during 1661–82, and 25 between 1683 and 1720; thereafter the expansion all but stopped. The new drive was lead by militant *dévots* and by religious orders such as Vincent de Paul's Lazarists. The later sixteenth century had seen the growth of *collèges de plein exercice* in France, offering a wide range of subjects that overlapped or exceeded those in seminaries. It was only in the seventeenth century that seminaries and *collèges* diverged, the former focusing on older trainees and distinctly theological curricula. In the eighteenth century the seminaries became more orthodox, more like universities, and more closely under episcopal control.

Education as a science began to be taught in German universities in the eighteenth century, with other European countries following the German example from the end of the century. The first secular teacher-training college in Denmark was the one at Blågård outside Copenhagen, begun in 1791 with two masters, a singing teacher and 14 students. Graduates of this institution needed no further proof of their qualifications to secure a post. Others had to show they could read, explain the Lutheran catechism intelligently, count, write legibly and grammatically in Danish, and sing the psalms clearly and correctly (Gold 1977: 61–3).

Whatever their formal qualifications, some teachers made frankly outrageous claims about their pedagogic skills, the range of topics they could offer and the results which they could achieve. There were *leccónistas* who came to Madrid from other Castilian towns during the second quarter of the seventeenth century to try their hand at teaching in competition with the licensed masters of the guild. They had a reputation for extravagant claims and modest standards (Kagan 1974: 15–17). Across Europe, writing masters were notorious for hyperbole. In eighteenth-century Lyon the worst charlatans were the Italian language teachers who, in order to enhance prestige and fees, claimed that they could produce accent, grammar and vocabulary of a high standard almost overnight. Séraphin Maglione arrived there in 1767 full of promises and not even the fact that he was forced to open an *épicerie* in 1771 to keep body and soul together could stop his stream of patter (Garden 1976: 150; Tóth 2000: 133–4).

These sorts of claims were almost certainly far-fetched. However, establishing the 'average' standard of teachers is difficult, partly because of the lack of quantifiable evidence and partly through problems of assessing typicality in qualitative material. Surviving documentation dealing with the quality of schooling most commonly refers to low standards, though these adverse comments may not be typical. In 1591 a Dutchman called Valcooch published a handbook written in rhyme in the hope of improving the standards of what he described, in terms hardly calculated to endear him to some readers, as the 'deeply ignorant parish schoolmasters' (de Booy 1980a: 264). When authorities visited a school, they dwelt long on any shortcomings that were uncovered, devoting to a competent teacher only a terse statement of his acceptability – or no comment at all. Villages unhappy with a teacher might refuse to pay him or even sack him; contented communities might never refer to their master. The voice of children is very rarely heard in early modern sources except retrospectively when adults recalled beatings and favouritism, or good teaching and acts of kindness.

Many early modern teachers were outsiders and many did not stay very long in a community. Virtually all the teachers who worked in the French commune of Vallorbe were strangers until the end of the seventeenth century when the Glardon family began to establish itself as a sort of teaching dynasty in the village. Turnover could be considerable. The grammar school at Ribe in Denmark had 25 *rektors* between 1536 and 1660, only one of whom stayed more than ten years (Dixon 1958: 14). In the Rhineland duchy of Zweibrücken (1556–1619), half of all town teachers stayed less than two years in the same school, 57 per cent of village teachers and 76 per cent of assistant masters in the towns. Poor and irregularly paid salaries, mediocre lodgings, conflict with the head teacher or the clergy or the parents, and outright dismissal for incompetence or moral transgressions account for the footloose character of many teachers (Vogler 1976: 333–4).

More permanent migration streams complemented this often local, short-term turnover. Men from mountainous areas of south-east France and northern Italy migrated to the plains during winter to hire themselves as teachers and notaries. The southern Alpine valley of Safien was known in the eighteenth century as the 'valley of the schoolteachers' (Viazzo 1983: 162). These movements were usually seasonal, but in the Netherlands the political and military disruptions of the 1560s and 1570s produced a substantial and permanent migration of teachers from south to north. Some 442 teachers migrated north between 1575 and 1630 and two-thirds of all the educators in Leiden during this period had come from the southern provinces (Parker 1979: 250). A similar inflow to the Netherlands, this time from France, occurred after Louis XIV revoked the Edict of Nantes in 1685.

Teachers could be paid by two means. Either they received a salary from the community in which they worked or the parents of the children they taught paid them fees that depended on the length of time they were in school and the sort of lessons they were being given. The normal practice was to blend the two sources of funding into a composite income, sometimes with the addition of jobs, officially sanctioned or otherwise. Suligny in the Aube region of France paid its teacher 455 francs for the year 1813, made up as follows: 90 francs of salary, 90 francs for singing, 100 francs from wine donations, 150 from school fees, and the right to cut firewood was assessed at a further 25 francs (Furet and Ozouf 1982: 110). No standard balance existed between the different components, but in schools for the poor where fees were either non-existent or very low, basic salaries tended to be higher than in other establishments. Communes such as those in Baden (Germany) which owned substantial amounts of communal property could afford to pay salaries high enough to allow the teacher to live by charging only very low fees. Around 1800 roughly 25 per cent of a teacher's income came from fees, compared with nearly 90 per cent in regions such as the Vaucluse in south-eastern France where the cost of education was not subsidised by communal funds (Maynes 1979).

Teachers' total incomes also varied. In the province of Utrecht, salaries ranged from 24 guilders per year at Kudelstaart (1624) through 48 at Kamerik (1631) to as high as 120 at Jutphaas in 1635. Communities in upland areas of eighteenth-century Languedoc tended to employ teachers on short contracts for sums of 30–60 livres, whereas in the low-lying regions 100–150 livres was the norm, suggesting year-round employment. At the end of the eighteenth century most Prussian teachers were earning between 100 and 250 talers a year though some received less than 100 and a handful more than 350. The *rektor* or headmaster of the school at Frankfurt-am-Oder got more than 400 talers a year, or roughly twice the remuneration of his five staff. In Spain, good pedagogues were in short supply and could earn more by moving around from month to month or season to season (van Deursen 1978: 61; Laget 1971: 1404–5; Neugebauer 1985: 310–11; Kagan 1974: 41).

Even allowing for variations and income supplements, there is no escaping the fact that as an occupational group, early modern teachers were poorly paid. Take the case of the Hjerm area of west Jutland at the end of the eighteenth century. In this poor, rural part of Denmark, teachers' salaries varied from just 8 to 82 *rigsdaler* a year. At this time, the daily wage paid to an unskilled Copenhagen labourer was 28 *skilling*. Assuming that the labourers worked five days a week throughout the year, their total annual income was roughly 76 *rigsdaler*. Though the cost of living was slightly cheaper in rural Jutland, there is no escaping the fact that the bulk of teachers there were getting less than common labourers (Gold 1977: 50). In seventeenth-century Paris, teachers are always found in the lowest taxation brackets and across the Habsburg monarchy the average income was well below that of a minor state official. This was not true of Turin where, in 1608, an elementary teacher received a salary in line with the better-paid public officials, nor of the teachers at the Calvinist school of Gyulafehérvár, paid by prince Gábor Bethlen of Transylvania, who received a handsome salary. Yet other central European pedagogues were paid only a half of the income of a humble parish priest and teachers as a group were poorly remunerated (Cipolla 1969: 30; Adler 1974: 39). Low pay often meant low prestige. One of the carrots held out to the teachers by the Polish National Education Commission in the 1770s was to form them into a hierarchical guild and thereby enhance their social standing.

Yet the most dynamic men continued to use teaching as a springboard to a career in the clergy, bureaucracy or as a notary.

Given their highly variable backgrounds and qualifications, it might be thought that some teachers deserved their low rates of pay. However, it is also possible that the poor remuneration rendered the profession unattractive to the most gifted individuals. As the clergy of Ribe in Denmark petitioned in 1789, what teachers 'have to live on is nothing more than hunger and poverty, which is why none want to be school teachers and we have to make do with poor, miserable, infirm wretches' (Gold 1977: 50). Teaching could attract those too weak or sickly to hold down a manual occupation. Sebastiano Vongeschi, a Pistoian monk convalescing in the small village of Cutigliano in the spring, summer and autumn of 1513, taught counting for five *soldi* a month, grammar for ten, primer, catechism and psalms for seven. He records in his diary that he did a roaring trade. Had he been useless, he would probably have starved (Lucchi 1978: 597).

For some it was their main source of income, but few depended solely on teaching for a living. Indeed, the catalogue of educators' by-employments covers almost the full occupational spectrum of early modern societies. In countries like Scotland, Denmark and the Netherlands it was usual for the official parish schoolmaster to double as deacon, sexton, clerk and precentor for the church; in some cases he also held the office of gravedigger (de Booy 1977: 352). The background or by-employments of 432 sextons and village schoolmasters from Brandenburg are known for the years 1668–1806: 71 per cent of them were connected with tailoring or other areas of textile working. This was acceptable to the local authorities and was not held to be incompatible with teaching. The same cannot be said of other additional occupations. Some teachers held classes in the kitchen or brewhouse while the normal functions of those rooms were being exercised. London schoolmasters might be scriveners, cobblers, tailors, fishmongers or pawnbrokers. Some in eighteenth-century Vienna moonlighted as beer-hall musicians and one even ran a bar in the very room where the children were reciting their catechism. A Dutchman called van Barendrecht used his classroom to organise a lottery contest (O'Brien 1970: 546; van Deursen 1978: 60).

Teachers could be fiercely protective of their privileges. Appealing to the laudable end of maintaining educational standards, the schoolmasters of Europe were in fact concerned principally with maintaining their salaries and fees against the competition of those who sought to infringe their privileges. Teachers and authorities in Scotland did not even bother with this pretence, stating that unlicensed (or what they sometimes called 'unfree') schools in the towns were prejudicial to the financial interests of the official parish master or 'dominie'. Teachers who obtained a licence might have to pay for it out of their own pocket. A certificate from the Parisian authorities cost 32 livres a year in Louis XIV's reign, roughly a tenth of the annual income of the average teacher. The *petites écoles* of the French capital were controlled by the Grand Chantre of the Cathedral Chapter of Notre Dame, a guild that policed other types of school such as the charity ones to ensure that their privileges were not infringed (Bernard 1970: 261–2, 279). A community of sworn master writers, specialists in the art of calligraphy, sprang up in Paris at the end of the sixteenth century. They won the exclusive right to run public writing schools and to act as expert court assessors of written documents alleged to be fake. For over 200 years the history of the guild involved a tenacious and sometimes vicious struggle to maintain its privileges, thrown into question in the seventeenth and eighteenth centuries by growing literacy and the related spread of a purely technical and no longer aesthetic knowledge of writing (Métayer 1990). Antwerp had a flourishing schoolmasters' guild in the sixteenth century which dated from the 1460s, and in Madrid the teachers formed a confraternity, *La Hermandad de San Casiano* (1666) in an effort to exclude competition from unlicensed teachers (Parker 1979: 21; Larquié 1981: 157; Soubeyroux 1987: 255–6). In Germany, the guild of Frankfurt-am-Main had, during the seventeenth century, secured the right for members of the *Gesellschaft der Deutschen Schulhalter* to pass on the privilege of holding a school to their sons, irrespective of their aptitude or ability (Friedrichs 1982: 374).

The posturing which could result from disputes between licensed and unlicensed teachers is beautifully illustrated by a case from seventeenth-century Braunschweig in northern Germany. Braunschweig in the middle of the seventeenth century was a substantial town of some 15,000 people with three élite Latin schools, two franchised municipal German schools and 30–40 *Winkelschulen* or 'corner schools' that were deeply hated by the two franchised vernacular teachers. In 1648 the monopoly of teaching reading and writing in German held by the municipal schools was challenged by the arrival of a wild young man called Melchior Schurdan. His challenge was all the more galling as he had once been taught by one of those with whom he sought to compete. Schurdan's methods were unorthodox. At one stage he employed his mother to accost boys in the street and encourage them to leave one or other of the franchised schools in favour of the one run by her son. The official teachers, Pöpping and Overheide, were livid and mounted a campaign against the young upstart. They alleged four reasons why the illegal school should be shut down. First, Schurdan taught only reading, writing and arithmetic, neglecting instruction in religious knowledge. Second, Pöpping and Overheide were encountering growing problems with discipline in their own schools. Any attempt to adopt a strict stance over infringements of the rules simply drove scholars to the illicit school. Third, their earnings were suffering. Fourth, schoolboy taunts about the quality of the respective schools were spilling over into adult conversation and therefore threatening to disrupt the peace of the town. Schurdan's school was duly closed, but the *Winkelschulen* persisted. There were 39 in the city in 1673, their numbers a testimony to the demand for secular elementary instruction (Friedrichs 1982: 371–4).

Schoolmistresses

Men dominated the 'teaching profession' both numerically and in the educational hierarchy. Women teachers were probably fewer in number than men and the sort of education they provided was almost always of a more elementary kind than that of the masters. The contrast in numbers is stark. Records relating to the town of Lyon in south-eastern France reveal the presence of 87 schoolmasters at some stage between 1490 and 1570; only five female teachers turn up in the same documents (Davis 1975: 73). A more glaring imbalance is apparent in a survey of Venetian schools conducted by the authorities in 1587. Some 258 male teachers were enumerated alongside a sole female, though it is likely that this investigation (like most official surveys of European education) under-recorded women educators. Rome in 1695 had just 16 registered schoolmistresses among a population of more than 130,000 people. The only educational institutions in Catholic Europe dominated by women were the schools attached to nunneries, on the one hand, and the specialist reformatories, on the other. There were places such as the *Zitelle*, the Venetian home for the daughters of prostitutes, in which 12 sober and moral ladies were employed to prevent the coming generation from learning the errors of their mothers. At the other end of the spectrum, in the eyes of contemporary moralists, were the religious orders, prominent among whom were *Les Béates*, the third order of the *Congrégation des Soeurs de l'instruction de l'Enfant Jesus*. Founded by one Anne-Marie Martin in the countryside of Puy (France) in 1688, this order worked in sparsely populated rural areas such as the Massif Central. The sisters worked in everyday clothes, generally alone, and lived with the families of the poor, to whose children (mostly girls) they taught reading and catechism. About 150 were at work in the diocese of Metz in eastern France in 1789 (Cholvy 1980; Furet and Ozouf 1982: 177–9; Laget 1971: 1409).

The eighteenth century saw a marked increase in numbers and improvement in status of female teachers in some parts of Europe. Lyon, where licensed masters outnumbered mistresses seventeen to one in the first half of the sixteenth century, could boast 50 male and 50 female teachers by the mid-eighteenth century (Garden 1976: 139). The French commune of Vallorbe first formally employed a schoolmistress to teach girls up to the age of ten as late as 1778, though girls' schools and women teachers had clearly been in existence long before this date. In 1730 there were at least 2,000 female teachers in England out of a total 'profession' of 12–17,000. By the time of the 1851 census 70 per cent of teachers were women. In the 1800s there were at least 20,000 'Persons employed in the education of youth, including universities' according to J. C. Colquhoun. There are no known female grammar schoolmistresses, but the majority of teachers in petty or dame schools were probably female. Indeed the sort of education which women could provide was deliberately restricted to the most basic classes and the youngest pupils or to girls, all learning simple skills such as the catechism and the elements of reading. The town of Namur in the Low Countries expressly forbade women to teach writing. In practice, this meant that schoolmistresses taught religious knowledge by rote, sewing and spinning, housewifery, a little reading and possibly the rudiments of counting.

Discovering the scholastic background and qualifications of women teachers is harder than for men. The only certainty is that none of them had been to university. Most were single. Of 121 who worked in Lyon during the eighteenth century, 22 were married and 15 were widows. Women principally used school teaching as a way to fill the time between leaving home and getting married, which was usually in their mid-twenties in France at this date. Keeping a school was one of the few non-manual occupations open to a woman who wished to remain single, as roughly one in ten did in eighteenth-century France. Some evidence suggests that women tended to spend longer in a teaching post than men, an unexpected finding since females were more geographically mobile than males in the early modern period. At Lyon between 1732 and 1792, only 9 per cent of 121 mistresses stayed in teaching in the town for four years or less compared with 19 per cent of 149 men. Of women teachers, 32 per cent remained to teach in Lyon for more than 25 years, compared with 19 per cent of men. Their social background is similarly obscure, but in the Rhineland duchy of Zweibrücken, the women whose backgrounds are traceable were often the daughters, wives or widows of teachers or clergymen (Garden 1976: 142; Vogler 1976: 356).

As recorded in official records, the role of women in education seems at best marginal. Confined to elementary teaching, their numbers were few and their function seems to have been as child-minders. With exceptions, the evidence is consistent with a picture of their involvement in very basic book-learning, practical skills, religious instruction and moral guidance. Women were generally confined to the lower echelons of the educational hierarchy and are never found teaching in grammar schools, colleges or universities. In terms of the quality of the learning instilled, their situation as a group was inferior to that of schoolmasters. There was, of course, overlap at the bottom of the profession, and there were many more female teachers than the records show. Beneath the officially recognised establishments were many which served local needs, perhaps just one street, and which women ran.

Chapter 4

HIGHER EDUCATION

Universities

The late fifteenth and sixteenth century saw an unprecedented increase in both the number of universities and in the proportion of the population who attended them. Many universities had flourished during the high Renaissance, *c*.1450–*c*.1520, and many continued to expand during the rest of the sixteenth century. Growth in higher education was achieved both by increasing the number of universities and by adding new colleges or by expanding the number of students at existing colleges. A formal charter giving the right to award degrees was the distinction of universities. Most early modern universities were organised on lines similar to the ancient foundation of Paris, with professors, faculties and centralised teaching. A variation was the Oxford or collegiate model with decentralised teaching. Finally there were the smaller institutions of Scotland or Spain which blended the first two forms.

England had just two universities throughout the early modern period. Growth came from new colleges within Oxford and Cambridge and an increased intake into existing ones. The latter institution had nearly 1,300 students in 1564 and 3,000 by 1622. At the other extreme were countries that had never had a university before the start of the early modern period. Ireland secured its first university (Trinity College, Dublin) in 1591, and Finland in 1640 (at Turku, now Åbo). Spain too relied principally on new foundations. There were six universities in Spain in 1450, 33 by 1600 and further establishments were set up in Spain's New World colonies. In most countries a combination of all three modes of expansion were used, including Scotland, Italy, France and Germany, the latter having 3,200 students in 1500 compared with nearly 8,000 in 1600. No less than 184 universities existed at some time during the early modern period, even if some were abolished or merged, and more than 100 colleges were founded 1502–1783 (Engelsing 1973: 33; De Ridder-Symoens 1996).

Expansion of universities as a whole, albeit at different rates and in different periods, disguises important variations in the areas of study which were attracting students. The largest universities contained four faculties: arts, theology, medicine and law. Theology was 'the queen of subjects' in the sixteenth century, jurisprudence in the seventeenth, and philosophy in the age of Enlightenment. The expansion of Oxford and Cambridge was based on intakes into theology and philosophy, and students could indeed take no other course since the London Inns of Court produced the nation's common lawyers. Spain's new students, on the other hand, sought out places in law faculties expanded to fill the need for trained officials. At sixteenth-century Padua, Pisa and Naples in Italy, 75 per cent of all students studied law. In contrast, Paris's legal faculty stagnated until Louis XIV's reign (Brockliss 1978; Kagan 1986: 163). Scotland's late sixteenth- and early seventeenth-century growth in university numbers was fuelled by demand for training in Protestant theology, while its eighteenth-century expansion was principally associated with legal and medical education. Scotland's universities provided the medical education England's lacked, producing nine out of ten British medical graduates between 1750 and 1800.

Nor was growth universal and contemporaneous in all parts of Europe even during the Renaissance. Lisbon university was shut down in 1536 and not re-opened until just before the First World War. The universities of central Europe went through a period of contraction and crisis between the time of the Reformation and the Thirty Years War. Matriculations at Cracow peaked around 1520, following a hundred years of fairly steady increase, then fell and stagnated for much of the rest of the century (Kaniewska 1986a: 117–18, 128–31). Prague was badly affected by its associations with the Hussite heretics and by the political unrest in the region. Its 'golden age' ended in about 1420 and the sixteenth and seventeenth centuries saw stagnation. Like Vienna and Cracow, failure to embrace Protestant theology held back matriculations. The proportion of foreigners at Cracow fell from 23 per cent in 1510–60 to less than 1 per cent in the eighteenth century (Kaniewska 1986a: 119–20; 1986b: 141). Fewer foreign students (*ultramontani*) attended post-Tridentine Italian universities than in the fifteenth and early sixteenth centuries. Confessional divisions reduced matriculations by foreigners in many universities. Across Europe, princes tried to keep their subjects at home as much as possible for political reasons (Kagan 1986: 167, 169; Šmahel 1986: 84).

Over most of northern Italy, university populations rose during the sixteenth century, a notable success story being Padua with some 300 matriculations a year in the 1550s rising to around 1,000 by 1610. Others peaked in the late fifteenth century, Perugia and Siena for example, and had a thin time in the following two centuries; Ferrara had *c*.550 students enrolled in the 1550s compared with some 70 around 1700 (Kagan 1986: 157, 160–61, 166). At the same time, some of the growth was short-lived or illusory. Of 22 new German universities set up between 1540 and 1700, only seven survived into the nineteenth century and some never attracted more than a hundred students at a time. The university of Évora in eastern Portugal (1550) offered a limited curriculum little different from that in a contemporary French *collège* until it was remodelled in the 1770s. Finally, the university of Paris hardly grew at all during the sixteenth century and by 1700 had closed 9 of its 43 colleges open in 1600. All French academies and universities were abolished in 1792, though soon re-established (Kamen 1984: 221; Bernard 1970: 260; Marques 1972: 299; 414; Kagan 1986).

Universities came under much closer state control in the sixteenth century, and indeed governments were important in new foundations – in Italy, for example. From the 1530s the rector of Coimbra in Portugal ceased to be elected from within the university and became a crown nominee (Marques 1972: 197). State support for universities was increasingly explicit in the German lands after the Thirty Years War in the interests of training bureaucrats (cameralism). Cameralism reached its apogee in the Austrian lands under Maria Theresa and Joseph II as universities were strictly regulated and supervised by the state. The successes and failures of early modern universities reflect their dependence on political and social developments, and in particular their responsiveness to fashion and to demand from church and state for clergy and bureaucrats.

Indeed, the process of growth was far from irreversible for those universities that flourished in the sixteenth century. Most experienced severe difficulties in keeping up their student numbers after the middle of the seventeenth century. There were three reasons behind this: the causes of the original expansion, the nature of the curricula on offer, and changes in the social, economic and political context in which the universities had to operate.

Up to a point, the growth of higher education in the Renaissance was a product of a new desire for learning in itself, a humanist belief in the power of knowledge to improve individual and society. Humanism involved new notions of time and space, new horizons in research, and an awareness of change. Some students went to university fired by such ideas, others went simply to have a good time and come out as fuller human beings, and others still looked only to the career opportunities which a university training could open up. Comments about students, which are less useful if more common than those by them, concentrate on the careerist aspects of the search for office. Doctor Juan Queippo de Llano, president of the *chancilleria* (modern *cancilleria*) at Valladolid, remarked with sadness that 'the love of letters brings only a few to the colleges' (Kagan 1974: 78). It is also true that some fathers intended their sons' university careers to finish them as gentlemen. One Richard Holdsworth, a former member of the college, wrote in 1635 to the master of Emmanuel, Cambridge, on behalf of a friend's son: 'his father means not to have him a scholar by profession but only to be seasoned with the varnish of learning and piety which is remarkable in many under your government' (O'Day 1982: 125). University attendance came to be part of the making of the early modern upper classes.

Some graduates could become self-employed doctors or lawyers; some could work as teachers or bureaucrats. A study has been made of the job destinations of 782 graduates of Prague university who wrote books, tracts or poems in Latin between the fifteenth and seventeenth centuries. It shows that 1 per cent died before obtaining work, 72 per cent initially took employment as schoolmasters, 14 per cent went straight into professional posts, and the careers of 13 per cent are unknown. Most of those who went into teaching as a first job did not end their days there (just 12 per cent of the original 563), and the majority went on to become clergy, academics, merchants, municipal administrators and members of the liberal professions (Šmahel 1986: 77–81).

There were two major public employers of university graduates at this time: church and state. Both demanded more and better-trained officials to cope with the competition for souls between Catholic and Protestant, and the drive for uniformity and order in the secular world. Thus, the university of Marburg in Germany was founded in 1527 explicitly to produce state servants. That at Leiden (1575) was a Protestant foundation to rival Catholic Douai and Louvain. The university of Tübingen was important for the consolidation of Protestant orthodoxy in south-western Germany. However, when the demand for officials stabilised, when the heat went out of confessional struggles, and when alternative paths to lucrative employment became available – attendance at specialist academies in Germany or French *collèges* for example – the universities began to suffer. The orientation of Italian universities towards legal studies is part of the reason for their decline in the seventeenth century since they had little to offer when new studies in science and the liberal arts became fashionable. They were side-tracked by new generations of students looking for 'education' rather than 'certification'. Italian *collegi dei nobili*, of which there were more than 40 by 1700, attracted élites away from universities; the one at Parma drew in *c*.300 students a year at this date. Jesuit colleges offered particularly stiff competition since they were sometimes able to win over the official patronage of both secular and ecclesiastical authorities from universities in the same town (Kagan 1986: 163–78). As higher education became more expensive and as élites were increasingly able to buy offices for their offspring, as job opportunities contracted and as fears about the over-production of highly educated men grew, as the upper class came to monopolise the paths to better jobs and as the bourgeoisie found alternative outlets in commerce, so the universities lost their primary role.

This development was far from inevitable. Had the universities been able to move with the times, they might have been able to accommodate social, economic and political change, as happened in Germany and Scotland. As it was, their archaic organisational structures and ossified curricula more commonly condemned them to stagnation and decay. All suffered from similar problems of intellectual inertia, for an increase in student numbers did not necessarily mean developments in teaching methods or curricula. Medical faculties were among the most traditional. In early eighteenth-century Germany, anatomical lecture theatres were almost unknown and students had only an indirect knowledge of anatomy. One disenchanted Hanoverian official of the time believed that medical schools existed only to 'create ten or fifteen young angels of death so that the people may be buried methodically' (McClelland 1980: 30). Throughout the university system, the problem was one of unchanging standards and rigid curricula. The 'new learning' of the humanists, which became fashionable in the early sixteenth century, was simply grafted on to the existing scholastic framework and traditional professionally-oriented courses. Rather than the leaders of intellectual development during the sixteenth and seventeenth centuries, universities were bastions of orthodoxy. In sixteenth-century France the defenders of Catholicism against all Protestant heresies and most new ideas, in the seventeenth and eighteenth centuries the developers and promoters of the intellectual underpinning of absolutism. In Portugal, intellectual developments during the sixteenth century took place largely outside a university environment. What Marques (1972: 204, 300–301) calls the 'revolution of experience' associated with geographical discoveries tended speedily to outdate certain areas of scholarship in that country. Scientific developments seemed to follow a similar path. Copernicus and Descartes never held university posts, Galileo and Newton left theirs. Literary and biblical scholarship owed more to publishers like Plantin in Antwerp than they did to any university press.

Curricular developments rarely amounted to modernisation of what was taught, since the universities continued to see their role as imparting a given body of knowledge rather than expanding or altering it. In the eighteenth century the new academies in which the ideas of the Enlightenment were hatched and dispatched left most continental universities as backwaters of conservatism. Scholasticism of a rather sterile, imitative kind remained strong in the French universities at a time when experimental and mechanical science was making strong headway outside them. Literary and philosophical innovations took place largely in the private *salons* and clubs or societies of the eighteenth century (Morgan 1978; Kagan 1974; McClelland 1980; de Ridder-Symoens 1996). Latin was still used as the main teaching medium in universities like Copenhagen as late as the 1790s. Early modern universities have been accused of sins of commission as well as omission. The universities of Basel, Geneva and Tübingen were notoriously nepotistic. Sale of degrees to men who had never been near their campuses occurred at Bourges, Orléans and Reims.

There were developments taking place within them nevertheless. In France, for example, they transmitted and popularised new scientific and philosophical ideas that played an important part in the intellectual ferment of the Revolutionary period (Brockliss 1987). Padua, the leader in medical studies in the seventeenth century, was responsible for educating the great English physician Harvey. At the same time, some universities reformed teaching and curricula, and there are some signs of a European-wide recovery in university attendance in the later eighteenth century. In Spain, for example, numbers attending 11 universities for which reliable statistics survive grew by more than a half between *c.*1760 and *c.*1800 (Kamen 1984: 222; Peset and Mancebo 1986: 192).

The difficulties faced by universities after the political, economic and military crises of the mid-seventeenth century are plainly demonstrated by the example of two countries, most of whose institutions of higher learning effectively solved them. First of all Scotland, a small, poor and relatively unimportant country which nevertheless possessed some of Europe's most prestigious universities. Student numbers rose from just over 1,000 to 4,400 between 1700 and 1820, at a time when population less than doubled, attracted to Scotland's institutions of higher learning by important changes in teaching methods and curricula. Until 1708 at Edinburgh, 1727 at Glasgow and 1747 at St Andrews, 'regents' took students through all the years of their university career. These non-specialist teachers watched over student life and morals, offering instruction by dictating chunks of text to large, passive classes. The pursuit of knowledge and independent thought were restricted by this stress on expounding set texts. The abolition of regenting was followed by the creation of a number of new specialist professorships, notably at Edinburgh, filled by gifted teachers and original thinkers such as William Robertson, Adam Ferguson and Dugald Stewart. The curriculum too began to be modernised from the end of the seventeenth century. Newtonian ideas were incorporated into science teaching and there were developments in theology within an Aristotelian framework. Francis Hutcheson, professor of philosophy at Glasgow, began lecturing in English rather than Latin from 1729. Medicine and the law were famous throughout eighteenth-century Europe for their advanced teaching methods and courses, and were important in changing Scotland's universities from glorified seminaries to much broader institutions which nurtured the distinctive ideas of the Scottish Enlightenment (Camic 1985: 165–84; O'Day 1982: 231–6, 273–9).

Not all Scotland's universities participated in these developments for St Andrews languished during the eighteenth century. The development of Germany's universities was similarly patchy. Some began to reform their curricula and teaching methods after the Thirty Years War and there were, unusually in Europe, new foundations, notably Halle in Saxony (1694) and Göttingen (c.1733). Under the stimulus of competition from the new *Ritterakademien* and of quickening interest from governments and élites, the best German universities began to change the subjects they offered and the way they taught. The overall fortunes of institutions of higher learning in eighteenth-century Germany were better than those of France, which had attracted so much criticism and so many enemies that they were swept away in their entirety during the French Revolution. In the 1600s there were 20 universities in the German lands with around 8,000 students, 28 in 1700 and some 9,000 young men, and 31 by the 1760s, though with a reduced number of students (about 7,000 in all); by 1820 this number had been thinned down to 20, giving Germany the leanest and fittest higher education system in continental Europe.

German universities succeeded where others failed for a variety of reasons. First, they had all been subject to state control from an early date. Second, they had a monopoly of the training of the higher bureaucracy in a state where that bureaucracy was a powerful force. Third, they legitimised the status of existing élites and offered a route by which other social groups could attain standing. Noble aspirants to office-holding were forced increasingly to have the same (usually legal) qualifications as their non-noble competitors – even if the nobility had a much better chance of advancement. The middling and upper ranks in German society took a close interest in curricula, admissions standards and employment openings (Vierhaus 1988: 55–7; Jahns 1995).

Local circumstances dictated how successful the adjustment was. These were political fragmentation, the ability of rulers directly to influence their universities, the need for trained bureaucrats and the rise of cameralism. Catholic universities remained traditional in the main and Protestant ones were the pacemakers. Catholic nobles might even send sons destined for state service to Protestant universities. Those German universities which survived and flourished during the eighteenth and early nineteenth centuries were those which responded to the new needs of state and society. Those in Germany and elsewhere that did not, went to the wall. The fortunes of higher education depended on the social and political context and on the responsiveness of institutions to it.

Who went to University?

Patterns of attendance at institutions of higher learning were, not surprisingly, dictated by the same social and economic forces which determined who might go to school. University attendance was largely the province of the middling and upper classes while the nature of the course studied and the general experience of university were dictated by social origins.

Universities varied enormously in size and curriculum. During the sixteenth century the Spanish university of Salamanca took in between 5,000 and 7,000 matriculands a year, dwarfing institutions like Seville, Granada or Baeza. More modest and much more typical of European universities was Pisa with 100 new students a year and a total size of 600–700 in the middle of the sixteenth century. Prague at this time had suffered from political and religious wrangles, possessing only a philosophy faculty and a mere hundred students. The range of size is neatly illustrated in the case of German universities. Around 1600, Greifswald in Pomerania could claim approximately 100 students compared with the 900 at Leipzig in Saxony. Total attendance at the Scottish universities in 1700 was just over 1,000, rising to well over 4,000 by 1820 (Kagan 1974: 197–8; Schmitt 1974: 8; Evans 1974: 1–2; 1981: 189; de Ridder-Symoens 1996).

The number of universities per million inhabitants in 1790 was 0.2 for England and Wales, 0.9 for France. For Ireland the figure is the same as England. Scotland had the highest ratio in Europe at 3.3 per million. The proportion of the eligible population able to attend was, while small in absolute terms, impressive in a historical context. The expansion of universities in the age of the Renaissance meant that as many as 2–3 per cent of young men were able to enrol in university faculties during the early seventeenth century, a figure not equalled again until the early twentieth century. Estimates of attendance must remain tentative for two reasons. First, matriculation records do not always survive and those that do may be registers of oaths of loyalty that could be taken at any stage in a university career. As many as a third of those admitted to three Oxford colleges 1612–31 never matriculated (Stone 1969: 49–50). The position is further complicated by the medieval tradition of moving from one university to another – the *peregrinatio academica*. Andrea Alciato, a noted jurist born in 1494, began his studies at Pavia in 1507, enrolled at Bologna in 1511 and graduated from Ferrara in 1517 (Kagan 1986: 156). Graduation records are more reliable. Yet even they do not offer a perfect indication of attendance, since throughout most of the middle ages, and well into the sixteenth century, taking a bachelor's degree was simply a qualification to read in a higher faculty. Passing-out rituals of the kind modern graduates experience came when taking a doctorate.

The drop-out rate was also high. At the university of Alcalá in Spain between 1550 and 1702, two-fifths to two-thirds of students left before the end of their second year of studies and a third of those at Pisa before the end of their third year. Of matriculands at the six élite *Colegios Mayores* during Philip II's reign, 9 per cent died before completing their course, and 16 per cent in that of Carlos II. Half of those who enrolled at Cambridge (1590–1640) did not finish, 15 per cent of matriculands graduated BA from Cracow 1510–60 (4 per cent MA) and only one student in 20 ever graduated from Heidelberg (1550–1620). What is more, the graduation rate fluctuated, making it difficult to generalise about attendance. At the university of Toulouse the proportion of students taking degrees rose in hard times and fell when the economy prospered. However, the long-term trend was towards graduating. For example, the proportion of students taking degrees at Oxford rose from 39 per cent in 1650 to 58 per cent in 1800 (Kagan 1974: 132, 178; 1986: 156; Ferté 1980: 319–20; Kaniewska 1986a: 127; Kamen 1984: 225; de Ridder-Symoens 1996). The trend reflects a Europe-wide change in relationships between universities and society exemplified in the Netherlands. In the century to 1680 the number of Dutch students rose strongly and steadily. People from a wide range of backgrounds sought education. Thereafter, the university was the resort of middling people in search of certification (Frijhoff 1981).

A second difficulty arises when trying to measure attendance. The concept of an eligible population, which can be defined quite closely for modern societies, was much more vague in the early modern world, the reason being that the age at which boys went to university varied considerably. The average age at matriculation to Spanish universities in the sixteenth century was 18, compared with 16 two centuries later. In contrast, the average age at first registration in the university of Paris was just 10 in the first half of the sixteenth century, rising to the late teens by the end of the seventeenth as students increasingly trained at provincial *collèges* before matriculating in the arts faculty. These averages disguise a substantial range of ages among the student population, many of whom were full-grown adults. The Paris arts faculty included men and boys more than a generation apart in the age of the Reformation. By the eighteenth century the age range had narrowed to roughly 15 to 30 (Kagan 1974: 17; Brockliss 1978: 519). At Oxford and Cambridge in the 1630s nearly all entrants were aged 15 to 19 (Stone 1964: 57).

A third problem exists in estimating the proportion of eligibles in a given country, that of the high numbers of foreign students. For all their faults, early modern universities remained cosmopolitan institutions: 242 German students matriculated at Bologna university 1600–1601 and 2,555 at Siena 1590–1609. Between 1433 and 1509, 44 per cent of Cracow's matriculands were foreigners, 23 per cent 1510–60 (Engelsing 1973: 33; Kaniewska 1986a: 119–20). Some universities attracted students because of their high reputation: Pisa for medicine, Leiden for law, Paris for philosophy. Others depended on shared traditions. The Reformed Protestant universities of Scotland and Holland developed a special relationship during the seventeenth century, for example. In some cases the lack of native alternatives drove young men to study abroad. Until the Reformation, Finnish scholars went to Paris, after it to Erfurt, Leipzig and Stockholm, and some continued to do so even after the first university in Finland was founded at Turku in 1640. Irish Catholics had perforce to go to continental foundations such as Louvain throughout the early modern period, Norwegian, Icelandic and, occasionally, Greenland youths to Copenhagen. Staff too moved around Europe, including the famous sixteenth-century Scot George Buchanan who worked briefly in the university of Coimbra in Portugal before falling foul of the Inquisition.

The universities of the late middle ages had been truly cosmopolitan institutions. Teaching and learning was in the international language of Latin. Until the Reformation, the lack of confessional differences also allowed easy mobility among both students and staff. Thereafter, hardening political divisions and the growing variety of theological training available created barriers. So too did the apparently benign spread of vernacular education in the seventeenth and eighteenth centuries. This potentially widened the social catchment area. It also narrowed the geographical one compared with when Europe had had a meaningful *respublica litteraria*. Mobility declined and recruitment areas contracted. Arguably at least, universities became more nationalist. If the Reformation and Counter-Reformation re-invigorated some institutions (especially the Jesuit foundations of France and Spain), their long-term consequences profoundly altered the nature of the university.

Catchment areas became nationalised at their broadest, regionalised at their narrowest. Most Parisian students of the seventeenth and eighteenth centuries came from north-eastern France, those who went to Seville from west Andalucia, to Granada from the east of that province. The smaller and less significant the university, the more localised its geographical intake. Thus areas well-served by universities, such as northern Spain, had higher than average percentages attending compared with less favoured southern regions, and towns like Madrid had nearly double the Castilian average in the middle of the eighteenth century (Kagan 1974). Central European universities recruited overwhelmingly from the towns. Fully 91 per cent of Bohemian graduates of the university of Prague 1433–1618 came from towns, a figure that is almost the exact reverse of the proportions of the total population living in urban and rural areas (Šmahel 1986: 76).

The problems of quantifying attendance have been discussed at length because they illuminate the diverse and changing fortunes of universities and the equally varied experiences of students. Cautious estimates of attendance rates can nevertheless be made. At the start of the sixteenth century, the rate was about 1 per cent in western Europe. With the expansion in university places during the century of the Reformation, the average rose to around 2.4 per cent in early seventeenth-century England, and 2.8 per cent in the United Provinces of the Low Countries at the same time. Nearly 3 per cent of males aged 15 to 24 attended in Castile, which contained most of Spain's population. Attendance peaked in the middle of the seventeenth century, falling away to levels of 1 per cent or less by the time of the French Revolution. Levels held up well in some regions: 1.5 per cent in Holland, and over 2 per cent in Castile and Scotland. Elsewhere the eighteenth century was a time of stagnation and decay. In 1700, some 1.5 per cent of young men attended England's universities. As a percentage of the eligible age group, Oxford drew in 0.6 per cent in 1700, but its graduation rate was just half that at

0.3 per cent; in 1800 the figures were approximately 0.2 per cent and 0.1 per cent respectively. For France the matriculation rate was approximately 1 per cent at the end of the *ancien régime*. To this figure could be added that for college attendance. In eighteenth-century France there were places in *collèges* for 2 per cent of teenagers (though some towns may have schooled 10 per cent), and in 1789 nearly 50,000 young men were in *collèges* (Roche 1998: 430).

Through the three centuries, absolute numbers remained small. As late as 1775, Scotland's universities, among the major European success stories of the eighteenth century, were only enrolling 2,000 students a year, despite their attractive new curricula and teaching methods, low entrance standards, low fees and bursaries to help poorer students. Germany's 31 universities took in under 7,000 and Russia's only proper university in Moscow drew approximately 100 undergraduates from an imperial population of 40 million during the 1790s (Alston 1969: 11; Kagan 1974; 1986; Frijhoff 1979).

The social distribution of students was restricted. At its height in the reign of Philip II, the universities of Castile drew in 20,000 students a year. However, somewhere between 25 and 35 per cent of boys from the gentry (*hidalgo*) class attended and virtually none from the ranks of ordinary peasants. Two-thirds of English society was made up of yeomen and husbandmen farmers, but these groups contributed only one in eight of the seventeenth-century student intake of Oxford and Cambridge. The élitism of England's universities grew in the eighteenth century. The proportion of Oxford students classed as 'plebians' fell from 27 per cent in 1711 to just 1 per cent in 1810. In the second half of the eighteenth century, Oxford and Cambridge drew four-fifths of their students from just three social groups which made up less than one twentieth of the population: gentry, clergy and military. Those from a mercantile or professional background comprised 29 per cent of those at Cambridge and 6 per cent at Oxford. Between 1762 and 1829 the proportion of students from military families going to Oxford rose from 25 per cent to 50 per cent. Even the humbler provincial universities of France rarely took more than 5 per cent of their students from the peasantry. By contrast, 65 per cent of matriculands at Douai were sons of professionals or officials. Law faculties were particularly élitist. Two-thirds of the nobility in German universities of the eighteenth century were to be found in law departments (Kamen 1984: 224; Morgan 1978: 153–4; Chartier *et al.* 1976: 277–8).

There are indications of some broadening of the intake at Cracow in Poland and at some Spanish universities in the eighteenth century as the percentage of noble youths fell: at Cracow from about a quarter to a tenth over the century (Kaniewska 1986b: 144; Peset and Mancebo 1986: 192). There were also certain excluded groups who began to gain access. Over much of Europe, Jews were barred from universities – and from many other forms of formal training that had religious content or sanction and from most professions. Some Italian universities, notably Padua and Siena, admitted Jews during the early modern period. So too did certain German universities, even if Jews were not allowed to graduate until late in the eighteenth century. At this date the university of Königsberg attracted more Jews than any other in Prussia (de Ridder-Symoens 1996; Ajzensztejn 1994). Women were not formally admitted to Europe's universities until the late nineteenth century. Universities generally drew students from the middling and upper reaches of male Christian society.

On the grounds of attendance, educational experience and destinations, universities cannot be associated with substantial levels of social mobility at any period, and certainly not in the eighteenth century. The church took between 57 and 62 per cent of graduates from Oxford in the eighteenth century, and most graduates from theology faculties in Scottish and German universities at this time looked only to the comparative security and prestige of a clerical career. The ultimate careers of those who attended university depended closely on their social origins. At the university of Paris in the eighteenth century, the humbler students looked only to the church, the wealthier to the law and artisans to a return to bourgeois life; medicine was considered a dubious profession for the well-born and only one man of noble status (Joseph Piton in 1696) graduated with a medical degree. The great nobles often did not bother with higher education, relying on travel to broaden their horizons. In eastern Europe they positively despised universities and academies until forced into them by state pressure. For the upper classes as a whole, university simply created alternative avenues to positions which the students would have enjoyed anyway (Brockliss 1978: 533, 539).

The social distribution of students was determined partly by attitudes and perceived opportunities, partly by the sheer cost of attendance. Fees, board and lodging (if the student did not live at home) and the payment for taking a degree all added up to a formidable charge on the parental purse. Fees in the university of Paris arts faculty were fairly low at between 12 and 36 livres during the sixteenth and seventeenth centuries, and were abandoned in the eighteenth. However, boarding in a pension cost something like 300 livres a year in 1700 (double for a single room), an impossible sum for a day labourer whose annual total earnings were less than 100 livres. Fees for taking a degree were 30 to 50 livres for arts and law in the sixteenth century, still a bargain compared with 800 livres for medicine. At least the cost of attending university in France rose in pace with costs in general. It cost a provincial 75 livres a year to be a student in Paris around 1500 and 750 livres in 1800. In contrast, it cost around £50 a year to support a young man at an Oxford college in 1720, not much more in real terms than a century before. However, the figure had soared to £80 plus by 1750 and to over £200 by 1850. The cost of higher education rose more than twice as quickly as living costs and earnings overall. Only in Scotland did it become cheaper in real terms to attend university in the eighteenth century. The importance of cost is clearly shown by short-term trends in enrolments to the provincial French university of Toulouse. During years of bad harvest or trade dislocation, the number of students who matriculated in the law faculty and who came from the diocese of Rodez was halved. Students of modest means preferred the cheaper provincial universities to Paris, but costs might push even these beyond their reach (Brockliss 1978: 528–30; O'Day 1982: 198; Ferté 1980: 317–18).

To combat the inhibiting effect of cost on attendance, all universities had some kind of bursaries for poor but able students. Renaissance learning included the idea that talent was equally divided among all ranks of people and that a state should encourage all able men to be useful to it in some way. Thus, sixteenth-century Spain had six *Colegios Mayores*, four at Salamanca and one each at Valladolid and Alcalá. These were self-governing institutions where 100–250 students could obtain scholarships and accommodation. By the beginning of the seventeenth century, wealthy students had increasingly infiltrated these institutions, admission to which became more and more dependent on patronage and money rather than poverty and ability. In the eighteenth century they were nothing more than élite colleges where the nobility and officials sent their sons to be trained as bureaucrats (Phillips 1977: 348). The same thing happened to colleges for the poor but gifted at the university of Paris during this period and, indeed, the story is familiar across Europe. Between 1543 and 1604, four new residential colleges were founded at the university of Pisa, two by the Grand Dukes, two by cardinals. However, abuses similar to those in Spain and France soon became apparent and in 1598 Grand Duke Ferdinando I noted with disgust that prospective students made a show of poverty to get into his college. Once there they showed off as though they had enough of everything and did very little work (Schmitt 1974: 9).

Official curricula were, of course, only a part of the university experience. Students were subject to many influences, both harmful and benign, material and intellectual. Enlightened tutors or the large body of printed material available could counterbalance archaic curricula. Poorly and irregularly paid professors in some Italian universities offered private tuition for fees – several at Naples were gaoled for this illegal practice in the 1620s – and students are said to have found these *lettori privati* much more useful than in-house university courses (Kagan 1986: 171–2). Cosmopolitan ideas and lifestyles, of the kind that confronted provincials at Madrid, Paris or Rome, could widen horizons and create a network of friends and patrons far more important than paper qualifications in a world where contacts were all. This is why some members of the upper classes treated their varsity careers as a sort of finishing school cum employment agency. Young men from monied and titled backgrounds had a completely different experience of university to their humbler fellows. Their attendance was brief and distracted. The sons of grandees and *titulos* at institutions such as Salamanca lived in style, dressed lavishly, had a degree course one year shorter than other students because of their supposedly superior preparation for university, enjoyed the services of additional tutors, employed servants to attend their lectures for them and normally did not take their degree (Kagan 1974: 184–5, 199). Some parents complained at the lack of supervision of their sons at university and, indeed, fighting, drinking and whoring were notorious in student areas of a town. Riots between Italian and Spanish students at Pavia in 1594 left several dead, and in one parish close to the university of Salamanca, 60 per cent of all the children baptised in 1558 were illegitimate (Kagan 1974: 203; 1986: 175; Houston and van der Heijden 1997).

The substantial expansion at all levels of the complex educational hierarchy fully merits the title 'an educational revolution'. More people than ever attended schools and universities, while educational institutions were reorganised to reflect changing religious alignments or social needs and the new power and demands of the state. Continuities too were strong at all levels of education, notably in teaching methods and materials, and in the structure of the teaching 'profession'. At the same time, existing attitudes and social structures limited the impact of change, notably the way in which the wealth of parents and the sex of a child dictated access to post-elementary education. The variety of experience of educational change was enormously varied across Europe and the fortunes of the universities highlight the important fact that progress in education was not linear and that educational institutions depended intimately on the social and political environment in which they operated. Education's impact on society was dependent as much as it was independent. Schooling played a more central role in the process of growing up for most western European children in 1800 than in 1500.

Supply is only one side of the equation, for demand had to exist to fuel the drive towards education and literacy. Nor were schools the only place in which the acquisition of literacy might take place. An understanding of the nature of demand for literacy and the ways in which that wish could be satisfied are central to the way literacy developed and the uses to which it was ultimately put.

Chapter 5

WAYS OF LEARNING

Schools were of enormous importance in raising the literacy of a broad spectrum of the early modern population. They were one of many ways of learning. Others included familial instruction from parents, siblings or neighbours; lessons on particular subjects from anyone including a pastor, notary, widow or even a passing foreign-language speaker; temporary or permanent evening or Sunday classes; catechism and religious instruction; self-teaching; formal or informal apprenticeships; service (Caspard 1996: 98). Young and old alike used different components for different reasons at different points in their lives.

Schools were certainly not the only positive force behind developments in literacy. After all, even when schools are provided not all parents will wish (or even be able) to send their children to them. Some form of compulsion must be exercised or, more significantly in early modern Europe, *demand* for education must exist to encourage families to bear its cost. Schools were most effective when they were an integral part of family and community life rather than alien impositions of outside authorities or social groups. Nor does the whole explanation for structures and trends in literacy lie with schools. Some type of formal instruction was probably essential to mastering basic skills such as deciphering letters and syllables or using a pen, even if little information could be transmitted to a child during the brief and intermittent schooling he or she received. Formal, scholastic learning was important since such knowledge was not be generated spontaneously. Nevertheless it was only one way of acquiring the skills of reading, writing and counting. Learning in adulthood could reinforce earlier instruction or even make up for its absence. Indeed, for many people, education in a school was only part of a much wider process of learning that encompassed the home, peer groups and work experience.

For many from the lower classes who made up the bulk of the population, schools were only a small part of growing up. Learning also involved a wider experience of socialisation that shaped their consciousness and informed their everyday lives.

When discussing elementary and post-elementary education in an earlier chapter, it became clear that childhood was arguably shorter than in modern western countries and certainly spent differently. At the present day, the teenage years are wholly or largely passed in formal education. In north-western Europe between 1500 and 1800 males and females spent the period between puberty and marriage living and working away from their own family as a servant or (for boys) as an apprentice. Service was a characteristic part of growing up in early modern Europe. It gave people the opportunity to save up to get married, something which happened about the age of 26 for women and 28 for men in the late seventeenth century England and 23 and 25 in the early nineteenth century. French women married at about 25–26 in the seventeenth and eighteenth centuries. Service also gave young men and women some experience of independence – or at least a different form of dependence from that of childhood – and a chance to learn both manual and other skills, like literacy or numeracy. England in particular was an indi-vidualistic society with an acquisitive and competitive ethos. At the end of the seventeenth century, nearly one English person in five was a domestic or agricultural servant, though that proportion had fallen to one in ten by 1820. For France on the eve of the Revolution the figure is one twelfth – two million individuals, of whom 100,000 lived in Paris. One duty of masters was to catechise their families, included among whom were live-in servants. Of the same age as servants, apprentices were mostly urban and had higher social standing; nearly all formally indentured (contracted) apprentices were boys.

Outside the School

Relatively brief formal education and a distinctive experience of vocational training meant that non-scholastic learning supplemented schooling or in some cases substituted for it altogether. Learning outside of formal schools could take place in all sorts of contexts, of which the most obvious was the home. The best-known example of learning in the home is that of the Renaissance aristocracy. In countries as diverse as England and Spain, affluent families employed private tutors to teach their sons the skills of the gentleman. The very few girls who learned Latin in Renaissance Italy did so with male household tutors (Grendler 1989: 93). Where schools were in short supply anyway, as in sixteenth- and seventeenth-century Finland, private tutors might be the only way of educating the children of the rural gentry and nobility.

Privately tutored boys from the upper ranks were taught the elements of literacy alongside more advanced skills such as Latin or modern foreign languages. The final gloss was provided by instruction in riding, fencing, dancing and the other trappings of gentility. At the time of Napoleon's invasion of Russia, prince Barjatinskij's son was receiving this sort of wide-ranging, practical and mainly personal instruction which, as with many aristocratic youths, culminated in travel abroad (Eeckaute 1970; Engelsing 1973: 50–52). Personal tutors might accompany the aristocracy on their travels. For the lesser gentry and for the daughters of the nobility, a stay in another gentle household could provide a similar training at less cost. During the eighteenth and nineteenth centuries the use of governesses spread down from the upper classes into the homes of the prosperous bourgeoisie who used them to give their children a grounding in elementary learning and etiquette, and to train girls in the ways of the middle-class spouse. The resort to private tutors declined in the west after the sixteenth century as land-owning families began increasingly to send their sons to urban grammar schools and then university, their daughters (if they were formally educated away from home) to the newly fashionable 'finishing schools'. However, private tutors remained central to the education of the children of nobles and gentry who did not follow the official religion of a country – seventeenth-century English Catholics for example – since the only alternative for those who did not wish their offspring to be brought up in a different faith was to send them abroad.

Education in the home was not the exclusive preserve of the upper classes. Guillaume Masenx, born in southern France sometime during the 1490s, received a little basic instruction from an uncle who was a priest at Castelnau – not that it did him much good, since he spoke only the local dialect, knew no Latin or French and the documents on which his hand appears reveal poor writing and spelling. Three centuries later, John Jones, a servant from near Birmingham in England who wrote an autobiography, told of his brief stay at a dame school around 1780 followed by two years of lessons from a retired stonecutter in the winter evenings (Le Roy Ladurie 1974: 125; Vincent 1981: 94).

In Russia and the Scandinavian countries, where properly constituted schools were rare before the nineteenth century, home learning was the norm. A Russian *Domostroi* or household guide of the sixteenth century shows that the family was conceived of as the basic social and political unit. It was dominated by a father who had a duty to educate and raise his offspring to glorify God and the Czar (Black 1979: 15–16). In the contemporary archbishopric of Milan, the reforming cardinal Borromeo recommended that while children should attend Schools of Christian Doctrine, fathers should also read aloud to their families from a devotional book after meals. Domenico Manzoni's *Libretto molto utile* (1546) was for fathers who took these religious exhortations seriously, though it offered no pedagogic advice on reading (Schutte 1986: 15). Domestic encouragement from mothers was also important to learning for girls. Recalling her Bohemian girlhood in the 1730s, Anna Nêmeçková told how her mother was an avid reader of Protestant books: 'She forced us to read them, but as for us, we amused ourselves more willingly with other things, like all young people' (Ducreux 1989: 211).

Religious reformers of all churches recognised the power of learning in the home. Luther spoke of householders being 'bishops in their own homes' and specifically commended the ecclesiastical constitution of the town of Leisnig in Saxony. It said that 'every householder and his wife shall be duty-bound to cause the wholesome, consoling Word of God to be preached to them, their children, and their domestic servants' (Strauss 1978: 4). The Lutheran literacy campaigns in Sweden and its dependencies relied solely on teaching by priest and parents in the home. A Swedish royal decree of 1723 actually transferred responsibility for children's education from the church to parents (Guttormsson 1990: 22–3).

These schemes required parents to teach children and masters to instruct servants. However, the younger generation might educate the older in situations where children were being taught outside the home and then brought their new found skills into the household. After prescribing the way in which his donation for a charity school at Stratford-upon-Avon should be spent, John Smarte added that when the children 'can read in the Bibles that they may have them to church with them and that they read them at home before their parents at least 3 tymes in the weeke (for parents are oftymes taken more with their children's reading than with what they heare at church)' (Richardson and James 1983: 149). The seventeenth-century Lancashire apprentice William Stout attended grammar school. Then when his father died he took a three-week cramming course in writing and arithmetic before entering his apprenticeship. Once installed, his master used Stout's talents to educate his son. The young were similarly important in spreading the English language into Gaelic-speaking parts of Ireland and Scotland during the eighteenth century. English was taught in schools whereas most adults were

Gaelic speakers. Whichever way information flowed, the home was an important place for exchanging practical and intellectual skills.

Learning did not stop at the door of the school or the front step of the home. Peers were as important as parents in the process of socialisation. One observer remarked of the people of Sweden in 1631 that they were 'so fond of letters that although public schools are very few, nevertheless the literate instruct the others with such enthusiasm that the greatest part of the common people, and even the peasants, are literate' (Kamen 1984: 210). Familial ties or simple personal friendships might generate these contacts. A Protestant linen-weaver from Cambrai in France explained to a court in 1566 how he 'was led to knowledge of the Gospel by . . . my neighbour, who had a Bible printed at Lyon and who taught me the psalms by heart . . . The two of us used to go walking in the fields on Sundays and feast days, conversing about the Scriptures and the abuses of priests' (Davis 1975: 189). Even within formal apprenticeships, young men learned from books or other apprentices and masters as well as their contracted employer and instructor.

Within the large classes in most schools, older children helped younger with their lessons. Learning from friends and neighbours, classmates and playmates could take place informally, on a very personal basis. Under certain circumstances, these associations could become more formal. In south-western France there were organised youth groups made up of young men and women in their teens and early twenties. These groups were principally recreational, but they also constituted a sort of moral police force. They went beyond the boundaries of household and family to encompass all the youth in a village. In parts of Germany, groupings achieved a regular status in the form of the winter evening *Spinnstube* or spinning circle. The *Spinnstube* (and its French equivalent, the *veillée* or evening gathering) was a type of work sociability where unmarried girls in particular met to spin, knit and talk. Most of the interchange was of gossip and tales, but there were also opportunities to practise reading and to learn other practical skills (Medick 1984: 317, 334–5).

All of these ways of learning could be a valuable addition to self-teaching. Schooling was brief for the majority of the population. They consolidated and expanded what they learned in order to make full use of elementary skills first learned at the age of six, seven or eight. Among lower-class writers of autobiographies, most had received very little formal education and had sought out reading and writing for themselves later in life. Writing of his late eighteenth-century schooldays, the German autodidact Gottlieb Hiller recalled that he went to school in winter, but had to work in the fields in spring, summer and autumn. Thus, he easily forgot what he had learned in childhood and had to make up the loss later in life through his own application (Engelsing 1973: 70). Some ordinary people never attended a school and had to rely on their own efforts or the help of friends if they were to master the basics of literacy. The seventeenth-century Puritan Englishman Adam Martindale took his first steps in literacy with a primer and the help of a young man who came to court his sister.

With the spread of printing and a growing interest in learning for religious and economic reasons, it is small wonder that the sixteenth and seventeenth centuries saw a proliferation of do-it-yourself literacy manuals. Strasbourg saw a spate of publishing of ABC primers as early as 1480–1520. From Venice in 1536 came Tagliente's *La Vera Arte de lo Excellente Scrivere* and from Lyon later in the century a *Brief Arithmetic* which promised to instruct a tradesman within 15 days and offered mnemonic verses to help him learn. Italian ABC books of this period commonly used verses in alphabetic order to help memorisation, in which the first word of the stanza gave an example of the letter (Davis 1975: 213; Lucchi 1978: 603–4; Chrisman 1982: 121–2; Roggero 1992). The frequent publication of such books in northern Italy may indicate the comparative significance of self-teaching in that part of Europe in the sixteenth century, though some of them were also used in schools.

A ready market for self-teaching aids is evident throughout the early modern period. From 1776, newspapers available in Finland contained sections specifically set out to help people learn writing. Early nineteenth-century almanacs even detail the use of a stick in a sandbox or snow, or charcoal on a piece of bark, or even a finger on a steamed-up windowpane for those who wanted to practise without pen and paper. They advocated starting with capitals then progressing to cursive script, practising by taking dictation or copying chunks from the Bible (Luttinen 1985: 44–5). Of course, self-teaching had its limitations. For readers it could lead to misunderstandings; for writers to rough handwriting, uneven lines, irregular or phonetic spelling, poor punctuation and capitalisation, and erratic grammar. One had to be able to read a little before one could understand the autodidactic literature. Tagliente's *Libro Maistrevole* (1524) was targeted at young people and adults who wanted to learn to read or to improve basic, possibly forgotten, skills. Still it required a volunteer instructor to guide the individual through the letters, syllables and words (Schutte 1986). It was not intended for the classroom or for young children and possessed a secular, practical, vernacular emphasis rather different from what was practised in formal, scholastic education.

Self-teaching or learning from peers was probably of greater significance in parts of Europe where schools were in short supply. Some regions seem to have had a tradition of 'collective autodidacticism', learning a wide range of literacy and other skills from family, friends and neighbours rather than in any formalised way from a teacher or expert. Contemporaries remarked on this among, for example, the Welsh and the Neuchâtelois (modern Switzerland). Explanations varied from the quality of the air and an egalitarian social ethos to poverty and the need to make a living by holding down multiple jobs (Caspard 1996: 97–105; Jenkins 1997). The Neuchâtel region is an eighteenth-century example where self-learning was both an outward manifestation and an integral part of social and political independence. Self-learning was not only an alternative to formal education; it could precede it; or it could supplement schooling. In parts of France and the Low Countries self-learning and schooling flourished together from the sixteenth century, suggesting that both came out of a desire to learn. Dutch *klopjes* or secret schools for Catholics after the Reformation were run by women and followed a model of mutual learning rather than the formalised instruction found in the Protestant public schools (Frijhoff 1996).

The significance of informal learning may also have differed by subject. Basic counting was probably learned at home whereas more sophisticated numerical skills like algebra were taught by mathematics masters; learning a second language was partly done by seeking out a native speaker for practice, partly from a language teacher for vocabulary and grammar (Caspard 1996: 84–5, 90). Self-learning was particularly good for basic skills, less so for the more advanced abilities where instructors versed in complex knowledge were required.

Important as it might be for some individuals, the significance of self-learning should not be exaggerated when explaining the literacy of groups. Of 806 defendants before the Spanish Inquisition of Cuenca, two-thirds said they had learned to read in school or from a schoolmaster, one seventh from the parish priest or sacristan, and one sixth had been taught by family members or friends – an experience that seems to have been especially common among women (Nalle 1989: 75). Between 1545 and 1560 a blind man called Miguel de la Iglesia made a living by teaching women their prayers on the street (Nalle 1992: 126). Pure autodidacts were rare. There was generally, though not invariably, a connection between the density of schools in a region and the reading and writing abilities of its inhabitants. In the countryside of early nineteenth-century Emilia, communities with schools had twice the level of male literacy as those without, while for females (whose level was very low) schooled communities could boast nearly three times the level of signing ability found in unschooled (Marchesini 1985: 130). At a group level, it is best to see both literacy and schooling coming out of a wider social and political consensus about both the demand and supply of cultural resources (François 1977).

Desire for Learning

Church and state could provide educational facilities. Compelling attendance was difficult unless there was a desire for learning and therefore a prepared-ness to devote time and money to education. Unfortunately, the surviving documentation does not allow systematic interrogation of the motives that encouraged an adult to seek command of literacy, or which decided a parent on a costly educational programme for a son. There are no early modern questionnaires to reveal whether people felt that literacy would enhance their prestige, broaden their horizons or help them find a better job. Individual examples gleaned from diaries and autobiographies offer insights into motiva-tion, while inferences can also be made from changes in the economic, social, cultural and political environment.

Both positive and negative forces determined demand for literacy. On the positive side there was the pull of economic need, the desire to maintain or change occupation or social status, and the wish to attain qualifications required for certain (mainly bureaucratic) posts; prestige and the possibility to form different social, occupational and patronage relationships; a richer spiritual life and the chance for vicarious experience leading to intellectual development. On the negative side there was a sense that literacy was needed to avoid exploitation, notably by the representatives of secular and ecclesias-tical authorities or by landlords and employers, or to defend a faith or culture against attack. Three developments underlay this. First, economic change expanded the need for reading, writing and counting. Second was the grow-ing influence and power of the state in everyday life, notably through armies and bureaucracies. Third came the development of religious pluralism and the ideological intolerance of confessionalism from the Reformation onwards. In their different ways they exerted a pervasive and powerful influence on the demand for literate skills.

At the end of the middle ages a 'European economy' did not exist. In its place there were hundreds of parcellised if overlapping local and regional economies. What trade there was took place overwhelmingly in foodstuffs and other agricultural products such as wine, skins and timber. However, only a tiny proportion of gross production ever found its way into the networks of overseas trade, and subsistence farming formed the focus of economic life for most of Europe's people. Transport was difficult and expensive, marketing poorly developed except in certain luxuries and bulk goods transportable by sea or river. Money was scarce and the patterns of transactions simple, dominated by face-to-face interactions in a marketplace or on a quay.

The sixteenth, seventeenth and eighteenth centuries saw pronounced if gradual changes in this scenario. A much larger proportion of both agricultural and (expanding) industrial output found its way into the marketplace as economic relationships became more commercially oriented. Cash replaced barter and payments in kind while financial instruments such as bills of exchange (the forerunner of modern banknotes) and prolonged credit developed which allowed long-distance trade to expand. Trade became more diverse and accounted for a growing proportion of the wealth of European states as merchants opened up the New World and created mass markets for new cloths and for products such as tobacco, tea, coffee and sugar. Internal trade was fuelled by population growth – Europe's numbers roughly doubled in the sixteenth century alone – and by the growing concentration of people in the towns. Around 1500, just 3 per cent of England's population lived in towns of more than 10,000 people. By 1800 the figure was 24 per cent. Half the population of sixteenth-century Holland lived in towns, an exceptional proportion by contemporary standards.

The social implications of this urbanisation and commercialisation were considerable. Many more people required the skills of reading, writing and counting. Farmers with an eye on profits had to keep account books and try to follow prices and developments in other regions. A sixteenth-century Friesland farmer stipulated in his will that of the three sons who were to share his legacy, 'he who turns out the most learned will have the major part of the property' (Parker 1979: 21). Merchants and carriers in particular required far greater awareness of the market and a more sophisticated approach to dealing with it. One trading company based in Szczecin (Stettin) ordered in 1756 that ships' captains should not take on sailors unless they could repeat the catechism. Skippers themselves, except those close to retirement, had to display facility in writing, counting and keeping journals (Engelsing 1973: 47).

Early newspapers were principally concerned with informing traders of political and economic circumstances in different parts of Europe germane to their commercial dealings. There was, for example, little point in shipping goods to Marseille in 1720 if the port was in quarantine for plague. Early newspapers were compilations of commercial intelligence. One genre of early printed books was the practical guide for working traders, known variously as merchants' books, commercial dictionaries or *Gesprächbüchlein*. These were multilingual phrase-books whose aim was to help traders to cope with the bewildering array of objects which were being traded, the diversity of legal systems and tariffs, and the huge variety of weights and measures in use. Sometimes presented in dialogue form, language and format were standardised and simplified to help the merchant find lodgings, describe his wares, negotiate terms, discuss the weather and political conditions, be polite and friendly, write a receipt. These pocket-sized books were published in England, France, Germany and the Low Countries from the end of the fifteenth century and usually covered two to four languages, though some ran to eight (Perrot 1981). An example is Griffin's *The English, Latin, French, Dutch, scholemaster. Or, an introduction to teach young gentlemen and merchants to travell or trade* (1637).

Merchants' books give examples of the new uses to which literacy could be put and the incentives which economic change created to learn literacy. Greater use of literacy for practical purposes established confidence in literate ways of doing things and thus generated further demand for practical skills like writing. The volume of paper produced by commercial transactions was enormous even in the fourteenth and fifteenth centuries, especially by the most go-ahead merchants of the day from the city states of northern Italy. The business archive of Francesco Datini of Prato between 1384 and 1411 includes 125,549 commercial letters from 267 places of origin and the total correspondence runs to 600,000 pages (Hyde 1979: 114). As early as the fifteenth century, the use of written instruments in business permeated the lowest ranks among Florentine artisans, presupposing a knowledge of reading, writing and arithmetic alongside a certain habit of mind about keeping records (Goldthwaite 1980: 312–13). This passion for paper extended to north-western Europe during the sixteenth and seventeenth centuries.

Economic change was a powerful force behind the spread of literacy. Significantly, those parts of Europe which enjoyed low levels of commercialisation and urbanisation were generally less literate than economically advanced regions. In seventeenth-century Russia, roughly 1 per cent of the population lived in towns. The peasantry treated money not as a universal means of exchange, but as another crop like rye or oats. Large tracts of eastern, central and southern Europe were 're-feudalised' during the sixteenth and seventeenth centuries, reducing the legally weakened peasantry to poverty while allowing their lords to participate in the expanding trade in foodstuffs. Of course, economic development did not necessarily produce literacy, and backwardness did not condemn a population to ignorance. The mountains of south-western France and northern Italy contained pockets of highly literate people who valued reading and writing as a way to escape the poverty of their homelands. A general connection exists between economic change and literacy, but it is by no means automatic and invariable (Smith 1983: 293).

The penetration of marketing and of production for exchange into the most remote areas of early modern Europe was paralleled by the growing intrusion of the state into everyday life. Medieval polity had effectively comprised a large number of separate political and legal units loosely bound together by monarchies. The history of the early modern period is dominated by the search for integration and domination of these quasi-independent localities by increasingly powerful central governments. Their weapons were armies, bureaucracies and the law, the expansion of which created a demand for literacy among both personnel and subjects. On the one hand, the state needed more servants with literate skills, on the other the people had to be able to cope with the demands which courts, administrators and soldiers placed upon them.

The early modern period witnessed substantial changes in military tactics and in the size of armies. A force of 30,000 men was counted large in the sixteenth century. Louis XIV had armies of 300,000 at the end of the seventeenth century (on paper at least) and Napoleon's numbered over half a million. Armies needed food, clothing, weapons and ammunition, and they had to be paid. They caused economic and social changes that touched virtually every person in Europe in some form or another. The new tactics that transformed the face of warfare in the seventeenth century needed more literate and numerate officers and soldiers. The Russian army came increasingly under central control and high-ranking officers complained of being swamped with paperwork. Officers had to understand written orders, sign for their pay and for supplies, write reports, requisitions and orders for others. Literate troops could read orders, understand firearm manuals and write home to their families, improving efficiency and morale. Literature on military matters proliferated in Italy and France from c.1550. Military academies first appeared in sixteenth-century Italy and by the eighteenth century had spread as far afield as Russia where they formed an important component of the slender educational resources of Peter the Great's empire.

The military revolution could touch all ranks. Swiss troops in service abroad commonly had to sign a special register for their pay while those of the French *Compagnie des Indes* had their own enlistment book. A Venetian of the early seventeenth century argued that command of literacy was essential for naval gunners. In fact, however, military developments were restricted to officers and sergeants since most infantry had only to master a few basic techniques. A petition from 30 gunners and riflemen at Oudewater in the Low Countries in 1618 includes not a single signature (Stephens 1980; Corvisier 1979: 105–6, 180–81; van Deursen 1978: 70).

Central bureaucracies ultimately controlled the vast continental armies of the later seventeenth and eighteenth centuries. Officials proliferated to deal with warfare and its 'sinews' – money, food and weapons – and to administer towns and villages across Europe since an orderly and well-run country was a strong one. Governments needed diplomats, tax collectors, clerks and judges – even inspectors who perambulated the towns of eighteenth-century Prussia sniffing out unlicensed coffee houses.

In the early days, bureaucrats were in short supply, and many of the innovations in post-elementary and higher education during the early modern period were deliberately aimed at improving the supply of capable servants for the state. Gustavus Vasa, king of Sweden 1523–60, was chronically embarrassed by the lack of trained secretaries at his disposal as he struggled to administer his country in the same way he would a huge estate. Young men had to be sent abroad for training and Vasa was sometimes driven to dealing with the German language correspondence himself, complaining bitterly of the 'drunkards and ale-hounds, debauched and beastly tosspots' who were thrown up by the defective educational system in his realm. Peter the Great summarised the need felt by many rulers for a cadre of men fitted to enter 'church service, civilian service, and ready to wage war, to practice engineering and medical art' (Roberts 1968: 112–13, 170–71; Alston 1969: 4).

The influence of the state extended deep into society to touch the humblest local officials. Seventeenth-century Sweden had its *postbonde*, or 'postal peasant'. Located every hundred kilometres or so along the main highways, these men had to be able to read addresses on letters and packets in order to dispatch them in the correct direction to the next appropriate *postbonde* or to deliver them to recipients in their own area. The work of the state required literacy and encouraged its acquisition. Parish officials too tended to be more literate than average. Village counsellors at Aniane in the Hérault valley of southern France were only 10–20 per cent illiterate in the 1660s compared with perhaps 80 per cent of their male constituents. Reading and writing were required of those who wished to sit on the town council of Buchorn (later Friedrichshafen) in southern Germany (1752) (Le Roy Ladurie 1974: 305; Engelsing 1973: 47). Absence of a developed infrastructure of communal administration may help explain limited writing ability for males in eastern Westphalia. This contrasts with Hesse where a decree of 1739 regulating bailiffs specified that officials must be 'those subjects who were practised in reading, writing, and the necessary arithmetic' (Hofmeister *et al.* 1998: 344). Illiteracy did not prevent men from becoming local officials, but its disadvantages were potentially serious. Jacob Jacobsz. of Nieuwport in the Netherlands, nominated as an alderman in the early seventeenth century, announced that he was honoured by the call and would be delighted to take it up – if only he could read and write (van Deursen 1978: 70).

The growing power of the state was achieved partly through its armies, partly through its bureaucracies and partly through the law courts. The pursuit of order, conformity and integration was furthered through the mechanisms of justice. Again, some educational developments were geared to the needs of a legal career, others were aimed at helping those on the receiving end of the state's intrusions to defend their interests. Göttingen university began in 1746 to offer new courses in *Reichsprozess* or imperial trial law, tailored to be attractive to nobles who were fighting off the more arbitrary administrative innovations of the new absolutist state (McClelland 1980: 45). Magnates too found the law and written forms useful in establishing and protecting their privileges. In eastern Europe the lord's court remained more important than the central courts throughout the early modern period. Estate papers of the seventeenth century are full of written papers to the lord's officials and of written receipts for sums disbursed; even for alms paid out in church in the Polish Zamoyski papers. Thus a demand for scribes and men with a legal training existed (Pośpiech and Tygielski 1981). In England royal justice had supplanted that of individual lords during the middle ages. In France royal jurisdiction ran parallel to seigneurial courts, of which there were some 40,000 on the eve of the French Revolution.

Legal developments placed many demands on ordinary people. Since most privileges enjoyed by Europeans were enshrined in the law, a knowledge of its basics was essential for anyone who had contact with the agents of the lord or the state. Written documents and the law certainly could be instruments of state or magnate power. Yet they also fixed and guaranteed the rights of ordinary people, meaning that there was a defensive as well as an offensive need for command of literacy and legal precepts. For all it appears to be fixed and ideologically neutral, writing could be a tool in power struggles.

Written records of current practice tended to be produced at strategic moments in disputes over land or use rights as apparent evidence of long-established relationships that were generally favourable to the party who introduced the medium. From the sixteenth century there are examples from the German Peasants' War and in England from both agrarian and industrial disputes (Wood 1999). Nascent British trade unions of the later eighteenth and early nineteenth centuries appreciated the importance of education for their members and the fact that ignorance made exploitation by employers easier. The drawbacks inherent in illiteracy were sometimes clearly perceived and sometimes felt as a vague sense of unease, an awareness that it was just another of the disadvantages suffered because of being poor and powerless. As early as the sixteenth century, a Durham farmer called John Taylor suspected his half-brother of shady dealings in trying to take over his land by 'bringinge certain writeings to me which I could not certainly tell what they were' (Wrightson 1982: 195).

Two final examples summarise the positive and negative aspects of the legal revolution that pushed and pulled people towards literacy. In France, the guardian of a minor had to be able to write, and if illiterate was forced to the expense and inconvenience of employing a professional notary to deal with all legal acts relating to the child's inheritance. The German city of Nürnberg required all that died in its bounds to have their goods inventoried by a licensed appraiser or *Unterkeuflin*. These men and women had to be able to read book titles, assess the value of goods, add up the total wealth and write the inventory (Chisick 1981: 80–81; Wood 1981: 8).

New demands for servants of the state and practitioners of the law greatly expanded opportunities for employment in the early modern period. Alongside economic change, these offered an avenue to occupational mobility in a world where population growth had made advancement increasingly difficult. Becoming literate was a way of preventing downward mobility in an uncertain world. Some parents clearly wished their children to improve as well as maintain their social and economic standing. Literate parents could promote learning among their children, but ignorants could aspire to provide their children with the education they had never had. For example, only a minority of the parents who subscribed a 1653 petition to set up a school at Kudelstaart in the Low Countries could sign their names (Voss 1980: 256). A *Universal Treasure* of *c*.1530 was directed to Venetians, 'especially to the sons of every father who desires his son's welfare'.

The state offered growing employment opportunities. From the later sixteenth century, impoverished Polish gentry and ambitious members of the commonality took jobs as clerks, court messengers and baillies, while some of the poorer townsfolk of Muscovy earned a modest living as scribes and clerks in the chancellery-secretary's office (Pośpiech and Tygielski 1981: 76). Literacy became increasingly important in the army too. After the reforms of Choiseul in the 1760s, sergeants of the French military had to be able to read and write, thus closing off promotion prospects to the illiterate. Opportunities for occupational and social mobility existed mainly for the middling and upper classes who could afford the advanced education necessary to enter the expanding ranks of the professions. Even here, notions of entrance by merit were strictly circumscribed. Mathematical skills rather than basic literacy were formally tested for entrance into an élite military academy in France during the second half of the eighteenth century. However, a man's lineage and *honnêteté* were also crucial to a successful application (Julia 1989). Regardless of the growing use of a university path, class and birth crucially determined access to legal careers in early modern Germany (Jahns 1995).

The significance of economic, political and legal developments on demand for literacy and learning is evident. Beginning in the sixteenth century, changes gathered pace in the seventeenth and became still more compelling during the century of Enlightenment and Absolutism. There were pressing, practical reasons to learn reading, writing and counting, and to advance beyond these to specialist training in navigation, accounting, law and military affairs. Basic literacy was only of limited value for the lower classes, though in areas such as the Hautes Alpes of south-eastern France and Alpine Italy it might, for example, provide a would-be migrant with the chance of becoming a schoolteacher in the less literate lowland areas nearby. Some negative incentives existed which can be reduced to the avoidance of risk, and these really only required elementary learning.

Basic reading and writing was also becoming increasingly important in social and familial life. The advent of printing brought reading into the mainstream of cultural activities, and writing enhanced the breadth and complexity of social exchanges. One example is the family memorandum book cum diary, known in France as a *Livre de Raison* and in Italy as a *Ricordanza*. These day books of the sixteenth and seventeenth century were kept mainly by patricians and bourgeois, but also by a few ordinary folk such as a Milan carpenter and a builder from Bologna. They record marriage settlements, inheritances and business deals; births, marriages and deaths in the family; remarks on the weather, plagues and politics. Self-written on cheap materials, they dealt with everyday, ephemeral, mainly private matters. Their existence also reflects a growing awareness of the utility and pleasure of reading and writing (Hyde 1979: 116–17; Marvick 1976: 261; Burke 1987).

The groundswell of demand for basic education was fed by the prestige attached to reading, writing and religious knowledge as much as it was by the perception of concrete advantages. Often this pride in literacy only becomes apparent when mentioned with approval by educated contemporaries. The desire for basic literacy among the Scottish Lowlanders at the end of the eighteenth century was forcefully contrasted with the alleged indifference of the Highlanders. At the same time, there was developing in Finland an attitude which related signing to social standing among the ordinary farming population. In some parts of central Europe this was linked to developing nationalist sentiment as it furthered a sense of self-confidence and independence among dominated peoples. Ukrainians are said to have prized education and literacy more than Muscovites and to have provided many of the Russian empire's most able thinkers and bureaucrats in the nineteenth century (Houston 1985; Viazzo 1983: 166; Luttinen 1985: 43; Saunders 1985: 43–4). Potentially indicative as they are, such comments need to be treated with caution, for they were generally made to drive home a nationalist, particularist or even racist point about the superiority of one region, lifestyle or people over another. Commentators often exaggerated mass literacy (Tóth 2000: 209–10).

Groups of literate people could develop a sense of identity and an enhanced feeling of worth, their skills being displayed as a badge of belonging. One example was the 'literary' confraternity set up in the small Polish town of Koprzywnicy during the fifteenth century. A religious confraternity was an association of people who lived in the same neighbourhood, or who worshiped at the same church, or who belonged to the same occupational group. In this case members had to be able to read and write. Participants in the eighteenth century were drawn principally from the prosperous bourgeoisie and nearly all were men: this was a powerful and exclusive body, prestigious in town life and significant in economic and political affairs as well as religious. The pride in shared literacy that had initially distinguished them from their fellows in the fifteenth and sixteenth centuries was reinforced in later generations (Ruciński 1974). Learned clubs proliferated in the eighteenth century and became central both to the spread of Enlightenment ideas and, by becoming a focus of sociability, to the development of middle-class identity. Reading in the eighteenth century was a sign of cultivation that denoted a leisured life. Leisure for women was a symbol of wealth and status. Therefore reading was, as much as a personal and social pleasure, a way of advertising and adding to a family's status (Grafton and Jardine 1986: 56–7). At Marshall's circulating library in Bath, women made up 35 per cent of readers in 1793 and 22 per cent in 1798 (Brewer 1997: 179).

The desire for learning had roots in Renaissance humanism. With its stress on learning as a good thing and its advocacy of reading classical texts, humanism created a revived interest in reading, writing and the classics among the élites whom it touched. Renaissance influences permeated eventually to the masses. Ecclesiastical leaders of the late middle ages also began actively to promote education in order to christianise populations tainted by what they saw as heresy, ignorance and paganism. As early as 1496 the bishop of Saint-Brieuc ordered his clergy to instruct their parishioners in the catechism and to examine them regularly (Croix 1981: 1200, 1205). As early as 1480 the synod of Alcalá in Spain ordered priests to possess a parchment on which were to be written the articles of faith, the Ten Commandments and a list of sacraments, vices and virtues. This was to be posted in a prominent place and read out to the people on Sunday. Worried about the defective religious knowledge of the people, the synod also advised priests to employ a deputy who could hold a school. These campaigns were reinforced and extended by the Council of Trent in the 1560s (Dedieu 1979: 263; Nalle 1992). A new interest in religious matters was also evident among the laity from the end of the fifteenth century, shown positively, for example, in the spread of prophesying and in membership of religious confraternities, and negatively in attacks on abuses within the established church.

For ordinary men and women the coming of the Reformation was both a more immediate and more powerful force. Competition for souls gave a fresh urgency to campaigns begun in the late fifteenth century. Protestants sought to win over converts, Catholics to prevent this or to win back those who had been seduced away. With Luther came a new emphasis on the individual's relationship with God mediated through the only source of truth, the Scriptures. Protestants across Europe advocated personal knowledge of the Word of God, and sought to provide members of the reformed faith with the means to achieve a new, personal relationship with God: a vernacular Bible and the skills of reading it. 'Luther made necessary what Gutenberg made possible: by placing the Scriptures at the centre of Christian eschatology, the Reformation turned a technical invention into a spiritual obligation' (Furet and Ozouf 1982: 59). Swedish literacy campaigners spoke of all being able to read in the Bible for themselves while in Scotland Janet Home's 1702 renunciation of popery before the church authorities of Edinburgh included a statement which faithfully represents the views of the Kirk: 'I doe believe it is the duty of every Christian who can read to be diligent in reading the holy Scriptures and meditating upon them, and that it is sinfull and unlawfull to forbid the people the free use of the holy Scriptures in a language they understand.' Protestants were particularly anxious to spread religious knowledge to the ordinary people and were arguably more successful. Catholics too strove from an early date to promote certain forms of basic literacy, even if they resisted the spread of the vernacular Bible. Both carrot and stick were used. From the mid-sixteenth century Spanish godparents had to prove they understood their responsibilities in the eyes of the church (Nalle 1992: 107). Those wishing to use church rites in Louis XIV's Brittany were obliged to be able to expound the principles of the faith and to recite prayers. A French act of April 1736 required witnesses to marriage ceremonies to be both godly and literate.

In practice, the reformers of the sixteenth and seventeenth centuries had to adopt a modest strategy of offering instruction in the catechism, psalms, Creed, Lord's Prayer and Ten Commandments. However, their stress on reading did begin to influence an increasingly wide range of people. Elementary teaching texts were mostly religious, and a large percentage of those who owned books had mainly or exclusively religious titles. Zealously religious men and women of accomplished literacy used their skills to take shorthand notes of sermons, a method of teaching writing in Calvinist countries such as Scotland and Holland. Many extant diaries of the seventeenth century were written for spiritual purposes, recording hopes and fears, prayers made and granted, feelings of unworthiness of God's grace. The first-generation religious campaigns of the Lutherans had had essentially negative and defensive goals. They wanted to provide basic literacy for the masses and, like the state, more advanced education to train clergy and administrators. Calvinists were more important in fostering personal religiosity of a kind which made men and women search out reading material and write down their thoughts for private reflection or publication.

Limitations

The list of forces that pushed or pulled people towards education and literacy is lengthy and impressive. Economic, political, religious, social and cultural imperatives created an apparently compelling demand for learning which nourished the spread of schools and the growth of literacy in early modern Europe. Yet, why did more people not achieve the ability to read and write? There are four reasons. First, the cost of education could be prohibitive.

Second, the occasions on which people needed to be able to read and write *in person* were not numerous for many groups before the eighteenth century in north-west Europe and before the nineteenth and twentieth centuries in the far south and east. Professional writers and vicarious literacy through the aid of friends, neighbours and relatives could be quite adequate. Third, attitudes to learning were not standard among all classes and were not uniform across Europe. Fourth, oral, aural and visual culture – learning by talking, listening and watching – remained vital and pervasive (see Chapter 9).

Looked at more closely, the decision to educate was based on three factors: the direct and indirect cost of formal schooling, children's status in society and the perceived benefit of literacy. First of all came financial considerations. Even if the monetary cost of education was within the means of ordinary people, there were other factors to be taken into consideration. Most important of these was the loss of earnings by the child. For most poor families in early modern Europe, survival or prosperity depended on the labour of all members of the household. Women too performed all but the heaviest tasks alongside their menfolk, both in the fields and in the urban workshops. For a married woman to enjoy the position of 'housewife' was a luxury too remote to contemplate for the majority of the population, though it did become more fashionable among urban middle classes in the second half of the eighteenth century. Women were conventionally allocated a domestic economic role, even if they also participated extensively in the outside labour force and therefore produced for exchange as well as use.

Children too were an important component of the workforce in the sixteenth, seventeenth and eighteenth centuries, making a small but significant contribution to the family budget. Their role was particularly extensive in agriculture where boys and girls were used for routine, time-consuming tasks in order to leave their parents free for more arduous jobs – scaring birds, weeding, gathering firewood, collecting dung for fertiliser, or shepherding, for instance. One girl from the village of Codesal in Castile told investigators in 1569 that she had herded her parents' cattle from the age of ten onwards, and legend has it that the adventurer Francisco Pizarro spent his boyhood herding pigs in the hills above his home village of Trujillo in the same part of Spain. Older Spanish children might hire themselves out as *mozos de soldada* (servants) (Vassberg 1983).

Children's contribution could grow in importance in times of labour shortage, as happened in Spain during the seventeenth century, or when landlords demanded an increased number of days of labour service from their serfs or tenants, as happened in Bohemia and Moravia during the eighteenth century. When a natural disaster afflicted their community, they were mobilised to help. Plagues of locusts were a common problem in southern Spain in the sixteenth century: children joined their elders to gather them by hand and burn them. Pests on the vines were another natural disaster: the village of Turégano in Segovia organised the youth for aphid hunts in 1589, 1590 and 1591 (Vassberg 1983: 67–8). What evidence there is suggests that children recognised they would have to leave school early or to forgo an education entirely in order to contribute to the family budget.

Use of child labour was not as universal in towns as it was in the countryside. True, children were employed in the silk industry of Lyon from the age of seven, sometimes earlier. Yet the difference between town and country is clear in the holidays allowed to pupils. The town of Namur in the Low Countries allowed children eighteen days off during the year, but most rural schools in its hinterland only opened their doors between October and April. Attendance was too poor at other times to warrant the teachers' presence. Of the 187 schools in the diocese of Reims in the eighteenth century, 108 operated only between November and March (Ruwet and Wellemans 1978: 33; Julia 1970: 406). Rural parts of sixteenth- and seventeenth-century Germany had specific *Winterschulen*, so called because of their highly seasonal nature.

The final factor that informed parents' decision to educate was their perception of the value of education. Being illiterate generally carried fewer penalties than it does in the modern world because fewer careers required reading and writing. Parents might be eager to push a boy's schooling, but they normally did so only if he showed an aptitude for book learning. There were plenty of ways to make a living for sons with less academic inclinations. For this reason, certain mental dysfunctions which make it difficult to learn were similarly less of a handicap. One example is dyslexia or 'word blindness'. This shows itself through difficulties in learning to read and slowness in reading and writing. The definition of dyslexia is related to the culture in which it is experienced, as is the degree of handicap it imposes. A language like modern English, which is unpredictable both as to pronunciation, spelling, and reading, will show up dyslexia much more easily than will one such as Italian which is more regular. A disorder such as dyslexia, if it existed in early modern Europe, would have been less obvious (and less of a handicap) than it is now because orthography was generally not consistent. There were fewer rules about spelling until the eighteenth century and individuals might even spell their own names in several different ways on different occasions. Furthermore, schooling to a standard where dysfunction could be identified was unusual and teachers must have been well used to the inhibiting influence of irregular attendance on progress in learning. Picking up problems would also have been difficult for teachers because tests of ability were usually confined to reading passages that could be memorised.

Adults knew that those to whom an education had been denied, or who had suffered from its premature completion, were not completely divorced from the products of literacy. They could generally find a literate friend, relative or neighbour who could read or write for them. Learning was not essential, and it might well be cheaper in the long run to hire or beg the services of a lettered person on occasions when it was needed. The alternative was to expend time and money on learning a skill which would rarely be used and which was not, at the basic level which ordinary people might attain, of much help in promoting upward social mobility.

Meeting this need at a commercial level were writers, usually called notaries public. They could write for those who, through ignorance or physical incapacity, were prevented from so doing in person. Second, their small numbers and distinctive signatures kept the pool of writers to proportions where it was simple to check on the authenticity of a document. By providing regular forms, by their record-keeping procedures and by authenticating letters and contracts, notaries reduced the chances of error and fraud in written records. For some purposes it was essential to use a notary. Except for a brief period during the Napoleonic occupation, legislation in the state of Savoy denied the validity of holograph wills. Notaries were familiar in the towns of continental Europe, carrying a box of inks and pens and a portable writing desk, working in shop doorways, marketplaces, clients' houses or in their own small shops. The smallest house in modern Salzburg is a former scrivener's shop, a *Schreibstube*. Some 'writers' were educated professional men with a legal training – Scottish 'Writers to the Signet', for example – but others were humble clerks.

Professional writers were more important to social and commercial life in Mediterranean societies than they were in northern Europe and more in areas of Roman than of customary law since the former placed more stress on written procedures. There were approximately eight notaries for every 1,000 people in Florence as early as 1427 and at Verona in 1605. Savoy had 1,000 notaries to serve its 600 parishes in 1700, or one for every 320 inhabitants (Siddle 1987). Some societies showed an active preference for professional scribes, partly through exigency and partly through fashion. The aristocracy of fifteenth-century Spain were not noted for their literacy, opting to delegate reading and writing to lowly clerks or to merchants who had to indulge in the trade which was so despised by the nobles. One early seventeenth-century Genoese patrician, Andrea Spinola, chastised many of his fellow nobles for the shameful way in which they preferred to depend on scribes and clerks to write for them rather than learning accounting and a clear hand for themselves. Early modern Italy was, and probably had been since the eleventh century, a 'notarial culture' where professional scribes dominated writing. This was true of much of the Christian Mediterranean, distinguishing it from England where personal writing was the norm from the fourteenth century or earlier. Clerks wrote most surviving documents from sixteenth-century Muscovy, even private correspondence. The decision to write in person depended less on mere literacy than on the social status of the individual and the nature of the communication (Franklin 1985: 8–9).

The existence of notarial cultures helps to explain why personal command of literacy was not essential. Nor was there a consensus among Europe's political élites that education was necessarily desirable for the masses. Popular attitudes too could be ambivalent. Hostility or apathy towards schools had several causes that cannot simply be attributed to ignorance or obscurantism. For religious minorities in a region or a country, the schools controlled by the 'official' faith might be seen as an artificial imposition. Protestant schools in the mainly Catholic Highlands of Scotland and Catholic ones in the Protestant zones of southern France in the later seventeenth and eighteenth centuries were alien agencies of religious evangelisation. A 'minority' or subordinate religion could set up its own schools, though there was always the chance these would be suppressed. In areas where faiths co-existed, but where one dominated, education might therefore suffer. For example, in the sixteenth-century province of Utrecht, efforts to establish Catholic schools were quickly squashed. Well-off parents could hire a private tutor or send their children abroad to a Catholic country. Most were faced with a choice between a Protestant education for their children or none at all. Some chose the former. Yet the low literacy of Catholics in some Protestant-dominated parts of Europe suggests many took the latter course. It was not until the later eighteenth century that Calvinist attitudes became less dogmatic in the village schools of Utrecht (de Booy 1977: 353–4).

A comment by a Protestant writer on another dominated people, the Irish Catholics, reveals a further reason for less positive attitudes towards schooling. In a letter written in the middle of the seventeenth century, John Dunton tried to explain why the standard of the Irish priesthood was so low by highlighting their humble social origins and poor native training facilities (most trained on the continent, if at all). Anti-Catholic as he was, Dunton made the perceptive remark that 'they who had such estates as capacitated their children for liberal education ... seeing the small prospect to be had of a future livelihood by it, bestowed them otherways' (MacLysaght 1969: 348). In other words, even those with the resources to educate their children might view their future job opportunities so pessimistically as to forebear spending money on an education. For the peasants in southern Italy or southern Spain or huge tracts of eastern Europe, the benefits of education might seem remote indeed. 'The almost complete attachment of the peasant to the land, the increased villein exploitation and the general decline of cultural standards deprived even the educated peasants of any prospects of social advancement' in early modern Poland (Litak 1973: 60). Literacy may have seemed irrelevant to everyday life, its benefits too intangible to warrant investment of time and money.

Education's value was not always immediately apparent. Especially in eastern Europe, specific social groups had to be persuaded or even threatened into accepting that education and literacy were worth having. Take the case of the Polish National Education Commission, whose educational reorganisation provoked considerable resistance from the nobility and teachers. The latter were relatively easy to deal with: the authorities removed the most recalcitrant and bullied others into compliance. A carrot accompanied the stick in the form of a higher status designation for teachers and their organisation into an hierarchical guild. The nobles were more of a problem. The state had to use threats – denying public office to those without the school diploma – and persuasion – informing them about the new ideas and organisation while flattering their position as the leaders of society – in order to gain a grudging co-operation (Bartnicka 1973). Nobles and teachers alike recognised that the new schools were being imposed by the state for its own ideological purposes. They had to be 'educated' to believe they too could have an interest in the new system.

Attitudes to the statute of 1786 proposing a school network for Russia were similarly ambivalent. One town council responded in a blunt and irritated vein. 'Schools are not necessary for the children of merchants and craftsmen. Therefore, we do not intend to send our children to school. We have no desire to support the schools and we see no value in them for us' (Alston 1969: 18). This opposition was not confined to the peasantry or the urban middle classes. Seminaries for training priests in early eighteenth-century Russia had very low attendance figures and attempts in the 1730s to enforce training were met by stiff resistance from those clergy who were supposed to send their sons (Freeze 1974: 652–3). Literacy might be considered useful, but far from essential.

Indeed, it might be viewed with apathy or even outright hostility. One writer on the charity school effort in eighteenth-century Shropshire (England) despaired: 'The grown-up People are mostly illiterate, and ... are willing their children should be so too.' Some families may have feared lest an education beyond the very basics of reading and religious knowledge should distance their children from them. Stephen Duck, an early eighteenth-century English thresher and poet, recalled that his mother had taken him away from school at the age of fourteen in case 'he became too fine a gentleman for the family that produced him' (Watt 1972: 42–3). Literacy could be a mixed blessing, especially for the lower orders, since it could distance ordinary men and women from their peers by giving them views distinct from traditional folk knowledge and received wisdom. Some may have ended up ostracised by their fellows, whose attitude towards 'intellectuals' was decidedly hostile (Vincent 1981: 177–95).

Variations in attitudes could be highly localised. In an area as small as the duchy of Zweibrücken in the Rhineland, some villages displayed a firm belief in education, shown in their petitions to the authorities to appoint teachers. An equal number were indifferent or antagonistic, either because they needed their children to work or because they were hostile to the local clergy or teacher. Positive or negative attitudes to education were at least partly a function of the general level of relations between the local community on the one hand and the secular and ecclesiastical authorities on the other. The low literacy of Brittany was partly an expression of resistance to the intrusion of French and of written forms which were viewed as instruments of central control over a region with fiercely particularist sentiments. By contrast, the villagers of Boissy-sous-Saint-Yon, fearful lest their esteemed schoolmaster should leave for a better-paid job elsewhere, clubbed together to offer him a larger salary and better lodgings. In some Italian rural communities where wealth and power were concentrated in a few, distant hands, collective petitions for relief from rent or tax payments may have seemed pointless and the desire for literacy therefore remained low. By contrast, the village council of Casteldelpiano in Tuscany expressed the opinion, when hiring a teacher in 1571, that it 'could hardly find any other reason or occasion in which so conveniently and honestly to spend the money of this community, having regard to the utility and well-being of both the community and its individual members' (Vogler 1976: 343–7; Cipolla 1969: 27).

The effect of social and cultural attitudes on reading and writing for the levels of literacy in different parts of Europe is neatly encapsulated in a final example from the Netherlands. In the northern provinces, the Protestant tradition of education and personal religious involvement through the Bible produced signing ability one and a half times greater than in the Catholic southern areas. There, the visual culture of the Baroque enhanced the power of oral culture and made custom and collective memory more significant than the written forms which prevailed in the north (van der Woude 1980: 258). The significance of cultural factors, educational opportunity, social status and demand for learning is apparent in the profiles of literacy that obtained in early modern Europe.

Chapter 6

SOURCES AND MEASURES OF LITERACY

Push and pull factors explain the expansion of education in early modern Europe. When it comes to evaluating literacy, a similarly helpful simplification is to distinguish between direct and indirect measures. As with causation, these categories are more nuanced in practice than the simple dichotomy would suggest. Most indicators are subject to quantification and therefore to statistical analysis. Historians disagree sharply about the value of qualitative rather than quantitative approaches to literacy and its uses. Robert Darnton (1971; 1986) offers a wide-ranging critique of attempts to measure readership. However, analysis of statistics and of the uses and meanings of literacy should be regarded as complimentary rather than mutually exclusive. Historians also differ about the validity of certain measures of the broad spectrum of skills which was early modern literacy (Schofield 1968). It seems that the most trenchant opinions are expressed by those not best known for their work in literacy studies, and are often justified by the flimsiest of evidence or by appeals to questionable logic.

Indirect Measures

Three main types of early modern source furnish the historian with 'indirect' measures of literacy. The first is the number of schools. Educational growth was somehow associated with increasing literacy, but what was the exact nature of the connection? Whether a growing number of schools provided by church and state produced more literate people or whether a more literate and informed population demanded better education is rarely considered. There is usually a relationship between abundant schooling and widespread literacy, but this link is not always consistent over time or between countries.

Sweden offers the example of a country with high levels of reading ability and very few schools. Furthermore, educational advances were not equally beneficial to all classes of people, lords and peasants, males and females alike. Boys from the middling ranks of society filled the growing number of school places, leaving attendance rates for the lower orders and girls unaffected. An understanding of the complex relationship between education, literacy and society is crucial to elevate a plausible connection into a proven one.

A second source is the production and sale of books. The body of literature on this subject is enormous and again the line of argument is familiar: more books mean more literate people. The problem of interpretation is similarly plain: who bought the books, who read them and how were they understood? These issues are discussed in a later chapter. Meanwhile, a simple example highlights the difficulties. During the 1660s in England approximately 400,000 copies of popular almanacs and chapbooks were sold every year. There were about one million families in England at this time. It is therefore possible that one family in every two or three could have bought one of these cheap pamphlets annually: some said that the Devil himself always possessed a current almanac. An alternative and equally plausible figure is that one family in ten bought four chapbooks or almanacs in any given year. The first figure implies a large and diverse reading public, the second a far more restricted one, and the historian is equally justified in believing either.

Figures from elsewhere in Europe are equally difficult to interpret. Spanish publishing was in the doldrums throughout the eighteenth century, but literacy began to rise from 1750 following the stagnation of the 'Golden Age' (Viñao 1990: 579). A French example confirms the doubts. The peak of chapbook publishing there came in the seventeenth century, and the contraction in the numbers produced during the eighteenth is difficult to square with evidence from other sources of increasing literacy during that century (Capp 1979: 23; Bollème 1969: 23). Subscription lists provide another indicator of the extent of the reading public. In this case, people paid in advance to have a volume printed and their names were listed at the back, sometimes with addresses and other personal information. However, not all subscribers are included; others are mentioned who were patrons rather than readers and represent salesmanship rather than a cross-section of reading tastes (Darnton 1986: 11).

An inventory of possessions left by individuals at their death is a third widely used source. Inventories were usually compiled in cases where the person's estate had to be settled. In England and Scotland, neighbours and friends were charged with producing a list of movable goods, while in France and Germany licensed appraisers did the job. Regional, national and temporal differences in the level of detail recorded in inventories can make comparisons difficult. Some publications, like cheap chapbooks, might escape mention because they were not valuable enough to list or because they had been given away before the person's death. Analysis of book ownership can therefore produce confusing results. The provincial town of Amiens had twice the proportion of inventories with books as the French capital in the sixteenth century. Given the disparity in size and wealth of the towns, the opposite might be expected. In certain Rhineland towns the proportion of inventories without books rose appreciably and the number with ten or more titles fell between the mid- and late eighteenth century, this despite the fact that book production trebled and literacy was growing. In the year 1714 some 628 new works were published in Germany compared with 3,900 in 1800 (François 1982: 359–60; Vierhaus 1988: 72). Some 88 per cent of inventories for the Rhineland city of Speyer mention at least one book 1744–50, 79 per cent 1780–86. A similar figure is reported for late eighteenth-century Tübingen and slightly higher than Frankfurt 1746–50 (77 per cent). These levels are far higher than for nine towns of comparable size and literacy in western France studied by Quéniart (37–38 per cent for the 1750s and 1780s). At Speyer 56 per cent of inventories mention five or more books in the first period, 32 per cent in the second (François 1982: 355).

An associated issue is readership. That a man or woman did not own a book did not prevent them borrowing one, and the simple fact of possession does not prove that a volume was read or consulted very often. Books might be bought for show. Take the case of Mathieu Lalemant, an Amiens lawyer who died in the winter of 1519. He was literate, but the ten books mentioned in his inventory cannot have been extensively used since the appraiser found them locked in a chest in his attic (Labarre 1971: 105, 393–4; Schutz 1955: 2). Giovanni Zonca, an Italian mercer, pleaded to the Inquisition that tried him that he had not read his collection of heretical works and pointed to the layers of dust on the volumes by way of proof (MacKenney 1987: 184). The ambiguities in these indirect sources are considerable and they must be used with great care.

Vaguer still as indicators of the distribution of reading and writing are the comments made by contemporary observers. The wealthy and powerful who travelled around Europe had a rich variety of experiences to record about the appearance of those they met, their social customs, their mode of government, their religion and even their climate, cleanliness and honesty. They tended to focus on differences between their own society and the one they encountered, to the extent of making sweeping generalisations on the basis of a frequently brief and selective experience. Viscount Molesworth said of Danish society in 1692, 'the common people do generally write and read'. What does this implicitly quantitative statement mean (Dixon 1958: 16)? Between April and September 1549, crown prince Philip, son Charles V and heir to the vast territories ruled by his father, visited his lands in the Low Countries. One of the future king's entourage, Vicente Alvarez, noted in his diary of the tour that 'almost everyone', men and women alike, knew how to read and write. This fleeting impression hardly commands respect. Weightier are the observations of the Florentine Lodovico Guicciardini who lived in Antwerp for a number of years and travelled extensively within the Netherlands. In his *Descrittione di Tutte le Flandre* (1567), Guicciardini observed that there were not only a great number of well-educated leaders there, but also that most ordinary countryfolk could read and write. These sorts of comments give some idea of the extent of literacy, yet they suffer from being imprecise and based on both uncertain criteria and undefined comparisons – in the above examples, possibly between the Dutch town-dwellers and the rural populations of Italy and Spain who are known from other sources to have been highly illiterate (Voss 1980: 257; Parker 1979: 21; Gibbs 1971: 345).

The observations about literacy made by contemporaries depended on the level of their own skills, their status in society and the point they were trying to make when they wrote. James Lackington, eighteenth-century bookseller and religious evangelist, regretted that 'in giving away religious tracts I found that some of the farmers and their children, and also three-fourths of the poor could not read'. In sharp contrast, Dr Johnson described the English at almost the same date as a 'nation of readers'. Edmund Burke's estimate of the 'reading public' in late eighteenth-century England was 80,000, a figure presumably confined to those who read newspapers, periodicals and political pamphlets (Watt 1972: 39–41). Contemporary comments can, of course, prove useful by suggesting broad differences between countries or between social groups. Unless they can be set in context and reinforced by less impressionistic sources, they should be treated with caution. Indirect measures and anecdotal information are useful, but only when backed up by more substantial evidence.

Historians are compelled to rely on such imperfect sources in some parts of Europe. One careful and nuanced study of eastern Europe has been made from publication figures. The number of published primers (*azbuki*) and follow-up readers (*bukvari*), and the ratio of these to population has been used to estimate literacy in seventeenth-century Muscovy. No more than one person in 10 (probably closer to one in 20) had rudimentary literacy (equivalent to painstaking reading of commonly recited prayers); intermediate literacy (defined as the ability mechanically but easily to read over familiar texts) was the preserve of 1–3 per cent of the people; almost nobody had full literacy, which was the ability to read and understand the unfamiliar word and to write (Marker 1990: 88–9). Similarly for Renaissance Italy, systematic quantification of literacy is difficult. Using school attendance rates as an indirect measure, Grendler (1989: 45–6) estimates a third of Venetian youth aged 6–15 years were literate in the 1580s and an eighth of girls.

Used with care, indirect sources can substitute for more direct measures or they can amplify or qualify findings from them. In contrast, one short article illustrates the problems with using suspect sources and vague measures in an attempt to dismiss signing as a valid indicator of the wide spectrum of skills called literacy (Smout 1982). T. C. Smout has used the records of 110 almost certainly atypical people out of thousands who attended the famous religious revival at Cambuslang near Glasgow in 1742. The clergyman who wrote about these individuals selected them not because they were representative, but because they were special. The record he compiled was designed as a piece of advertising. The source is quite unable to support the interpretative burden placed on it by Smout. It states the *reported* level of education and religious knowledge displayed by these select few, leaving unclear how either reading or writing ability was measured. Smout offers a wide range of one-third to three-quarters of men able to sign: figures which cover all known levels of literacy across western Europe at this time (1982: 121). Comparisons are drawn with Scandinavia without acknowledging that Sweden had a tradition of home learning which educated with almost no schools, whereas formal education was much more significant to eighteenth-century Scots. Smout also cites literary evidence to support the notion that Scotland's people were particularly literate – without assessing the value of these attributions or asking whether the same thing was said about England (which it was) or any other part of Europe.

Direct Measures

Smout's article raises two hoary issues. First, how valid is the most direct measure of literacy, ability to sign one's name on a document? Second, what sorts of documents give the most representative cross-section of the population? In view of the shortcomings with many indirect measures of literacy, a firm benchmark exists in the form of the subscriptions made on documents by everyone from princes to paupers. During the late medieval period, the keeping of written records became much more common for the state, the church and the individual. Archives across Europe bulge with bodies of paper produced mainly by professional scribes. Documents were also authenticated or, less commonly, written by ordinary men and women. These include petitions, contracts, wills, testimonies of witnesses before secular and ecclesiastical courts, and marriage registers. Many of these papers had to be subscribed by the person involved. In discussing the relative merits of these sources, it is important to recognise that the main requirement is for a set of documents that either represent the population or where enough is known about their biases to make allowances. For example, some sources only cover males; others embrace only the better-off members of a community; more provide evidence on only one occupational group.

Potentially useful in providing large bodies of signatures or marks are petitions, bonds and oaths. Across Europe, groups of people banded together to beg, cajole or threaten those in positions of power to grant favours, to agree on a particular course of action, or to assert their loyalty to a cause. One of these occasions was to request a school, as happened at Lifford in county Donegal in 1682. Eighteen 'burgesses and commons' banded together, of whom 15 were able to sign their names in full. A generation later, more than 300 Ulstermen petitioned the governor of Massachusetts for permission to migrate there. In this case, illiteracy was confined to some 5 per cent of subscribers. These petitions cover particular social groups and cannot be taken as representative of the whole population of north Ireland. Desire for a school might be stronger among those already convinced of the need for reading and writing, while emigrants may have been drawn from the more literate and mobile (Protestant) sections of Ulster society.

As long as their biases are recognised, petitions or bonds can be useful in providing a 'snapshot' picture of literacy. A well-known example is the Protestation Oath subscribed by all adult males in England during 1641 and 1642 to assert their loyalty to the nation and to the established Protestant religion. In this case the section of society included is known (Cressy 1980: 65–8, 71–8). With most other sorts of document, the position is much less clear. One example is an oath of loyalty entered into by a group of Dutch sailors in 1616. While serving on the vessel *West-Vrieslant* they hatched a plot to take it over by force and devote themselves to the lucrative trade of piracy. A written oath of loyalty they compiled to bind themselves to each other said on it that 28 of them in a circle had signed it. However, there is no way of knowing how many had to resort to marks or initials (van Deursen 1978: 70).

Sources that cover small groups or particular sections of society are legion. Oaths and petitions are two examples, others include leases, receipts and contracts. Biases in these sources are usually obvious. A receipt for poor relief was signed by eight of 18 men at Letterkenny, county Donegal during the early years of the eighteenth century. They are described as 'poor decayed Protestants'. More commonly, contracts were made by the other end of the social spectrum, those who had property to buy or sell. Land leases, abundant in all European countries, are biased towards men from the middling levels of society and seldom include women or poor people. Dowry contracts entered into between families with cash or land to bestow on their offspring have been used to study literacy in and around Turin in northern Italy during the eighteenth century. However, between 1710 and 1790 only two-fifths of couples whose marriages are recorded in parish registers for the area entered into dowry contracts which were formally booked by notaries, these mostly from the middling and upper ranks of Piedmont society (Duglio 1971: 486–8).

This bias against the lower classes is also found, if to a lesser extent, in wills. All across Europe, the sick, the dying or simply the careful expressed hopes for their souls and wishes about the ways in which their goods and chattels should be distributed after their death. Geographical coverage is not even since in some areas will-making was not the custom, while in others (notably eastern Europe) the concept of personal property which could be disposed of by an individual was less developed than in the west. As with many early modern manuscripts, some have simply disappeared, been destroyed by damp or fire, used as wrapping paper or for scribbling, discarded as wasteful of space.

The testator sometimes wrote these documents himself (less commonly herself, because married women generally did not make wills), though it was more common to have the task carried out by a scribe or notary, amateur or professional. The use of notaries to make wills fluctuated over time. For example, it increased in Madrid in the second half of the eighteenth century, but decreased in other Spanish towns (Soubeyroux 1987: 263). The problem with wills is two-fold. First, the poor are under-represented, since they had few means worth a formal disposal. Second, people who in health were literate might be forced to make a mark or ask someone else to subscribe for them because of an infirmity. In some parts of Europe it was held to be unlucky to make a will except when death seemed imminent.

More comprehensive in their coverage are some military records. Russian pay books of the seventeenth century include only officers. Eighteenth-century registers of national regiments in Habsburg service, *Musterlisten* (preserved in the military archives of Vienna), are more socially representative because they contain the subscriptions of all recruits rather than simply commissioned and non-commissioned officers. From the end of the eighteenth century states began to conscript young men into their service. For the Low Countries, conscription registers do not begin until 1843 (Ruwet and Wellemans 1978: 15–16). But for their late starting date and the fact that conscripts were drawn disproportionately from certain regions and from the less favoured social classes, conscription records would be useful in providing information about young adult males.

The number of different types of document testifies to the importance of literacy. From the sources listed so far, it may appear that the problem for the historian is one of embarrassment of riches rather than paucity of documentation. In reality, sources must be chosen with great care. Many sorts of document provide a partial or even distorted impression of the distribution of literacy among the people of early modern Europe. Some favour males over females, others rich over poor. A practical example of the adjustments needed comes from comparing the literacy of males and females who subscribed notarial acts with those authenticating marriage registers in early nineteenth-century Anderlecht. Among males, 26 per cent could not sign notarial acts in full compared with 55 per cent of men who married. The female figures are 38 per cent and 64 per cent respectively (Ruwet and Wellemans 1978: 63). It is immediately obvious that those men and women who subscribed legal instruments drawn up by a notary public, a professional scribe, were nearly twice as literate as those who put their names or marks to the marriage registers of this small town near Brussels. Why should one literacy profile be more credible than the other? The answer lies in the nature of the source. Notarial acts tend to include the propertied sections of the community who were more literate than average. In contrast, the vast majority of the population married, and marriage registers can be accepted much more readily as a source of reliable information about the community as a whole.

Marriage registers are an excellent source because they cover 80–90 per cent of the population at some stage in their lives (most for the first time in their mid-twenties in north-west Europe) and because they sometimes afford information about the occupation or social status of the couple which can be useful in presenting a more precise profile of the distribution of literacy. Marriage registers are common to all European countries, beginning (nominally at least) over most of western Europe in the sixteenth century. However, the extent of personal subscription by the bride and groom varies.

The city of Amsterdam was unusual in requiring subscription of the betrothal register from 1578 (van der Woude 1980: 261; Kuijpers 1997). French marriage registers had to be subscribed from 1686, and extensive studies of Gallic literacy have been possible using this source. A retired schoolteacher called Louis Maggiolo at the end of the nineteenth century carried out a national survey of the numbers of brides and grooms able to sign their names in selected periods of years. Numerous articles and monographs have used these documents, the most comprehensive being Furet and Ozouf (1982). Recently, however, scholars have questioned the representativeness of Maggiolo's survey for some parts of France. In the middle Garonne region, eighteenth-century parish registers are too badly kept to allow the evaluation of literacy levels by counting the signatures of newly married couples in marriage acts. In rural parishes, future spouses were three times more likely to sign their marriage contract at the notary's study. Based on parish registers, the traditional method used by Maggiolo does not produce credible statistics and may overestimate rural illiteracy (Astoul 1992; Poussou 1993).

The priest rather than the couple signed the marriage registers of early modern Spain, meaning that other sources have been used in conjunction, including wills, notarial documents and *declaratións de pobre* (poverty) (Soubeyroux 1987: 229–31). Regrettably, the Spanish situation is typical and few countries insisted on the bride and groom subscribing the register until the late eighteenth or nineteenth century. England's marriage registers record signatures and marks from 1754, but Scotland's not until the beginning of civil registration of all vital events in 1855. Prior to the late nineteenth century, subscription was not required on Italian marriage registers except during the Napoleonic occupation between 1806 and 1814 (Vigo 1972–73: 129). The same is true of north German territories which adopted French administrative procedures from the 1790s and which kept *Zivilstandsakten* or civil registers (Hinrichs 1982; Hofmeister *et al.* 1998).

Where marriage registers are lacking, a similarly trustworthy source can be used: depositions of witnesses before secular and ecclesiastical courts. Civil and criminal courts alike normally kept records of testimonies relevant to the case in question. Men and women made statements, ranging from a few words to tens of thousands, about themselves, their neighbours or complete strangers (Ginzburg 1980; Houston and Frith 2000). Those so described were usually not typical of their peers. In contrast, those called upon to give evidence about criminal or other deviant behaviour form a cross-section of local communities. True, men were preferred over women, rich over poor, old over young because their judgement was regarded as sounder. Yet the young, poor and female did find their way into the courts. At the same time, most witnesses provided biographical summaries at the start of their testimonies, furnishing detail on their age, occupation or social status and residence. In order to authenticate their evidence, witnesses were asked to sign or mark their testimony. This valuable information allows deponents to be grouped together by social characteristics, and the social distribution of literacy to be analysed.

Some depositions are still more detailed, taking the historian into the realms of reading and religious knowledge. The Spanish Inquisition, in particular, examined accused persons about their beliefs: what they thought, what they had read to develop their ideas, with whom they had discussed heretical concepts, whether they could write, and how well they could read. The Inquisition started questioning defendants closely from the 1550s, and from the 1570s they were asked to recite the Lord's Prayer, Creed, Hail Mary, Salve Regina. Then, from the 1570s, they had to repeat the Ten Commandments and other articles (Nalle 1992: 121–2; Viñao 1990: 576). One study of the Inquisitions of Toledo and Cordoba during the sixteenth, seventeenth and eighteenth centuries is able to distinguish 11 different levels of literacy from examinations. For example, a Morisco (Moorish) healer called Ramirez told his interrogators that he possessed a number of books, but that he could only read with difficulty and could not write a word (Rodriguez and Bennassar 1978: 23–4; Bennassar 1982: 269). Such finely detailed information is fascinating, and adds flesh to the bare skeleton of literacy skills derived from depositions. Yet systematic comparisons are difficult. Judges graded the religious knowledge of the accused from good through mediocre to bad (wholly ignorant). There were at least 70 different judges at the Toledo tribunal 1540–1650. Not all asked the same questions and not all exercised their subjective judgements on ability in the same way (Dedieu 1979: 272–6).

The ability to sign a name on a document is a universal, standard and direct measure of literacy that involves few problems of inference. However, it is reasonable to ask where signing lies on the wide spectrum of literate skills, between stumbling through a few words and writing a diary or a theological text. In other words, what does it say about literacy as a whole? Was early modern Europe full of people like Ramirez or was his literacy unusual? Some superficial studies highlight the problems with signatures in order to dismiss them as a viable indicator, often without assessing the typicality or weight of the examples used. Marking rather than signing could be the result of choice rather than inability. In Hungary, making a cross had symbolism even for those who could sign their name (Tóth 1989: 536).

A person might write his or her name in full, while being unable to read or to write more than their name. In seventeenth- and eighteenth-century France, the writing teacher might copy out the pupil's name on a slip of paper or *modèle* so that it could be copied when the need arose. One man from Becherel in what is now Belgium claimed that he could sign his name. When put to the test he had to admit that he could not manage without his *modèle*. Of course, first steps in writing were copying, and whether a person needed a crib is irrelevant to the fact that he or she could use a pen. The practice of using a *modèle* was not, however, usual and one study of Falaise in Normandy during the years between 1670 and 1789 concludes that people did not learn to sign without also learning to write words and phrases other than their name (Ruwet and Wellemans 1978: 73; Longuet 1978: 222; Nalle 1989). Quality of writing was also related to orthographic proficiency. Around 1800, members of the community council of Caldern, a village north of Marburg, were required to authenticate a petition. Those with the best signatures were most successful in spelling the unfamiliar word *Municipalrath* (municipal councillor) placed after their signature (Hofmeister *et al.* 1998: 334–5). That there was a connection between parts of the literate spectrum is shown in an earlier example. Those from Cuenca diocese who said they could read and write when they appeared before the Inquisition were more proficient at prayers than were illiterates in the sixteenth century. However the gap had narrowed to just 10 per cent by the period 1610–61 (Nalle 1992: 126–7). From Portugal to Hungary, signing was in practice closely correlated with other literate skills (Magalhães 2000; Tóth 2000: 61–9, 102–10).

Regrettably, nearly all early modern sources give only one signature at one precise point in a person's life. Only by chance, or by the painstaking reconstruction of a local community, is it possible to tell how facility in writing changed over time. Work by Belgian scholars on towns near Brussels at the start of the nineteenth century shows an encouraging consistency in signing among those married more than once. Marriage registers for Turnhout and Anderlecht confirm that for more than 80 per cent of males and females (and in 97 per cent of cases for the men of Anderlecht), the quality of signature was the same from one marriage to the next. At Turnhout, 84 per cent of women used the same sort of subscription, 6 per cent had improved their writing over time and for one in ten it had deteriorated. This example is drawn from a period when familiarity with writing was greater than in earlier centuries, yet the consistency in subscriptions over time is encouraging and suggests that men and women had learned their writing well enough for it to be a robust skill (Ruwet and Wellemans 1978: 77). Signing was not simply a one-off trick.

Other sources permit the historian glimpses of levels of writing ability far in excess of simple signatures. On some Russian legal documents it was not sufficient merely to sign one's name. A signature and an affirmation together were too difficult to muddle through for someone who had only learned to write his name. These attestations were called *rukoprikladstva*. Officers in the Russian army of the seventeenth century had to make out receipts for their salary. In person or by proxy, they were required by the paymaster to write their names, and to specify in writing the amount of money or payment in kind they had received, and the period for which this was due (Stephens 1980: 116). In sixteenth-century London, the guild of ironmongers ordered that those who were bound apprentices to members of the company should write and sign an oath of obedience. Between 1520 and 1550, 72 per cent managed to do so, and during the second half of the century this figure had risen to 94 per cent (Rappaport 1983: 116). These were formal requirements imposed by institutions, and they indicate that for those involved writing was more than just reproducing their name. The very demands placed upon them might have encouraged men to broaden their literacy. Less formal were the New Year's wishes which Dutch children of the eighteenth century gave to their parents or to other family members. Well-written on paper printed with historical or Biblical illustrations, these felicitations were usually copied from a book of examples and were sometimes written for the boys and girls by adults. Usually the children wrote them themselves, as was the case with Cornelis Jubaan, a 12-year-old who lived and went to school in a poor area of Rotterdam. His greetings to his grandfather are clearly and competently written, and the corrections he made suggest a good command of language (van der Laan 1977: 310). Epistolatory manuals offering collections of model letters were available in France throughout the early modern period (Daumas 1993).

The division between signing a name in full and making a mark is to some extent an arbitrary one that disguises the remarkable range of subscriptions which men and women made on documents. Some marks were crude, little more than a scrawled line or cross or circle; sometimes they included inverted letters. Others were ingenious and must have required some level of manual dexterity. In sixteenth-century Languedoc an artisan might draw a rough hammer, a peasant a ploughshare or a rake, a stonemason a square or a trowel. Among signatures too, there are clear differences in quality. Languedoc sword makers or *espaziers* usually signed with more ease and fluency than

other artisans. Indeed, it is possible to make subjective judgements about differences in the quality of signatures as well as their quantity. The larger towns
of Normandy, such as Rouen and Rennes, had higher proportions of clear
and practised signatures than was the case in the smaller towns (Le Roy
Ladurie 1974: 161–4; Longuet 1978: 223). In Hungary, people either made a
cross or wrote their name, only rarely initialling a document (Tóth 2000: 58).

In recent years some historians have tried to move beyond simply dividing
signatures from marks. One Spanish study distinguishes five different levels
of ability: (a) signs well; (b) signs; (c) signs badly (for example, separating
letters); (d) does not know how to sign; (e) cannot sign because of illness
(Soubeyroux 1987: 232–3; Astoul 1992; Magalhães 2000). The problem here
lies in comparisons with earlier studies that simply used the ability or otherwise to sign in full, and with nineteenth-century census statistics which
simply summarise the numbers capable of signing.

Only with diaries and journals is it possible to be sure about the full extent
of literacy. They show high-level skills like composition and record examples
of reading and other parts of the literate spectrum (Frijhoff 1995). Commonly, these 'ego-documents' tell about a sole individual. At best they also
give indirect information about his (rarely her) immediate family. John Clare,
son of a Northamptonshire labourer born towards the end of the eighteenth
century, wrote a diary-cum-autobiography. In it he told of his mother's total
ignorance of letters and of his father, who could read parts of the Bible if
necessary, but who preferred ballads, stories, prognostications, telling tales
and singing songs over a mug of ale with his friends. Clare's father knew
more than a hundred ballads by heart. An earlier example is Adam Eyre, an
English gentleman who wrote an account of life during the period of the
Civil Wars in the late 1640s. He was fully conversant with writing, for otherwise he could not have set down his thoughts and deeds. He could read
fluently; he wrote and received letters himself and on behalf of others. He
records in his diary that at one point in the winter of 1647 he 'spent most of
the day in reading'. At that period he was working his way through Foxe's
Book of Martyrs, which he began in October and finished in December.

The very fact that Eyre wrote a diary marks him out from the great
majority of seventeenth-century people. He was not alone by any means.
Other examples include Sebastiano Arditi, a sixteenth-century Florentine
tailor; Nehemiah Wallington, a seventeenth-century London turner; Pierre-
Ignace Chavatte, a Lille weaver of the same period. During his course of
studies at the university of Salamanca in Spain, a young Italian patrician
called Girolamo da Sommaia kept what he liked to call *Ephemerides seu Diarii*,

included in which was a record of his sexual exploits written in Greek (Burke 1987). However, until the eighteenth century, diary keeping was generally confined to the deeply religious and/or the highly educated. In some parts of Europe such as Denmark, it was an unusual activity for any social group until the nineteenth century. The changing nature of 'ego-documents' reflects changing mentalities. In the eighteenth century, 'The new biographies and journals were accounts of the pursuit of a better life as a matter of self-explanation and understanding, not the interrogation of the soul before the divine inquisitor, or the pursuit of civic and political virtue' (Brewer 1997: 110).

Diaries and autobiographies give accounts of reading (and understanding) texts. Reading may have been the most significant of the spectrum of skills called literacy because it gave access to vicarious experience and may therefore have opened up new avenues of thought and action. Few documents offer any direct insight into this important capacity, though most authorities assume that a greater proportion of the population could read than could write. Because reading was taught before writing and schooling was brief, many children may have left with basic reading and nothing more. Library registers sometimes reveal who borrowed books and when. Like inventories they give no certain and direct evidence of reading.

Fortunately, systematic records of reading were kept in some parts of Europe from the second half of the seventeenth century. In the territories where Lutheranism was dominant, records of a community's religious literacy began to be kept in the seventeenth century. Religious literacy is understood as the capacity to read familiar texts in print. Swedish church examination registers called *husförhörslängder* begin in the mid-seventeenth century, though they were not commonly kept until the early eighteenth century. In Iceland the main source is the catechism or 'soul' registers (*sálnaregistur*) which survive in abundance from the late eighteenth century (Guttormsson 1990: 24). In the German lands these were called *Seelenregister*. In both Lutheran and Calvinist areas of Germany, *Hausvisitationen* by clergy give detailed estimates of reading ability and religious knowledge. For example, in the canton of Zurich at the end of the eighteenth century three-quarters of men can be counted as readers (von Wartburg-Ambühl 1981).

Sweden has particularly fine registers that record directly and systematically the extent of reading ability among the population at large. Following a church law of 1686, most parishes began to keep examination registers of reading and religious knowledge. The priest divided parishes into examination districts and then surveyed by household. Individuals are named, and their age, status and relationship to the family head is recorded alongside their skills, typically split into ten categories such as prayers, Luther's explanation of the five articles, and five reading levels from 'cannot' through 'begun to read' to 'can read'. These registers were principally intended for children and youths, but usually also cover all the population aged above six. The quality of reading ability is difficult to assess because the clergy who kept the records judged the candidates subjectively. Nevertheless these registers, which are also found in different forms in other Scandinavian countries, are invaluable to the historian of literacy (Johansson 1981: 168).

Sweden was unusual in its stress on reading and because of the absence of schools. Its experience has sometimes been erroneously attributed to other European countries (Smout 1982). The implication is that reading was extremely widespread everywhere in Europe and among all classes and both sexes. However, the only other region in which people learned *only* to read was in southern France. This was linked to a particular form of Counter-Reformation Catholicism and cannot be generalised (Furet and Ozouf 1982: 178–9, 183; Hébrard 1988). When the experience of such regions can be reconstructed from the very detailed census investigations of the 1860s and after, a most intriguing finding emerges. In France (and Italy) in the 1860s, just 5 per cent of the population could read without being able to write. The figure is actually higher in areas where more people could read and write (such as north-east France or northern Italy) than it was in, for example, Languedoc or southern Italy where comparatively few were literate. In this context, at least, being able to read without being able to write looks like a phenomenon associated with societies which value literacy and were becoming literate rather than with those which did not regard it highly and which had very low literacy. In northern Italy, it was at the stage when full literacy was highest that partial literacy reached its maximum – albeit still less than 20 per cent of adults. Furthermore, a higher proportion of north Italian males than females could only read, suggesting that reading alone reinforced rather than counterbalanced inequalities of achievement in full literacy (Sallmann 1989: 212–13).

Chapter 7

PROFILES OF LITERACY

The ability to read and write was a function of access to schooling, demand for basic learning, prevailing social and cultural attitudes to literacy. Commercial, religious, administrative and intellectual 'revolutions' of the fifteenth century onwards enhanced the supply of education and fuelled a growing demand for instruction. This chapter deals with the net effect of these developments on structures and trends in literacy.

In the western world today, basic literacy is treated almost as a birthright. All but a few possess the simple skills of reading, writing and counting. Those who do not are regarded as suffering serious social disadvantages. The position in early modern Europe could not have been more different. Access to education was uneven and the need for literacy variable. As a result, the social distribution of literacy was heavily skewed towards certain sections of the population. Put simply, this meant those who could pay for an education or whose social, cultural and economic life required them to learn were literate. What this amounted to in practice was a world in which command of writing was disproportionately in the hands of males from the middling and upper classes.

The extent of divisions between social groups varied over both space and time. In the sixteenth century when literacy was restricted, virtually all those who could read and write came from the landlord, mercantile or professional classes. Beneath them lay a yawning chasm of illiteracy. This stark differentiation was tempered over time as more members of the middling and lower orders – artisans and farmers, for example – picked up the skills of the book and the pen. For England, lowland Scotland, the Netherlands, northern Germany and north-eastern France, an expansion of literacy for the middling ranks had occurred by the end of the seventeenth century. Poland and Russia retained a restricted literacy regime deep into the nineteenth century.

Early modern education favoured some skills over others. Until the eighteenth or nineteenth century, schools taught reading before writing and both before more esoteric training in arithmetic, geometry, languages or accounting. Reading took from one to three years to learn, writing the same again. Learning was firmly sequential and markedly gendered. In the schools of Küstenmarsch (in the Niedersachsen region of north-west Germany), reading was taught mainly to those aged 6–11 years. Writing was taught with reading from 8 to 14 years, with more boys than girls learning the additional skill. Counting was only taught to those aged 11 and above; only boys learned it in the late seventeenth century and a tiny number of girls from the mid-eighteenth century (Norden 1980: 136–40). The stratified learning process and frequently brief periods of school attendance meant that writing was rather restricted in its scope, reading more evenly distributed. In some parts of Europe only reading was learned.

Rich and Poor

Across Europe between the Renaissance and the beginning of the nineteenth century, literacy was intimately related to wealth, occupation and social position. The most literate were landowners and professionals, followed by urban merchants and artisans, prosperous farmers, rural industrial workers, urban labourers, cottagers and rural labourers. Take the case of Spain between 1580 and 1650. All clergymen could sign their names, as could the *letrados* (qualified bureaucrats), merchant élite and most of the upper nobility, but not the poorer *hidalgos* or lesser nobles. Between one-third and one-half of artisans, shopkeepers and the better-off farmers could sign. Among employees, the nature of employment and the status of the employer were important. Servant retainers of noble households were usually literate. In contrast humble tavern staff or journeymen were largely illiterate, as were virtually all the day labourers (Bennassar 1982: 270). At the other end of the continent, among the inhabitants of the Palatinate of Cracow (1564–65), 9 per cent of officials and bourgeois were illiterate compared with 22 per cent of the richer nobility and 78 per cent of the taxpaying peasantry (Wyczanski 1974: 708). A similar profile existed in later sixteenth-century Languedoc. Urban merchants were almost all literate; two artisans out of every three could sign a lease or bond in full, one in ten farmers, but only three out of every 100 labourers (Le Roy Ladurie 1974: 161–4).

More than a century after this (1710), merchants from Turin were 47 per cent illiterate, artisans 89 per cent. And two centuries later, the profile was still apparent in the large silk-working and agricultural community of Vigevano in northern Italy. Men involved primarily in farming were 84 per cent illiterate compared with 46 per cent for craftsmen and tradesmen, and 32 per cent among those in the service sector (Duglio 1971: 509; Vigo 1972–73: 134). Position in the social hierarchy remained an important determinant of literacy throughout the early modern period. In north-western Europe these steep contours of illiteracy between the peaks of attainment reached by the élites and the modest achievements of the lower orders were moderated, yet the same distinctions remained.

Occupation is usually a reliable indicator of social position in the early modern period. Wealth was commonly associated with occupation and status, and therefore with literacy. For the Palatinate of Cracow, tax documents show that landowners paying the lowest assessment were 71 per cent illiterate; the next band in wealth showed illiteracy of 47 per cent, whereas the richest nobles had only one in five illiterates in their ranks (Wyczanski 1974: 708). In the hinterland of Turin at the time of the French Revolution, 65 per cent of those entering into dowry contracts where 700 lire or less was involved were unable to sign the papers compared with 20 per cent of those in the 800–6,000 lire bracket (Duglio 1971: 508).

Breaking down literacy attainments by social groups creates an impression of discrete categories. The occupations and status groupings used to structure the above analysis of literacy's relationship to the social hierarchy are based on the main divisions in economic function and wealth. In reality, there were literates and illiterates in each class of society and the distribution of literacy is most accurately envisaged not as a set of clusters, but as a spectrum. The example of the military shows that within occupational groups there existed a finely graded hierarchy of literacy. Officers in the Russian army of the seventeenth century had to write a receipt for their salary. A pay-book survives with the names and subscriptions of 243 officers from 14 regiments stationed at Belgorod in 1669 and 1670. Among this cosmopolitan group, 44 per cent were illiterate, 23 per cent signed in Russian and the remaining 33 per cent in some foreign tongue such as German or English. Literacy followed rank: 18 of 21 colonels were literate, 42 of 67 captains and 35 of 92 lieutenants. The 85 per cent literacy of those above the rank of captain, classed as staff officers in the 1647 Russian translation of a German military manual, came from their dealings with the central government as well as soldiers and their special need for reading and writing skills (Stephens 1980: 116–23).

Men and Women

The differences between 'degrees of people' were not simply those of wealth and status, a fact that becomes evident when comparing the literacy of men and women. Educational theory, practice and outcome were profoundly gendered. One of the constants of early modern literacy is that men were far superior to women. This gulf is particularly obvious in the ability to sign one's name on a document. Only 28 per cent of the women who subscribed contracts made in the French town of Lyon during the 1560s and 1570s did so with their full name (Davis 1975: 72). This pattern is repeated to a greater or lesser extent all across Europe. One man in three and two out of every three women could not sign the parish register when they married at Amsterdam in 1630. By 1730 the figures were 24 per cent and 49 per cent illiterate and by 1780 15 per cent and 36 per cent respectively. For rural France in the 1740s, just one woman in eight was literate compared with one male in three. What is more, the quality of women's signatures is generally much inferior to those of males even when they were able to sign in full (van Deursen 1978: 68; van der Laan 1977: 310; Houdaille 1977: 68).

In southern and eastern Europe the gap between men and women was more extreme than in the north-west. For every 100 literate men living in the hinterland of the northern French town of Rennes at the end of the seventeenth century, there were 64 literate females compared with just 25 in rural Provence (Chartier et al. 1976: 94). At Madrid in the 1790s there was 17 per cent male illiteracy compared with 64 per cent female, a gap much more pronounced than in comparable studies of other parts of late eighteenth-century western Europe. Looking at only one socially selective source, in late eighteenth-century Paris illiteracy among male will makers was only 10 per cent (20 per cent female) whereas for female Madrillenos it was 39 per cent (males 7 per cent) (Soubeyroux 1987: 238–9; Viñao 1999: 44). Of Peter the Great's Russia, one authority concludes that 'to be a woman . . . was to be illiterate and a virtual slave to father and husband' (Black 1979: 152).

The evidence of a yawning chasm between the signing of males and females is narrower when it comes to their reading abilities. Because of sequential learning and brief schooling, it is likely that poorer men and women as a whole enjoyed much closer levels of simple reading skills than writing. Indeed, it may be that in countries like Italy and France two or three women could read for every one who could write. In the Scandinavian countries with literacy campaigns directed solely towards reading, the sexes were effectively equal in literacy by the second half of the eighteenth century. However, more advanced reading (with understanding) and writing was the preserve of those middle and upper-class young men who had had a longer formal education. Yet, in some Scandinavian countries such as Iceland and probably Norway, the reading campaign failed to iron out differences between social classes or sexes by the 1750s. In a group of nine Icelandic parishes between 1748 and 1763, 75 per cent of fathers could read well compared with 47 per cent of mothers; for male and female house servants the figures are 49 per cent and 36 per cent. The literacy gap between the sexes was still evident (Guttormsson 1981: 148).

That women as a group were less literate than men does not mean that all women were illiterate. Even the most disadvantaged groups had some literate members. Overlap existed between the literacy of women as a sex and the lower classes among men. At the same time, women from gentle, aristocratic and upper bourgeois origins enjoyed reading and writing abilities comparable with those of male categories such as richer peasant farmers and urban craftsmen and tradesmen. By the end of the eighteenth century the wives of town-dwelling Provençal notables had achieved the near total literacy of their husbands. The same was true of contemporary Koblenz. Men from the upper classes in this Rhineland town were universally literate and women from that section of society only 3 per cent illiterate.

Some unusual females from these social ranks achieved standards of learning equal to those of men: no small accomplishment in a world where education for girls was severely circumscribed and where the prevailing male attitude to the literate female was summed up by the phrase 'learned beyond her sex'. One prodigy, Louise Sarrasin, the daughter of a Lyon physician, began to be taught Latin, Greek and Hebrew at the age of eight. Others mastered the male-dominated world of print and used it to attack the prejudices levelled against them. Susanna Parr criticised the Reverend Lewis Stockley in 1659 for his blasts against what he saw as 'weake women (who are not able to speak for themselves in *Print* . . . so well as men)'. And there were prominent women who both wrote and patronised the arts: Marguerite of Navarre was an important patron for Protestant writers of both sexes in sixteenth-century France. All this was an uphill task, for women writers operated in a negative, censorious and dismissive climate generated by men (and, not infrequently, other women). James I of England, presented with a 'learned maid' able to speak and write Latin, Greek and Hebrew, remained ostentatiously unimpressed, enquiring dryly, 'but can she spin?' (Davis 1975: 72). Learned women were viewed with incomprehension or hostility in the Renaissance world (Grendler 1989: 93). In the eighteenth century female learning became more acceptable, and was indeed an important part of the Enlightenment.

During the sixteenth century most of the literate women came from the nobility and upper bourgeoisie. In late sixteenth-century Poland, more than 90 per cent of all literate women came from these groups (Urban 1977: 257). During the seventeenth century, literacy began to percolate through to the lower layers of society, more peasant and artisan women joining their wealthier and more socially exalted sisters in possessing a command of reading and writing. However, the social hierarchy of literacy for women remained evident. Below the élites, social position had a much weaker impact on the literacy of women than men. By the middle of the eighteenth century, only 20 per cent of bourgeois women at Lyon were illiterate, compared with 50 per cent of the wives, widows and daughters of artisans and more than 80 per cent of those from the poorest classes (Garden 1976: 135). In late eighteenth-century Koblenz, there was 8 per cent male illiteracy among crafts, trades and officials compared with 40 per cent for women. Male day labourers were 33 per cent illiterate, their womenfolk 60 per cent (Vogler 1983: 444).

Town and Country

The ability to read and write was not evenly distributed among all ranks of people in early modern Europe. Men were more literate than women and the higher social groups enjoyed far superior achievements to those of peasants, artisans and labourers. This uneven distribution of reading and writing skills is equally apparent when considering residence. Three main spatial patterns are evident: first, the extreme variations which existed even within small areas; second, pronounced regional and sometimes national differences in literacy; third, the generally superior literacy of towns and cities.

Aggregate figures for literacy are bound to disguise the rich variety that existed. For example, 54 per cent of men from the English county of Essex who subscribed an Association Oath in 1696 made initials or a mark. However, variations between parishes in the proportion of males who could not sign this anti-Catholic oath of loyalty were considerable. Within a radius of 10 kilometres in the north of the county there existed one parish where 41 per cent of adult males were illiterate and another with 71 per cent. Over England as a whole in the early 1640s the range was from just 9 per cent in one London parish to 94 per cent in certain parishes in Lincolnshire and

Westmorland (Cressy 1980: 73, 100–101). The geographical distribution of literacy in seventeenth-century England was very uneven, again a feature common all over Europe. In northern Italy, one Alpine valley such as Alagna might boast high literacy during the seventeenth century, while of another nearby it was said that only the clergy were literate (Viazzo 1983: 163).

Substantial local variations in literacy are clear, and were related to the wealth, occupational structure, educational facilities, commercial orientation and cultural values of particular communities. On the surface the variations lack an obvious explanation. The Dala deanery of Iceland enjoyed 51 per cent reading ability among its parishioners in 1744–45 compared with a mere 23 per cent in the Arnes area (Guttormsson 1981: 158). Yet, beneath the apparently random variation there are patterns to be found. In seventeenth-century Ireland the north was more literate than the south, illiteracy in county Wexford being nearly twice the level obtaining in county London-derry, for example. Male illiteracy in Provence at the beginning of the French Revolution was 68 per cent, but in the adjacent Dauphiné it was just 51 per cent (Vovelle 1975: 94). No firm line existed between an area where literacy was common and one where it was still unusual. Over France as a whole, departments in the north and east had levels of literacy far in excess of the remainder of the country. The 50 per cent level attained in the most favoured regions by the late seventeenth century was not matched in the least until 1866. In the Low Countries, illiteracy levels for males and females were one and a half times greater in the southern parts than in the north around 1800. The level for Brussels in 1845 had been reached in the towns of Holland as early as 1600 (van der Woude 1980: 258, 261–2). The place where a person lived might reinforce or counteract other environmental influences, as in the case of these differences between towns in different areas. Day labourers in one high-literacy area of France might be as accomplished in signing their *acte de mariage* as farmers in another with low scores. Artisans in different areas of France had widely differing levels of signing ability (Furet and Ozouf 1982: 152).

Scandinavia too had marked internal differences in literacy achievements. Sweden, Finland and Iceland had a tradition of home instruction whereas in Denmark and, to a lesser extent, Norway schooling was a more central part of literacy's development. In terms of reading ability, Sweden leads the Nordic league table in 1700 followed by Iceland, then Finland (Guttormsson 1990: 16). Denmark may not have equalled Sweden in its reading rates, but it had far higher levels of writing. Approximately 40 per cent of young people were unable to sign their declaration of engagement in three Danish market towns of the late seventeenth century, and 86 per cent in five rural parishes. The figure for six rural parishes in Scania (Sweden) was 93 per cent and for two urban parishes 84 per cent (Guttormsson 1990: 17). The push of the literacy campaign increased reading ability for all, but the pull of economic need remained selective.

In explaining the differences between regions of a particular country, rather than between one country and another, it was not simply factors such as wealth, social structure and the availability of schooling that mattered. The languages used for different purposes in different areas also influenced literacy. Despite the development of nation states during the early modern period, Europe remained highly fragmented politically, administratively, culturally and linguistically. Most countries had a dominant, 'official' language such as English, French (*langue d'oeil*) or *castellano* in which education was conventionally provided. Alongside these existed both dialects and distinct languages such as various forms of Gaelic in Ireland and Scotland; Provençal, Breton, Poitevin and others in France; Basque, *catalan* and *gallego* along with Arabic and Hebrew in Spain (Viñao 1990: 573). Education was commonly provided only in the main language of church, law and government, meaning that children who grew up among, say, Irish or Welsh monoglots had to learn another language (English) before they could begin to understand the rudiments of reading and writing. The stress on linguistic unity was an instrument of religious and political assimilation in countries such as Britain (including Ireland) and France which had serious repercussions on literacy (Ó Ciosáin 1997; Jenkins 1997: 317–41).

Scotland provides a clear example of this. In the fifteenth century half of all Scots spoke Gaelic, a language quite distinct from English. During the sixteenth century, Scots, a version of English that had been spoken since at least the early middle ages and had been gaining ground since then, spread quickly over most of the lowland areas of southern and eastern Scotland. By 1700 Gaelic was confined to the Highlands and the Western Isles, and to perhaps a quarter or a third of Scotland's population of roughly one million. This decline was the result of greater economic and cultural intercourse between Scotland and her rich and powerful neighbour, coupled with the growing political and economic dominance of Lowland over Highland Scotland. The decline of Gaelic was hastened by a deliberate policy of assimilation which was pursued with increasing vigour after the Protestant Reformation of 1560 and the union between the English and Scottish crowns in 1603. That policy involved active proscription of social and cultural forms held to be inimical to peace and stability, prosperity and civility. The Gaelic-speaking areas in the seventeenth and eighteenth centuries were seen as Catholic and lawless, their clans a threat to the peace of the Protestant Lowlanders. Thus the educational campaign mounted by the state in the seventeenth century and continued by charitable bodies in the eighteenth sought to provide schooling only in English.

Deliberate policies and organic developments served to condemn the Gaelic-speaking areas of Scotland to deep illiteracy until well into the nineteenth century. Between 1660 and 1770 the average illiteracy of farmers in the Lowlands was just over one-third; in the Highlands and Islands the figure was over two-thirds (Houston 1985: 70–83; Durkacz 1983). In Highland Scotland, the overlap between Gaelic language and illiteracy was nearly complete. Gaelic monoglots were condemned to low reading and writing abilities. In Wales this was also the case until the eighteenth century, when the circulating and Sunday schools set up by the evangelists Griffith Jones and Thomas Charles respectively went against two centuries of English-language education and used Welsh as their medium of instruction (Jenkins 1997).

Elsewhere it might be the transitional, bilingual zones that were the least favoured. The Low Countries affords a good example of the detrimental effect of dual languages on literacy. In the northern provinces, Dutch was the principal language while in the south (what is now Belgium) Flemish and French predominated. In general, Dutch towns were far more literate than those in the southern Netherlands. However, the linguistically mixed areas of both zones had the lowest literacy. Dutch-speaking communities in the French areas had literacy levels much lower than French-speaking ones. Around 1779 towns in the southern or Walloon area show 34 per cent male illiteracy and 50 per cent female compared with 43 and 55 per cent respectively for the Flemish speakers (van der Woude 1980: 258–60; Ruwet and Wellemans 1978: 24–5). The issue was not simply one of language since areas like the southern Netherlands, the Basque country and Brittany had a strong oral culture which actively resisted written forms, especially if they were in an 'official' language (Furet and Ozouf 1982: 297–8). Ruthenian- and Romanian-speaking parts of the Austro-Hungarian empire were far less literate than German areas. In some parts of Europe, dual-language zones had poor educational provision. Schools tended to cluster in regions of homogeneous Bulgarian speaking rather than of ethnic or linguistic transition. In the late eighteenth century Greek schools replaced Bulgarian-language cell schools in peripheral places such as Târnovo and Sliven.

When making such regional or national comparisons, it is vital to specify the environment. For those who lived in towns of more than 2,000 to 3,000 inhabitants enjoyed higher levels of reading and writing ability than did country dwellers. For much of the sixteenth century the only literate French people were the landlords and those who lived in towns. In the countryside around Nantes in western France, rural illiteracy hovered around 99 per cent through the whole century. The only men who could sign their names were nobles, officials and merchants, most of whom lived in the towns of the region. Two centuries later, in the 1740s, a national sample covering the whole of France shows that rural males were 65 per cent illiterate compared with 40 per cent of urban men; female figures were 87 and 60 per cent. Areas of France with nucleated villages were more literate than those of dispersed farmhouses or small hamlets. In one of his many quotable phrases, Michel Vovelle describes the countryside of eighteenth-century Provence as '*le ghetto culturel rural*'. As a general, if not infallible, rule the denser the settlement of a region the higher the literacy. People living on the plains of central Italy were usually more literate than those in uplands villages (Meyer 1974: 346; Houdaille 1977: 68; Vovelle 1975: 113; Marchesini 1985: 134–8).

Towns almost invariably enjoyed superior literacy, though size was important in determining the extent of the gulf between urban and rural signing. In central London during the 1750s, 92 per cent of bridegrooms could sign their names in full and 74 per cent of brides. Levels for the much smaller provincial town of Northampton were appreciably lower at 70 and 44 per cent, though still superior to rural Bedfordshire's 52 and 28 per cent literate (Malcolmson 1981: 95). Meanwhile in France, illiteracy in the smaller towns remained close to rural levels. Communities of less than 1,000 people in seventeenth- and eighteenth-century Provence had the same profile as deeply rural parishes. The next threshold came at about 2,000 people while urban concentrations of more than 10,000 could boast the highest scores (Vovelle 1975: 99–104).

Spanish illiteracy was higher in towns and villages with less than 500 households where more than four-fifths of the population lived. Tax documents of 1635 relating to northern Spain show that about a third of male household heads in ports such as Santander and San Vicente de la Barquera were literate; slightly more than a quarter in the larger towns of the interior such as Medina de Pomar or Mojados. Villages near the main towns of Burgos and Segovia could reach 10–15 per cent, but for the mainly rural parts of Galicia the figure never exceeded 10 per cent literacy (Kagan 1974: 23–5; Bennassar 1982: 270). Urban–rural differences persisted until the nineteenth century in areas where literacy was low, such as central Italy. Male illiteracy in five cities of Emilia (including Parma and Bologna) was just over 50 per cent

1806–14, female 80 per cent. In the rural hinterland of these cities 95 per cent of women and 85 per cent of men could not sign their marriage documents (Marchesini 1985: 125–8).

The high literacy of European towns in the early modern period can be attributed to two principal causes: the type of people who lived and worked there, and the 'hothouse' effect of urban living thanks to the concentration of cultural features associated with reading and writing. Most urban centres performed a variety of functions. Characteristically they provided services in the form of lawyers, doctors and educators, retail and wholesale trades, along with crafts of various kinds ranging from specialists like goldsmiths and coach-makers to humbler and more basic industrials such as textile workers and blacksmiths. These crafts, trades and services were not wholly absent from the countryside, but were less common than in the towns and not as spe-cialised. Artisans, tradesmen and professional men were more literate than the average peasant and concentrations of such people produced a uniquely literate environment. However, enhanced urban literacy cannot be attributed entirely to the composition of town populations. For in these concentrations of people, men and women were constantly in contact with the instruments and the products of literacy (Houston 1994).

Schools, and especially post-elementary ones, were generally located in towns. Both density of places and variety of establishments were superior in urban areas. For those with the ability to read and write, towns and cities afforded unique opportunities to participate in literate culture. It was in com-munities such as Antwerp, Amsterdam, Venice, St Petersburg, Augsburg and Nürnberg that there lived and worked the printers and booksellers who made and sold the products of literacy. City dwellers might find a publisher or a bookseller on their own street. Given that few early modern towns took more than half an hour to traverse on foot, books, pamphlets and broad-sheets were never more than a short walk away for literate men and women with a few coins to spare. Amsterdam could boast 270 printers and book-sellers in the last quarter of the seventeenth century. Bookstores blossomed in St Petersburg at the end of the eighteenth century: one sole establish-ment in 1768, 29 by 1800. Indeed, most Russian broadsheets and pamphlets of the eighteenth century used city life as their background, since that was where the printers and the reading public were to be found (Ovsyannikov 1968: 17).

Printers liked to work in towns. Christopher Plantin arrived in Antwerp in 1549 and stayed there 34 years to produce 1,500 different works and to employ, at the height of his fortunes in 1574, 16 presses and 55 printers and journeymen. His impressive premises are now a museum. Plantin himself summed up Antwerp's attractions.

> No other town in the world could offer me more facilities for carrying on the trade I intended to begin. Antwerp can be easily reached; various nations meet in its market-place; there too can be found the raw materials indispensable for the practice of one's trade; craftsmen for all trades can be easily found and instructed in a short time. (Parker 1979: 26)

Plantin's remarks point towards the general function of towns and cities as intellectual entrepôts. The Dutch Republic was particularly significant here both because of its concentration of cities – no town of the 'Randstad' was more than 25 kilometres from another – and because of its domination of European trade in the sixteenth and seventeenth centuries. Amsterdam was a commercial centre that linked several regional and national networks of commerce and finance. It became a focus for the exchange of information which was both a by-product and a commodity of trade, the seventeenth century seeing an expansion of the postal service, of specialist information-brokers (among whom Leo van Aitzema was the most famous), and of commercial newsletters such as the *Hollantsche Mercurius*. Among its functions, this sheet announced the return of the all-important East India Company fleet, on which the fortunes of many merchants and financiers rested. The company (*Verenigde Oostindische Compagnie* or VOC for short) had numerous stations in the far east which sent reports to their Javan headquarters in Batavia (now Jakarta) for collation and dispatch to Amsterdam. The city dominated the production and sale of Hebrew books for Poland and Lithuania until the late eighteenth century (Raven 1993: 6, 12–13). It had a particularly strong culture of discussion, both in person and in print or writing. Small wonder that Amsterdam was a mine of information and a hothouse of literacy (Smith 1984; Gibbs 1971).

The importance of the urban environment in forcing literacy is apparent when aggregate levels are broken down into town and countryside. Such a division reveals that towns did not simply bring more literate people together, but also enhanced the reading and writing skills of those who might otherwise have remained illiterate. High levels of literacy are demonstrated in Europe's great cities as early as the sixteenth century. Between 1523 and 1537 some 102 artisans, merchants and professionals living in Rome's Trastevere made entries in an account book at a pork butcher's. Of these, 95 could write themselves (Petrucci 1978). At London in 1598, 99 grocers were required to authenticate a receipt for repayment of a loan made by their company – 98 did so with their full names, a figure without parallel anywhere else in England. A similar document survives dated 1606, in which the only illiterate person among 126 subscribers was a widow called Elizabeth Coles (Rappaport 1983: 116). As early as 1600, male illiteracy among natives of Amsterdam who married there was just 30 per cent, female 55 per cent (Kuijpers 1997: 507). Urban living intensified the need for literate skills. Urban priests who subscribed legal documents in seventeenth-century Russia were more literate than rural ones, and book holdings among clergy in towns like Nizhnii Novgorod (1621–22) were superior to those of their rural counterparts.

Towns and cities concentrated literate people, presented them with schools, writing and books in relative abundance and demanded of them greater familiarity with reading, writing and counting. This is not to say that towns were a uniform social or cultural environment, or that literacy was equally high in all their quarters. Printers and booksellers were concentrated in certain parishes or even in specific streets. Shops of German *Briefmaler*, who printed single-leaf woodcuts for an artisan and peasant audience during the seventeenth century, were generally located in the suburbs of cities like Augsburg and Nürnberg since it was cheaper to have premises there and easier to reach their customers. More up-market, the booksellers of Dublin were mainly to be found in Castle Street and Skinners' Row. Sixteenth-century Venetian book-men favoured the central districts of San Marco, Sant' Angelo, the Rialto bridge, Santi Apostoli, San Zanipolo and Santa Maria Formosa for their shops, while some hawked books from stands near the Rialto bridge or round the Piazza San Marco (Grendler 1977: 5).

The effect of differences in residence according to occupation, wealth and social status is plain in the spatial geography of literacy in the towns. Early modern towns differed from those of the present in that the rich lived in the central parishes while the poorer classes, and especially industrial workers, tended to congregate in the suburbs. At Rouen during the reign of Louis XIV, merchants and professionals clustered in the western parishes near the Seine where ships unloaded and their goods were transferred into barges for the journey up the river to Paris. The eastern suburbs were the home of weavers and spinners, a poorer and less literate part of the town. Central Luxembourg had only 32 per cent illiteracy in the later eighteenth century, compared with the 62 per cent of the poor suburban parish of St-Jean Grund. Suburban parishes were usually more literate than the surrounding countryside which tended in fact to benefit from proximity to a high literacy environment. Rich town parishes of the southern Netherlands at this time could boast female illiteracy as low as 25 per cent; less favoured ones had figures close to 70 per cent (Ruwet and Wellemans 1978: 30–31; Art 1980: 270). In some areas of Europe, suburban and inner-city dwellers even spoke different languages. In predominantly Ruthenian-speaking (and illiterate) areas of sixteenth-century Poland, towns tended to be islands of Polish-speakers (and of literacy). In bigger urban communities such as Lvov the outer parishes were inhabited by Ruthenian-speakers in the later sixteenth century while Polish was the prevailing tongue in central streets (Martel 1938: 196–7).

Concentrations of literate people and the 'hothouse' effect made most towns into centres of literacy. At the same time, urban job opportunities encouraged the more dynamic rural dwellers to take their skills and aspirations into the towns. Natural increase played a small role in maintaining and increasing urban populations. The most significant influence was immigration from the countryside. Between 1650 and 1750, London drew in and retained at least 8,000 people every year, while half of the populations of the French towns of Caen and Lyon were not born there during the second half of the eighteenth century. Substantial proportions of early modern populations had experience of living in a town. At any one time between 1650 and 1750 one in six of England's people were living in London or had lived there at some point.

For some towns these migrants provided a boost to literacy levels. In the case of the growing textile town of Leeds in Yorkshire, immigrants were appreciably more literate than native-born people during the 1760s, and between 1760 and 1792 four out of every five men and women who moved into Rouen in France could sign their names (Grevet 1985: 622–3). These figures suggest that dynamic and possibly upwardly-mobile people came from other towns and from the countryside to make their lives in an urban environment. In England, the period after 1760 saw a proliferation of pocket-sized town guidebooks and of full-sized town histories at a time when rural guides were almost unknown (Clark 1983: 106, 118). On a hypothetical 'cultural balance-sheet', immigrants represented a gain for the receiving town. This pattern was not, however, universal. Those who moved into mid-seventeenth-century Madrid from elsewhere in Spain were slightly less literate than the native born and only foreigners were clearly more accomplished than the indigenous inhabitants (Larquié 1981: 152). Immigrants to early seventeenth-century Amsterdam were much less literate than those born there, but the gap was narrower in mid-century and there was little to choose in 1700 (Kuijpers 1997: 507). Among natives of eighteenth-century Koblenz, there were 86 literate females for every 100 males. The ratio for immigrants was 53:100, suggesting that immigration was selective of less literate women:

domestic servants and prostitutes for the garrison. The same pattern of immigration characterised contemporary Bordeaux (Vogler 1983: 445; Furet and Ozouf 1982: 209–10).

Immigration could also bring cultural problems. The rapid rise in numbers experienced by the towns of Dordrecht, Rotterdam, Delft, Leiden and Haarlem in the Low Countries forced up illiteracy between 1600 and 1650. An influx of young and less literate people, coupled with resulting high birth rates, strained educational resources. Ghent saw a 32 per cent decrease in the number of children receiving formal education between 1650 and 1789 despite an increase in the total population (Lottin and Soly 1983: 294). Extremely fast population growth, especially that brought about by the immigration of unskilled workers into the manufacturing towns of the north of England, central Scotland, north Germany, 'Belgium' and north-eastern France from the end of the eighteenth century, tended to reduce aggregate literacy levels (van der Woude 1980: 261; Furet and Ozouf 1982: 203–13; Hofmeister *et al.* 1998: 374–81).

Old and Young

Most migrants entered towns in the prime of life, commonly between the ages of 15 and 35. For most people this was the time of their lives when writing abilities were at their peak. Memory of what had been taught in school was still fresh, and opportunities to practice literate skills were expanding with their need to make their own way in life, both materially and socially. Indeed, some men and women were actually becoming more literate under these influences, practising or adding to the manual skills which they had obtained while at school or in some cases learning for the first time what their truncated education had failed to teach them.

The effect of non-scholastic education after the age at which formal schooling was likely to end is neatly demonstrated by the case of indentured servants who migrated to the British colonies of North America in the late seventeenth and early eighteenth centuries. They made up one half of the total white migration there. David Galenson has analysed the indentures of 812 servants registered at the Middlesex Quarter Sessions court during 1683–84 and 3,187 listed in London between 1718 and 1759. The youngest servant was 14 and therefore likely to have finished school. Mean age at indenture was about 20 for women and 22 for men. Servants came from diverse social backgrounds and from both towns and rural communities. Yet, even allowing for the impact of these factors, it is clear that the older they

were, the more literate they became. Older servants could sign more frequently than younger ones, suggesting that they had picked up or honed their
abilities through practice rather than through schooling. This influence was
not uniformly felt. Servants who had 'skilled' occupations were already more
literate than their less skilled peers even at relatively young ages, and the rate
at which their signing improved was slower. Most skilled servants who were
literate had become so before learning their trade or craft. For the less skilled,
informal learning while in work was more important, producing increased
literacy with age. Reasons for educating early in life are summarised in
Campbell's *London Tradesman* of 1747.

> There are some Parts of Education that are useful and necessary . . . The sooner
> these Helps are given, the greater and more lasting Effect they will have; and though
> the Child might acquire them in the Course of his Apprenticeship, yet it is more
> advisable to let him learn the Rudiments of them before he enters: By this Means,
> he is facilitated in learning his Trade, and acquires it with greater Ease. (Galenson
> 1981: 824)

The effect of advancing years on literacy was not always a benign one. As
people grew older they became more susceptible to debilitating conditions
like blindness and arthritis that early modern medicine could do little to
alleviate. Subscriptions to wills and comments made by scribes upon them
illustrate the resulting damage. In a mid-seventeenth-century will which he
had written, one notary recorded that Catalina Ortiz y Millan from Madrid
suffered from an infirmity in her right hand which prevented her from
signing. Isabel de Albornoz had gone blind and could not take the pen that
the scribe proffered for her use (Larquié 1981: 136). Some people had simply forgotten how to use a pen. Others on their death-beds may have felt the
effort of signing their name not worth making. What is certain is that those
above the age of 60 were less literate than those in the prime of life.

These examples reflect a decay of signing ability caused by age-related dis-
abilities. In other respects too, the older generations could be isolated from
literacy. Directed at children, who were impressionable, rather than at their
parents and grandparents, who were seen as obdurate and ignorant (at least
by some observers), the literacy campaigns of the late seventeenth and
eighteenth centuries had the short-term result of creating a literate youth,
while leaving the older people largely uneducated. The best examples of this
come from the Scandinavian nations with their eighteenth-century reading
campaigns because the rate of change was, in historical terms, rapid. In the
Swedish parish of Tuna in Västernorland, the parish priest between 1688 and

1691 examined 370 persons in reading and religious knowledge. Of those aged over 60, 47 per cent could not read and 37 per cent of those in their 40s, compared with only 14 per cent of men and women aged 21–25 and just 2 per cent of the 11–15 cohort (Åkerman *et al.* 1979: 181). For a group of Icelandic parishes during the 1750s, 45 per cent of the over-50s could read the catechism well and 5 per cent could provide a decent explanation of it, compared with figures of 89 and 84 per cent for the 15–19 age band (Guttormsson 1981: 151). Young people were receiving instruction in reading and religious knowledge from the parish priests, then passing it on slowly to their elders. Eventually, as the older members of communities died and as the literate younger generations came to take their place, the whole society became literate. Meanwhile, a 'generation gap' must have emerged.

Age differences are a way of measuring rates of change prior to periods for which the first documentation survives. At Althessen in Hesse 57 per cent of brides could not sign compared with 8 per cent of grooms; 78 per cent of mothers and 10 per cent of fathers were illiterate, showing a rapid rise for females in the previous generation. Proportions able to sign in Halberstadt increased only slightly for males 1745–1804, but nearly tripled for females (Hofmeister *et al.* 1998: 337, 342–3, 364). The cultural effects of such a gap are difficult to assess. Where, as in early modern Europe, material, political and cultural resources were concentrated among older people (predominantly males), the possessor was more important than what was possessed. Growing literacy did not enhance the status of the young because they were dependent.

Catholic and Protestant

The importance of religion in creating both a demand for literacy and a drive from ecclesiastical authorities to instruct the people has already been discussed. To a large extent, Protestant and Catholic churches alike sought to win ordinary men and women from the traditional communal, medieval religious observances that were deemed 'magical' and 'pagan' by the leaders of the Reformation and Counter-Reformation, and turn them into committed, individual religious believers imbued with God's Word. Whatever their shared goals, they also competed for the hearts and minds of Europe's people. Protestant parts of Europe usually enjoyed superior educational facilities to Catholic. The implication of these differences for literacy has exercised considerable debate among historians. They generally agree that Protestantism and literacy were associated, and that denominations fostered literacy in their different ways, both through the provision of schools and the desire of individuals for direct access to Scripture. 'God's people were to be a literate people, taking in God's Word from the printed page' (Stone 1969: 79).

At the simplest level, this proposition is quite correct. Protestants tended to be more literate than Catholics within areas where they co-existed, and countries where the Reformed faith was the official religion were usually more advanced in literacy than Catholic neighbours. The mainly Protestant Dauphiné community of Saint-Jean-d'Herans could boast 65 per cent literacy among its artisans around 1690 and 44 per cent among farmers; by contrast, Catholic Saint Ismier's craftsmen were 55 per cent literate, its peasants a mere 10 per cent (Chartier *et al.* 1976: 105–6).

The distinction between the faiths may have been greater in the sixteenth and seventeenth centuries than it was at later periods. Until the Revocation of the Edict of Nantes, Protestants in Bas-Quercy were more literate than Catholics. When forced to give up their schools, Protestants refused to patronise Catholic schools. In the eighteenth century, therefore, Protestant rates of literacy became equal to those of Catholics, despite an overall increase (Astoul 1994). Elsewhere there were still differences, even in the eighteenth century. A study of the cosmopolitan city of Amsterdam in 1780 shows the crude distinctions between denominations. Most literate among bridegrooms were the Calvinists (13 per cent illiterate), followed closely by Lutherans (14 per cent). Roman Catholics were half as illiterate again at 21 per cent. The hierarchy for women is similar: 31 per cent illiterate among Calvinist brides, 35 per cent for Lutheran, 47 per cent Roman Catholic. In the Maasland area of southern Holland a generation before this, the Catholic–Protestant gap was less for males (18 per cent compared with 13 per cent illiteracy), but greater for women (61 per cent for Catholics rather than 39 per cent). Protestants as a group were more literate than Catholics (van der Woude 1980: 262).

The case for connecting Protestantism and literacy seems compelling. Particularly fervent Protestants tended to have very high literacy. In England, Protestant sects such as the Quakers were all able to sign their names on marriage registers after 1754 whereas two-fifths of men and two-thirds of women in the rest of the (largely Anglican) population could not (Stone 1969: 80). However, the nature of the relationship between religious affiliation and the ability to write is by no means straightforward. To understand why, it is essential to realise that Protestants and Catholics were not distributed equally among all sections of society. This is particularly obvious among Calvinist minorities in Catholic countries such as Poland and France. Lutheranism made little headway in sixteenth-century Poland. Calvinists were much more successful in establishing a foothold, principally because of their policy of targeting important nobles and gentlemen who could espouse and protect the faith on their (substantially independent) estates. Thus Calvinism in late sixteenth- and seventeenth-century Poland was essentially an élite movement with limited grass-roots support. A similar though less extreme social imbalance is clear among members of Calvinist congregations in late sixteenth-century France. Protestantism was a minority faith, concentrated in towns such as Toulouse and La Rochelle, drawing its adherents disproportionately from the middling ranks of society. The peasantry remained 95 per cent Catholic and, as Natalie Davis puts it, 'A printer, a goldsmith, or a barber-surgeon was more likely to disobey priests and doctors of theology than was a boatmaster, a butcher, or a baker' (Davis 1975: 80; Astoul 1996). Protestants in these states were not drawn exclusively from the middling and upper classes, but were recruited disproportionately from the most literate sections of society.

When early modern populations are broken down into social and religious categories, the wide difference in aggregate literacy between Protestants and Catholics is reduced. Among rural male leaseholders in north-west Ireland during the eighteenth century, Catholics were far inferior in literacy to Protestants. However, Catholics held smaller and poorer plots of land than Protestants and this accounts for at least part of the difference. The economic and social standing of the Catholic population was lower than that of the Protestants who dominated landholding in Ulster. In this Irish example, religious differences remain the most significant differentiating factor in literacy profiles, more important even than wealth. The same is not true of rural areas of the Dutch province of Utrecht at the beginning of the nineteenth century. A gap of some 10 per cent existed between the literacy of Catholic and Protestant men as a whole. Among social groups composed of all denominations, the gulf was far wider. Between day labourers on the one hand and artisans and farmers on the other there lay fully 40 percentage points. No significant difference existed between Catholic and Protestants in the latter group, but Catholic labourers enjoyed only three-quarters of the literacy of their Protestant equals (van der Woude 1980: 263). In this example, the differences attributable to status were greater than those grounded in religion.

The association between Protestantism and enhanced signing ability was not consistent over either time or space. Aggregate literacy levels in

Protestant England were, for example, approximately equal to those in Catholic north-eastern France. Sometimes Catholics were more literate than Protestants. In the Protestant Duchy of Oldenburg (Germany), 17 per cent of men could not sign the marriage register introduced during the Napoleonic occupation of 1811–14; for women the figure is 58 per cent (Hinrichs 1982). This is inferior to part of the Mosel (a Catholic area), where men marrying between 1798 and 1802 were 13 per cent illiterate and women 40 per cent (François 1977). Four-fifths of men marrying in the predominantly Catholic Mittel-rhein area of Germany towards the end of the eighteenth century could sign, along with two-thirds of women, achievements clearly superior to contemporary England and marginally better than Lowland Scotland. Meanwhile, the ferociously Protestant Cévennes region of south-east France was highly illiterate. And in Vas county (Hungary) in the early eighteenth century, Protestant and Catholic literacy was equally low (Graff 1987: 188; Chartier et al. 1976: 106; Tóth 2000: 55–6).

The picture becomes even more complex in parts of northern Germany. In Hesse religion made no difference to male literacy, but Catholic brides had only half the signing levels of Calvinist and Lutheran women. The impact of religion was mediated by other cultural influences (Hofmeister et al. 1998: 338). Indeed, the diversity of experience among Protestants was sometimes greater than among Catholics. There was a 16 per cent superiority in the male and female literacy of Lutherans over Catholics in the Hildesheim-North region of Germany around 1800. In the environs of Göttingen, Lutheran grooms and brides had 19 per cent lower illiteracy (12 per cent illiterate rather than 31 per cent for grooms, 52 per cent not 71 per cent for brides) than in Hildesheim-North. In the Göttingen area Calvinist grooms were seven percentage points higher than Lutheran, brides fully 20 points (Hofmeister et al. 1998: 353).

Literacy figures may nevertheless disguise important qualitative differences in the way Protestants and Catholics related to literacy and its products. Reading for Protestants was an essential act of faith. That their relationship to the book was special is shown in both ownership and usage. At any level of wealth and status, Protestants in late seventeenth-century Metz had twice or three times as many books as Catholics. In Protestant culture, books were both familial and familiar, reading itself a sacred as much as an instrumental activity. Catholic authorities were not necessarily against reading, but they were ambivalent about it. Reading for Catholics occupied a different place in a hierarchy of practices, taking not pride of place, but playing a subsidiary role after many other observations such as attending Mass, taking the sacraments, going on pilgrimages, saying prayers aloud, and reciting the Rosary. The Catholic church stressed oral and visual means of instruction: catechism, preaching, confession, music, processions, images and rites. Active hostility to certain types of books did exist. In the eyes of Austrian inquisitors, books made heretics. Simply possessing books which had not been approved by a parish priest was a cause of grave suspicion, even if these were not formally proscribed by the *Index*. Both clergy and laity normally equated illiteracy with Catholic orthodoxy. Raids on the houses of those suspected of possessing illicit works continued in the Bohemian lands until 1781 (Ducreux 1989). The Spanish Inquisition's prohibition against the printing, selling or possession of vernacular Bibles, passed in the 1550s, remained in force until 1782. Thereafter, translations were usually substantial and expensive folio volumes. Nor was it easy to change overnight the notion that Bible reading was an unwelcome Protestant practice (Viñao 1990: 580–81).

The divide between Protestant and Catholic (or even between emphases within Protestantism) was not the only religious rift in western Europe. The other fundamental distinction was between Christians and non-Christians (Jews and Moslems). Of 513 Moriscos (Moors) from four villages indicted by the Inquisition of Valencia in 1574, there were no women who could sign and 93 per cent of men were also illiterate (Viñao 1999: 45). The reason Moriscos had higher illiteracy than Christians is twofold. First was the repressive effect of forcible conversion to Christianity on Morisco life and culture following the completion of the reconquest of Spain from the Moors in 1492. Second was the Moorish emphasis on reading and memorising Arabic texts rather than on writing. Yet even a minority like Moriscos might have divisions. Some of those who inhabited sixteenth-century Ávila were highly literate, these being converts to Christianity who were also well integrated into the mainstream social and economic life of the town. More marginal groups in Ávila, and Moors anywhere where they were actively persecuted prior to their final expulsion in 1611, had inferior literacy (Viñao 1999: 45–6; Nalle 1992: 122). Moriscos and Jews were required to participate in Christian religious services and instruction. Yet Old Christians held them in disdain and non-Christians had little interest in abandoning their own culture. Over the period 1544–1661, 54 per cent of Moriscos could recite Christian prayers properly compared with 71 per cent of Old Christians. Jews or *conversos* were actually more accomplished (78 per cent), being the wealthiest on average (Nalle 1992: 127–9).

Elsewhere, and at a later date, Jewish literacy among men was unremarkable when compared with Christian. Among those marrying in Amsterdam around 1780, male illiteracy among the small number of resident Jews nestled between the main Christian denominations at 16 per cent. For women an exaggerated form of Christian patterns appears. At 69 per cent illiterate, Jewish girls were far less accomplished in signing than Catholics and twice as illiterate as Calvinist brides (van der Woude 1980: 262; Fournel-Guerin 1979).

Change over time is discussed in the last section of the chapter. The foregoing sections are concluded by reporting the results of an intensive study of part of northern Germany around 1800 which allows an assessment of the relative significance of factors that promoted or inhibited literacy. There was nearly universal male literacy in a line from Magdeburg/Halberstadt through Göttingen to Marburg; to the west of Hildesheim men were much less literate. The female pattern is less clear: transitions between zones were gradual and regions of high and low literacy existed side by side. Male literacy was high in areas with dense settlement, good soil, dispersed wealth, rural handicrafts; it was low in former ecclesiastical territories; in the middle was Minden-Ravensberg with the most industrial employment. It was not the level of economic activity alone, but the type that made a difference. Industrial penetration seemed to favour female literacy whereas the increasingly commercialisation of agriculture aided males. There seems to have been a strong connection between *rural* Catholicism and illiteracy. However, the attitude of the confessions to reading was similar and there is no reason to believe that Catholics had a distinctly hostile attitude to writing. In Protestant areas of eighteenth-century Germany, 'greater attention was paid to developing efficient school systems and to encouraging a greater sense of comfort with printed works'. It may be that curricula in Protestant schools were better for transmitting literacy than Catholic, and that qualitative improvements in teaching came earlier in Protestant than Catholic lands. Finally, the attitude of the population was vital to the successful reception of educational reforms. Minden consistory warned parents in 1803 to allow their children to learn to write as well as read. The admonition suggests that people were not persuaded of the benefits of extensive schooling, just as in the sixteenth and seventeenth century rural people had resisted attempts to compel them to send their children to any school (Hofmeister *et al.* 1998: 374–81).

Numeracy

Jews were the subject of both prejudice and stereotyping. Both are evident in their perceived and actual role as money lenders, an occupation where counting was essential. If the structures and dynamics of the spectrum of literate skills are well established for most of early modern Europe, those of numeracy are more difficult to ascertain. The first problem lies with definition. A criterion that requires facility with written symbols is too narrow because it excludes, for example, users of an abacus. At the beginning of Molière's last play, 'Le Malade Imaginaire' (1673), the hypochondriac Argan uses a counting-frame or abacus to reckon the cost of the remedies prescribed by his apothecary. He eventually arrives at a total cost of 'three and sixty pounds, four sous, six deniers'. This method of counting was quite common in Molière's time. Though written numeration had been known in the Latin West for several centuries, and paper was in general use, the abacus with counters was still often used in the seventeenth and even in the eighteenth centuries. Goethe's father, a municipal official, used an abacus for calculations while he himself used counters to map out the heavens (Roggero 1996: 639–40). The celebrated mathematician Leibniz also used an abacus, and Voltaire's famous correspondent Frederick II of Prussia took it as the pretext for a quatrain: 'Courtesans are counters/Whose value depends on their place:/In favour, millions,/Noughts in disgrace.'

Most people other than the very young and the mentally disabled can be classed as numerate, because exchanges of goods and/or money and counting of assets or elapsed time require it. Even in the middle ages, one common test of imbecility or idiocy was the inability to count to ten or to do simple addition or subtraction with coins (Houston 2000: 195–201). In a Scottish murder trial of 1800, defence counsel for David Hunter attempted to stop the proceedings on the grounds their client was an imbecile. Establishing the family history to reinforce his case, the lawyer reported of the accused's maternal uncles that 'the only employment they were capable of all their lives was herding a parcel of beasts [cattle], which they were unable to number, and indeed they were hardly able to count their own fingers'. In contrast, the ability to memorise, read and write was not necessarily a reliable indicator of mental normality (Houston and Frith 2000).

If basic numeracy was nearly ubiquitous, the ability to perform arithmetic and handle mathematical formulae was much more restricted (Tóth 2000: 24). Cohen (1999: 39) estimates that, at the end of the seventeenth century in England, 'fewer than four hundred men could be said to be mathematically minded'. Arithmetic was almost wholly identified with commerce across Europe and élite English public schools like Eton did not teach the subject until the nineteenth century. However, when it came to practical numeracy the bourgeoisie and later the upper ranks of the peasantry became increasingly comfortable with accounts and kept formal records as a matter of course by the end of the eighteenth century – as with the German *Anschreibebücher* or household books. Numbers became an everyday part of society and government.

Until the end of the eighteenth century, teaching and learning arithmetic consisted of a set of rules for the student to commit to memory. Students wrote these rules in their copybooks, along with one or two problems to illustrate the rule. They learned rules and examples by rote (as they might a catechism) rather than solving actual problems. Arithmetic was considered a difficult technical subject reserved for boys aged ten and older, and the problems and examples used to illustrate arithmetic were overwhelmingly drawn from the realm of commerce and money (Grendler 1989: 306–23; Granet-Abisset 1996: 130–36). Even in commerce, people with poor arithmetic skills managed by using 'ready reckoners', little booklets listing prices for multiples of products at a variety of costs. The need for these is clear, for the addition in early modern account books shows the hit-or-miss accuracy of counting, even by 'professional' book-keepers.

The Piarists had a special interest in the exact sciences like mathematics and their schools offered training in arithmetic to Catholic boys from the later seventeenth century (Liebreich 1985; 1986). In the late eighteenth and early nineteenth century teaching was simplified for younger pupils and counting was taught more widely in all types of school using tools like counting frames, and methods such as mental problem solving. Commercial developments explain this, coupled with a new premium put on an educated citizenry. Educational reformers advocated arithmetic because it disciplined the mind, encouraged inductive thought, and developed habits of precision, attention to detail, and a love of factual knowledge. In response to the increasing demand for education and with the backing of governmental authorities, new types of schools were founded in Italy in the late eighteenth and early nineteenth centuries to complement and eventually replace the Renaissance abacus schools. In late eighteenth-century Milan there were 12 schools of commercial arithmetic teaching 410 pupils. These schools, which were potentially open to everybody including the poor, taught reading, writing, and arithmetic. Yet fees were high (Roggero 1996: 629).

Although schools and teachers of 'commercial arithmetic' had long existed in Italian towns and cities, demand for the inclusion of mathematics in elementary education in the countryside only became notable during the eighteenth century. Many new textbooks became available. Yet they were not always reliable and required a certain degree of literacy on the part of pupils. The standard forms of calculation used in them were often beyond the comprehension of peasants who continued to use traditional methods that were adequate for their needs. The introduction of the metric system during the period of French domination at the end of the century added to the problems, even though the fact that it allowed comparison between the sizes and weights of different objects came to be seen as an essential part of education (Roggero 1994b). Modern Europe uses the metric system, even if some British people continue to think in 'imperial' weights and measures. Early modern Europe had dozens of different standards of weight and measure.

It has been claimed that 'numeracy cannot be measured' (Cohen 1999: 11). However, it is possible to infer (inexactly) changing numeracy from the changing use of numbers, just as literacy can be inferred (equally inexactly) from book publication and distribution. Furthermore, there are quantifiable measures of familiarity with numbers and precision in their usage. Between 1650 and 1750 developments in statistics were confined to data analysis, often without the use of any explicit probabilistic ideas or the notion of uncertainty. The best example of descriptive statistical analysis is John Graunt's 1662 *Natural and Political Observations made upon the Bills of Mortality*. The Scotsman Sir John Sinclair coined the word 'statistics' in the 1790s and, initially, it simply denoted facts about the state that it was useful for governments to know. By the 1830s, the word statistics had both broadened its compass and narrowed its meaning, coming to include all facts having to do with civil society. The most useful facts were numerical because they were precise, seemingly objective, and comparable (Fienberg 1991). It seems clear that people became more comfortable with precision in the use of numbers during the eighteenth century. Age reporting in documents became more exact. A tendency to round or estimate to base units such as 10 or 12, or their multiples (such as 30 or 36) or sub-multiples (5 or 6) and to prefer certain digits over others (such as 6 over 7) gave way to a more equal (and believable) distribution of numbers. The tendency to exaggerate age for effect also became less necessary as canons of proof in court cases changed during the eighteenth century (Tóth 2000: 167–77).

Data analysis was one branch of statistics, the other being probability and inference (the inductive process of generalising from a sample of observations to population quantities using a probabilistic argument). Just as proof in court often depended on 'common sense' and 'public opinion' (what would now be termed 'hearsay'), the concepts of statistical probability which developed from the late seventeenth century were located in subjective assessment and 'moral certainty'. If changes in data analysis came out of civil concerns, late seventeenth- and eighteenth-century developments in probabilistic theory and practice (as applied to annuities and insurance) derived as much from gambling as from pure science. It was only in the early nineteenth century that probability came to be defined in terms not of a 'rational' interpretation of likely outcomes made by a few thinkers (the traditional, classical approach), but by the quantitative analysis of the apparently irrational actions of the many (Daston 1988; Shapiro 1983).

Even before this happened, numbers had become a symbol of rationality and of the Enlightenment. Reckoning had been equated with reasoning by the seventeenth-century English thinker Thomas Hobbes and eighteenth-century thinkers conceived of intelligence (Condillac and d'Alembert) and moral feeling (Hutcheson and Bentham) as essentially forms of calculation. Even the celebrated Scottish philosopher David Hume spared 'abstract reasoning concerning quantity and number' from his penetrating scepticism. According to Grotius in *On the Laws of War and Peace* (Book 1, Cap. 1, Title X, 5), 'God himself cannot make twice two not be four'. As astrologers, surveyors and military engineers, mathematicians in the seventeenth and eighteenth centuries enjoyed a status (and wealth) they have since lost (Daston 1994).

Change

Structures of literacy among the people of early modern Europe reveal some clear patterns in spite of their rich variety. Ability to sign was stratified depending on who one was and where one lived. Basic numeracy, like basic reading, was more evenly distributed. Many of the patterns proved remarkably enduring in spite of dramatic changes. By 1800 over most of north-western Europe, more than half of adult males could sign their names and still more could read a simple text. Whole social groups had command of high levels of functional skills – reading, writing, counting and languages – and there was no class wholly devoid of literate elements. Female literacy advanced less rapidly and did not reach the level of males as a group. Nevertheless, countries like England, lowland Scotland, the Scandinavian cluster, much of Germany and north-eastern France could, in their own distinctive ways, boast mass literacy which set them apart from much of the Mediterranean world and vast areas of central and eastern Europe. Mass literacy had arrived, bringing with it accentuated social and geographical stratification.

These developments should be seen in the context of the ways in which change was won. Most significantly, the growth of literacy was extremely slow. Literacy campaigns in countries like Cuba or Nicaragua in the 1960s, 1970s and 1980s produced in a decade or less improvements in reading skills which took a century or more in early modern Europe. Changes in historic Europe were gradual, irregular, hesitant and far from complete, even in 1800. Literacy rose at different times and at widely varying rates in different areas and among disparate social groups (Arnove and Graff 1987).

Literacy rose quickest in countries which espoused the modest goal of inculcating a capacity for reading and memorising basic religious texts. National literacy campaigns in the Scandinavian states took two to three generations to secure near-universal reading ability among their people. In the Swedish parish of Möklinta, just 21 per cent of the total adult population could read in 1614. By the 1690s examination registers show a level of 89 per cent. The final drive to universal literacy could produce marked falls in ignorance over very brief time periods in parts of Scandinavia. Information survives about approximately 500 people who were tested for reading and religious knowledge at the time of their confirmation in the Icelandic diocese of Skálholt. In 1754, 13 per cent of them were considered illiterate. Just four years later the percentage had fallen to less than a half and in 1760 a figure of nil is recorded (Kamen 1984: 211; Guttormsson 1981: 162). The level of ability required was low, yet these two cases exemplify the fastest known rates of improvement.

They may have been paralleled in Catholic Europe more than a century earlier. The Toledo Inquisition asked those who stood accused before them about their upbringing, their travels and their beliefs. It also enquired about Catholic conformity, judged as ability to recite certain prayers and rehearse the essentials of Christian doctrine. Before 1550, 37 per cent of men were 'good' at reciting the four prayers (Ave, Pater, Salve and Credo), 25 per cent failed completely. For 1600–50 the figures were 82 and 5 per cent respectively. Between 1565 and 1574, 40 per cent were good at reciting the Ten Commandments and 45 per cent 'bad' (wholly ignorant), compared with 70 and 8 per cent respectively in 1600–50. By the reign of Philip IV the majority of males who came before the Toledo Inquisition possessed this '*bagage théolgique minimum*' (Dedieu 1979). The judgements on which these figures are based were subjective and the requirements were less than for Scandinavian examinants. The figures nevertheless show what could be achieved, even in the sixteenth century.

Developments in literacy came slowly and they were far from regular. Local variations could be considerable. Adjacent towns in a small country such as the Netherlands could display quite different profiles of change. Brides at the towns of Leeuwarden and Groningen saw a steady reduction of about 30 per cent in their illiteracy between the first quarter of the seventeenth century and the last quarter of the eighteenth. For young women living in most other Dutch towns, the first half of the seventeenth century was a time of rising illiteracy and at Nijmegen the years 1650–1700 were also a time of mounting illiteracy. Progress was far from uniform and could be reversed for decades on end. At the same time, rates of change varied considerably over the centuries. Between 1585 and 1700 the rate of growth of literacy was fastest at Amsterdam at the end of the sixteenth century (Kuijpers 1997: 507). Inability to sign among Amsterdam bridegrooms fell from 43 per cent in 1630 to 15 per cent in 1780. Between 1630 and 1680, illiteracy was cut by 30 per cent; a further reduction of 20 per cent (30 per cent down to 24 per cent) marked a slowing down of improvement between 1680 and 1730. The rate of change picked up again in the half century to 1780 when a reduction of 38 per cent was recorded. The trend is similar for women (18, 12 and 27 per cent respectively), albeit at a slower pace (van der Woude 1980: 262).

A similarly erratic pattern can be detected in most European countries. For men at least, Castile in the sixteenth century was on a par with France and England until the second quarter of the seventeenth century (Viñao 1993: 159). Between c.1620 and c.1740 it failed to develop at the same rate as France, but during the period of the Enlightenment (up to 1808) there was a recovery (Viñao 1990: 579). The literacy of Spanish women who gave evidence before the Inquisitions of Toledo and Cordoba fluctuated between nil and 7 per cent between 1515 and 1750, only improving to 18 per cent under the impact of the literacy campaign of the later eighteenth century. Their husbands, fathers and brothers saw a substantial and sustained rise from 57 to 93 per cent over the three centuries from 1515 to 1817. Yet this did little to stem a decline of literacy which put Spain in 1860 where England had been in 1660, with 75 per cent of her people illiterate (Viñao 1999: 51, 70–71). In the case of southern England, the fastest rate of improvement for most social groups was during the reigns of Elizabeth and James I (1558–1625), whereas in the northern counties the years 1660–1720 were the most favourable.

Apart from occasional decades when rapid advances were made, the pace of change throughout the remainder of the early modern period was slow. In some parts of Europe it was non-existent. Michel Vovelle describes the eighteenth century in Provence as a period of cultural stagnation when the graph of literacy was not surging into the nineteenth century, but was instead 'une courbe brisée' (Vovelle 1975: 140). The eighteenth century was also a time of stagnation in the Massif Central, Brittany and Acquitaine, indeed at very low levels of literacy. Haut-Vienne in the Limousin remained among the ten least literate départements in France from the mid-seventeenth to the mid-nineteenth century. Italy, a highly literate culture (in the towns of the north and centre at least) in the late middle ages, probably saw a contraction of education and literacy in the sixteenth and seventeenth centuries similar to what happened in Spain (Graff 1987: 189). Literacy also declined in the Palatinate of Cracow between 1650 and 1800 (Urban 1984). Over large tracts of western Ireland, illiteracy remained above 90 per cent for women throughout the eighteenth century, a time when it had been cut by nearly a half in Scotland (Furet and Ozouf 1982: 30–31, 41–2; Vovelle 1975: 140; Houston 1985; Daly and Dickson 1990). There was a dramatic improvement in signing ability of manorial peasants on certain estates in Jutland (northern Denmark) during the eighteenth century. Four-fifths of men could not sign around 1720 compared with just one tenth by 1800. This created a huge gulf in literacy between them and an estate near Odense in the southern province of Fünen where illiteracy hovered near 90 per cent throughout the century. The gap was not bridged until the middle of the nineteenth century thanks to a continuing fall in illiteracy in the south and a *rise* in the north, both areas settling at 30 per cent male illiteracy. In the easternmost parts of Europe, many of the basic patterns established in the west during the sixteenth century still did not apply in 1800. It was not until the last two decades of the eighteenth century that anything approaching a half of the nobles in the Vas region of Hungary signed documents personally; in the first half of the century the proportion had been less than a fifth (Tóth 1989: 545).

Illiteracy declined for both sexes and all social classes between 1500 and 1800. Yet change did not take place at equal rates for all groups. Indeed, the most characteristic pattern is not for simultaneous and uniform reductions in illiteracy among men and women, artisans and labourers alike. Literacy improved among the upper reaches of the social hierarchy and among men first, followed some time later by women and the lower orders. Küstenmarsch, to the north of Bremen, saw pronounced falls in illiteracy for both sexes under the influence of Pietism. A quarter of men and half of women could not read in 1675, nearly all could by 1735. Writing was more restricted. Half of men could write in 1675 and three-quarters by 1750 compared with 10 per cent of women at the first date and under a half at the second. No women could count in 1675 and just one sixth of men. Nearly half the men could count in 1735 and 7 per cent of women registered arithmetic skill (Norden 1980: 123–4).

Different groups reached 'ceilings' or 'plateaus' at different times, from which it might take decades to move. Take the example of one village in the Champagne region of north-eastern France. Male literacy at Vitry les Reims had climbed to 83 per cent by 1700. Only then could females drag themselves from no literacy at all to a figure of 60 per cent on the eve of the French Revolution. Over north-eastern France, the eighteenth century was 'the age of the take-off of female literacy *par excellence*' (Furet and Ozouf 1982: 37–8). The rate of improvement at this time was much faster for women than men. This was an important period for advances in female literacy across western Europe. After a century of stagnation, the second half of the eighteenth century saw much better progress for Madrillenos of both sexes: illiteracy fell by a fifth (from 39 per cent to 31 per cent for males and from 88 per cent to 71 per cent for females) (Soubeyroux 1987: 262).

Different social classes experienced distinct patterns of change even within the same area. Illiteracy was halved among tradesmen who lived in Northumberland and Durham during the sixteenth century. In contrast there was a fall of only a few percentage points for the farmers of the region (Cressy 1980: 159–63). In the larger towns of Provence the wives of artisans won substantial improvements in signing ability between 1660 and 1750. The servant girls whom they employed saw none whatsoever during this period (Vovelle 1975: 114). Turin merchants cut their illiteracy by two-thirds between 1710 and 1790, whereas artisans could only manage a reduction of an eighth (Duglio 1971: 509). There are exceptions to this pattern, for contemporaneous improvements for all groups did occur in some areas. Nevertheless the most common pattern was a socially staggered reduction in illiteracy.

Some parts of Europe hardly participated at all in these fundamental changes. It is not possible to talk of a shift to mass literacy in southern Italy before the second half of the nineteenth century. The same social groups were at ease with writing in the early nineteenth century as had been in the sixteenth century: nobility, clergy, upper bourgeoisie, professionals, merchants, and a third of master-artisans. Towns were more literate than the countryside and Naples had the highest literacy in the whole of southern Italy. It was also the only location to see anything that could be called a progression in literacy. Male illiteracy fell from about 60 per cent to 50 per cent between *c.*1750 and *c.*1850, Naples still retaining its superiority over other towns of the south. There were illiterate nobles at the start of the sixteenth century, but not at its end, and the urban upper classes followed this progression a generation later. Outside Naples, levels of literacy were always lower, but there were variations from place to place depending on economic and occupational profile or the presence or otherwise of a school or active religious order offering teaching. Yet even in 1800 writing was still largely an urban phenomenon in southern Italy (Pelizzari 1989).

Looking at Italian towns more generally, the Marches and Umbria form an intermediate zone between the deep illiteracy of the south and the much higher levels in the north west. These are also the least urbanised parts of Italy; most so is the south, with 60 per cent of the population of Sicily in 1861 living in towns of 6,000 or more (Sallmann 1989: 199). However, the existence of (mostly small) 'agri-towns' did not mean that literacy was higher in the urban south. Levels in the towns of north-western Italy in the nineteenth century were close to those in France, and much higher than in the towns of the kingdom of Naples. Northern towns were much more than residences for farmers (Sallmann 1989: 190–91).

If there were three zones of urban literacy, rural Italy is divided between the superior literacy of the north on the one hand and the inferior achievements of the middle and south on the other. Northern Italy had a large gap between town and country, in the context of high overall levels of literacy. In the central areas there was also an urban–rural divide, but overall levels were lower; the towns were islands of literacy. Town and country were both deeply illiterate in the south. This pattern was a long-established and stable one. Less than 3 per cent of rural women could read and write in the far south of Italy in 1861 and less than 1 per cent in the province of Reggio Calabria (Sallmann 1989: 191–3, 200).

The only parts of Italy where literacy was high among significant social and residential groups, and where it was comparable with northern Europe, was a strip of the far north next to France and Switzerland. The quasi-structural illiteracy of southern Italy (Naples, Sicily, Sardinia) throughout the early modern period, which marks it out from much of northern Europe (and even from northern Italy), should make historians question notions of progress. The situation in southern Italy (and perhaps Hungary and even Portugal) can be explained by: the absence of a religious frontier which meant that there was no need for a campaign to educate those tempted by a competing faith or to win back converts; the ambivalent attitude of élites to mass education and of rural dwellers to the place of schooling in their communities; limited geographical mobility and commercial exchange (Pelizzari 1989: 635–6; Roggero 1999; Magalhães 2000). The dynamics of change, like the basic structures of literacy, reveal the intimate dependence of reading and writing on their social and material environment.

Chapter 8

BOOKS AND READERS

Changes in the medium of literacy, from syllabic to alphabetic writing in the ancient Mediterranean world, from written to printed texts in the fifteenth and sixteenth centuries, from type and paper to electronic technologies in the present day, have all potentially involved fundamental transformations in patterns of thought and communication. The printing revolution of the mid-fifteenth century and the explosion of publishing which followed it brought the printed page into the forefront of both popular and élite culture, creating a huge potential for both new reading and new patterns of thought. Rare and precious in the fifteenth century, books had by 1700 (if not earlier) become common all over western Europe. At the same time, political, commercial and religious change confronted more and more people with the products of print. How many books were produced and on what subjects; how much did they cost; how were they distributed; who owned books, who read them and, finally, what impact did the printed word have upon the mental world of early modern men and women?

Book Production

Until the fifteenth century, books had usually to be copied out longhand, meaning that they were few and expensive. Printing had existed in Europe in the form of fixed wooden blocks for generations before the birth of Johann Gutenberg. His outstanding contribution to the development of printing was the invention of movable metal type coupled with the development of an ink that would adhere to it and modifications to the screw press which made for greater flexibility in operation and improved legibility of the finished product. Printing by movable type began in Mainz in 1439, soon spreading to other major commercial centres: Cologne in 1464, Basel 1466, Rome 1467, Venice 1469 and to Paris, Nürnberg and Utrecht in 1470. It later spread to other centres such as prominent university towns. Indeed, the period from *c.*1450 to *c.*1550 marked the most dynamic phase: 'the creative century', according to Steinberg (1974: 12). By 1480 more than 110 towns had presses and by 1500 some 236 centres could boast one. Presses proliferated, though the high cost of paper (two-thirds of the cost of production) and uncertain markets meant that failure rates among printing enterprises was high. Some survived by moving from town to town, seeking out ecclesiastical or lay patronage for their skills. Important innovations during the creative century included the development of italic and other type-faces, Greek and Hebrew printing, pro-duction of musical scores and the introduction of pocket editions. Hebrew printing flourished in early sixteenth-century Italy following the expulsion of the Jews from Spain and Portugal in the 1490s. Primitive 'copyright libraries' were created – Francis I ordered the Parisian printer Robert Estienne to give him one copy of every Greek book he produced – and the growth of competi-tion is neatly attested by the apology of a Parma bookman who accounted for the numerous errors in a book by pointing out that it had been rushed out 'more quickly than asparagus could be cooked' (Steinberg 1974: 119).

The geographically expansive phase had come to an end by the third quarter of the sixteenth century in western Europe. Peripatetic presses settled in the main administrative and marketing towns, printers' privileges increasingly fixed in law. London's early dominance of printing (from Caxton onwards) was consolidated by legislation granting a monopoly of English printing to the London Stationers' Company in 1557. Once settled, print shops were usually located in premises that had been or still were private houses. They were often cramped and dirty. In Paris before the Revolution each of the 36 licensed master printers had at least four presses in their workshops. Technology was simple and operated by manpower, either the traditional two-strike press or the new, more efficient, one-strike press of the late eighteenth century. In the nineteenth century machine-made paper and then steam presses made books much cheaper and quicker to produce. Until then, increasing output involved more presses and more labour. A compositor could line up 1,000–1,200 characters an hour: one small (octavo) page. The man operating the presses could pull 1,200–1,500 sheets in a period of about 10–12 hours (though in 1776 Paris bookbinders struck for their working day to be *reduced* to 14 hours). However, total output per man per day was only about four pages (the equivalent of one printed sheet) including type-setting, proof-reading and correcting (Bennett 1952: 229; Birn 1981: 163).

Technological stability over three centuries did not prevent a massive growth in output. In Spain, roughly 300 editions were produced between the introduction of movable type (*c.*1472–73) and 1489. Double that number appeared during the 1490s and 1,307 in the years 1501–20 (Norton 1966: 117, 125). Some 5,100 titles were published in England alone between 1486 and 1605. Perhaps 20 million books were printed in Europe before 1500, and 150–200,000 editions between 1500 and 1600. Except for proven best-sellers such as Luther's works, which might demand an edition size of 4,000 copies, the average print run was probably about 1,000. In other words, 150–200 million copies may have been turned out during the sixteenth century (Febvre and Martin 1976). Several million copies of ballads and other 'ephemera' may have been circulating in late sixteenth-century England, and there are 15,000 ballads surviving in written and printed form from the early modern period (Watt 1991: 11). The number of editions produced and volumes printed increased dramatically in subsequent centuries. Some 400 titles were published in England in the 1500s, 6,000 during the 1630s, 21,000 in the 1710s and 56,000 in the 1790s. These figures take no account of manuscripts or imported publications. In the century between 1711 and 1811, approximately one million New Testaments were sold in Germany alone, plus two million complete Bibles, ten times as many as had been bought there between 1534 and 1626. During the eighteenth century, three million titles were produced in Europe as a whole; allowing for multiple editions this meant that roughly 1,500 million copies were printed and this total excludes popular ephemera. Towards the end of the eighteenth century somewhere between two and five million books a year were being printed in Germany alone (Gawthrop and Strauss 1984: 50; Ward 1974: 62). Trends in output differed between countries. Production rose steadily in France between the mid-seventeenth century and the mid-eighteenth. Its growth was less rapid than in Germany after 1750, where the population are said to have been seized by a frenzy for reading (*Lesewut*) (Darnton 1986: 8).

Western Europe was the leader in printing. Muscovy, by comparison, was a late starter and the level of production was low. Less than 30 titles had been produced there by 1612 and just 500 by 1700. At the time of Peter the Great's coronation, yearly output was about six or seven titles. Five new presses were set up in St Petersburg between 1711 and 1727, by which date the average annual output had risen to 45. The growth in output continued to accelerate, reaching 500 a year by 1790 when the Empire could boast 30 publishing houses (Marker 1982: 270, 277; Simmons 1977: 47–9). On Europe's northern fringes too, printing was slowly established. Only three

Norwegian towns supported presses in the eighteenth century (Lindberg 1981: 228).

Both the number of printing shops and presses proliferated as more people (nearly all men) took up jobs in the printing industry. Forty-two titles were produced at Geneva between 1533 and 1540. An influx of 130 Protestant refugee printers into the city in the 1550s raised that number to 527 editions 1550–64. There were 17 *Briefmaler* (literally letter painters) living in Nürnberg in 1571 compared with 27 in 1599, and those describing themselves as *Formschneider* (cutters of wood blocks) increased from five to nine (Alexander and Strauss 1977: 17–18). Before the London Stationers' monopoly was granted, printing had been established in nine English towns, only to disappear by 1559 (though it reappeared at Cambridge and Oxford in 1583 and 1585 respectively). The lifting of the Stationers' monopoly on English printing in 1695 was followed by the establishment of presses in 13 provincial towns before 1725.

Sixteenth-century printing had been a small-scale affair. The biggest enterprises in Venice at that time (Giolito, Giunti and Manuzio) turned out between ten and 20 titles a year (originals and reprints). More typically printers produced between four and six editions a year. The names of 500 publishers feature on the title pages of Venetian printings during this century, though there were only three or four dozen who were producing at least a title a year for any length of time (Grendler 1977: 4–5). Rationalisation also took place in the industry during the seventeenth and eighteenth centuries, enterprises becoming fewer and larger. Paris in 1644 had 75 printing shops with 180 presses compared with 51 shops and 195 presses in 1701. During this half century, the number of journeymen per master increased, meaning that employees' chances to become masters in their own right were reduced (Darnton 1984: 9; Febvre and Martin 1976: 192, 196, 315).

Publishing was a widespread enterprise in some countries. Germany, Spain and Italy had a number of interconnected book production and distribution centres. Thirty-one permanently located presses are known to have existed in Spain before 1510 and an unknown number that moved from town to town. Forty-nine Italian towns had a press at some point between 1501 and 1520. As early as 1480, 50 German towns had a press. All the Imperial free cities had at least one press in the early seventeenth century, Prague was a multilingual publishing centre and provincial towns as modest as Dobrovice and Königgrätz could boast presses. Certain towns were famous for specific types of publishing – Burgos in Spain and Troyes in France for chapbooks –

or as distribution centres – Frankfurt-am-Main and Leipzig (Norton 1958: xiii; Schulte 1968: 69; Evans 1979: 102; Raven 1993).

Other nations had a more centralised publishing industry. Paris and London had the lion's share of publishing, just as these metropolises dominated the economies and governments of France and England. Fully 95 per cent of all English publications in 1800 bore a London imprint, even if distribution in England was national. Copenhagen similarly dominated Danish publishing at this date, Russia's printers were to be found in a handful of major towns such as Moscow, Kiev and St Petersburg, and Iceland's only press before 1772 alternated between the diocesan seats of Skálholt and Hólar. Most publishing in sixteenth-century Portugal was centred on the ancient university towns of Coimbra, Lisbon and Évora. By the end of the eighteenth century the dominance of Coimbra and Lisbon had grown at the expense of minor centres such as Braga and Oporto (Macedo 1975; Lisboa 1991). Distribution networks also varied from the pan-European to the local. An example of the former is Amsterdam, which maintained a huge multilingual output of Bibles in the seventeenth century and was the principal source of books for eastern Europe into the eighteenth century.

Whatever the organisation of production and distribution, the importance of printing itself was not lost on contemporaries. Martin Luther spoke of print as 'God's highest act of grace' and the Elizabethan Francis Bacon believed that along with gunpowder and the compass, printing had 'changed the appearance and state of the whole world'. Governments were not slow to realise the potential of printing. James IV saw Scotland's first press (at Edinburgh, 1507–8) as a way of promoting his government through the printing of legal texts, Acts of Parliament, chronicles and service books. The epilogue to Diego de Valera's 1482 *Coronica de España* deplored the scarcity of manuscript texts and praised printing; two decades later the Spanish crown was eagerly fostering printing (Norton 1966: 117). In seventeenth- and eighteenth-century Russia, the state was the main force behind the propagation of print. Among the other contemporaries who appreciated the significance of making books cheaper and more available was Tomasso Garzoni who, in the 1599 edition of his *Piazza Universale*, claimed that printing had made esoteric knowledge available to all and had brought to light volumes of classical and humanistic literature which might otherwise have been condemned to obscurity. More conservative in his outlook was the Dominican Filippo della Strada who cautioned that print could spread unacceptable political and religious ideas to the common people (Lucchi 1978: 593, 595).

Modern scholars too have discussed the significance of the invention and dissemination of printing across Europe. Most distinguished of these is Elizabeth Eisenstein, writer of a monumental two-volume work, *The Printing Press as an Agent of Change* (1979), the major conclusions of which are summarised in a substantial article and a brief volume (Eisenstein 1968; 1983). Eisenstein's argument centres on the fact that print can produce more books at cheaper prices than manuscript copying, that it fixes concepts and facilitates the cumulative development of ideas, and that the new modes of thought which it requires alter both attitudes and human relationships. First of all, printing dramatically reduced the number of hours needed to produce a volume and therefore made books more accessible both in terms of numbers and cost. 'More abundantly stocked bookshelves increased opportunities to consult and compare different texts and this also made more probable the formation of new intellectual combinations and permutations' (Eisenstein 1968: 7). People could experiment with new ideas and form new ways of thinking. Furthermore, existing ideas were now available in a *fixed* and certain form, making cumulative intellectual advances easier and systematic progress more rapid. At the same time, learning by doing became less important than learning by reading, and the mental world of those steeped in oral culture was changed by familiarity with regular numbering, systems of dates, indices and the other trappings of printed volumes. Reading could be private and introspective, separating individuals and reducing the importance of communal participation. Thus printing touched the very core of everyday experience. It also eased economic developments. Standard printed works helped with efficient planning and rational calculation of profit; printing created new advertising possibilities. In the sphere of politics, print made possible the standardisation of language sought by increasingly powerful states and fixed both rights and obligations of rulers and subjects in an unprecedented way. Fixed, definite and international rather than drifting, vague and local, printing ultimately restructured cognition and all human relationships. It could even change the way people conceived of time. 'Subscribers to periodicals were in the new position of receiving a continuous, indefinitely extended, constantly updated series and this may well have contributed to a different sense of temporal flow' (Eisenstein 1992: 10). For Walter J. Ong, who influenced Eisenstein, writing restructures thought (Ong 1986).

Writing and print are said to promote objectivity, encourage exploratory thinking, separate the known from the knower, interpretation from data, past from present and learning from wisdom. However, the importance of printing is not as straightforward as it might appear. Its impact depended both on existing forms of communication (written and spoken) and on established intellectual tastes. Print was undoubtedly important in changing the ways in which people thought and, indirectly, in shaping economic, social and political developments in the early modern period. Yet its impact was neither immediate, nor direct, nor certain. The changes it won were slow and contingent, dependent on other features of society as much as it altered them. Printing itself may have been in part a response to an existing desire to promote mass communication for economic and political purposes. Like education and literacy as a whole, printing's importance depended on the existing social, economic and political context.

Eisenstein's arguments depend on the presentation of books, their numbers, content and the ways in which they were understood. In all these areas, her ideas are subject to qualification. In appearance and content, considerable overlap existed between the forms of manuscript books and those of printed volumes. True of France, England and Germany, this was also the case in Russia where the creation of a specific 'print' form did not occur until the seventeenth century. The form and content of printed books continued to follow that of their manuscript predecessors even during 'the creative century'. Lavishly illuminated manuscripts were still being produced throughout the sixteenth century, patronage of them being considered as an act of piety. Hand copying remained important during the early seventeenth century. It was geographically widespread and well integrated into distribution networks. As late as the seventeenth century, merchants and gentry in Norway sought out hand-written newspapers and manuscript versions were still available in eighteenth-century France and Germany (Høyer 1982: 16). Most Russian book collections of the sixteenth and seventeenth centuries continued to be composed predominantly of manuscript books and most printed volumes were imported, since there are no known books printed in Muscovy until 1564; in the west, printed books were in the majority by 1550. Moscow, and later St Petersburg, were the only centres in which large numbers of printed editions were available to the reading public, and then only in the eighteenth century (Marker 1982). Even in the west, manuscript books on esoteric subjects that did not attract publishers continued to be important to scholars and students. For a limited market, it might make more commercial sense to continue copying since it was not difficult to run off a few hundred brief volumes by hand in a large copying shop of the kind found in late fifteenth-century Flanders (Labarre 1971: 395). Major Scottish legal texts circulated in manuscript far into the seventeenth century.

In the early years, the advent of print did little to change the titles available. More than three-quarters of books printed before 1500 were in Latin and 45 per cent were religious in content, indicating that demand came principally from scholars and clergy. Titles such as the Bible, Thomas a Kempis' *Imitation of Christ* and Augustine's *City of God* were the most popular. Voragine's *Golden Legend* went through 88 Latin editions, 18 French, 5 English, 2 German, 2 Czech, 13 Flemish and 6 Italian in the late fifteenth and early sixteenth centuries alone. Classics too sold well, including 126 editions of Aesop's *Fables* before 1500 and 61 of Juvenal's *Satires* (Febvre and Martin 1976: 245–55). Publishers were in business to make money, and it is hardly surprising that books gave their audience what they wanted to read, which often meant established titles conveying an existing body of knowledge. Twice as many volumes were published about the Turks during the sixteenth century as about the Americas, and there was virtually no literature on Africa. Illustrations were of considerable, if diminishing, significance. The 1498 edition of *Tristrant* had 80 woodcut depictions, but the editions of the 1550s had 55 or less and that of 1570 had none at all.

Illustrations were sometimes employed for their appropriateness rather than strict accuracy. The 1493 Koberger edition of Hartmann Schedel's *Liber Chronicarum* had 1,809 illustrations, but only 645 woodcuts were used. Any one walled city was, for example, used to depict Rome, Paris, Jerusalem or whatever (Steinberg 1974: 158). In fairness, this Nürnberg edition was not trying to be a work of modern scholarship. In form and content it was a medieval chronicle and its use of illustrations followed the same guidelines as the selection of examples and settings in the oral narrative tradition. The publisher employed whatever was at hand or whatever seemed appropriate by way of example or setting. However, if books like this represent the world map of early modern people, then they had a distorted perception. Publishers preferred to print old favourites such as the fantastic Sir John Mandeville's *Travels* or Boemius' *Geography*, the latter reprinted seven times in French alone between 1539 and 1558 without any mention of north America. Maps and atlases proliferated from the seventeenth century, conveying a less stylised sense of place (Black 1997). Yet, while maps tried to represent space, they were also a statement of political or social aspirations. They asserted dominance and integration. Used partly as a help in progressing predictably from A to B, early modern maps were also designed to show that the maker or his patron ruled from A to Z (Hills 1996).

Early printing did not necessarily accelerate the spread of new knowledge or ideas. Instead it tended to popularise old beliefs, strengthen existing prejudices and give authority to established rather than innovative ideas (Febvre and Martin 1976: 278–9, 282). Bernard of Gordon's medieval *Lilium medicinae* expounded the stereotypes of Jews, including the notion that they had melancholic blood. The humoral medical theories on which it was based had come from Galen in ancient Greece. They had been preserved as Arabic texts before being transmitted to Latin in the early middle ages. *Lilium medicinae* was still a set text at the university of Vienna in the 1520s and continued to be printed until much later. Reading tastes tell a similarly conservative tale. As late as the third quarter of the eighteenth century, the catalogues of 500 private libraries in France show only one copy of Rousseau's *Social Contract* and Enlightenment ideas reached the educated élites by indirect means: book five of the more popular *Emile* rehearsed Rousseau's arguments (Darnton 1971: 215). In contrast, Rousseau's *La Nouvelle Héloïse* (1761) was allegedly such a runaway success that Parisian booksellers were swamped by demand and had to rent out copies by the day or even the hour (Darnton 1985: 235). However, it is worth asking if what appear fundamental texts to modern scholars may have been comparatively unimportant in the spread of new ideas to contemporaries.

Without print, it is hard to imagine the intellectual ferment of the later seventeenth-century Scientific Revolution, the debates on social and intellectual topics during the Enlightenment or the surge of revolutionary sentiment across Europe after the floodgates of censorship were flung open in 1789. Between *c.*1450 and *c.*1650 the expansion of printing made many more volumes available in the international language of learning, Latin, and thus made the ideas contained in them more accessible to the European élites who had command of that language. From the middle of the seventeenth century, the rapid increase in vernacular output made ideas more widely available, but broke up the unity of intellectual life created by Latin. That unity was to some extent recreated by the adoption of French as a diplomatic and scholarly language in the eighteenth century, at least in Catholic Europe and among the nobility of the Orthodox east (Eisenstein 1992: 38–40).

Censorship

Uniting or dividing, the potentially revolutionary impact of the book was explicitly limited by controls on what could be published and sold. In all the countries of Europe, censorship existed in one form or another throughout the early modern period. Nowhere was the freedom of publishers to print whatever they thought the market would bear recognised either in principle or in practice. Two means of controlling access were used. Before publication manuscripts were inspected by the publishing guilds for content. After publication sales were policed to uncover forbidden or clandestine texts, and those who broke the rules were punished. The officers of the book police and the representatives of the publishing industry oversaw printers and booksellers, settled and itinerant. The system never worked perfectly and the growing flood of publications and the ferment of new ideas at the end of the eighteenth century made the strains and imperfections all the more apparent.

Strict or lax, censorship was imposed before and/or after publication and could be effected by three means: direct control by the church, secular intervention by royal or local officials (including judges and university professors), and printing monopolies. The reality of patronage and economic necessity means that self-censorship must also have been practised. In countries like Iceland where all the presses were run by the church until the eighteenth century, the printers and the supervisory personnel worked cheek-by-jowl and were in some cases the same people. Administratively, the third option was the easiest and was used with success in England, where the London Stationers' Company held the monopoly of printing from 1557 until 1695 and in Ireland where the royal Print-Master General had a monopoly from 1609. The state's political interests were served by giving a monopoly of printing to a guild whose economic concerns would ensure that they forced out illicit publishers and policed what was being printed. In Scandinavia and the Netherlands too, censorship was principally handled by guilds. Between the early seventeenth century and the late eighteenth in Sweden, the binders' guild dominated the import and distribution of unbound books that comprised most of the trade. Similar controls over printing and publishing were exercised by the binders' guilds in Lithuania and the Ukraine (where the first book was published in 1574) (Lindberg 1981: 229–30; Raven 1993: 10). Post-production censorship was also practised in England, where men like Roger L'Estrange worked with the bishop of London during Charles II's reign. A variation on censorship for fiscal reasons was restriction of whole types of output by economic means. In the later eighteenth century, the English government tried to stem the flood of radical propaganda by placing a stamp tax on pamphlets that would price them beyond the reach of ordinary people.

By the end of the seventeenth century the French crown had established its control over all agencies of censorship which had previously existed independently (as they continued to do so in some other European countries): church, universities and law courts. The Sorbonne in particular lost its censoring powers at this time, while the church was only able to supervise theological publications. The power of the *parlements* or law courts was tolerated while they followed the royal line, though, like the church, they were increasingly restricted in the early eighteenth century to condemning and punishing rather than autonomously censoring. The 'Office of the Book Trade' (known as the *Direction de la Librairie* after 1750) examined some 500 titles a year in 1700, 1,000 in 1771; between 10 per cent and 30 per cent were proscribed. The Office operated a pragmatic and sensitive censorship that sought to curb certain types of title and to legitimate others rather than to limit overall production. God, king and morality were sacrosanct, the rest was left to publishers, authors and readers.

Post-publication censorship lay with the book police, modelled on and centrally controlled from Paris. In Paris itself, about 1,000 offenders against the book laws went to the Bastille 1659–1789, making up 17 per cent of all those imprisoned in that period. In the 1750s and 1760s the figure was 35–40 per cent. In the provinces, representatives of royal authority (including *intendants* and *parlementaires*) worked with local *chambres syndicales* made up of booksellers' and printers' guilds. These were potentially a formidable arm of the police for more than 1,000 printers and booksellers made a living in France in 1781. The lieutenant-general of police in Paris might send out officials to check up on local censorship. Local inspectors enforced royal ordinances of 1686, 1723 and 1777 by searching commercial traffic. Police worked with guilds to try to prevent clandestine print shops being set up. They examined works in licensed premises. Finally, they tried to prevent the importation of books from abroad. There were designated entry points for book imports (notably Lyon), shippers were monitored and even recipients of packages had to have them officially opened and inspected. Whether these measures were very effective (and they seem to have been increasingly lax as the eighteenth century went on) is less important than the statement they made about the need for public unity in politics and religion.

Book production in France was relatively easy to supervise because it was heavily centralised. The 3,000 ordinances and decrees regulating the Parisian publishing industry in the eighteenth century alone testify to the importance which royal government attached to it. Paris had a monopoly of new titles which meant that provincial printers in Rouen, Lyon, Caen and other centres had to rely on reprints of existing ones, albeit sometimes with alterations. Monopolies also served a fiscal purpose, since the recipient usually had to pay the crown for the privilege. In France, Holland and Spain printing privileges were (as in Scotland) for limited periods at the behest of the state. The highly lucrative monopoly of printing playing cards was much sought after in several countries during the eighteenth century. Philip II granted a share in the proceeds of a monopoly of Nebrija's Latin grammar, *Arte Grammatica*, to Madrid's largest almshouse in 1602 as a way of funding poor relief (Bennassar 1982: 272; Thomas 1979).

Most towns exercised some independent control over what was printed by their burgesses, representing the local and mainly secular version of censorship. Authorities tended to concentrate less on the politically polemical or theologically unorthodox than on libellous works which might damage the closely-knit fabric of urban life (Chrisman 1982: 28–9). Nevertheless, after 1708 the London government increasingly relied on Scottish burgh authorities to police religious controversies in print. Those in politically sensitive areas – the Imperial free cities of Germany such as Cologne and Nürnberg – had established codes of practice to govern printing, though the fragmented nature of the early modern German states made censorship, and indeed primitive copyright regulations, difficult to enforce. In the Spanish towns of Valladolid and Ciudad Real, control of the press after 1502 was vested in the presidents of the royal tribunals or *Audiencias*, while in the other principal towns such as Burgos this job was performed by the bishop (Norton 1966: 119).

Specific developments could increase or diminish the desire to censor and the effectiveness of controls. Countries like France were relatively free of censorship until the vicious 'truth war' between Huguenots and Catholics in the 1560s, even if scriptural writings had to be passed by the university of Paris's theology faculty as early as 1521. Francis I protected Rabelais against the Parlement de Paris and the Sorbonne, though attacks on the court in the affair of the Placards during the 1530s provoked a censorious backlash. Nor did Spanish authorities become strict until the threat of Protestantism appeared serious during the 1550s, and Venetian censorship was not at its peak until the 1560s. A flood of pent-up prognosticatory pamphlets was let loose when censorship was removed in England in 1640. Political fragmentation – the Holy Roman Empire had 330 political units within it – weakened the effectiveness of censorship in the German lands, except for (Catholic) Bavaria and towns where the local university monitored publication. However, tightening of controls was also possible. Frankfurt book fair's fortunes were eclipsed in the seventeenth century partly because of the activities of a censor, the Apostolic Book Commissioner, sent out by the Emperor and a resulting commission which proscribed Protestant publications (Smith 1979: 79, 93; Raven 1993). The apparently timeless tolerance of controversial works by the Dutch actually originated in the seventeenth century and was a result of weak political centralisation and the consequent difficulties of enforcing pre-publication censorship. Licenses to print had not been required since the late sixteenth century for all but the most controversial editions. However, the English and Scots governments put pressure on the Dutch to ban anti-royalist and religious nonconformist books in the 1630s, with some success. The need for licenses was completely removed by the province of Holland and the States General in 1650–51, after which the States felt they no longer had the power to censor (Groenveld 1987). Prussian authorities prevented the import of uncensored foreign papers, while allowing native publishers considerable freedom. This changed completely during the Seven Years War when Frederick the Great would brook no criticism of his policy (Smith 1979: 65; Burke 1978: 262–70).

Successes were achieved where there was a political will, even with the imperfect mechanisms available to early modern governments. A formidable battery of punishments could be called upon. If denounced for printing defamatory or inflammatory material, a publisher might theoretically face the death penalty in Renaissance Italy. The publishing of Jewish books stopped completely in Venice after the purge of 1553. Scotland's government banned all newspapers in the 1660s, even royalist ones, and they did not reappear until the 1690s. During the 1700s the chancellor of France, Pontchartrain, employed inspectors to seize anti-Jesuit, pro-Jansenist, anti-war and pro-Protestant literature. They mounted 142 successful raids between 1700 and 1706. Provincial publishing in France was subject to even closer scrutiny after 1760 through the appointment of 120 censors (Birn 1981: 159–61). A state-controlled board was set up in Portugal in 1768 to administer censorship, though its concerns remained mainly religious (Marques 1972: 415; Márquez 1980).

Sixteenth-century Venice had its own officials who enforced the censorship of the church, and a civil court, *Esecutori contro la Bestemmia*, which could order the burning of proscribed titles (Grendler 1975). Venice, ostentatiously different in many respects, nevertheless typified the towns of Spain and Italy which had local, secular censorship combined with local and national church Inquisitions. A list of banned volumes (*Index*) was printed periodically, though Venice only accepted the Papal Index in full in 1569. Approved books, on the other hand, were identifiable by an official *Imprimatur*. The various Inquisitions produced their own Indices, varying in length and the sorts of titles proscribed. The Spanish Indices (the most important issued in 1551, 1554, 1559, 1583, 1584, 1612, 1632 and 1640) were, for example, more liberal than those of Rome (Kamen 1965: 98). The Inquisitions of Spain and Portugal were vigorous enforcers of censorship. However the Papal Inquisition, with its famous *Index*, was not allowed to operate in the French or Austrian lands.

The censorship of the Inquisitions has achieved notoriety, thanks to Protestant polemic and the hindsight of more 'enlightened' ages. Cardinal Ximénes of Spain is said to have burned more than a million Moorish books during the reconquest of Granada at the end of the fifteenth century. Yet, the effectiveness of censorship was limited by three principal facts. The first was that the remit of Inquisitions left many areas of scholarship untouched. Of the seat of the Papal Inquisition in 1739, a French traveller opined: 'Freedom of thought on religious matters and sometimes even freedom of speech is at least as great in Rome . . . as in any town I know'. Second, as seen above, the fluctuations in the zeal with which illicit books were sought out and the limited personnel and effectiveness of any bureaucracy in early modern Europe made total or consistent control impossible. Third, the ready international market in books and pamphlets meant that a title banned in one country could be obtained fairly easily from another. It was said that Dutch people consulted the *Index* when looking for an exciting book to read. This is not as odd as it sounds, for censors sometimes put 'approbations' on books, explaining why they had enjoyed them (Darnton 1989: 96). In England, banned pornography was obtainable from France, while Frenchmen who wanted news or comment critical of their regime had only to look to the Netherlands. Despite inquisitorial censorship, the Moriscos of Aragon kept and read censored books in the sixteenth century. Scribes copied out Korans and clandestine schools passed on the traditions of Islamic culture (Fournel-Guerin 1979). The limits of existing censorship were increasingly apparent in the second half of the eighteenth century. The tribunal of Logroño informed the Spanish *Suprema* during the 1790s that 'the multitude of seditious papers coming from France makes it impossible to initiate prosecutions against all the people who introduce, keep, and distribute them'. Two decades earlier, a priest proclaimed of banned Enlightenment literature that it was 'sought after at any price . . . read with ardour and delight, and devoured . . . with the hunger of a disordered appetite excited by novelty and prohibition itself' (Kamen 1965: 268–9).

As many as 200 million books (large and small) were published in Europe during the sixteenth century alone. Demand for print must have existed to fuel such a vast production and for the determined it was always possible to get the books. The other side of 'censorship' was to foster certain kinds of output in order positively to shape opinion rather than simply suppressing the unacceptable. Indeed, many of the developments in printed literature, notably in newspapers and broadsheets, came about through the political will of governments or interest groups. Propaganda was probably more important in shaping public opinion than proscription of certain literature. Periods of political, military and religious crisis provoked an outpouring of print. Martin Luther's famous pamphlet, *To the Christian Nobility of the German Nation*, sold out its first edition in exactly seven days and within two years had been through 13 editions. The catalogue of pamphlets and broadsheets in the royal library at 's-Gravenhage (The Hague) in the Netherlands shows that, from a few dozen a year, the number of such works rose into the hundreds at times of fear and suspicion such as 1578–79, 1607–9, 1618–19 and 1647–48. Indeed, the Thirty Years War was one of the most productive periods of propaganda publication. Propaganda came of age between 1618 and 1648. Fifty-four pamphlets and broadsheets describing just one battle – the Swedish victory at Nördlingen – are known to survive and European archives are full of evidence of the flood of claim and counter-claim which was part of this vicious conflict. More than 4,000 political lampoons, *Mazarinades* (so-called after the royal minister), circulated in Paris between 1649 and 1652, more than 15,000 religious, social and political commentaries in England between 1640 and 1661 (Febvre and Martin 1976: 291; van Deursen 1978: 90–93; Langer 1978: 238; Kamen 1984: 216). Developments in the content and format of periodical literature were partly attributable to political initiative.

The early modern period saw important developments in censorship. There was a shift from licensing all books to targeting certain types of undesirable output. Central censorship became focused principally on political rather than religious subversion during the eighteenth century. Pre-publication licensing gave way to post-publication banning of titles. Finally, the draconian penalties of the sixteenth century were gradually replaced by more moderate sanctions against transgressors, including fines, confiscations and short terms of imprisonment.

Book Distribution

The volume of publication grew enormously throughout the early modern period. Warehouses bulged with bales of heterogeneous reading material from Bibles to bawdy pamphlets. The next task is to trace how they made their journey from print shops, lofts and store rooms into the hands of the readers. Some sort of distribution network, however informal, was needed so that men and women could enjoy the products of the revolution in printing. Fortunate individuals had their own ready-made outlets. As early as the 1470s, a Dominican called Petrus Nigri had his evangelical book addressed to the Jews published by Conrad Fyner at Esslingen; some sales he handled himself, others were made through his home monastery in Würzburg. During the same decade a group of Perugian booksellers banded together to publish books and have them sold through their stalls in Rome, Naples, Siena, Pisa, Bologna, Ferrara and Padua (Sprandel-Krafft 1983; Febvre and Martin 1976: 225). More commonly, wholesale and retail outlets were organised separately. Their variety almost defies classification. The discrete categories of type-founder, printer, editor, publisher and bookseller that came to exist by 1800 were blurred and overlapping in the early decades of printing. Sometimes the functions were performed separately, at others they were conducted by one and the same person or on the same premises. One noted authority (Paul Grendler) uses the term 'bookmen' to encompass the many facets of the trade, though it should be noted that there were female printers (Parker 1996). Broadly speaking, shops, chapmen and mail-order (perhaps associated with subscription) were the principal outlets to the reader, and fairs and personal links between publisher and retailer were the key to the wholesale trade (Steinberg 1974: 215–32). The German book trade offers an example of developments during the early modern period. The century between 1450 and 1550 was characterised by cash sales, an identity between printer and publisher, and distribution by travelling peddlers outside the main towns. Protestant authors, for example, distributed their own and friends' books in the 1520s and 1530s. The distinctive features of the years 1550–1750 were that sales on an exchange basis became common and book fairs became the accepted mode of transaction for traders. Literary patrons of booksellers were unimportant after the mid-seventeenth century. After 1750, publishing and selling came increasingly to be separated; sale or return developed and bookshops proliferated (Ward 1974: 92).

The market for books was restricted for much of the early modern period, dependent on the purchasing power of the reader and the availability of transportation. Most booksellers did not carry large stocks and most pur-chases were sight-unseen and by mail-order. In small and geographically favoured countries such as England or the Netherlands, delivery was not a problem. Isaac Thompson claimed in 1766 that his *Newcastle Journal* reached readers in 188 towns and villages in the north of England (Wiles 1976: 90). Books were nevertheless heavy, bulky, fragile and expensive to transport. In 1778 the director of postal services at Rotterdam complained to Etienne

Luzac, editor of the popular *Nouvelles Extraordinaire de Divers Endroits* (generally known as the *Gazette de Leyde*), that his packages destined for France were far too heavy. He suggested either reducing the weight of the bundles or paying for a second horse to carry them – or having the paper printed in France (Gibbs 1971: 334; Popkin 1989). As a result of transport costs and, sometimes, a desire to avoid customs officials, orders for books dispatched by publishers tended to be small. In the later seventeenth century, Guillaume de Luynes sent 24 copies of Primi's *Histoire de la Guerre de Hollande* to booksellers at Lyon, five to one at Nantes, eight to one at Reims, six to Bordeaux and four to Douai.

Lyon was a significant town for the book trade and was the location of the first major book fair in Europe during the sixteenth century. Fairs in strategic locations such as Lyon or later Frankfurt-am-Main attracted many buyers and sellers anxious to exploit their range of choice, efficient transport facilities and financial services. Lyon was the market for Italian, German, Swiss and Flemish publishers; major Italian publishers like Giuntas, Gabiani and Portonari all had branches there. Via the Loire valley and Toulouse, books were transported to different areas of Spain, Medina del Campo, Burgos and Valencia being the principal distribution points (Febvre and Martin 1976: 220–30). As well as fairs, there was a healthy wholesale trade between booksellers. For example, a Dublin or Edinburgh seller might order a bulk consignment by sea from London and distribute it locally.

Bookshops were uncommon in the sixteenth and seventeenth centuries, confined to capitals and to the larger provincial cities. In the provincial towns of western Europe, merchants sold books as part of a wide range of goods prior to the eighteenth century. In Norway, Sweden, Iceland and Finland bookshops were almost unknown until the nineteenth century. In Russia as late as 1750 the two bookshops belonging to the Academy of Sciences, one in St Petersburg and one in Moscow, accounted for the vast majority of domestic sales (Luppov 1981; Marker 1982: 280–81). Those who wanted to buy printed material had either to order it specially or to rely on mobile retailers. The same holds true for many other consumer goods across rural Europe. In Sweden the peddlers or chapmen were called *gårdfarihandlarar*, literally tradesmen who travel to farmsteads, or by local names. In Västergötland the slang was *knallar* (Dahl 1959). These men (and sometimes women) traded mostly in craft products such as cooking utensils and clothes not available locally. However, many also carried a few books and pamphlets as part of their wares. In sixteenth-century Italy, humble itinerants who specialised in the lives of saints were called *leggendaio*, in Russia *ofeni*, in

Germany *Jahrmarktströdler*, while in France the word *colporteur* describes the peripatetic trader. Illegal in some countries such as Sweden, chapmen were officially licensed in France, though they were stigmatised in a decree of 1660 as 'people who sell almanacs, ABCs, gazettes, little tales of *Mélusine* and the *Quatre Fils Aymon* to abate boredom, vulgar songs, dirty and nasty idle farces, and disgusting drinking songs' (Martin 1978: 86). Only 46 recognised *colporteurs* existed in 1611, though there must have been hundreds more who operated outside the licensing system. The number was restricted to 120 in 1725. By 1740 four times that number had licences and in 1848 the figure had jumped to approximately 3,500 (Capp 1979: 271; Bollème 1965: 64–5).

Between rural chapmen and settled sellers in towns were transient hawkers who sold the cheapest papers, sheets and pamphlets. In Venice, humble traders bought and sold second-hand books from open-air benches on the Rialto bridge or peddled religious pamphlets at the doors of churches. The hawkers advertised their wares by reading pamphlets and newspapers aloud from barrels, benches and street corners. A German broadsheet of 1630 shows one of them, clutching fistfuls of sheets in both hands; more are crammed into a large sack on his back; his pockets and waist pouch bulge with pamphlets and there are even papers stuffed into his hatband and garters (Smith 1979: 18; Langer 1978: 238). A contemporary estimated that there were some 300 street hawkers crying their wares in London in 1641, using oral means to promote literacy's products (Grendler 1977: 6; Capp 1985: 200). Even blindness did not prevent some Spanish street sellers from presenting a résumé of their merchandise to potential customers. One bi-weekly published between 1786 and 1791 was called the *Correo de Madrid o de los Ciegos* after its blind distributors. A clear, hearty voice was possibly more important than eyes to street-corner sellers (Schulte 1968: 108).

Crying the merits of a broadsheet or pamphlet was one way that a potential audience could be won over. In some cases the market for print was fairly certain: almanacs, Bibles and other religious works, topical news-sheets and certain recreational literature sold easily. They were the bread and butter of ordinary printers. Some publishers only produced works to order, assured by their contract that they would not be left storing quintals of unsold print. An alternative, which was pioneered in the sixteenth century and reached its heyday during the eighteenth, was publication by subscription. The merit of this arrangement was that printers did not have to sink large amounts of capital into production, stocking and distribution. The audience was 'captive, tame, pre-committed' (Rogers 1972: 1539). A sixth of all new German books published between 1770 and 1810 were subscription volumes (Darnton

1986: 11). For most specialist works, this was the preferred means of funding because of the necessarily small and dispersed audience. A Spanish translation of the Dutch political periodical *Mercure Historique et Politique* appeared in 1738 with 1,000 subscribers on the Iberian peninsula and a further 60 copies a month shipped to the Spanish colonies in the New World. German translations of English literature afford another example. Johann Joachim Bode's translation of *Tristram Shandy*, published at Hamburg in 1774, was subscribed to by roughly 600 north German professional men and 43 women (Gibbs 1971: 348; Fabian 1976: 166–7). Enterprising eighteenth-century publishers were able to extend the concept to include what were known in England as 'number books'. Smollett's *History of England (1757)*, for example, was sold a few pages at a time bound in cheap blue paper. Serial publications made these long and expensive books accessible to a wide market. Some were distributed weekly by the same people who delivered newspapers (Wiles 1976: 98–9).

Particularly fascinating are the means used to disseminate illegal literature. All countries of Europe operated some kind of censorship, but restrictions on the sort of material which could be printed, imported and sold could not wholly prevent clandestine publication and distribution. Indeed, the more extensive the censorship, the more ingenious and daring became the illicit book trade. Take the case of Italy at the height of the Counter-Reformation. Protestant bookmen such as the Venetian Pietro Longo had contacts with printers in key towns like Basel in Switzerland. In the 1570s and 1580s he carried contraband titles with him along with legitimate merchandise into Venice where its passage through customs inspections was 'eased' by sellers like Zilettia and Valgrisi, who also helped to distribute the illegal books to Protestants in Venice and its region. The clandestine trade could prove lucrative, especially for occult works, but it could also bring heavy fines and imprisonment or worse. Longo was drowned by order of the Inquisition for his heresies and smuggling in 1588 (Grendler 1977: 188, 193).

Smuggling flourished all over Europe in the century of the Enlightenment. Catholic countries which could be reached with ease from Protestant havens such as the Netherlands or Switzerland were particularly vulnerable to infiltration by illegal titles. Some publishers existed almost wholly to fill the demand for banned books in French, known generically in the trade as *livres philosophiques*. The archives of the *Société Typographique de Neuchâtel* for the later eighteenth century provide insights into the clandestine book trade between Switzerland and France. Take the example of Faivre de Pontarlier, described in the association's records as a hard worker who lived on his wits.

Faivre shipped crates of books by horse-drawn wagon from his storehouse in Neuchâtel to a secret location in the village of Les Verrières on the Swiss side of the border. He then employed teams of porters and mule drivers for the back-breaking task of lugging bales of books across mountain trails into France where he had a hidden warehouse near Pontarlier. This was a dangerous job, since the portage had usually to be done at night over perilous mountain paths. Worse, the porters might risk a stretch in the galleys if they were caught with banned books. They were paid in cash and drink, the latter perhaps welcome under the circumstances. French customs officials at the Frambourg post were either bribed or duped with fraudulent *acquits à caution* (discharge notes). Once in France, the books were crated once again and sent in wagons to Besançon or to other distribution points where dealers bought them for sale in Troyes, Lyon or Paris. This was an expensive and slow process fraught with difficulties. Books might be seized, abandoned by the porters or damaged, for most publishers shipped books as unfolded, printed sheets which did not receive a protective binding until they were sold to a reader. Smugglers like Faivre had to undertake to reimburse their clients in full for any books lost in transit. For those prepared to pay the understandably high prices, this network gave opportunities to enjoy illicit political, religious or pornographic works (Darnton 1971; 1976).

Newspapers

Censorship was supplemented by positive attempts to shape opinion by propaganda. Indeed, new forms were tried during the early modern period in order to 'inform' the political nation about events, objectives and (supposed) achievements. The best example is the development of the newspaper from its origins as a commercial information sheet to the status of a provider of more or less hard news of the kind which modern readers associate with the medium. The development of newspapers is another example of the interplay between institutions and social groups in the development of literacy and its products. Newspapers were born of merchants' need to be informed about political and economic conditions in the areas with which they traded. Intelligence was received from business representatives and semi-professional *rapportisti* or *avvisatori*, and collated by town authorities or by private companies like the Fuggers. The resulting news-sheets were available in both manuscript and print from the end of the fifteenth century. Circulating as *Avvisi* in Venice or *Zeitungen* in Augsburg from the 1550s, they provided a model for later newspapers (von Klarwill 1970).

Newspapers developed through four stages. First came sheets describing a single event: 'relations' such as the early sixteenth-century Spanish *Relación de lo que pasó al Emperador en Bornes [Worms] con Luthero en 1521*. *Relaciónes* were usually one-off single sheets folded once or twice. One or two a year survive on average for the reign of Charles V, nearly four for the early years of Philip II, more than five for his later years, 12 for the first half of the reign of Philip III and 26 for the second part. For the years 1599–1614, 159 different news-sheets survive and many more must have been published and all the copies lost. Not all seem to be 'hard' news. Some in verse told of sightings of monsters while one of 1617 from Granada was a report of a nun who, after 12 years in a convent at Úbeda, suddenly became a man after vigorous exertions (Ettinghausen 1984: 1–3, 12). Stories like these, apparently fantastic or light-hearted and recreational, often had powerful political overtones. Whether they were 'true' was less important than whether they were believable. 'Relations' telling of prodigies such as monstrous births or comets were commonly the work of a political faction that sought to use such events to condemn their opponents. Similarly, hagiography did not simply promote a saint, but was designed to further the interests of a place, party, or persuasion associated with him.

The second phase was characterised by the publication of a series of relations as a *coranto*, a form in which the Dutch specialised. During the 1620s, Jacob Jacobsz. produced a French *Courant d'Italie et d'Almaign*, pirated in Spain by Andres Mendoza as *Correos de Francia, Flandes y Alemania* – though it is not strictly fair to call editions 'pirated' if published in another country with different copyright laws. These sheets were regular (if infrequent) and kept to fixed titles. Next came the 'diurnal' which purveyed regular news about a particular event or body for a brief period: Robert Coles and Samuel Pecke's 1640s *Perfect Diurnall of the Passages in Parliament*, for example. Fourth came 'mercuries' such as the *Mercurius Gallo-Belgicus* published in Latin at the end of the sixteenth century (Smith 1979: 9–11; Schulte 1968).

These phases were not discrete and sequential since forms overlapped over time. Every European country has at least some claim to have published the first 'modern' newspaper, including, for example, King Mathias of Hungary's *Dracola Waida* (Devil Prince) in 1485 and the 1609 Augsburg relation. In fact, there was no Augsburg relation of that year, but there were two weekly papers with that title, one published in Strasbourg and the other in Wolfenbüttel (Ries 1987). Debate on the origins of modern newspapers is clouded by problems of definition: is permanence of title, nature of content or regularity and frequency of appearance the most significant criterion?

Newspapers were only formally defined from the eighteenth century, usually in the context of censorship or taxation. A British newspaper was defined in the 'Six Acts' of 1819 as 'any paper which contained public news, intelligence, or occurrences, any comments thereon or on matters of Church and State; and which was printed for sale and published periodically within 26 days; and which was no larger than two sheets and sold for less than 6d inclusive of duty'.

There is more agreement over the importance of the mid-seventeenth century in the development of regular newspapers. Newspapers proliferated in the decentralised German states during the seventeenth century and these territories were much more productive than France or England, which did not see similar expansion until the eighteenth century. Germany had over 200 newspapers before 1700, the Netherlands as many as 30. The first regular daily was produced at Leipzig in 1660 (*Einkommende Zeitung*) (Ries 1982). The *Gazette de France* was weekly from 1631. Florence had a weekly newspaper from 1636, Rome from 1640 and Madrid from 1661. In both numbers and frequency, the second half of the eighteenth century marks the next major phase of development. Countries already well-endowed with newspapers saw a further proliferation while in the northern and eastern states sheets and pamphlets began to be available on a more frequent and regular basis. Provincial England had 35 papers in 1760 and 50 by 1782, with total circulation doubling to nearly 400,000 copies a year. In 1779 Paris had 35 periodicals of any kind compared with 160 newspapers and journals published in London. A decade later London had increased its number to 205, Paris nearly five-fold to 169. Spain's first daily, *Diario Noticioso*, was started by the prolific Francisco Nipho y Cagigal in 1758 and Paris got its first daily paper in 1777. Scandinavia and the eastern countries lagged behind. Denmark got its first 'permanent' newspaper, *Berlingske Tidende*, in 1749 and the first regular, if short-lived, Finnish language paper was not started until 1776. The first Latvian newspaper (*Latweeschv Awihse*) came as late as 1822 (Thomsen 1982: 3; Kamen 1984: 218; Høyer 1982: 16; Schulte 1968: 91; Vīksniņš 1973: 157).

The significance of the first half of the early seventeenth century for the development of regular newspapers lay in improved communications, growing demand for political and economic news and a heightened awareness among rulers of the part which the proper manipulation of information could play in ensuring success abroad and peace at home. Part of the development of newspapers came spontaneously, part was orchestrated. Popular demand for commercial and then political news increased the numbers,

regularity and variety of news-sheets and pamphlets. In England, the Netherlands and the Austrian Habsburg territories, development was largely organic.
In France, Denmark and Russia it was closely influenced by the aims of absolute governments determined to convince outsiders of the strength of their
regime and those within its boundaries of the legitimacy and efficacy of their
policies. If sixteenth-century propaganda had been rhetorical and overstated,
that of the seventeenth and eighteenth centuries was increasingly sophisticated and imaginative, using reasoned persuasion to win over a better-educated
and more aware public. Serially published news periodicals mark a signal
adjustment to new patterns of taste and political culture. France's *Gazette*, the
principal newspaper of the seventeenth century, was wholly given over to
official propaganda. Peter the Great was determined that his policy of west-
ernising the manners, dress and attitudes of his Russian subjects and the military
development of his empire should be aided by the creation of a state-
controlled press. The Russian *Posolskii Prikaz* (department of embassies) took
seven Dutch newspapers alone in the early eighteenth century and employed
a battery of translators to scan Europe's news-sheets (Gibbs 1971: 338).

As much as their modern counterparts, early modern newspapers demonstrated one-sided coverage. Spanish *relaciones* of the reigns of Philip II, III and
IV illustrate the selective presentation of news. They tended to proliferate
in years of prominent national successes such as the defeat of the Turks at
Lepanto in 1571 or at times of celebration such as royal visits. Unpleasant
news tended to be filtered out (except for acts of God), publishers working
on the assumption that bad news is no news. They 'put out a consistently
reassuring interpretation of reality that is strikingly at variance with the
messages of contemporary satirists, moralists and reformers'. Their content
may have been inspired by the government, but it is also possible that people
preferred not to recognise that Castile was in serious economic difficulties
and that the Spanish empire was encountering growing military problems in
the early seventeenth century. Arguably, people propagandised themselves.
Presenting a picture of stability rather than change, *relaciones* were 'less reports,
selecting and distorting a set of events in the real world, than accounts put
together after the manner of literature according to a sense of what is necessary and appropriate' (Ettinghausen 1984: 14–16). They legitimised existing
power structures, boosted morale, fostered loyalty to the crown, united diverse
parts of Spain by emphasising joint nationality, and related victories and
miracles which showed that God and Spain were synonymous.

Newspapers could also serve separatist causes. The 1778 *Dublin Evening
Post* represented nationalist sentiment against English domination, and the

first Hungarian language newspaper (*Magyar Hirmondó*) of 1780 was followed by a wave of patriotic, anti-Habsburg imitators (Smith 1979: 92). Indeed, the press was used as an agent of change as well as a means of preserving existing social and political structures. The radical English Levellers used cheap print to propagate their ideas in the 1640s and the later eighteenth century saw an expanding use of printed propaganda for radical causes in England and Europe. Scandinavia had newspapers independent of government from the middle of the eighteenth century. However powerful the censorship mechanisms of eighteenth-century France, printed propaganda against the regime still circulated. In 1743 the chevalier de Mouhy told his employer, the lieutenant-general of police, that 'the true cause of the discontent' against Louis XV's government and of the 'agitation of the people' lay in the widespread reading of hostile broadsheets and gazettes (sometimes called *lardons* – literally little pieces of bacon) smuggled in by France's enemies (Kaiser 1983: 623). No country was 'watertight' and this example illustrates the potential of printing and literacy. Once printed material was available and a reading public existed, it was impossible to exert total control over the uses to which literacy could be put. The problem posed by topical printing for the authorities was summed up by Charles II of England's official censor Sir Roger l'Estrange when he opined that reading newspapers 'makes the multitude too familiar with the actions and counsels of their superiors, too pragmatical and censorious, and gives them not only a wish but a kind of colourable right and licence to the meddling with the government' (Burke 1978: 270).

Broadsheets and Chapbooks

The growth of newspaper output shows how commercial needs in the early stages of development were built upon by political will in the seventeenth century and then by extensive demand in the eighteenth century. Newspapers became cheaper and more common in the seventeenth and eighteenth centuries, but can hardly be termed a mass medium. It is also unlikely that the majority of substantial volumes could have commanded a truly mass market. Arguably, the only real mass medium for print in the sixteenth century was the illustrated broadsheet and in the seventeenth and eighteenth centuries the pamphlet or chapbook. With the exception of religious texts, most books were either too expensive or too abstruse for the ordinary man or woman. A literate form that used visual symbols rather than print or which kept the number of words to a palatable minimum was likely to reach much larger audiences than substantive literature. Popular literature was often illustrated in the early years of printing. A third of all volumes printed in Europe before 1500 were so embellished (Steinberg 1974: 158). What scholars understood from writing and print was communicated to ordinary people by pictures, or a mix of print and image. It is, for example, unlikely that more than 10 per cent of the population of Luther's Germany could read his work for themselves and most of these were middle-class urban males. Vernacular religious literature in late fifteenth-century Italy was semi-theatrical in presentation, showing the contemporary emphasis on visually oriented spirituality (Schutte 1980: 16–17). At a time when literacy was restricted to a small minority of men, people could nevertheless gain knowledge of the ideas of the Reformation by looking and listening rather than reading.

What they viewed were illustrated woodcuts. A picture was cut into the end grain of a block of wood and printed on to single sheets of paper using a press. Colouring, if done at all, was completed by hand after printing. When combined with text, images guided comprehension of that text in a way different from separate engravings, which were more open to varying interpretations. Integrated images invited the marginally literate into the world of text and encouraged interactions between words and pictures. Luther's preface to the Passional in his *Betbüchlein* of 1522 explained why word and image were linked 'above all for the sake of children and simple folk, who are more easily moved by pictures and parables to retain in their minds the divine history, than if they were simply read [to them] or taught [in sermons]' (Robinson-Hammerstein 1989: 30; Scribner 1981/1994).

Broadsheets continued to be an important means of communicating religious ideas in eastern Europe until the nineteenth century. Russian broadsheets and pamphlets were called *lubki*, after the limewood blocks used to make them. Some 3,000–4,000 copies could be printed before deterioration of the block. Broadside sheet almanacs were the precursors of modern wall calendars, posters the harbingers of the political graffiti of the present day. They could be posted on internal or external walls and doors, or even inside the lids of trunks where most people kept their clothes and other personal effects. Some woodcuts were crude and simple, but expert practitioners could produce definition close to that which could be obtained by engraving metal. Some were pictures alone; others combined word and image. In all cases the symbolism was rich and powerful. Human, animal, divine, earthly, pious, profane, monster, medical, morbid and mechanical images all were used to impart religious and political propaganda as well as social comment and pure entertainment.

The largest category of early seventeenth-century *lubki* comprised religion. Next came recreational subjects. Callot's depictions of Punch and Judy were introduced to Muscovy in the second quarter of the eighteenth century and Russianised as the beak-nosed *Farnos*. Drink, taverns and drunks were popular themes in broadsheets of the period. One, set out like a hagiographical icon, depicts nine scenes of what can befall the inebriate. *Lubki* of the early seventeenth century were primarily directed at upper-class audiences. By the eighteenth century they found their way on to the walls of humbler townspeople. They only became common among the peasantry in the nineteenth century, by which time they had long been out of fashion with the élites (Ovsyannikov 1968; Brooks 1985: 63). The propaganda potential of broadsheets was not lost on rulers or ruled. Peter the Great may have issued a picture of a barber cutting off the beard of an Old Believer as part of his westernisation campaign following his 1705 decree banning beards, though it may also have been a satire put out by his opponents. Old Believer propaganda, on the other hand, showed Peter as a cat, a crocodile, a witch-baby and even Satan. In eighteenth-century Russia western themes were adapted for propaganda by the Orthodox church or for entertainment purposes by enterprising publishers.

In the west as in the east, these broadsheets were not simply illustrations to accompany a text, but contained the central message(s) in their images. 'Like homemade gin', writes Scribner (1981: 5), the woodcut 'was cheap, crude and effective'. The range of subjects covered was substantial and changed relatively little over time. A major study of German single-leaf woodcuts has shown that, between 1550 and 1700, religious matters accounted for a third of all surviving broadsides, a fifth were 'folklore and superstition', a seventh involved social comment while the remainder dealt with politics or offered calendars, advertisements, maps and portraits (which were the only growth area between 1550–99 and 1600–1700) (Hanebutt-Benz 1983; Langer 1978: 238–9, 248; Alexander and Strauss 1977). The heyday of the broadsheet was in the sixteenth and the first half of the seventeenth century in western Europe.

It seems plausible to believe that, in societies with restricted literacy, visual and aural means of transmitting ideas would predominate. However, the importance of one or other medium cannot be taken for granted. For example, the accessibility of visual images should not be exaggerated, either in terms of what was available or how well it was understood. The Lutheran Reformation in Germany built on a flourishing late-medieval tradition of illustrated books and broadsheets. However, this tradition was much less developed elsewhere in Europe where illustrations tended to appear not in the cheaper publications, but in those intended for a more affluent, leisured market (Duggan 1989). Furthermore, the trend over the sixteenth century was for the number of images in books (and of books with images) to decline. The images are sometimes complex, even ambiguous, and while their meaning was far from closed to 'simple folk', the messages they conveyed may not have been those that modern scholars read into them. They contained many complex signs which the audience had to be educated in 'reading', just as they had to understand letters, syllables, words and phrases in print or writing. Visual literacy was as much a spectrum as that based on words. Because they had to be decoded, such images may have acted less as a medium of initial instruction (for example, in the ideas of the Reformation) than as a mnemonic for those who had learned first by hearing from a priest or through the catechism. One enterprising printer from Basel, Pamphilus Gengenbach, produced booklets to accompany carnivals pillorying the clergy of mid-sixteenth-century Germany which explained the more obscure allegorical references in ritual and image (Bercé 1976: 65–6).

Two centuries later, another potentially mass medium was more restricted than its apparently popular appeal might suggest. The English political prints of famous cartoonists like William Hogarth and later James Gillray were expensive, produced in small numbers, and required prior knowledge to decode their often complex message (Nicholson 1996). Political broadside ballads of the mid-eighteenth century in England were printed in expensive forms which made them the preserve of the moneyed urban classes. Simple and accessible as they appear, seventeenth-century French *placards* and *libelles* or eighteenth-century English cartoons, designed as means of political representation and persuasion, had many layers of meaning and may also have had a restricted circulation. They could certainly be interpreted in different ways depending on their political, intellectual, and social context. What seem basic and rather obvious productions to educated readers, early modern or modern, may have been less easily fathomable by early modern viewers. For example, forms associated with basic schooling could be used for teenagers and adults as well. The woodcut anatomical leafed sheets of the sixteenth century, reminiscent of 'pop-up' books, were intended for medical students, though not solely bought or used by medical professionals (Carlino 1994).

In Germany, *Flugblätter* were broadsheets. With more pages and more print, chapbooks and pamphlets (*Flugschriften*) were the most significant mass media of the second half of our period. Known as *Skillingtryck* (farthing prints) in Sweden, *literatura de cordel* or *pliegos de cordel* in Spain (also *pliegos sueltos* – 'loose pages'), and as *Fatras* or the *bibliothèque bleue* in France (because of the cheap blue paper in which the pamphlets were bound) this inexpensive, brief and ephemeral literature circulated extensively. It is hard to overestimate its popularity. Chapbooks were priced low enough to be afforded by ordinary peasants and labourers or even by servant girls. Output was correspondingly huge. In Spain, mass production of chapbooks began in the 1510s while as early as 1548 Guillaume Godard, a Paris bookseller, died leaving a stock including 1,000 ABCs, more than 10,000 verse chapbooks, 275,000 service books and 148,000 Books of Hours (Schilling 1985; Marco 1977; Martin 1978: 73). Educational writers all over Europe complained that people loved nothing better than to waste their time reading idle and frivolous tales, romances and fables rather than studying Godly and improving texts, one critic being the Spaniard Pascual Valejo in his *Discurso sobre la necesidad de una reforma en los métodos de educación . . .* (1791).

The range of topics covered in chapbooks was enormous because almost any title which was available in a substantial bound volume could have an approximate equivalent in chapbook form, from reprints of medieval romances such as *Amadis of Gaul* to condensed versions of contemporary best-sellers. Defoe's 1719 *Life and Most Surprizing Adventures of Robinson Crusoe* (a substantial volume of more than 400 duodecimo pages costing about five shillings) was available some years later as *Voyages and Travels: Being the Life and Adventures of Robinson Crusoe of York, Mariner,* a pamphlet which ran to just eight pages and did not take the reader much beyond the hero's shipwreck. Shortened editions or serial publications were targeted at a market approximating to that of the full version. The eight-page Crusoe exemplified chapbooks in being fragmented, 'hasty, formulaic, with no sense of tempo or climax, and no relation beyond plot outline to the original text' (Rogers 1985: 168, 171, 196; Watt 1972: 45–6). It was aimed at a lower-class readership.

Brevity and simplicity were not necessarily related, and not all short books were chapbooks. Less than a quarter of titles printed at Glasgow in the first four decades of the eighteenth century were longer than 50 pages, most of these demanding religious and political works. Some French pamphlets were addressed to highly sophisticated and restricted audiences. The *Grand Calendrier et Compost des Bergers* seems, for example, to have been targeted at rural landowners and the urban middling sorts (Chartier 1995: 92). Popularisation of sophisticated material involved breaking it up into short, simple, autonomous units; shortening sentences and paragraphs, increasing the number of chapters, dropping complex sub-themes and the development of characterisation; clichés were substituted for elegant prose, a few short, simple words for extensive vocabulary (Darnton 1986: 23). Not all popular literature was a vulgarised and condensed version of 'serious' books, but most chapbooks were not written for their market from scratch. They were usually a selection and alteration of 'mainstream' works which were thought saleable. For example, a Spanish classic of the early seventeenth century, *Life of Buscón*, metamorphosed into a popular French pamphlet. The main difference between 'popular' and 'élite' literature lay in presentation, form and price rather than in its subject.

The topics dealt with in chapbooks were religion, death, success, ruin, violence, power, vice, love, travel, crime, miracles, marriage, injustice, fashion, politics, war, history and medicine. Most popular in France were chapbooks dealing with traditional piety and morality, and practical guides such as the *Calendrier des Bergers*. This was a sort of abridged encyclopaedia in which a shepherd offers cures for psychological and physiological ailments, traditional medical lore, recipes, prayers and fiery accounts of hell, refurbishing and retelling old and familiar truths. Marvellous topics were also popular and people seem to have delighted in monsters and the grotesque. Gastronomic extravagances, another frequent theme, must have represented an exact reverse of meagre everyday fare. Histories were often jingoistic. Because they were generally published to cash in on recent events, what purported to be histories of world from the Creation gave as much space to these events as to the birth of Christ, the Black Death or the Norman Conquest of England. The youth market was important to chapbook producers and many tales dealt with the experiences of young people, including courtship. Farce and crude humour, known generically as *Tabarinades*, included Grosley's finely tuned, if obscene, *Description of Six Kinds of Fart*. Some were in prose, some in verse. Certain Spanish chapbooks related current affairs in verse. Some were illustrated, some text only. Most shared brief chapters, frequent repetition, summaries and a slow rhythmical progress suited to those who were used to oral forms such as story telling, ballads and church litanies (Martin 1978).

One important variety of chapbook was the almanac. Originating in fifteenth-century Italy, almanacs also took root in Spain in the sixteenth century and the genre flourished in Germany and the Netherlands until the late seventeenth century, in France until the nineteenth century. Almanacs contained two strains, the first involving accessibly presented intellectual astrology and the second representing a set of generalised beliefs in heavenly influence. Like the *Calendrier des Bergers*, these were handbooks-cum-diaries, essentially tables or calendars of terrestrial, astronomical and astrological events with predictions for the future. They might also contain medical or farming hints, weather forecasts and lists of fairs, tides and interest rates. Prognostications, dismissed by Rabelais as drunken fantasies, were a popular subset of almanacs.

English almanacs were usually borrowed from continental examples until the early seventeenth century, then began to develop on their own. English almanacs were more practical than French, their agricultural information, for example, including during the seventeenth century new techniques from Holland being tried out by agrarian innovators (Capp 1979; Sührig 1981). Interest in astrology was on the wane in Europe from the mid-seventeenth century. However it flourished in an intellectualised form in England. German calendars or almanacs were changing to reflect new tastes during the eighteenth century. Astrology gave way to household tips, weather forecasts, and tables of interest rates (Petrat 1985). In France too, almanacs slowly changed from being prophetic to informative and historical (Roche 1998: 94–9). However, Lombard almanacs of the late eighteenth century remained dominated by astrology. In Piedmont the genre metamorphosed again after c.1800 to include more news and realistic commentary (Montanari 1988; Braida 1990). The popularity of almanacs was huge. A quarter of all titles printed in seventeenth-century Sweden were almanacs, featuring astrological predictions, biblical tales, snippets of history, and advice on medicine and economic life (Hansson 1986). In Piedmont 170,000 copies of 30 almanacs were produced in 1789 alone. The *Badische Landeskalender* was produced in runs of about 20,000 a year towards the end of the eighteenth century, while in England the phenomenally popular *Vox Stellarum* or 'Old Moore' was printed by the London Stationers' Company in vast quantities: 107,000 for 1768, 220,000 for 1789 and 353,000 for 1800 (Engelsing 1973: 58).

Before leaving the subject, it is important to recognise that chapbooks, like all forms of literature, could be approached at different levels. They might contain classical allusions or literary references which were accessible to the highly educated, as well as an apparently simple narrative for basic readers and listeners. Form alone is not a wholly reliable guide to readership. However, most brief and basic literature with a large print run, a stress on visual aspects and with potential for being read aloud was probably intended for a mass (lower- and middle-class) audience. More demanding literature was not denied to ordinary people, but their limited education frequently did not equip them for it. At the same time, most volumes beyond simple pamphlets were beyond the means of many of Europe's men and women.

The Price of Books

In the century after the invention of movable type, printed books were expensive, though probably much cheaper than their manuscript predecessors. Just how expensive is clear from the proportion of income which a worker had to set aside to buy various categories of literature, or how much food a family had to forego in order to substitute the mental satisfaction of reading for the more down-to-earth pleasure of a full stomach.

In the early years of the Reformation in Germany, few could dream of owning a Bible. A New Testament published in 1522 cost the equivalent of a week's wages for an ordinary artisan, and the first complete German Bible (1534) the equivalent of more than a month's earnings for a common labourer (Gawthrop and Strauss 1984: 116). A basic arithmetic cost a French person the same as half a loaf of bread in the 1530s, a sermon on poor relief roughly a whole loaf. Buying an account of the siege of Rhodes could mean postponing the purchase of a new pair of children's shoes. Even the lowliest publications were not a negligible expenditure for ordinary people (Davis 1975: 212). Throughout the early modern period, specialist texts on law, surgery, science and the classics were far beyond the reach of the bulk of the population. The 3,931 subscribers to the first edition of the *Encyclopédie* (1751–65) – a key Enlightenment text – must have been affluent to afford its high price. Later editions were smaller, simpler and cheaper, but purchasers were still largely urban professional men. The *Gazette de France* had just 12,000 regular subscribers on the eve of the French Revolution because a subscription cost more per annum than the average peasant's entire disposable income for a year.

An expensive luxury in the late fifteenth and sixteenth centuries, books gradually, if intermittently, became more affordable as time went on. They became cheaper in real terms in England 1560–1640 because nominal prices remained constant. In contrast prices rose appreciably in real terms in contemporary Scotland before starting to fall after the Restoration. It was not until the mid-eighteenth century in England that book production, especially in the form of cheap pamphlets, became a powerful motor for raising literacy as incomes rose and production costs fell. By 1711, the cost of a German Bible had fallen substantially in real terms to just one and a half days' wages for a labourer thanks to more efficient printing techniques (Gawthrop and Strauss 1984: 49). Falls in real prices did not progress without interruption and some barriers to widespread book-ownership remained. Religious works, drama and recreational material (usually in unbound form) were relatively affordable. In contrast, illegal titles smuggled into France or Italy continued to command high prices and some of the new reading available (like novels) was priced for a middle-class market. And costs were never negligible. Even in the eighteenth century, a 16- to 32-page recreational pamphlet from the *bibliothèque bleue* cost the same as a pound of bread.

There were, of course, ways round the high cost of certain books. One strategy was borrowing, another was to buy the volume with others. Some *ex libri* annotations in French and Italian books of the sixteenth century include the phrase *et amicorum* alongside the owner's name, implying that the volume was shared with others (Davis 1983: 83). Another option was to purchase it, read it, then sell it again if it had not already fallen to pieces. A ready traffic in second-hand books existed. The Jews of central Europe in the eighteenth century were well known for selling second-hand clothes and used books, though the association lay principally with selling old things rather than with the products of literacy. People seem usually to have kept only works of reference, books of sentimental or religious value such as family Bibles, or particularly valuable volumes such as an illustrated Book of Hours. Publishers and booksellers helped by reducing the selling price and by finding ways of spreading the cost over time. James Lackington set up a major second-hand bookstore at Finsbury Circus in London in 1774 and pioneered the practice of remaindering publishers' surplus stock (Porter 1982: 95). Widespread pirating of popular works in eighteenth-century Germany made them cheaper and more accessible. Novels could be made more accessible by serial publication or by splitting one tome into several smaller volumes. Fielding's *Tom Jones* (1749) was produced in a six-volume edition, though its total cost was still more than a week's wages for a labourer.

Book Ownership

Given the cost of books, and especially of bound volumes valuable enough to be mentioned in inventories and strong enough to survive use and misuse, the restricted social distribution of ownership is understandable. In early sixteenth-century Paris, 105 of the 173 inventories of movable possessions at death which mention books refer to the estates of men who worked in the law or bureaucracy; 17 were those of medical men, 11 clergy, 2 teachers, 38 merchants and booksellers (Schutz 1955: 6). Of 4,442 inventories of inhabitants of nearby Amiens (1503–76), 887 mention books. Of these, 143 relate to clergy, 259 to merchants, 144 to lawyers and nobles and 32 to doctors (Labarre 1971). Book ownership was mainly the preserve of the professional classes in urban France at this period. It was also more common among men than women. Just 140 of the 887 Amiens inventories pertained to wives and widows, and in the Spanish town of Valencia during the seventeenth century 34 per cent of male inventories mention books compared with 16 per cent of female (Bennassar 1982: 275).

Over time, book ownership became more evenly spread throughout society, though it remained heavily biased towards the middling and upper ranks. Artisan ownership of books was almost unknown in Paris at the start of the sixteenth century, except among printers. Those who worked in print shops were unusually literate at an early date (Parker 1996). However by 1560 the proportion of craftsmen whose inventories contained books had risen to levels which were not exceeded until the second half of the seventeenth century. Among Valencian artisans, the average number of books per inventory between 1490 and 1518 was three. This had risen to five during the next half century. Around 1700, 28 per cent of merchants' inventories at Frankfurt-am-Main contained no mention of books, a figure which had fallen to 16 per cent by 1750 (Engelsing 1973: 46).

Wealth and social standing remained an important determinant of ownership. At Amsterdam in 1700 it is possible to compare taxable wealth with patterns of book ownership. Those in the top category, with average net wealth of about 72,000 guilders, had an average of 138 books each. At the lowest taxable levels (c.3,000 guilders – well above the poverty line) the average was six. However the majority of inventories with books show nothing more than a Bible and a hymn book (Faber 1980: 152–3). The continuing expense of the Bible in some parts of Europe meant that the most common book in the ordinary household was the psalms. A quarter of homes in an Icelandic sample between 1748 and 1763 had a Bible, two-thirds a psalm book (Guttormsson 1981: 138). Indeed, while book ownership in countries like France, Spain and England had ceased to be the preserve of élites and professional groups by c.1600 and had spread well down the social hierarchy by the end of the seventeenth century, in Finland it was not until the second quarter of the eighteenth century that urban inventories other than those of clergy, teachers and merchants record books and not until the closing decades that artisans finally came into possession of volumes worth recording (Lindberg 1981: 237–8).

The sorts of books which people owned can be crudely compartmentalised into those used for entertainment, those necessary to their spiritual welfare and those to their worldly prosperity. One Parisian woman who lived in the sixteenth century died leaving a single example of each: a Lancelot (epic), a Book of Hours and a book on how to make jam (Schutz 1955: 11). In seventeenth-century Amiens, 9 per cent of all inventories mention 50 or more titles, but half of the artisans whose inventories show they owned books had a single title. Some 90 per cent of all the single volumes were religious and of these four-fifths were Books of Hours. Religious works and reference books dominated collections, with half the books recorded of practical use (Labarre 1971: 262, 398). True of the Calvinist Netherlands and Catholic France, this distribution was also the case in Lutheran Germany and Orthodox Russia.

Full and wide-ranging private 'libraries' were rare at any social level before the eighteenth century. Fifty-five book owners left inventories of their possessions in the Franconian town of Kitzingen-am-Main during the seventeenth century: 20 had 5 books or less, 24 had between 6 and 20 titles, nine had 21–50, one had 62 and one could boast 74 (Weyrauch 1985: 469). The word 'library' can mean a number of things from a catalogue of books which can be bought or consulted to a private collection to a publicly accessible stock of borrowable volumes (provincial booksellers could turn their stock into a library, charging for the privilege of reading) to an abstract or real store of knowledge (Chartier 1994: 61–88). 'Private libraries' – substantial personal collections – were more common than public. Any collection of books which had significant financial value, and especially any which were worth compiling into sale catalogues that survive for the historian to study, belonged to members of the professional and landed classes. Catalogues survive for 377 private libraries in late fifteenth- and sixteenth-century France. Of these, 28 per cent belonged to churchmen, 33 per cent to lawyers, 18 per cent craftsmen and tradesmen, 8 per cent soldiers and the rest to nobles and other professional men (Febvre and Martin 1976: 263). Other libraries were extensive. When don Fernando of Aragon, duke of Calabria, died in 1550 he left 795 titles, a quite exceptional number by the standards of contemporary Spain. The library of Jörgen Seefeldt at Ringsted, captured by Charles X of Sweden during his invasion, contained 26,000 volumes and was probably one of the largest anywhere in Europe. More typical was the collection of Johann Langepeter, pastor of Kapellendorf in northern Thuringia (Germany), who reported 77 titles when asked about his literary possessions by his superiors in 1570. Or Jehan Myramont, a student at the university of Toulouse who around the same time made a hasty departure from the town leaving five dirty shirts, two torn doublets, a sheaf of lecture notes, 27 books and an unpaid bill for three years' lodging (Bennassar 1982: 276; Hermannsson 1929: 52; Strauss 1980: 161–2; Davies 1983).

While the preponderance of religious and practical works among recorded collections persisted throughout the early modern period, reading tastes could be extremely varied among those who moved away from the staple fare. Those who sought out contraband titles in sixteenth-century Venice showed a fascination with the occult, interest in which was fostered by curiosity, greed and a desire for power, wealth and success. Humanist titles were also popular among those hungry for knowledge about intellectual developments taking place in northern Europe (Grendler 1977: 196–7). Given the problem of omissions from inventories and catalogues and the scarcity of library catalogues, historians have tried other methods to discover the literary tastes of the reading public. One approach is to investigate the trade in clandestine books for later periods. The presence of censorship in all European countries meant that certain titles could not appear in public or legal documents. However, records relating to booksellers who specialised in the clandestine trade make it possible to illuminate the sometimes shadowy world of reading tastes. One such specialist was Mauvelain, who operated an undercover 'trade in the taboo' from Troyes east of Paris. The archives of the Swiss printers who supplied him show the sort of titles which Mauvelain ordered for his customers, allowing compilation of a sort of 'best-seller' list of prohibited titles for this area of eighteenth-century France. Top of the list by far was *Les Fastes de Louis XV*, a political libel, with 84 copies requested; in descending order of popularity after·this were the *Muses du Foyer de l'Opéra* (pornography), *La Chronique Scandaleuse* (scandal), *La Papesse Jeanne* (religious satire), *L'Espion Dévalisé* (political libel), *Dialogue des Morts* (topical politics) and the *Portefeuille de Mme. Gourdan*, all with 31 or more volumes ordered. The 15 most popular titles were all concerned with politics, pornography and scandal, and the number one best-seller was, not surprisingly, a mixture of all three (Darnton 1976: 49).

No one source affords an absolutely true-to-life picture of reading tastes and, indeed, different sources sometimes reveal contradictory patterns. Nevertheless, there is enough overlap between the different perspectives offered by inventories, publication records and booksellers' lists to allow a convincing montage to be created. Religious literature was of central importance in the early years of printing. Between 1465 and 1501 about a fifth of Italian incunabula were in the vernacular and thus available to ordinary people. Religious titles account for 35 per cent of this vernacular output at Bologna, 46 per cent at Venice and 70 per cent in Florence. Moral treatises, works about the life and passion of Christ and the Virgin, and works depicting models of religious piety were particularly popular, notably Tommaso Gozzadini's *Fior di*

Virtù which went through 42 editions 1465–94 (Schutte 1980: 8–16). During the sixteenth century, the most significant trend was an increase in the proportion of religious material in publishers' lists. Religious titles accounted for about a fifth of the approvals for new books issued by the Venetian Inquisition between 1551 and 1575, compared with one-third between 1578 and 1607. The house of Giolito counted religious titles as 7 per cent of their output in the 1540s, compared with ten times that level by the 1570s (Grendler 1977: 132–4). The proportion of religious titles fluctuated depending on the political and religious climate: 29 per cent of 169 titles published at Paris in 1598 compared with 38 per cent of 456 in 1645 (Kamen 1984: 213).

The most significant shift in reading tastes after the middle of the seventeenth century was an increase in the proportion of historical, scientific and fictional titles at the expense of religious works. At Speyer in the Rhineland the number of religious books mentioned in inventories decreased by 32 per cent between the 1750s and 1780s (Vogler 1983: 448). Leipzig book fair catalogues of newly-printed works show that 19 per cent of titles were religious literature for the layman in 1740, 11 per cent in 1770 and 6 per cent in 1800, while novels, drama and poetry increased from 6 to 16 per cent, reaching 21 per cent in 1800 (Ward 1974: 33). Given the continuation of a strong demand for religious material, especially cheap Books of Hours, psalters, catechisms and lives of saints, it is probable that the new secular demand was a supplement to existing tastes as much as a substitute for them.

Conceivably, the rural masses and urban lower classes retained a taste for traditional material while the middling and upper groups sought out the newly fashionable novels and periodicals. If the new taste for the secular and profane took root principally among the middling and upper classes, the polarisation of taste between social groups may have been enhanced during the eighteenth century.

The secularisation of reading tastes should not be exaggerated. Nearly one-third of all those dying in Amiens during the seventeenth century and whose inventories mention books had only a Book of Hours (Labarre 1971: 397). Even after the first flush of the Counter-Reformation had passed, saints' lives remained popular in Catholic Europe. As late as 1789, 8 per cent of the inventory of Etienne Garnier, a Troyes printer, was made up of hagiography. On the eve of the French Revolution, 63 per cent of the volumes published in provincial France (excluding Paris) were religious in flavour, mostly practical, devotional works such as liturgies and Books of Hours rather than high-flown theology (Brancolini and Bouyssy 1970: 11). A similar emphasis is clear in Protestant Europe. Half of the 1,034 titles recorded in seventeenth-century inventories from the German town of Braunschweig were religious, and fully two-thirds of the 691 at Kitzingen-am-Main (Weyrauch 1985: 469). Book ownership remained dominated by religious titles in many areas of Germany throughout the eighteenth century. Even in its closing decades, no more than a fifth of books owned by people from Tübingen had an obviously secular tone. In the Swabian village of Laichingen the figure was close to zero and more than a half of books owned were spiritually oriented (Wiswe 1975; Medick 1991). Religious books made up 84 per cent and 80 per cent of the total owned at Speyer in the 1740s and 1780s respectively (François 1982: 356). However, this does not mean that readers had the same mind-set as in the sixteenth century. Books may not have changed, but understanding of them may have. The emphasis on religious texts is found everywhere, regardless of the extent of book ownership. An analysis of probate inventories for 1,040 households in rural Jutland 1760–80 shows that one fifth had books, nearly all of them religious. The first purely secular Moscow-printed book did not appear until 1647.

A new taste for the profane is nevertheless clear in the growing demand for pornography. Markets for libertine pictures and literature had always existed. However, the seventeenth century saw an expansion of production and the development of a ready international trade in erotic tales. The French *Ecole des Filles* (1655) was quickly translated into English as *The School of Venus*: Samuel Pepys bought a copy in 1668 and, after reading it 'for information sake', records that he burned it. The popularity of the genre made it an attractive target for moralist fraud. A spoof *Ecole des Filles* was produced, the first 24 pages of which promised a spicy dialogue between mother and daughter, thereby sucking in the reader for the remaining 120 pages which told how to expunge unclean thoughts and deeds by prayer, masses and confession. Taste was moving away from the more artistic, allusive tales of professional whores made famous in the classic early sixteenth-century dialogues or *ragionamenti* of Aretino towards more explicit and domestically situated material such as Defoe's *Moll Flanders* (1722). In eighteenth-century France, enterprising publishers produced pornographic political propaganda, *Libelles*, about Louis XV and XVI's court and especially about Madame du Barry, whose career from a brothel bed to influential mistress of Louis XV made her the perfect target (Foxon 1964; Goulemot 1994).

Whether destroyed after reading, as Pepys claimed, or secreted away, an erotic book probably had a single reader. For more mainstream (and more socially acceptable) topics, book purchase might be supplemented by borrowing. Most borrowing and lending was personal and non-commercial before the eighteenth century, existing on an extensive but unquantifiable scale. Together with reading aloud, this meant that the potential reading public was far larger than most documentary sources suggest.

Medieval libraries were private and closed, created for monasteries, ecclesiastical officials or academics. University collections and private libraries were on occasion opened up on an individual basis to scholars. One such was the library of the Academia Gustaviana, set up by the Swedish king in 1632, and later to become Tartu university. In the later seventeenth century, the books were accessible for three hours a day on Wednesday and Saturday. Students were granted a twice-weekly visit to the library 'for looking through its good books and reading them, and making abstracts of them'. Students were not supposed to borrow books, a hangover from the days when the staff read books and passed their contents on to students in class, though the lending register for the years 1692–1707 shows otherwise. Indeed, staff and students were not the only borrowers: doctors, clergy, army officers, city councillors and other townspeople were among them. One depiction of the university library at Leiden in 1610 shows rows of books chained to shelves and users standing up to read from shoulder-level counters, protected against the cold by heavy cloaks and against cramp by a foot rail. Catalogues, where available, were often unhelpful (Darnton 1986: 13).

Libraries were still not 'open' even in the eighteenth century and the first real lending library in Britain, that attached to the shop of the Edinburgh bookseller Andrew Ramsay in 1725–26, was an offshoot of a commercial enterprise (Steinberg 1974: 255–9). Private libraries of the seventeenth century did, however, sometimes form the core of later public ones. For instance, the library of Pescia in Tuscany was based on the collection of Romualdo Cecchi, who died in 1648, bequeathing his volumes to the cathedral chapter for general use (Brown 1982: 196). The ducal library of Wolfenbüttel, whose borrowing register dates back to 1666, did lend more readily than most and during the 1760s the number of books borrowed every year doubled; borrowers from social levels below the professions begin to appear at this time. Berlin had a public library from 1704. However libraries were far from common in Germany until the last quarter of the eighteenth century. Bremen 'public' library in 1660 was open only on Wednesdays of alternate weeks (Ward 1974: 103). St Petersburg imperial library, founded in 1795, became open to the public after 1814 (Darnton 1986: 11; Ward 1974: 107).

The seventeenth century was the great age of private libraries. In the eighteenth century it became more common to club together to buy books, which were kept for consultation and borrowing by members of reading societies. In eighteenth-century Ulster, three sorts of group purchase existed: subscription libraries; county reading societies patronised by artisans and schoolteachers who pooled books; and societies which did not keep a library, but disposed of the books once read. All had the common aim of spreading the cost of buying and avoiding duplication as far as possible. Some were highly successful, including the Downpatrick literary society, founded in 1793 and able to boast 827 volumes by 1804, and the Doagh book club in county Antrim, set up by a local schoolteacher in 1770 and burned down by anti-Radical elements in 1798. At least a dozen reading societies existed in Ulster by 1800 (Adams 1980). A variation on this theme was the circulating library. These flourished in England from the 1740s onwards, members paying on average three to five shillings a quarter. The money was used to buy books which were then lent out. There were 122 circulating libraries in London in 1800 plus 268 in the rest of England (Porter 1982: 253; Brewer 1997). In all cases, members had to pay to use the library, though it might be 'seeded' by a philanthropic figure. The owner founded the library for the lead miners of Wanlockhead in southern Scotland after a serious labour dispute in 1756. However it attracted little interest and few members from the workforce until the 1780s.

Membership of reading societies was generally select and prestigious. One adult in 500 belonged to a reading society or *Lesegesellschaft* in Germany at the turn of the nineteenth century. There were two such bodies in the German town of Wunstorf whose total complement was around 60 in the mid-eighteenth century: some 4 per cent of the town's population. Schaffhausen reading society's membership amounted to 1 per cent of the inhabitants in 1770 or 10 per cent of the burgesses; those of Mainz in 1788 had 300–450 members among some 22,000 inhabitants (Fabian 1976: 166; Ward 1974: 105–6; Engelsing 1973: 63). Much less exalted were coffee houses where newspapers and periodicals might be available. Paris got its first coffee house in 1672 and had 380 by 1723; in 1739 there were 551 coffee houses in London; Vienna had at least 60 by 1760 (Brewer 1997: 35). More informal still were groups of Swabian peasant women who met to read the Bible and pray together as a way of resolving generational conflicts and reconciling themselves to a life of toil (Gawthrop and Strauss 1984: 54).

Book Readership

Book ownership was restricted in the late fifteenth century. It spread gradually and intermittently through society to feature among the possessions of growing numbers of humble people by the end of the eighteenth century. Religious literature remained important even in 1800, but secular titles became increasingly significant and with them came other changes in reading tastes. Sold by shops, chapmen and hawkers or directly by publishers, books, pamphlets and broadsheets issued from the printing house into the hands of the reader. Books were finding their way into the homes and hands of growing numbers of ordinary people and literacy figures reveal a large potential readership even in the seventeenth century. Plausible connections can be posited between the production and distribution of books and the extent of the early modern reading public, associations which must be investigated closely to discover the extent of book reading, its social distribution, the sorts of titles which readers preferred and the possible impact of literacy on the thoughts and deeds of ordinary men and women.

The particular audience intended by the author and publisher can be inferred from statements in the preface to a text. Books and pamphlets might be targeted at a specific section of the population. Some contain dedications which set up the framework for understanding the text and establishing the context in which the author wished it to be seen. In 1570 the printer Antoinette Peronet dedicated a translation of Marcus Aurelius to the provincial governor of Lyon in return for his patronage. The book was an expression of goodwill, a request for aid and an offer of advice on the art of good government (Davis 1983: 75, 78). Others were deliberately coy about their contents. The 1794 chapbook, *Le Messager Boiteux de Bâle*, asked educated men and the widely read not to judge the almanac too harshly, since it was really intended for the lowest classes who were not in the habit of reading a great deal. Yet this excuse in itself suggests an élite readership (Bollème 1969: 11–12, 65). The content of seventeenth-century Swedish almanacs (including attacks on the increasingly unfashionable astrology) and their dedications suggest that they were aimed more at the well-educated townsman than at the peasantry (Hansson 1986). Addresses to 'the ordinary reader' cannot always be taken at face value, since they were a standard apology for basic presentation. One English medical pamphlet of the sixteenth century was directed to the commonality, even if its suggestion that tennis was a useful form of exercise meant it had scant relevance to the lives of the masses. Many of the most popular medical pamphlets in sixteenth-century England were written not by physicians, but by (and for?) lawyers, clergymen and officials. Indeed, most surviving collections of popular chapbooks were made by gentry such as the Englishman Samuel Pepys and by aristocrats. Francis I, king of France, had a copy of the 'model' almanac, *Calendrier des Bergers* (Slack

1979: 257–8, 273; Davis 1975: 191). There was no hermetic seal between élite and popular culture in the sixteenth century and it is possible that all classes read chapbooks, even if it was the 'romantic revival' of the late eighteenth century, with its stress on rural values, which made the reading of *Volksliteratur* chic. Similarly, men were avid readers of *The Ladies Diary*, founded in 1704 and selling 30,000 copies a year in the 1750s (Capp 1979: 246). The intended or assumed audience was not always the actual one.

Direct evidence of readership is unusual and never simple to interpret. Ownership of a volume did not necessarily mean that it was read. Some Books of Hours, hand-illustrated or decorated with silver, semiprecious stones and mother-of-pearl buttons, may have been bought and kept as much for decoration or investment as for devotional purposes. Books were fragile and those which survive or were recorded in inventories represent an uncertain proportion of those produced and used. Borrowing and lending was certainly widespread. A collection of extracts from popular prophecies published in Germany in 1522 exhorts the reader to pass the pamphlet to others when finished and to discuss its contents with them (Scribner 1981: 6). One sixteenth-century Italian miller, whose mental world will be considered shortly, borrowed from priests, women and kinfolk while belonging to a reading circle which included a painter and a farmer. The miller, Menocchio, obtained Voragine's *Legendario de Santi* from his uncle, Domenico Gerbas, but since it had 'become wet, it tore' (Ginzburg 1980: 30–31). Six of the eleven books which Menocchio possessed at the time of his trial for heresy were borrowed. He may simply have read what he could get his hands on.

By buying or borrowing, people had access to a large volume of printed material. The next step is to determine the size, composition and tastes of the reading public. Estimates of the proportion of the population who could read are of only marginal use here, since this ability did not mean that a person could necessarily be described as a reader. Two surveys covering Arras and Saint-Omer in the Pas-de-Calais during the eighteenth century showed that, despite high levels of signing ability, fewer than 5 per cent of the country people could be classed as 'well educated' (Grevet 1985). Between 1787 and 1812 the Republic of Lucerne in Switzerland saw the establishment of four libraries accessible to everyone – at least in principle. Their promoters' motives ranged from philosophical to commercial, their efforts aimed exclusively at their own patrician and burgher class. They did not intend to enlighten the lower classes. Of the town's 4,337 residents in 1800, close to 40 per cent are estimated to have been illiterate, 30 to 40 per cent attained a level of semi-literacy, while only 5 to 10 per cent sustained the culture of the book

(Kamber 1991). Until late in the early modern period, teaching methods concentrated on particular texts and on rote learning rather than on instilling critical understanding; reading and writing represented a strain for many 'literate' people. Necessarily, the reading public must have been smaller than the numbers of those able to read.

Contemporaries made guesses and claims about the extent of the audience for books, newspapers and periodical literature. The sixteenth-century Spanish writer Cervantes posited the existence of a reading public among peasants and labourers in his *Don Quixote*. Such claims or estimates are often tendentious. Financial interest lay behind some boasts of large circulation. Joseph Addison, editor of the *Spectator*, claimed in 1711 that 20 people read each copy. In 1712 one stamped (taxed) newspaper was produced for every two adults in England; there were three by 1760 and six for every two adults by 1800 (Barker 2000: 46). Approximately 16,500 newspapers a day were sold in mid-eighteenth-century London. Depending on the number of different people who read these papers, readership could have been a quarter to a half of the population. Provincial readership was probably much lower at about one twentieth of the population in 1750 and one twelfth by 1780. Provincial readers were principally gentry and better-off townspeople. Issues were borrowed, read in coffee houses, barbers' shops and anywhere time had to be killed; the second-hand market was probably enormous. However inflated Addison's claim may have been, others echoed it. Thomas Abbt also reckoned on 1:20 as the ratio of copies to readers of newspapers and periodicals in Germany in 1765, though another contemporary went as high as 1:40 or even 1:50. The *Hamburgische Correspondent*, the most widely read political newspaper in Germany and Austria during the 1780s, was published in editions of 21,000 and was therefore potentially read by between approximately 400,000 and one million people (Engelsing 1973: 56–60).

Direct estimates of this kind are both unusual and approximate. Book subscription lists offer an alternative insight, this time into the social stratification of readership. Such lists appear inside the back cover of volumes. There is no guarantee that subscribers actually read (or even owned) the book in which their names appeared. Some perhaps subscribed in order to advertise their social and literary standing. However, subscription lists do show that the reading public was a highly stratified entity. Pat Rogers has analysed lists in two early eighteenth-century publications, one a translation of the *Aeneid*, the other Oldmixon's *History of England during the Reigns of the Royal House of Stuart*. The subscribers shared certain common features. They were overwhelmingly male and drawn from a close-knit circle of wealthy and highly educated persons. But the precise social breakdown differed between the volumes and the subscribers to Vergil were generally younger than those who are named in the history book. Far from homogeneous, the reading public was 'a sharply stratified array of separate audiences' (Rogers 1972: 1540). Similarly, the account books of Jean Nicolas, a mid-seventeenth-century Grenoble bookseller, show that his sales were mainly to lawyers, officials and members of the local *parlement*; purchases by other elements of society were infrequent (Martin 1978: 70). In eighteenth-century Germany there was a market for reading material in English and French. The first French book-shop was opened in Berlin in the early 1700s, the first English one in Ham-burg in 1788. However, nobody pretended that this was anything more than the upper crust of the literate public.

There were three regular reading publics: academics and reviewers; the educated middling and upper classes; and a limited number of 'unlettered' general readers. To these might be added a fourth: the bulk of the barely literate population who were attracted to devotional and recreational chap-books and pamphlets. In eighteenth-century Germany, and indeed over much of Europe, the reading public was specific to certain social groups and envir-onments and it grew in layers rather than evenly across the whole of society. Urban professionals were the most precocious, the reading habit spreading down through successive layers of urban society in stages until, at the end of the eighteenth century, only the rural masses and town-dwelling labourers had still to be assimilated. The latter groups were not necessarily illiterate. However their educational standards, pockets and tastes meant that they sought out traditional literature such as Bibles, psalm books, almanacs and chapbooks rather than the new and varied material that the middling and upper ranks had begun to crave (Fabian 1976: 168; Engelsing 1973: 64–5).

Basic literature had one important feature in common with more substan-tial and demanding volumes. It was not meant to be read swiftly and silently, but to be perused closely and probably rendered aloud. The most significant development in reading during the early modern period was the shift from this intensive reading to extensive. The timing of this change varied across Europe. Beginning in the late seventeenth century, it was concentrated in most western countries during the eighteenth century. From analysis of book ownership, borrowing and reading, it is clear that for most literate people, reading until the eighteenth century was an intensive affair. A few volumes were closely examined, and perhaps studied more than once. Devotional literature in particular was read repetitively. English Quaker meeting-house libraries of the late seventeenth and eighteenth centuries lent out books on average once a year to any given individual. The same is true of a mid-eighteenth-century Scottish library, that at Innerpeffray in Perthshire. Between 1747 and 1757, 241 books were borrowed by 130 individuals, two-thirds of whom only borrowed once during the 11 years. Even the most avid borrower took out just one volume a year over this period. Particularly interesting is the case of John Roben, a weaver. In April 1754 he took away a religious text called *Gospel Revelations*, returned it and then borrowed it again in January 1755. At Christmas of the same year he picked *The Fulfilling of the Scriptures*. Seven months later he returned to his favourite *Gospel Revelations* (Houston 1985: 174–9). This example illustrates the important general point that apart from courts, noble households and scholars, men and sometimes women were in the habit of reading in detail a narrow range of books, carefully poring over them for every nuance. People came into contact with a limited number of texts, though these may have circulated widely. Thanks to their comparative scarcity before the seventeenth century, bound volumes may have been treated with particular reverence. Literates and illiterates alike were influenced by the settings in which they saw books, especially in churches and law courts, settings which lent authority to books through their rituals. Intensive reading, both privately and aloud, meant that texts were effectively memorised and became truly internalised as part of the individual (Engelsing 1974).

Two main developments in reading tastes came during the eighteenth century: the search for novelty and a more extensive approach to reading. The craving for the topical and for the new rather than for ancient wisdom is shown in the development of periodical literature. Readers looked for more and more varied material. Scholarly periodicals were on the wane as well-educated readers in countries like Italy came to demand literature on current affairs such as the *Gazzetta Veneta* or *Caffè*. Venice had 66 journals and 44 almanacs at one point or another between 1661 and 1797, Russia more than a hundred 1755–1800 though most of these enjoyed small circulations and brief lives (Georgelin 1978). Periodical literature developed particularly rapidly in Germany. Typical were the moralist weeklies growing in popularity from the 1720s, periodicals such as *Der Patriot* and *Die vernünftigen Tadlerinnen*, the latter said to be available in 18 towns, the former in 40. Twenty-eight new moralist weeklies were set up 1741–45 in Germany, 27 1746–50, 44 1751–55. German journals of the late eighteenth century wrote of a craze or mania for reading and *Das gelehrte Teutschland* listed 4,300 living authors in 1776 ready to meet that demand (Ward 1974: 23, 60; Darnton 1986: 9). In England, topical pamphlets such as bishop Sherlocke's *Letter from the lord Bishop of London to the*

Clergy and People of London on the Occasion of the Late Earthquakes (1750) sold well, as did the periodical *Gentleman's Magazine* (Watt 1972: 39).

During the eighteenth century the growth of newspaper and periodical literature encouraged recurrent, extensive perusal of printed matter by providing new material and thus fostering a climate in which novelty was demanded. As far as full-scale books were concerned, skimming for ideas became increasingly common. The second major development of the eighteenth century was the rise of the novel, a fictional prose narrative of everyday events which built on literary developments in Golden Age Spain. Cheaper than full folio editions, novels moved away from the traditional, eternal and invariant themes so common in chapbooks (and the 'heavyweights' from which they commonly originated).

Before the eighteenth century, authors mixed factual writing with fictional work. Hans Grimmelshausen (who died in 1676) was a producer of calendars as well as the author of the famous *Simplicissimus*, and in the tales of Eberhard Happels traditional moral and didactic strains remained prominent. The novel form did not catch on in Germany until the mid-eighteenth century and cannot be seen as genuinely 'popular' until the early nineteenth. Readers had to have a wide knowledge of other literary products to derive the maximum enjoyment from early novels (Ward 1974). In Germany (and Finland), many readers continued to demand a practical or edifying content until late in the eighteenth century (the nineteenth century in the case of Finland) (Lindberg 1981: 237–8). Written in the vernacular, the English novels of Defoe, Swift, Dryden, Pope, Addison and Fielding offered scenes from lives recognisable to their bourgeois and gentry readers (Watt 1972; Knight 1985: 936; Fabian 1976: 169–72). Historians of literary development see the novel as a dependent, uncertain and psychologically elementary form until the nineteenth century. Nevertheless they acknowledge the significance of the period after the 1680s in its early development, and of the eighteenth century in its maturation, with the publication of three seminal novels in England, France and Germany: respectively, Samuel Richardson's *Pamela* (1740), Rousseau's *La Nouvelle Héloïse* and Johann von Goethe's *Die Leiden des jungen Werthers* (1774) (Darnton 1986: 9).

Novels and periodicals exemplify the spread of extensive reading. However, rather than seeing a shift from one type of reading to another, it may be more fruitful to see intensive and extensive reading side by side. Different approaches to reading co-existed, but the divergence became more obvious in the eighteenth century with an increased availability of items (Darnton 1985: 242–5). Whatever the growth in new fare, the same religious titles and same authors were popular in Rhineland towns during the 1780s as had been in the 1740s, a fact which may show the continuity of traditional, intensive reading of the kind identified by Engelsing (François 1982: 364–7). Further light is thrown on types of reading by the records of a reading society in the late-eighteenth-century German town of Trier. The society had 83 members, but only two-thirds of these ever borrowed books in the years 1783–93 and eight readers account for around half of the total number borrowed. The others presumably sought out the company which the reading society had to offer as much if not more than its books (Engelsing 1973: 63). Whatever the continuities, there were also important changes taking place. When people with access to many books read only one or two over and over at one period, then read multiple items in another, it is justifiable to conclude that a *Lesererevolution* – a change from intensive to extensive reading – had begun. There was not one 'reading public' in early modern Europe, but several, each with different tastes and capacities.

Understanding

Printed matter of all kinds was widely read throughout early modern Europe. Readership moved down the social scale over time and people were reading a much wider range of material in 1800 than they had even a century before. Men from the middling and upper groups in society, people who lived in or close to a town and those who inhabited the more economically and politically developed states of western Europe almost certainly participated in a widespread and highly diverse literate culture. Having located books and pamphlets and broadsheets in the hands of ordinary men and women, analyses of literacy conventionally stop. Breakdowns of book production or sale or ownership tell about the relative popularity of different genres, but not about how influential certain titles were compared with others. During the 1980s and 1990s, leading cultural historians such as Roger Chartier and Robert Darnton probed the reception of texts, seeking to understand the meaning of the printed word for individual readers.

Concentrating on ideas and their transmission in print, historians have until recently tended to shy away from any detailed investigation of the way in which facts and concepts were received by the reader. They conventionally assumed that early modern people read and understood the printed page in the same way as modern scholars. This is a dangerous supposition, for the ability to read does not automatically bring with it a complete understanding of the text and certainly does not imply the capacity for independent or original thought. After all, there are three major actions involved in reading. First is identifying and recognising printed words; second, understanding the meaning intended by the author; third, using the meanings and understandings derived for some further purpose. These processes are: a response to graphic signals in terms of the words they represent; a response to text in terms of the meanings the author intended to set down; a response to the author's meanings in terms of all the relevant previous experience and present judgements of the reader. The way readers fashioned meanings from texts is particularly complex. For Robert Darnton, 'reading . . . is not merely a skill; it is an active construal of meaning within a system of communication' (Darnton 1985: 210).

Three French scholars stimulated debate about chapbooks, politics and culture during the 1960s and 1970s. They variously argued that popular literature was written to be understood in a particular way. For Geneviève Bollème, the French *bibliothèque bleue* shows a collective mentality which changed little between the fifteenth and nineteenth centuries and which desired the entertaining and the useful from its reading. Chapbooks, for Bollème, were written by and for the people and served no other purpose (Bollème 1965: 70–89). Ordinary people were certainly subject to multiple insecurities and threats to their life and happiness from natural and human agencies. Perhaps they used chapbooks as an innocent way to forget their problems or to cope with them in a practical way. However, themes such as the inversion of the normal social and political order found in some pamphlets could, if read aggressively, help to free peasant minds from oppression and injustice. Indeed, Bollème's portrayal of the relationship between chapbooks and popular mentalities is too simplistic.

More sinister, if not less problematic interpretations are possible. Robert Mandrou proposed that chapbooks were composed by the alienated lower orders as a substitute for class consciousness. He argued that popular literature was essentially escapist and prevented ordinary people from understanding the harsh realities of their exploited lives. However, he also implied that author, printer, seller, peddler and censor conspired to enforce submission to authority and hierarchy through popular literature, thus legitimating the existing social and political order (Mandrou 1975). Robert Muchembled developed these views, claiming explicitly that the *bibliothèque bleue* was written by members of the élite as a way of pacifying or 'acculturating' the masses: 'like drugs', chapbooks 'tranquilized a popular world that was alienated, crushed by taxes, and tempted by revolt' (Muchembled 1985: 292).

If chapbooks contain a very basic, 'conservative' world picture, their origins and content are far from simple. Was literature for the people also of them? The answer is that chapbooks cannot be taken as a simple indicator of the mental world of ordinary people. This is because of the chronological and social distance between context of production and reception of texts; the gap between the author's intent and the reader's reception; and the fact that texts belong to many fragmented genres and traditions.

Many pamphlets were written by the educated middle classes, including the clergy who wrote most of the religious tracts destined for a mass readership in late seventeenth-century England. However, the early modern author is a shadowy presence compared with the modern literary world. From the author's point of view, the concept of a reading public was an eighteenth-century development. Until then serious writers tended to produce for patrons. Only polemicists and hacks wrote for a mass market. What people wrote was often altered to suit production and marketing needs, meaning that 'The writer was not *the author* but a protean figure whose value lay in his ability to assume a number of authorial roles' (Brewer 1997: 148). Booksellers were the real power behind publishing in eighteenth-century Europe, and their principal interest was in making money. The English novelist Samuel Richardson was also a printer. In the 1750s he had 9 presses employing 40 journeymen and even more apprentices.

Furthermore, most popular literature was hybrid in form and content. Detailed study of one particular chapbook reveals that different themes could co-exist in a single text. François Lebrun has analysed *L'Enfant Sage à Trois Ans Interrogé par Adrien Empereur de Rome*, first known in 1516 and popular in numerous editions until well into the nineteenth century (Lebrun 1984). The format is questions posed by assorted worthies and the child's answers, resembling that of the catechism systematised by Calvin in 1541. The content is a mixture of fantasy, religion and social comment. The questioners are composite medieval figures including a duke, an archbishop and a knight. While the text is theologically sound on infant baptism and salvation according to the tenets of the Catholic church, it allows the reader to drift into fantastic situations in the text. There is no questioning of the social order and the values expressed are deeply traditional. When questioned about the hopes of farmers for salvation, the child answers that 'most will be saved because they live by honest toil and God's people eat the fruits of their labour', unlike the deceitful tradesmen. *L'Enfant Sage* had a religious purpose, but it was neither an imposition by the élites nor a spontaneous expression of popular culture. Like much literature before the emergence of the novel as a clear literary form in the early eighteenth century, it was designed to be use-ful as well as entertaining and was almost certainly written by an educated man. Some elements of the chapbook were based on traditional folk culture, some on a vulgarisation of élite literature and some on a specific religious viewpoint which the church wanted to put across. In a single chapbook, there is thus evidence to support the viewpoints of Bollème, Mandrou and Muchembled. Discussions of the role of popular literature in social stability and change run into difficulties over the issue of understanding and of iden-tifying which components of a text are the most meaningful to the reader.

Indeed, discovering the intention of the author is child's play compared with assessing the impact which a work made on the mind of the reader. One example from the records of the Venetian Inquisition highlights the problem. In 1574 the tribunal examined an elderly lawyer and druggist, Marcantonio Valgolio, who had a shelf of banned books, most of them written by humanists. Admonished by the judge that his 18 prohibited titles would foster evil in his mind, Marcantonio replied cleverly that this would only be the case if the reader's intention was mischievous (Grendler 1977: 197).

While literacy potentially offered a singular commodity, the ways in which people related to its products were emphatically plural. Reading and writing involve a complex process which is not simply passive reception. Instead it should be understood as creative adaptation, selective appropriation, and productive re-creation. As Chartier has argued, there are multiple relations between reading, writing and speaking, between texts and performance. The need is to understand not a cultural act or a cultural form like chapbooks, but the ways in which shared cultural acts and forms are appropriated differently by individuals and groups: to take account of 'plural uses and diverse under-standings' (Chartier 1995: 89). Is any reading truly 'passive' when individuals or groups can resist, alter or reappropriate what they read? Readers could take as imaginary real-life situations or stories to which they could not relate, actively producing culture and meaning as well as consuming a commodity. Chartier indeed writes of the 'reader as poacher' (1994: 5). Even when intended for one purpose, such as religious evangelisation, viewers could creatively adapt cultural forms such as broadsheets. It is by no means certain that the same iconographical universe was inhabited by all classes. Overlap there was in readership and reading, but it is unwise to insist, as does Tessa Watt (1991), that a yeoman, artisan or labourer in rural England interpreted a picture in the same way as the artist, or even as a well-off London book-seller. Texts and symbols should not be seen as transparent registers of cultural meaning which can be read by the historian just as they were by early modern people (Mah 1991).

Understanding depended on a reader's existing mind-set and the context in which reading took place. Readers seem to have looked for works to reinforce their own point of view, or to have read books for ideas that confirmed those they already had. Before he became a Quaker, the Yorkshireman Josiah Langdale deliberately refused to read books owned by an early employer of his, lest he be 'drawn to the Belief of the Quakers'. The physical layout of the text may also have been important to the way it was understood. Some Englishmen were apparently influenced by the astrological almanacs they read. Richard Shanne, a Jacobean yeoman, entered astrological rules into his family memorandum book. Henry Best recorded that he delayed gelding his lambs until the full moon had passed. Shanne seems to have copied from almanacs, but Best's beliefs in lunar influence were strongly rooted in popular wisdom. Perhaps he only chose certain ideas from his reading (Thirsk 1983). Indeed, the evidence strongly suggests that reading was a very selective process and that readers only took on board certain aspects of the intellectual content of a text. Once read, the ideas were transformed by the existing mental climate of the reader. Marginalia show the way a reader related to a text he annotated, while printed margin annotations helped guide and structure the use of a text (as with the Geneva Bible).

A full and fascinating picture of this active process of selection and transformation in print is Ginzburg's study of the mental world of the miller Menocchio. Born in 1532, Menocchio lived at Montreale, a small hill town in the Friuli district of Italy, until he was denounced to the Inquisition as a heretic in 1583. Recognised by his neighbours as a reader and a vigorous debater, he was questioned intensively by the tribunal on and off over a period of years. His testimonies reveal the world picture of an ordinary person during the sixteenth century. Menocchio cannot be seen as 'typical' of all early modern people, for he was an individual possessed of a distinctive cosmology. Yet, in the broadest terms, he illustrates their mental world.

Menocchio owned or borrowed at least eleven books ranging from a vernacular Bible through the *Decameron* and Mandeville's *Travels* to the Koran. He read others borrowed from friends and neighbours, steadfastly asserting that 'my ideas came out of my head' rather than from either books or discussions with other people (Ginzburg 1980: 27, 28–31). His claim was a ring of truth, since a close comparison of the passages of the books that he mentioned with the conclusions which he derived from them reveals significant gaps and discrepancies. For example, Menocchio had read in the *Historia del*

Giudico (a fifteenth-century religious poem) that it was good to give charity to a beggar. In the story the beggar was Christ. He went on to make the connection that if Christ is a neighbour and a beggar, it would be better to love one's neighbour than to love Christ, since He could exist in all one's neighbours and was certainly more accessible in that form than in others (Ginzburg 1980: 36–41). Interpretation involved more a change in the emphasis of the text rather than outright distortion. Stressing certain ideas over others altered the sense. Menocchio did not passively accept ideas from a book nor the opinions of others. The way he read was 'one-sided and arbitrary', heavily influenced in the sorts of interpretations he made by the literal, materialist emphasis in popular thought. Some ideas he ignored completely in the printed texts he consulted, others he altered significantly. Some books, such as Mandeville's *Travels*, helped hugely to expand his mental universe to encompass pigmies and cannibals. Others, such as *Il Fioretto della Bibbia*, provided him with the linguistic and conceptual tools to express his view of the world, albeit a view composed not of discrete ideas, but of a mass of composite elements. Menocchio pondered phrases for years, ruminating them until they had been assimilated, transposed or even completely remoulded. A critical or analytical approach to reading was unusual, but active interpretation was normal, so that the concept of a fixed 'source' with unequivocal meaning is difficult to maintain (Ginzburg 1980: 44–7, 60–61). Creating a radically non-Christian view of the world from Christian texts, Menocchio's assertive style of reading appears 'a discontinuous process that dismembers texts, decontextualizes words and sentences, and assumes a literal meaning' (Chartier 1995: 94).

Unusual as his conclusions were, Menocchio is an example of a common process of selective reading. Understanding how people read sheds light on how they thought. Deeper immersion in print and discussion of ideas with others might eventually help to form an interpretation. For the self-taught, ambiguities must have remained strong. Jean Ranson, a prosperous merchant from La Rochelle, provides an example of a more educated reader. His letters ordering books from Neuchâtel (1774–85) show a concern with the quality of paper and binding, the proportions of the typeface, the quality of the printing. The book to Ranson was a cherished artefact whose aesthetic quality was an important part of the pleasure of ownership. As for content, Rousseau had tried to shape readers' lives and to direct the way he was read. Ranson's letters (on topics far more intimate and weighty than simply buying books) show an implicit and sometimes explicit attempt to live by the great man's precepts. Family relations are a prominent example of how the master inspired

Ranson and helped him to make sense of his life. According to the letters Rousseau received, readers across Europe showed a strong emotional reaction to works like *La Nouvelle Héloïse*. Ranson's letters show that intensive reading had not wholly been supplanted by a desire for novelty and cursory entertainment. In the way he related to Rousseau, Ranson was an old-fashioned 'intensive' reader. What may have happened in the late eighteenth century was a change in the way readers responded to texts. 'Rousseau taught his readers to "digest" books so thoroughly that literature became absorbed in life' (Darnton 1985: 244). Ranson treated the author less as a distant authority than as a member of his own family. Reading changed not only how people like Ranson lived, but the way they chose to rationalise their deaths. Suicide notes changed their form in Germany after the publication of Goethe's *Wertherfieber* in 1774 (Darnton 1989: 90).

What slender evidence exists of the way early modern people related to the products of literacy shows a mental world very different from our own. It was shaped by reading and writing, by visual, oral and aural forms, and by cultural influences such as intense religious belief and magical assumptions that are weaker in (or even absent from) modern societies. One of the differences is that 'reading and living, construing texts and making sense of life, were much more closely related' in early modern Europe than now (Darnton 1989: 89). For example, folktales 'told peasants how the world was put together, and they provided a strategy for coping with it' (Darnton 1985: 59). England developed the nursery rhyme, but lacked the rich repertory of folk tales found in France. French tales are 'realistic, earthy, bawdy and comical' whereas German tend towards 'the supernatural, the poetic, the exotic, and the violent' (Darnton 1985: 57).

Eighteenth-century reading was a physical process which involved bodily preparation (like diet and posture – did one read standing or sitting down?) as well as relating to the book as an object, including the typeface(s) and the quality of paper. Their varied lengths, layouts, costs and subjects suggest that books had different target audiences. Even size could convey a message. Small-format works could indicate that they were for less affluent readers, but in England in the 1790s this could be extended to an association with political radicalism because small books were less conspicuous.

The appearance of a book also determined how seriously, even reverentially, it was treated, for readers had a 'typographical consciousness' which has largely disappeared in an age of mass production. Books were not abstract texts whose appearance was irrelevant to their meaning. For example, between 1500 and 1800 there occurred 'the definitive triumph of white over black'.

This means that books came to have more paragraphs with indentations to break up long passages, fragmenting the text into units (Chartier 1994: 11). The English philosopher John Locke lamented the way Scriptures had begun to be formatted into chapter and verse, claiming that this fragmentation made God's word harder to comprehend. However, for some readers this made understanding easier and thus gave freedom to the audience. In the century after Locke wrote, 'dictionaries, encyclopaedias, collections and critical histories helped to order and evaluate the proliferating genres of knowledge' (Brewer 1997: 191). Changes in form as well as content were significant in the development of early modern reading. Paper superseded parchment; print largely replaced handwriting in books; copperplate engravings took the place of woodcuts. Pages became simpler in appearance during the eighteenth century, perhaps in order to win over a wider audience. In short, the medium was part of the message.

Chapter 9

LANGUAGE, ORALITY AND THE USES OF LITERACY

Language

In the sixteenth century the vast majority of printed literature was available either in Latin or, in Russia, Church Slavonic, both of which were understood only by a small élite. Of the 6,000 books in Oxford's Bodleian library around 1600, just 36 were in English (Thomas 1986: 101). The triumph of the vernacular as a literary medium certainly made literature more accessible. Eight of the 88 books published at Paris in 1501 were in French, 38 of 269 in 1528, 70 of 332 in 1549 and 245 of 445 in 1575 (Febvre and Martin 1976: 321). This development came later in Germany. In 1650, the ratio of Latin to German books sold at the Leipzig and Frankfurt book fairs was 71: 29. By 1700 that ratio had been reversed to 38:62 (the 1680s was the key transitional decade). Vernacular output continued to grow at the expense of Latin. The ratio was 28:72 in 1740 and just 4:96 by 1800 (Steinberg 1974: 118; Knight 1985). Literature was more widely available provided one had reading skills in the language of everyday communication.

However, as one barrier was overcome, another came into view. One language was made the official medium of communication in the church (when Latin was not in use), law courts and bureaucracy and it was in that language that the bulk of vernacular literature was printed until the end of the eighteenth century. Speakers of dialects or different tongues were left with a restricted or even non-existent body of literature upon which to draw. Italy in the fifteenth and sixteenth centuries illustrates a problem common to much of Europe. 'There was,' as Harvey Graff writes, 'an Italy of many dialects, but no true literature, and an Italy of courtiers, oligarchies, and the learned, with one language and one great literature' (Graff 1987: 89; Burke and Porter

1987). For the literate, print helped to unify cultural experience. For the millions who did not possess the language of literature there might be little change in their intellectual horizons. The map of Europe was pock-marked by 'black holes' of illiteracy, but it was also blotched with linguistically distinctive areas which escaped or resisted cultural integration. As the geographer Sebastian Munster noted in his *Cosmography* of 1552: 'Formerly regions were bounded by mountains and rivers . . . but today languages and lordships mark the limits of one region from the next, and the limits of a region are the limits of its language' (Parker 1979: 35).

Many different families of languages existed in early modern Europe. There were Germanic, Romance, Celtic, Slavic, Albanian, Greek, Turkish, Basque and Finno-Ugric languages among those with identifiable geographical locations. In addition there were Arabic, Judeo and Romani languages used by specific ethnic groups across the continent. Then there were the many dialects or patois. Together they made linguistic unity within the boundaries of a state unusual in early modern Europe. In some parts of the Austrian Habsburg lands, German vied with Czech, Serb and Croat; in the Swedish empire, Swedish with Finnish and German (among others); in Scotland, English (or Scots) with Gaelic; in Spain, *castellano* with Basque, *catalan*, *gallego* and Moorish.

The way a language is described illuminates the complexity of the processes by which cultural change took place. Some languages which are 'lesser used' now were extensively spoken in the early modern period. Nor can they always be described as 'minority'. For one thing, what later became the dominant language may not have been the tongue of a majority. For another, 'minority' may refer to their status in political units that were still being formed. Furthermore, the social domains in which a tongue is used may be as important as its geographical extent. If a word like 'minority' may be quantitatively accurate, one like 'subordinate' is value-loaded and potentially pejorative.

Despite developments in trade and communications, European society remained highly localised, one feature of this being the diversity of vocabulary, intonation and phraseology used by the inhabitants of a particular area. For example, an investigation of 1790 led by abbé Grégoire revealed some striking facts about language and dialect use in France. French was the dominant language in just 15 of 89 departments; 6 million Frenchmen could not understand French at all; a further 6 million could understand it, but spoke it only imperfectly; 30 patois were spoken plus foreign languages like Flemish, German and Basque; only 3 million could speak French properly (Higonnet 1980). Other parts of Europe were similarly affected at this date. Seven out of ten of the inhabitants of Wales were monoglot Welsh speakers in 1800 and more than a half of Ireland's people born in the 1770s spoke only Irish, these concentrated in the western counties.

Cornish, the only separate language in England in 1500, was marginalised during the sixteenth century. Yet England was still divided into dialect zones. Travellers remarked on the problems which ordinary people had in under-standing the natives of a different county and one said of Tyneside: 'They speak very broad: so that, as one walks the streets, one can scarce understand the common people, but are apt to fancy oneself in a foreign country.' One prose and verse chapbook, printed by J. Kendrew of York in 1809, offered *Specimens of the Yorkshire dialect. To which is added, A Glossary of such of the Yorkshire words as are likely not to be understood by those unacquainted with the dialect.* Socially aspiring bourgeois provincials of eighteenth-century Scotland and England responded well to newspaper advertisements which promised to eradicate traces of dialect and train them in 'standard' English (Malcolmson 1981: 94; Febvre and Martin 1976: 322). It also became increasingly fashionable for grammar books and pronunciation guides in later seventeenth-century Germany to offer examples of 'proper' pronunciation and expression, thus creating a distinction between 'fancy' and 'common' speech (Schenda 1985: 449).

Scots was the dialect which the poet Robert Burns so confidently used. In contrast, the literati of Enlightenment Edinburgh aspired to pronuncia-tion and orthography which conformed with the best London practice, exemplified in the English man of letters Samuel Johnson's first English dictionary. Certain Scottish poets like Robert Fergusson wrote in Scots and English. Celebrated among contemporaries, their work also proved import-ant for later Romantics and eventually modern nationalists. English rather than Scots became the tongue of Scotland's landed, professional and aspirant mercantile classes during the eighteenth century. Indeed, the drive for linguistic and grammatical standardisation produced distinctive results in countries which pursued it. Eighteenth- and nineteenth-century British society was overtly class-based and produced a hierarchy of forms of speech. In nineteenth-century France it was not accent, but variations in phrasing and spelling which distinguished social groups, principally the bourgeoisie taught in the *lycées* from the rest (Higonnet 1980: 69). Dialect differences were less of a problem in the vast Russian territories than in countries like Italy, though the communication difficulties occasioned by fluidity in language (the fluctuating relationship between Church Slavonic and the more vernacular East Slavonic) and alphabet were not finally removed until the end of the eighteenth century (Auty 1977a: 32–6; Franklin 1985: 2).

While Europe's largest countries contained great variety, even small states might encompass several different languages and dialects. The Netherlands, that great political, religious and intellectual melting pot, offers an example. In the core provinces during the sixteenth century there were two languages, French and Dutch, and the dialects based on them such as Walloon, Picard and Flemish. In the eastern lands, Low German was spoken and written while to the north, in more isolated Friesland, Fries was spoken. Even Dutch was divided between that spoken in the east (Oosters) and West Dutch which was later to become dominant (Parker 1979: 35–6). In Pembrokeshire and on the Gower peninsula of west Wales, it was said that an hour's walk separated 'Englishries' from 'Welshries' and that in an extreme case one side of a street spoke English, the other Welsh (Jenkins 1997: 54–60).

Linguistic and dialect differences had social as well as spatial dimensions. Broadly speaking, the urban middle classes and the gentry and nobility in the countryside were less prone to use dialect and were more likely to speak and read the official language in multilingual zones. Male members of the Welsh gentry spoke, read and wrote Welsh, English and Latin thanks to their education in grammar schools, universities and Inns of Court. They were able to participate in pan-European Renaissance culture and to acquire a breadth of outlook far wider than their social inferiors. In France, the nobility of the north-western provinces had abandoned the local dialect, Breton, in favour of French (*langue d'oeil*) as early as the twelfth century. In contrast, English only superseded Gaelic (in its different forms) among the land-owning classes of Ireland and Highland Scotland during the later seventeenth and eighteenth centuries. The Norwegian nobility spoke Danish rather than their own tongue, those of Finland preferred Swedish, and the Lithuanian upper classes opted for German. Eighteenth-century developments in publishing in Iceland, such as the monthly *Islandske Maaneds Tidender* (set up by Magnús Ketilsson in 1773, it ceased publication in 1776), were nearly all in Danish. The market was made up by officialdom and the educated élite who understood that language best (Cullen 1980: 18; Kessler 1976; Hermannsson 1918: 6–7).

Officials of church and state too might conduct their affairs in a language which was not that of their subjects. What this meant was that in some circumstances those with knowledge of more than just the local language or dialect acted as translators for the monoglots, in the same way as literates mediated the products of literacy for illiterates. At the end of the fifteenth century, the city fathers of Montreal, to the west of Condom in south-western France, could not understand correspondence in French and had to have it translated into Gascon. Meanwhile the local bishop, Antoine de

Pompadour, employed a clerk to translate petitions and letters in Gascon into French for him (Loubès 1983: 317). In contrast, local officials working in the Habsburg monarchy during the eighteenth century had to be bilingual in German and the native tongue of their area (Burian 1970–71: 86).

Language use was socially and geographically complex. Schoolteachers and religious instructors in eighteenth-century Norway were usually native Danish speakers who could also manage Norwegian. The Norwegian–Icelandic written language of the middle ages – the language of the sagas – had fallen into decay by the sixteenth century when Danish was the dominant written language. Danish was the language of the towns and of administration, Norwegian dialects belonged to the peasantry. In the west of Norway the dialects resembled Icelandic and Faroese, in the east Swedish and Danish, making Danish readily intelligible in the east and the reception of Danish as a written language easier. What was called Norwegian after the political split of 1814 was almost the same as Danish. In eighteenth-century Finland too, rural dwellers spoke Finnish, more educated urbanites Swedish. Sweden had an élite cadre of Russian-speaking interpreters who worked in diplomatic negotiations, interrogated prisoners of war, translated the Lutheran catechism into Church Slavonic and collected political, military and economic information from Russian travellers and businessmen. In northern Norway and Finland Lapps were taught reading in Norwegian. Lapp was not introduced as the language of religious instruction in Finnmark until 1820. In contrast, the Danish government favoured using the vernacular in missionary and educational contexts in Greenland, producing better results there than in Finnmark (Guttormsson 1990: 27; Tarkiainen 1972).

Knowledge of more than one language gave these 'brokers' a position of power in local communities. The overlap between high social status and bilingual skills reinforced the dominance of the gentry and nobility over their monolingual peasants. Yet even ordinary people might enjoy some standing because of their ability to translate. Irish peasants who spoke English seem to have done so very poorly, taking a Gaelic sentence and translating it inaccurately into English. Yet a humorous literature existed which required an awareness of the differences of grammar and vocabulary between Gaelic and English and the potential for error. This suggests that a bilingual market existed. In the Mediterranean and the Baltic, phrase books helped merchants in the rudiments of conducting business, Finally, there were some parts of Europe where the population was induced by their circumstances to become multilingual. In the hills of northern Italy, men required a knowledge of Italian for dealings with bureaucracy, and of German and French if they wished to emigrate temporarily from their village or trade with neighbouring areas (Bliss 1976: 556–7; Viazzo 1983: 168).

Separate dialects and languages came increasingly under attack by governments during the early modern period. Rulers equated the lack of a uniform tongue within a state with the persistence of provincial loyalties, which weakened or actively opposed the consolidation of centralised power. Leading the field in the search for linguistic unification was the Tudor state which introduced a 'language clause' into the Act of Union between England and Wales (1536). This required English to be used for government and the law. The French crown followed soon after with its 1539 ordinance of Villers-Cotterets establishing standard French (the *langue d'oeil* used in the north east) as the official language of the law courts. France had numerous dialects and languages – Poitevin, Picard, Gascon, Provençal and Breton, for example – and uniformity was not achieved overnight. In 1668, Louis XIV set up a *Collège des Quatre-Nations* on the model which his former minister, Mazarin, had outlined in his will, the aim being to educate gentry boys from the extreme north-east and south-west of France in French and to encourage them to accept central domination of their ostentatiously separatist homelands. The campaign was still active in the eighteenth century, when Rolland D'Erceville, spokesman for the Parlement de Paris, expressed the hope that educational expansion and an insistence on the use of standard French would hasten national integration (Febvre and Martin 1976: 272; Trenard 1980: 99; Leith 1977: 17).

The Revolutionary government after 1789 continued this policy, suspecting non-French speakers and dialect speakers of federalist and counterrevolutionary intentions. Abbé Grégoire's investigation brought awareness of linguistic diversity and for a time government communications were translated for non-French speakers. Yet within a few years the eradication of patois again became the government's goal because it seemed to impede political integration and social change (Higonnet 1980). A stress on a standard language like French may seem oppressive. However it could act as a social leveller since élites tended to have patois and French, common people only patois. The divisive effects of language choice are plain in seventeenth-century Acquitaine. Protestants there were keener to have education in French so that their people could read biblical texts, compounding a religious divide with a linguistic one because Catholics favoured religious instruction in patois (Astoul 1996: 60).

France was just one of the European states formed in the late medieval period from an amalgam of distinct provinces. The problems of diversity and the drive for integration through uniformity of language, laws and government were common to all of Europe. In the seventeenth century the Swedes tried actively to assimilate provinces of the Finnish frontier by insisting that Swedish should be the language of education (Whittaker 1984: 7). From 1607, James VI and I sought explicitly to eradicate the Gaelic tongue spoken by his Scottish Highland subjects because of its association with the unacceptable religious and political aspects of that region: Catholicism and clans. And in the vast Habsburg territories of central Europe at the middle of the sixteenth century, Ferdinand I's reforms of government and the courts involved a substitution of German for Latin. However, Czech remained the administrative and legal language of Bohemia until the 1620s (when only some 10 per cent of the population there were German speakers) and it was not until the late eighteenth century that German became generalised as the language of government, official communication, military command and the courts in all but the Italian and Belgian provinces of the empire. After the first partition of Poland (1772), the Austrian authorities tried to insist on teaching in German in the schools of Galicia 'to contribute to the unification of provinces varying in national structure and religions, into a single, strong State organism'. And Joseph II spoke for generations of fellow rulers when he extolled in 1785 the 'advantages which the whole state will gain if the different provinces of one and the same government are more closely united with each other through the common language' (Krupa 1981: 82; Burian 1970–71: 84–5).

The decline of certain minority languages and dialects was not always the product of a deliberate drive for conformity on the part of secular authorities. In fact, straightforward proscription of a language seems to have had a limited effect on its survival or decay. Certain languages and dialects persisted throughout the early modern period, others experienced erosion and decline. What determined their differing fortunes were their political standing, the extent to which literature was available in the minority tongue and the relative significance of the dominant language in economic and social life. Take the case of the replacement of Ruthenian by Polish as the language of the middling and upper classes in zones such as Lithuania, Byelorussia and the Ukraine. Until 1696 legal documents had to contain an introductory and concluding clause in Ruthenian. It was not compulsory to write documents in Polish, but it was rare to have a whole document written in Ruthenian after 1640. There was no institutional reason for nobles, clergy and bourgeoisie to drop Ruthenian in favour of Polish unless they had lost faith in their native tongue for other reasons. Leaders of the Russian Orthodox church realised the perceived and actual weakness of local vernaculars when they selected a language of service and literature to combat militant Counter-Reformation Catholicism, opting for Church Slavonic as their weapon (Martel 1938: 54–66; Jakobson 1955: 33).

Sometimes the reasons for loss of confidence in a tongue can be identified. Sir John Davies commented that the spread of English criminal assizes across the whole of Ireland caused a movement away from Irish from the reign of Elizabeth: 'because they find a great inconvenience in moving their suits by an interpreter, they do for the most part send their children to schools, especially to learn the English language'. And in the reign of James I, the chronicler Connel ma Geoghagan wrote of his fellow authors: 'Because they cannot enjoy that respect and gain by their said profession as heretofore they and their ancestors received, they set naught by the said knowledge [of bardic culture], neglect their books, and choose rather to put their children to learn English than their own native language' (Ó Cuív 1976: 529).

The early modern period witnessed a contraction in both the geographical areas where separate dialects and languages were used and in the social spread of the users. The change occurred sometimes quickly as a result of a traumatic event, sometimes slowly as a result of creeping erosion. The main period when Irish suffered at the hands of English was the seventeenth century while, in Highland Scotland, Gaelic retreated most rapidly during the eighteenth and nineteenth centuries. In Spain, the dominance of *castellano* was quickly achieved in Valencia and Aragón during the fifteenth and sixteenth centuries. In contrast it remained a foreign tongue in Catalonia, the Balearic Islands, the Basque lands and in much of Galicia in the seventeenth century. Literacy in Catalonia developed in *catalan* during the eighteenth century, and it was not until the mid-nineteenth century that a campaign to use *castellano* for reading and writing began to be effective. In Galicia as in Catalonia, *castellano* was the language of the wealthy and powerful, while *catalan* or *gallego* belonged to the masses. In Galicia *castellano* was also the language of schools and people there learned to bow to the superiority of *castellano* rather than actually learning to read and write it. Since the seventeenth century *catalan* had had a political significance which *gallego* lacked (Bennassar 1982: 259; Viñao 1990: 573; Benítez 1997: 507).

Languages and dialects which avoided decay were, broadly speaking, those which had a practical use in a number of domains, being used for religious, cultural, legal, administrative and economic as well as social and familial purposes. Breton, for example, was not taught in schools, but from the late seventeenth century there was religious (and some recreational) literature which helped to perpetuate it. Two-fifths of the stock of 30,000 volumes held by the Quimper printer Marie Blot in 1777 were in Breton. It survived as a medium of religious instruction and in the theatre, oral culture and chapbooks. In 1807 there were nearly a million people regularly speaking Breton (le Menn 1985: 230, 239).

Irish was slightly more fortunate than Scots Gaelic. Its widespread use as a written (less so as a printed) language distinguished it from Scots Gaelic and allowed it to revive as a focus of nationalist feeling in the late eighteenth and early nineteenth centuries (Cullen 1980). By contrast, Welsh, which was formalised as a language of religious worship by the publication of a Bible and Book of Common Prayer in the 1560s, enjoyed much greater stability and permanence than either the two forms of Gaelic or Breton. Welsh-language printing flourished, giving rise to 500 titles 1660–1730 and a total of perhaps 3,000 works before 1820. With a population ten times the size, Ireland could only boast 200 works in Irish before 1800. Scotland did not have a Gaelic New Testament until 1767 and there was no complete Gaelic Bible until 1801. English did make headway in Wales during the seventeenth and eighteenth centuries, notably in the towns and in the bilingual zone in the east of Wales. Yet seven out of ten of the inhabitants of Wales were monoglot Welsh speakers in 1800 compared with one-fifth of Scots who were Gaelic speakers (Durkacz 1983; Williams 1971; Ó Ciosáin 1997: 163; Jenkins 1997: 48).

The success of Welsh as a religious language was because it was never associated with opposition to Protestantism and political centralisation in the sixteenth and seventeenth centuries. In the eighteenth century, Protestant dissenting churches or chapels catered especially to Welsh speakers. There were also important social reasons for the success of Welsh. The landowning political élite of Wales was important in introducing English, but the Welsh language was preserved and developed by a middling sort lacking in Scotland and Ireland. In the Highlands and Islands of Scotland the cultural 'brokers' were often outsiders or outward looking: economic middlemen such as estate factors and mobile cattle drovers who favoured English. What Wales lacked until the eighteenth century was a commitment to education in the Welsh language. When that came about through the actions of Griffith Jones, the movement stemmed from native Welshmen, rather than being imposed from outside by Anglicisers. Until then there were English-language schools which had existed since the sixteenth century. Education was one of the domains where separate traditions of language use and literacy obtained: reading and writing in English, reading in Welsh. More generally, 'Although English was the dominant language in domains like government and administration, law, commerce, science and polite society, Welsh held sway on the hearth and in the workplace, in church and chapel, in literature and poetry, in recreation and popular culture' (Jenkins 1997: 122).

The story of what were eventually classed as 'minority' or 'subordinate' languages was therefore not always one of decay. During the second half of the eighteenth century the developing nationalist movements of eastern Europe began to foster the use of their local languages and dialects as a way of asserting their independence from central, imperial power. In Hungary from the 1790s, nationalists tried to promote Magyar in public life rather than German or Latin, and in 1805 14 county assemblies decided to conduct all official correspondence in Magyar. The first 'best-seller' in Magyar was the 1788 *Etelka* extolling Hungarian virtues and denigrating German cultural influences. The Finnish Aurora society, founded in 1771 by Henrik Gabriel Porthan, sought to promote national consciousness by fostering language and oral traditions. The period after 1814 saw the rise of 'New Norwegian', a recreation of ordinary speech before the Danish take-over (Bárány 1966: 29, 34; Tóth 2000: 133–44; Whittaker 1984: 8).

Linguistic and dialect variety were not the only obstacles to pan-national or pan-European culture. Print lettering was not uniform during the sixteenth century. The two main faces in use in western Europe were Gothic (also known as textura, *Fraktur* or 'black letter'), which dominated the first century of printing, and Roman face, also called Latin or 'antiqua' face. Italic face, developed in Italy from the late fifteenth century, had restricted usage. The clergy and notaries of sixteenth-century Rome used italic; craftsmen and tradesmen used merchant hand (*mercantesca*) (Petrucci 1978).

Acts of Parliament and proclamations from the English crown used Gothic type in the early sixteenth century, as did elementary teaching aids, making it difficult to gain familiarity with Roman type (Thomas 1986: 99). Roman type only became dominant over most of western Europe from the end of the sixteenth century, stagnation in the development of Gothic type-faces from the early seventeenth century announcing its surrender to Roman type as the principal literary face. After the Reformation, Scottish Bibles followed the Genevan example of using Roman type in preference to the Gothic face preferred by Lutheran Scriptures. Germany, Scandinavia and parts of eastern Europe held on to Gothic type until the eighteenth and nine-teenth centuries – the first known Danish book to be published in Roman type came in 1723 – when intellectuals came to realise that Gothic face was provincialising their culture. The indigenous population of Greenland during the eighteenth century read and wrote in Roman letters whereas most

Danish literature was in Gothic and both traders and officials of Norwegian and Danish extraction used Gothic (Gadd 1985). Not even numbers were standardised. Roman and Arabic numerals co-existed, and there is also evidence across Europe of 'peasant numerals' – symbols representing numbers which may have been derived from Roman numerals, but which were distinctive (Roggero 1996: 634–5). People did not relate to literacy as a single object, but as a collection of objects in different languages and type-faces; in manuscript or print; as letters, pictures, or sounds.

Political as well as literary considerations influenced choice of type-face as it did choice of the language of printed communication. Archbishop Laud insisted that the controversial prayer book he imposed on Scotland in 1637 be printed in textura, adding to its unpopularity among contemporary Calvinists. Something as apparently neutral as type-face could be used to assert a political position. As conceived by the Austrian government after 1774, education in Bohemia was intended to use German Gothic script for writing Czech words. However, from the early nineteenth century rounded, humanistic script was favoured – and became a way of asserting nationalism.

The varieties of script used in the west were less of a barrier to communication than was the case east of the river Elbe. Russians and Finns used calendars made of wood (*birka*), multi-faceted sticks a foot or two long notched to mark days and marked with signs (often pictograms connected with agricultural tasks) and Cyrillic letters (featuring a forest of accents and diacritic marks) to show saints' days and festivals. Printed calendars, which became more current in the eighteenth century, retained the same form and letters (Smith 1983: 283). An important change took place during the reign of Peter the Great, involving the introduction of a streamlined, civil alphabet called by printers 'secular face'. During the eighteenth century, ecclesiastical face (which was to secular what Gothic was to Roman in western Europe) came increasingly to be confined to religious works as the simplified alphabet was used to print new works. The first book using this type-face was a geometry text of 1708 (Simmons 1977: 49; Auty 1977a: 36).

In Poland the position was more complex and more fluid, especially during the sixteenth and seventeenth centuries. Court documents of the Grand Duchy of Lithuania show a gradual replacement of Cyrillic by Latin over this period. Unlike Galicia to the south, ruled by Casimir the Grand, Ruthenian was not banned outright in Lithuania. Instead it was gradually pushed eastward by the spread of Polish. The transition can be dated quite precisely in the documents. The nobles who signed contracts and agreements did so in Cyrillic until the 1580s when they began to use Latin script. By 1620 the only ones who signed in Cyrillic were the lesser nobles. Of 23 from the Kiev region who petitioned the king in 1629, only six did not use Latin letters. The transitional phase can be identified in a paper relating to the purchase of a building by a religious order, dated 7 June 1590 and registered at the tribunal of Vilna. The text is in Ruthenian; of the 15 signatories, six use Cyrillic letters followed by a legal clause in Ruthenian, while the other nine employed Latin characters with a Polish formula. Russia, Poland and eastern parts of the Holy Roman Empire were the only areas of Europe where language divisions were accentuated by the different scripts in use (Martel 1938: 54–9).

The implications of linguistic and dialect divisions were profound. Keen to shake off his own accent and dialect, Martin Luther tried to encourage the standardisation of High and Low German dialects (the former spoken in the south of Germany, the latter in the north) to make his message easier to transmit in print. Yet, areas in which a dialect or minority language obtained were often poorly served by printed literature. Flemish, spoken by 90 per cent of the population of eighteenth-century Brussels, was a culturally marginal language. The 15 major periodicals available there were all in French and of 218 stage plays put on in the middle years of the century, 95 per cent were in French and the rest were in Italian (Lottin and Soly 1983: 293). Only a handful of books were printed in Breton or Basque during the sixteenth century, these usually religious in nature. Some agricultural tracts were printed in specific Italian or German dialects at this time, but most were in Latin or one of the mainstream tongues such as Tuscan or French (Beutler 1973). Two centuries later (1788–89), 76 per cent of French books were produced in the north-eastern half of the country, with Toulouse and its hinterland the only part of the Midi where substantial production and demand existed (Brancolini and Bouyssy 1970: 19, 32). Breton endured, but areas where it was widely used still had lower literacy than the French-speaking *départements* immediately adjacent. Brittany was also a part of France which had high proportions of men and women who could read but not write as late as the 1870s, suggesting that the advantages conferred by attachment to print culture brought only a restricted literacy. Using patois was part of a cultural preference for oral communication. The same is true of southern France, where variants such as Provençal had no written form and the dialect versions of French used for education and administration were not commonly spoken. The north-western province of Galicia may also have had different cultural priorities from other parts of Spain which were similarly expressed in language use. For one thing it was poorer, and when school attendance statistics become available in the nineteenth century it had low levels comparable with the deep south and much inferior to the north-east of Spain.

Even if they could obtain the full range of literature through the rudimentary distribution networks, inhabitants of these zones had not only to be literate, but also to be versed in a language which was probably not the one which they spoke in everyday life. As with education, the transfer of ideas through the medium of print was seriously inhibited by linguistic and dialect divisions. The triumph over much of Europe of English or Tuscan or standard French or German or Polish tended, in many areas, to mean that town-dwellers spoke a different tongue to that of rural peasants, while the rural gentry and nobility were distanced from their lower-class neighbours by speech as well as education, wealth and life-style. Social as well as intellectual divisions could be widened by the expansion of printing and of literacy. That some of the peoples inhabiting interstitial regions like the southern Netherlands or northern Italy managed to combine linguistic pluralism with high literacy should not detract from the general association between language and literacy outlined here.

Innovation and 'Modernisation'

Extensive communication of ideas through the medium of print was an innovation of the late fifteenth century, and historians like Eisenstein have claimed that it marks a revolution in intellectual and practical life. Reading printed material is said to create new possibilities for thought and action. Writing too can help to restructure thought and create new forms of communication. By breaking through the barriers erected by 'irrational custom' and traditional oral transmission, print and writing create fresh opportunities for individual and societal improvement and help substantially to hasten economic change (Eisenstein 1979; Ong 1986). Intellectual contact and cross-fertilisation of ideas were certainly facilitated by printing. Yet when it came to imparting practical knowledge the influence of print and writing was less straightforward.

Examining the relationship between literacy and economic change can test these ideas. Commercial development enhanced the demand for literacy and was itself fostered by the expansion of educational facilities. The largest sector of the early modern economy was not, however, trade. Agriculture was the biggest industry and substantial developments in manufacturing did not come until the eighteenth century. Production of food was crucial to the economic well-being of a country and was central to something as basic as whether its people lived or died. With the exception of the Low Countries and areas of northern Italy, intensive, high-productivity farming was uncommon during the sixteenth century. During the seventeenth and eighteenth centuries there were major improvements in both organisation and techniques which increased output in certain regions of Europe so dramatically as to merit the title of an 'agricultural revolution'.

Literature on agricultural improvement existed from the medieval period, and has been studied for the sixteenth century by Corinne Beutler. These early tracts were written by gentry for gentry and were concerned with the growing of basic foodstuffs. A Polish treatise by one Gostomski offered information on how to run an estate, presented as a set of epistles advising how to raise rents, market produce and instruct peasants. Most such treatises were in prose, though some verse editions exist, including the early sixteenth-century Italian *Coltivazione*. Some were in Latin and 622 editions were reprints of ancient authors such as Vergil and Pliny. Konrad Heresbach's German *Vier Bücher über Landwirtschaft* was in fact first published in Latin in 1570, and was modelled on the Georgics. The practical usefulness of such volumes is questionable, and it is hard to escape the impression that many were little better than coffee-table books. Even vernacular editions were not particularly useful to the masses, written by highly educated Italian and German authors and presented in terms which were probably alien to the ordinary working farmer. Not all texts were like this. Some tried to be simple and practical, one even claiming to have been tested 'on the ground' by two gardeners from Nîmes in France. Yet sixteenth-century agricultural literature probably had limited significance in bringing about agrarian change (Beutler 1973; Thirsk 1983: 295).

Only in the seventeenth century did pamphlets begin to appear on specialist topics such as gardening and tree growing, and only in the eighteenth was there any extensive body of literature on experimental methods. England and Holland led the field in agricultural improvements during these centuries, the dissemination of best practice aided by a large body of literature on new methods. Arthur Young, the famous eighteenth-century agricultural improver, divided print on agriculture into two categories: the genuinely useful written by working farmers and the material composed by dilettantes for journals like the *Museum Rusticum* (Fussell 1932: 419). The former could certainly prove useful, and there are surviving examples of agricultural pamphlets marginally annotated by farmers using information obtained from practical experience of trying the recommended methods, or from discussions with farmers or from reading other literature (Thirsk 1983: 305).

Yet, caution is required when extrapolating from one or two examples to the whole process of disseminating new ideas on agriculture. To the issues of author's intention, potential market and reception (considered in an earlier chapter) can be added the problems of gauging the effects of literature on innovations in agriculture. Recent research on seventeenth-century England indicates that the channels by which new ideas and methods were conveyed were complex. Innovation travelled by two means. Gentry and richer yeomen farmers, the rural élite, read about novelties in books or in correspondence with other 'opinion leaders' elsewhere in England. They introduced the innovations first and by this medium ideas travelled over long distances and were introduced into an area. Extensive adoption of new techniques such as turnip husbandry depended on these opinion leaders showing other yeomen and husbandmen the means and merits of their improved farming. However, personal contact and the mobility of labourers trained in the new husbandry were more significant than reading and writing in the widespread dissemination of innovations. As William Ellis put it in his *Modern Husbandman* (1744): 'It is certain that no teaching of Arts and Sciences comes up to the practical way of doing it; and, therefore, Ocular Demonstration is the quickest and best Way of introducing new improvements in Husbandry' (Overton 1985: 216–17). Literacy was significant as a complement to traditional methods of learning by seeing and doing. Some eighteenth-century farmers scouted around for trained labourers and tenant farmers from other counties with experience of new methods in order to train their existing workforce, recognising the difficulties created by agrarian conservatism and the importance of example in changing attitudes.

The most effective improving texts were those which recognised the importance of example and leadership, and which therefore tried to show the educated how to direct opinion and work among the masses. Charles Estienne's sixteenth-century agricultural manual assured the French landowner that reading and writing were superfluous to the productivity of his tenant farmers as long as they were experienced and receptive (Davis 1975: 196). Established, socially prestigious figures in a community could act as opinion leaders who influenced discussion and innovation. There was, of course, no guarantee that their views would be adopted, or that their ideas would spread beyond limited social groups. Some British agricultural innovators of the eighteenth century were viewed as eccentrics by working farmers. However the mix of demonstration and literate media seems to have been the most successful means of disseminating innovations. The influence of literacy and print on agricultural practice depended on social contacts, cultural traditions and existing methods.

The same point can be made about inventions and new technology in industry. Until the end of the eighteenth century no part of Europe can be described as industrialised, though significant pockets of (principally textile) industry did exist. Most manufacturers were small in scale, decentralised, rurally located and used simple machinery which involved little fixed capital. However, important changes in technique were taking place during the seventeenth and more especially the eighteenth century. How they were introduced and systematised again illustrates the complexity of the relationship between printed or written means of communication and the human agent. As the Frenchman Trudaine de Montigny warned in 1752: 'the arts never pass by writing from one country to another; age and practice alone train men in these activities' (Harris 1985: 130).

The Italian historian, Carlo Cipolla (1972), has written a short but important article on this topic. In 1607, Vittorio Zonca published his *Nuovo Teatro di Machine et Edificii*, which featured illustrations of a hydraulic silk mill or *filatoio* capable of increasing significantly the output of manufactured silk. This book was available to the eager English as early as 1620, but they were not able to build a copy until decades later when an industrial spy called John Lombe 'found means to see this engine so often that he made himself master of the whole invention and of all the different parts and motions'. Lombe ran a great risk, since the Piedmontese government had decreed that seeking or revealing such information was punishable by death. They recognised that, without practical instruction, the mere reading of books would not enable competitors to build and run the mill. This example illustrates that practice and demonstration were every bit as important as the reading of printed material when it came to propagating innovations.

As was the case with agricultural change, mobility of skilled labour was of great significance in disseminating novel industrial techniques. In the sixteenth and seventeenth centuries, Protestant refugees from religious persecution in France and Flanders took new clothmaking skills to Holland and England; to Scotland and Scandinavia they took metalworking and clockmaking developments. Most of the prestigious royal manufactories in eighteenth-century Spain were worked by English, French and Dutch artisans. Eighteenth-century Swedish and Flemish craftsmen were attracted to Russia in order to introduce the technique of casting iron guns. Some of

the Swedes had originally come from Flanders, which was a leading technological zone in the sixteenth and seventeenth centuries. In the eighteenth
century, England was the most industrially advanced nation, and it was from
her that many European nations obtained their new technology. As early as
the 1690s, Swedes worried by Russian competition came over to learn from
the English. Other legitimate information gatherers followed clandestine
investigators like Odhelius and Swedenborg. Schröderstierna made 200 pages
of notes on Birmingham manufactures in 1749. As the pace of technological
change accelerated, secrecy became more important and downright spying
more common. Austrians, Germans and Russians were all active, as were the
French, one of whom posed as a naturalist in the 1760s to spy on mining
and metallurgical enterprises (Harris 1985; Mathias 1975).

The significance of personal demonstration and practical experience
to technological change and economic development highlights the place of
aural, oral and visual forms in everyday life. Increased literacy was important,
albeit tempered by existing cultural forms and social practices. As an agent of
economic change, literacy and literature depended on personal demonstration, social contacts or divisions and on deep, often oral traditions. Was it
nevertheless the case that those steeped in oral culture thought differently to
those who had mastered the art of reading and writing? To enter the mind of
any early modern person, and particularly those who left no written record
of their thoughts and deeds, is notoriously difficult. Gauging how broad and
'modern' the minds of literates were compared with illiterates is fraught with
methodological problems, not least of which is the widespread assumption
that the more recent a set of values or body of information is, the more
rational and enlightened it must be. Despite these difficulties, it is possible to
distinguish certain features which marked out different ways of thinking.

From the end of the Thirty Years War, if not sooner, religion played
a reduced role in international relations. In the course of the eighteenth century, European societies may also have become more secular in their outlook
and less dominated by religious concerns. Some historians have spoken of a
'dechristianisation' of Europe, signalled by scientific advances, the decline
of the belief in witchcraft and magic, and the growing dissatisfaction with
bodies such as the Jesuits who were committed to a supranational religious
ideal. With increasing literacy went a more secular outlook. There is some
support for this argument. Certain types of devotion became increasingly
the preserve of those who could not sign their wills during the eighteenth
century. Around 1710, half the wills of literate wage-earners from Marseille
asked for masses after their deaths, as were half the wills where the testator

did not sign in full. In 1730 all literate testators asked for a mass, but only half of illiterates. Within a decade the association between signing and religiosity had been reversed. From the middle of the eighteenth century to its end, three illiterates made the request for every one who signed his will. Literacy and a lack of expressed concern for religion seem to have become more strongly associated. Over the same period in another Provençal community (Cotignac, *département* de Var), the number of wills which contained clauses dedicating the testator's soul to God decreased appreciably for literates, but hardly at all for those unable to sign their names. Of those who asked for masses, half could sign in 1700 compared with just a fifth in 1800. Illiterates asked for masses and inserted dedicatory clauses much less than did literates until the very end of the eighteenth century when convergence was nearly total. Prior to 1800 literate people were godly by these criteria, illiterates much less so. By 1800 both had reached the same level of outward manifestation, albeit by following very different paths (Vovelle 1975: 136–7).

Illiteracy might therefore be linked with traditional attitudes, literacy with a greater receptivity to change. However there are qualifications to this argument. First, those who signed may simply have expressed their piety differently from illiterates (and vice versa), rather than being more or less pious. Second, even if the association is accepted, literacy and religiosity were linked in the early eighteenth century, but not in 1800. This suggests that literacy may have been associated with a willingness to change, rather than with one particular set of attitudes like strong or weak religious devotion at one point in time. Finally, it may be that literacy and a modern outlook both sprang from a similar set of social and economic circumstances, and that something other than literacy was the driving force behind changing attitudes.

In the secular world too there are intriguing, if similarly inconclusive indications that literate people had distinctive attitudes. The content of a national sample of rural *cahiers de doléances* (complaints about the *ancien régime* solicited from France's 40,000 parishes in 1789) has been compared with their region's literacy as measured by subscriptions to the 1786–90 marriage registers. In short, literacy made no great difference to the sorts of demands for change or continuity which were made by communities. Literate regions were more inclined to discuss the need to improve agriculture and industry, and were also more likely to address the structure, organisation and operations of existing institutions of government. They were less likely than low-literacy regions to refer to the workings of the forthcoming Estates General (Markoff 1986: 323–9). A study of Malmöhus county (Scania, Sweden) has shown a connection between literacy and a desire for agrarian change among hereditary peasants. The strengthening of proprietary rights during the eighteenth century caused a larger number of peasants to seek out literacy, to become more entrepreneurial, and to pursue enclosure. This in turn strengthened the demand for literacy in late eighteenth-century Sweden, with peasant freeholders paying extra to have their sons instructed in writing and also lobbying for parish schools (Pettersson 1996). However, some Scandinavian historians question the relationship between literacy and 'modernisation' (Markussen 1993).

There were differences in social and cultural life which may be attributable to literacy. In Hungary, regional patterns of marriage seasonality may have been related to literacy, among other influences (Faragó 1994). Literates married throughout the year, illiterates at certain times. For those who were not steeped in literate ways of thought, time was perceived as blocks punctuated by significant festivals such as May Day and by important events such as harvest or a change of employment or residence. Even in the eighteenth century, peasants in eastern and central Europe dated by ecclesiastical feasts, fairs and events in the agricultural year rather than by day and date (Tóth 2000: 72–5). Literates tended increasingly to relate time to a documented continuum of years, months and days, and they turned more rapidly to watches and clocks when these became widely available in the eighteenth century. However, the sixteenth century was also important in the shift from traditional to modern methods of dating in western Europe, and the transition was led by urban dwellers. In eastern Europe it took much longer, partly because the length of an hour, for example, was different in the province of Novgorod from that in the Moscow region. Notched sticks only began to be replaced by printed calendars in the eighteenth century and carved counting-sticks were used by Swedish and Finnish farmers to record the days worked by crofters until the late nineteenth century (Moran 1981; Smith 1983). Yet, even in the west measurement of time continued to be influenced in the eighteenth century by prominent natural events and the calendar of the church: natural and cosmic time. A growing precision in measuring time and a changing sense of time – a shift to exchange and clock time – may have been a result of growing literacy and numeracy as much as a cause (Pellizari 2000: 174–8; Roche 1998: 78–90).

Oral and Aural Culture

Those who seek to understand the distant past must use artefacts of one kind or another, including words written or printed on paper. Written words bear silent witness to the huge amount of correspondence which took place between businessmen, lawyers, bureaucrats and soldiers. Millions of printed books speak volumes for the intellectual curiosity of Europe's readers and thinkers. Because of the sources they use, historians may value the products of literacy more than other types of communication. The words of ordinary men and women as they went about their everyday lives have been lost in the utterance. Yet for the vast majority of early modern people, what was spoken and heard, seen and experienced may have been more important for social and economic life than what they read or what they wrote. This is clear from the preceding discussion of the dissemination of innovations. To measure just how important is, of course, impossible for the very reason that face-to-face interactions generally leave no trace in surviving written records. Transcriptions, even if verbatim, cannot convey the full force of the spoken word, with its pauses, stresses and cadences. Most important lessons in life were probably learned by seeing and doing.

In order to assess the part played by oral communication in shaping the social, cultural and intellectual lives of the common folk, it is necessary to rely on incidental and sometimes anecdotal information. These types of source are by no means inferior to the quantitative material which has provided most of the detail so far. Instead, they help to fill in the significant contours of experience sometimes lost in mere figures. Indeed, qualitative sources hint at a rich and densely textured oral and aural world with meanings and understandings every bit as subtle and important as those of written culture.

There was no firm dividing line between oral and literate culture. The two were face-to-face all over early modern Europe, their interaction eased by a number of factors. First, there was the prevalent practice of reading aloud, both when alone and in company. Medieval society had prized the idea that knowledge and books were best shared, and in Muscovy the verbs 'to read' and 'to listen' could be used almost interchangeably of a written text. When children were taught to read, they were expected to articulate the words, and this habit seems to have stayed with them into adulthood. In 1570 Arthur Chapman, a 30-year-old blacksmith from Wolsingham in the English county of Durham, was called before the diocesan Consistory Court for misbehaviour in church. He admitted that he had been attending morning service in his parish church one Sunday, and defended himself by allowing that he had been 'reading of an English book or primer, while . . . the priest was saying of his service, not minding what the priest read, but tending his own book . . . Marry, he read not aloud to the hindrance of the priest . . . but the priest after the first lesson, willed him . . . to read more softly.' He later added that he had owned the primer for more than a year. He was presumably using odd opportunities to improve his grammar, spelling and vocabulary, since he could already sign his name in full (Raine 1845: 231–2).

Reading aloud to oneself could be a very personal event, and may explain why many working-class readers preferred to follow their hobby in the open countryside. It also had wider social implications, for reading aloud in a group could be a way of transmitting ideas and information contained in written or printed material to illiterates. Some popular literature was clearly designed to be read out to an audience and street peddlers sometimes advertised the contents of sheets and pamphlets by doing so. In early sixteenth-century Germany, the verb 'to read' could also mean 'to read aloud'. Some works advised those who could not read or who had only rudimentary literacy to seek out a more accomplished friend to read out the harder passages. Popular propaganda for the German Reformation was often a hybrid form with printed words and pictures mixed; the process of transmission was probably also hybrid. A Nürnberg clerk called Erasmus Wisperger was arrested in 1524 for reading a proscribed religious work aloud in the marketplace (Scribner 1981: 6).

Few communities, however small and remote, can have lacked at least one person who could read, write and count, even if that person was a figure in authority such as a local priest or landowner. Cross-checking a plan of the parish of Montin in Savoy with family ties shown in parish registers and with literacy from notarial registers reveals that every illiterate family in the community during the eighteenth century had at least one literate kinsman living close by to whom they could turn (Siddle 1987). During the 1640s, the English gentleman Adam Eyre recorded in his diary occasions when, on behalf of one or other of his friends and neighbours, he drew up a petition, framed an apprentice indenture, made out a draft contract for the sale of some land and read out some writings which had been brought to him. His friends paid (either in cash or in ale) another man, the Lancashire apprentice Roger Lowe, for writing love letters, wills and bonds. The famous sectary, Ludovick Muggleton, a contemporary of Eyre's, was aware that his followers might not be able to understand 'print-hand' and had to have his message read aloud to them (Reay 1985: 6). Eighteenth-century Parisian illiterates could go to one of several public reading places to hear news being read out for a small fee. Professional gossips, *nouvellistes*, told paying listeners stories about court affairs, from their accustomed benches in the Tuileries or Jardin de Luxembourg (Smith 1979: 47–8). Even members of the literate population depended on vicarious literacy. Until spectacles or eyeglasses became widely available in the eighteenth century, older people with failing eyesight would have required someone to read aloud for them (Tóth 2000: 78–81, 113–15).

Reading in private required time, light and, in winter, warmth. How much more congenial it would be to read aloud or to listen with friends in a parlour, tavern or barn. Anabaptists at Augsburg in the 1520s and Cologne in the 1530s sometimes preached in inns (Scribner 1984: 242). Reading aloud communicated, but it also created or reinforced social bonds. Some forms of sociability created particularly favourable opportunities for experiencing vicarious literacy. The German *Spinnstuben* or spinning circles are a good example. Conducted in the winter evenings, these formalised gatherings of young men and women began with the sexes separated. The initial male assembly was called a *Gunckel* and typically involved the youths in set emulations of their elders. Thus the young men smoked their pipes, played cards, argued about politics and read the newspaper aloud. Only later did boys and girls meet. *Gunckel* and *Spinnstube* included a whole range of sociabilities, one of which was reading aloud and listening to texts. In southern France a similar institution existed in the form of the *veillée*. During the sixteenth century, the material which was read aloud at these meetings was rather old-fashioned, according to Noël du Fail, who wrote literary works such as the *Propos Rustiques* (1547) set in a peasant village. He picked out Aesop's *Fables* and *Le Roman de la Rose*. Those charged with reading out such texts might also have to change standard French into local dialects. Both the *veillée* and *Spinnstube* were special occasions and there must have been many more informal gatherings of family and friends where reading aloud occurred (Medick 1984: 334–5; Davis 1975: 196–8, 210, 213; Fox 2000).

Oral and literate culture interacted in these sorts of environments. The exchange was a fruitful one and by no means one way. Literacy could be an aid to oral communication rather than a substitute for it. Oral culture often provided the basis for what was written down, while printed texts fed back into the oral tradition to be retold and perhaps subtly changed. Interactions of this kind are clear in much of the ballad literature collected by amateur ethnographers during the eighteenth and nineteenth centuries. Sometimes portrayed as the pure waters of oral tradition, songs and tales did not in fact spring unpolluted from the depths of popular memory. Instead, oral and literate forms contributed to each other in differing ways over time. Oral forms were consciously or unconsciously changed when written down, perhaps modified for publication and modified again when reproduced orally. 'Cultural currents intermingled, moving up as well as down, while passing through different media and connecting groups as far apart as peasants and salon sophisticates' (Darnton 1985: 70). In Ireland and Germany, for example, some tales began in a written form in the medieval period, were adopted by oral tradition in the fifteenth and sixteenth centuries, then passed into and out of manuscript until they were eventually printed during the nineteenth and twentieth centuries. On the way, tales changed almost out of recognition. Little Red Riding Hood began life as a dark erotic tale of murder and prostitution, but is best known to modern readers as a nursery story whose message is not to trust strangers. On the other hand, the importance of oral influences is evident in the repetition, use of epithet, tortured rhymes, clichés and vague historical context displayed in much popular literature.

A good example of interactions between cultural forms is in jokes. Men went round taverns, coffee shops and private houses making collections of jests and witty stories. Written down and then printed, these jokes fed the conversation of readers in the same environments in which they had been found (Ó Cuív 1976: 537; Hermannsson 1914). Early nineteenth-century Berlin was the centre of German humour publication, with *Witzhefte* published in local dialects being particularly popular. All could have read them – around 1800, 90 per cent of Berliners could read – but their cost and marketing structure suggest a readership from the middling and upper ranks. Yet the joke is an example of the superiority of oral forms in some circumstances. Much of the effect of a joke depends on timing, tone of voice, facial expression, body posture, and audience reaction. Printed jokes lose much of their impact.

Representatives of the oral tradition such as jokes or ballads would almost certainly have remained unknown to modern historians had they not been collected, written down and often printed by those who saw it as their duty to record what seemed to be either a curiosity or the last remnants of a threatened culture. The early eighteenth-century commentator Pálsson, for example, started his collection because he believed that all the old women of Iceland who could remember the ballads were dying out. Many of the tales the amateur ethnographers gathered were designed to be nothing more than entertaining. Interesting differences nevertheless appear in the sorts of ballads preferred by men and women. In early nineteenth-century Norway, men preferred humorous tales, women magical ones; in eighteenth-century Scotland, men regaled audiences with martial stories and songs, women with more marvellous ones; Faroese men opted for heroic ballads, women for those on love, chivalry or the supernatural. There is some evidence that women were the repository of the ballads and, indeed, most written down in the eighteenth and nineteenth century were collected by men, like the famous Icelandic compiler Árni Magnússon, listening to women. The Englishman John Aubrey recalled that as a child his nurse recited a ballad version of the history of England from the Norman Conquest to the reign of Charles I.

The most important difference in cultural practices between men and women was arguably not orality versus literacy. Instead it is that different values were attributed to oral and literate forms according to the sex of the participant. Women were formally excluded from some important oral forms such as preaching and the composing and reciting of poetry. They were allowed to participate in something like gossip which was not valued and which therefore reinforced rather than detracted from their dependency. Women told their tales in the home whereas the menfolk enjoyed the quasi-professional status of public singers and tellers. Orality too had its hierarchy (Grambo 1983: 121; Ólason 1982).

Ballads and tales were not purely recreational. They could also serve important social and political ends. Singing at work about topics close to their lives helped to reconcile women to hard labour, resolve their genera-tional conflicts, unburden themselves of worries about husband and family, assimilate news about the living and remember the dead. For the whole community, a song about the virtues of past nobles might serve to highlight the shortcoming in a present landlord and thus help to alleviate feelings of injustice. A tradition of Gaelic political poetry began in late sixteenth-century Ireland, nurtured among men who had been exiled to Catholic Europe. The Irish bardic tradition contains a number of long political poems composed between c.1630 and c.1660 dealing with the partiality of the English courts, confiscations, transportations and the brutalities of troops. These are rhetor-ical and atavistic, offering little in the way of constructive alternative because of the structures of patronage within which bards operated. In seventeenth-century Scotland, spiritual songs helped preserve proscribed Catholicism among the Highlanders. The significance of the Gaelic poets as political propagandists was recognised by Charles II, who retained Iain Lom MacDonald as his bard to compose and disseminate loyalist, episcopalian ballads (Ó Tuathaigh 1980: 158; MacInnes 1950: 32, 37). Ballads show the ways in which oral culture could mould itself to a variety of practical ends: coping, resisting, propagandising and controlling as well as entertaining.

Oral culture is often portrayed as an unchanging morass of immemorial ideas. Custom is similarly misunderstood as a set of timeless and immut-able practices. Interchanges between written and memorised forms must cast doubt on this notion. Furthermore, the material which was transferred by speaking and listening was adapted to context and was far from invariant. Ballads which moved from one country to another tended to undergo creative adaptation which gave them a distinctively local or national flavour. Faroese imports from Denmark or Irish borrowings from England and France are an example. Eighteenth-century Iceland had three versions of the story of Griselda from the Decameron, all very similar, which had been introduced from Holland. The initial transfer was probably oral, but the tale was then written down. This particular story was never printed in chapbook form in Iceland as it was in most other countries, being propagated instead in prose or in verse *rímur*. Bardic traditions did not necessarily wither, to be replaced by print and writing. Both tale-telling and manuscript copying remained vital until the seventeenth century in Wales, for instance. As a result of a conscious and energetic response to the opportunities of print, the bardic tradition was modified, especially through religious works, to be encapsulated in new printed literary traditions (Williams 1971).

Some folk tales were invented or remodelled by the Jesuits for use in social and moral education. For example, in the seventeenth-century *König Drosselbart*, an arrogant German princess rejected several suitors, but was ultimately glad to accept one she had mocked. Similarly, some forms of theatre relied for their impact on the ability of the players to mix elements drawn from folk memory with comments on everyday life and motifs derived from printed literature. In sixteenth- and seventeenth-century Germany and Spain, Jesuits were active in mounting short plays (Spanish *farsas*) to make simple theological points. In sixteenth-century Seville they ran classes for actors who were to convey the message of the revived Catholic faith through drama (Hsia 1989: 94–100; Nalle 1992: 114; Robinson-Hammerstein 1989: 105–31). Ukrainian religious stage plays, performed by peripatetic students during their vacations from Orthodox Brotherhood schools or the Kiev Mohyla academy, used folk culture enriched with educated values and information derived from the products of literacy, fusing Scripture, theology, classics and foreign literature with folklore (Lewin 1977).

No area of early modern life was free of this complex interaction between oral and literate forms. Over the period, literate means of communication and record keeping came to dominate everyday life, at least in north-western Europe. Modern readers tend to assume that this was an inevitable result of the spread of literacy: written documents and written communication will automatically be more important than verbal exchanges because they are fixed and (notionally) unambiguous. The ultimate authority in any context will be the written or printed page. For early modern men and women, the reality was rather more complex. On the one hand, the products of literacy were not always of paramount importance as authentication. Many of the important events at which literacy was used contained acts and spoken words too. Scotland was one of the first European countries to instigate a centralised register of land transfers in 1617. The written 'instrument of sasine' was recorded in official volumes. The actual transfer usually took place on the land itself, and involved the handing over of a clod of earth from the seller to the buyer before witnesses. The proportion of Hungarian land sales where writing was used (the alternative was to call the old men of the village to testify to the existing ownership of a holding) grew substantially between 1646 and 1762 in three villages close to Körmend, then stagnated 1762–1812. Only after 1792 did written documentation come to be preferred over the word of elders. Local variations in usage of written proof were pronounced. In one village in 1762 just 5 per cent of agreements were written, 88 per cent in another (Tóth 1989: 541).

This Hungarian example could be written off as coming from a 'backward' region on the margin of Europe. However, a similar emphasis has been documented for seventeenth-century England, one of the most economically advanced and literate countries in Europe. For witnessing and communal memory rather than account books or formal contracts remained important in authenticating business dealings. Economic events were not simply transactions of commodities, but were seen and remembered as social exchanges. Across Europe, then, 'the memory of transactions was woven into the fabric of the community as much as they were written into diaries or private account books' (Muldrew 1997: 64). In the Hungarian example it was men who authenticated. In England too men comprised more than 90 per cent of witnesses in disputes over customary rights heard before central courts. Both examples suggest that the role of women as the guardians of communal memory has been overstated (Wood 1999: 264).

Oral and aural forms permeated early modern culture. Indeed, Daniel Woolf has questioned whether the period saw a transition from the 'age of the ear' to the 'age of the eye', as Lucien Febvre suggested. Woolf argues that the senses were complementary. Whatever their promotion of the printed word, Protestants valued preaching and singing, humanists oratorical excellence. Classical training in rhetoric stressed a person's vocal and oratorical qualities (Waquet 1993). In short, 'the early modern historical mind sprang from oral and aural roots – rhetorical roots – as much as from visual ones . . . the early modern mind was fully capable of balancing aural and visual perception, despite the increased assault on the eyes provided by print . . . in so doing it merely maintained and developed a "perceptual equilibrium" present in the later medieval mind rather than shifting from one mode of perception to another' (Woolf 1986: 160).

Literacy did not necessarily dislocate memory. It could reinforce oral and local cultures. For authenticating personal documents, a seal was counted as good as a signature in countries such as Poland and Hungary until well into the early modern period, a practice that also says something about the aspirations of the magnates to royalty. Eastern Slovakian officials used picture seals to authenticate documents until the eighteenth century (Novák 1992; Tóth 2000: 61–3). For all the voluminous documentation they created, civil and criminal court cases were fundamentally oral and theatrical. Those who had something relevant to say about the case and who were present when it was heard were generally obliged to present their evidence in person. Witness credibility was dependent at least partly on demeanour, including the tone of voice used. Oral testimony meant the defendant was informed of the evidence against him or her and knew those giving it. The point of these examples is to show that ritual, orality and symbol were often mixed with bureaucratic and literate forms, and that the importance of the latter should not be taken for granted. Written documents were an (admittedly important) complement to public, personal acts, rather than a substitute for them. A document could be valued for its mystery and symbolism as well as a record, authentication or replacement for memory (Franklin 1985: 24–36; Tóth 2000: 83–5, 155–62).

Literacy was not always privileged over orality. At the same time, its products – books and writings – had a symbolic or totemic significance which depended only partly on the words they contained. Books became a symbol of Czech nationalism from the fifteenth century thanks to their association with the Hussites and later the Protestants after the forced re-Catholicisation of the 1600s. They also symbolised the Enlightenment in late eighteenth-century paintings and prints, just as the Book had been the symbol of the Protestant Reformation (Ducreux 1989). There were further differences in this part of central Europe in what were regarded as legitimate uses of the book, ways to read and methods of interpretation. Different readers invested reading with different expectations and meanings. For example, religious reading had different 'rules' to commercial reading. When questioned about their use of books, Bohemian heretics of the eighteenth century had diverse ways of relating to print. Some used the book as an icon, others knew only the chapter headings, each related to the text in their own fashion.

The Bible was not simply a mediation of God's word, but also a material object which gave that word a real presence. The Czech word which signifies the ability to read (*čtení*) also signifies the Gospel (Ducreux 1989: 216; Tóth 2000: 83–5, 91–3).

Books (and writings of all kinds) were used in a symbolic and instrumental way. A printed catechism may have had a different importance for a person who could read it than it did for someone who simply heard and repeated what was in it. Oaths on a Bible depended more on what the Bible symbolised than what it contained, and the cross which usually adorned the front of any large edition might be the sole focus of veneration for an illiterate peasant. In all European countries, the Bible's cultural significance went far beyond its textual content. Revered as the touchstone of the Protestant Reformation, it was used as an icon, a talisman, for social display, to cure illness, find lost goods and even forecast the names of future lovers. Martin Martin recorded in his 1703 account of a journey in the Highlands and Islands of Scotland that on Colonsay it was the custom to fan the faces of the sick with the pages of the Bible. Books were objects of awe, playing a role in eschatological expectations such as visions of the afterlife in which a 'Book of Life' is consulted to assess the soul's fate in Heaven or Hell. In sixteenth-century Italy, the legend of Santa Margherita was believed to possess healing powers and, if read out to or placed on the stomach of a pregnant woman, to help in childbirth. Books were useful gifts in sixteenth-century France because they were less loaded with meaning than flowers, animals or clothes (Cressy 1986).

These examples of oral-literate interaction point towards an important feature of communication in early modern Europe. Information could only travel as quickly as the human beings responsible for disseminating it. This is an important point about all communications before the advent of electrically transmitted signals, and one made by the famous media guru, Marshall McLuhan (1973). Until the nineteenth century, communication and human transportation were synonymous. Take the example of the fastest postal service in Europe, that for carrying diplomatic mail. The German Imperial postal service (with the post horn as a symbol of its monopoly from 1505) had already developed quite extensively by the time of the Thirty Years War. Competition from the posts of individual states produced an increasingly dense and frequent (if no quicker) network thereafter. Thurn und Taxis' imperial postal couriers did the journey from Augsburg to Venice in six days, two days faster than the town's official news service. There were few professional couriers and vital communication might rely on a chance meeting. Sir Edward Stafford, Elizabethan ambassador to France in 1584, saluted his queen in a letter posted 'out of an alehouse upon the river of Loire where I met with this bearer'. Crossing the Alps, other messengers might have to wear special studded boots. All had to avoid bandits and their country's enemies who might deprive them not only of their mail, but also of their lives (Allen 1972). In short, news usually travelled only as fast as a person on foot or horseback or in a boat. At its speediest, that meant perhaps 50 miles a day. Smoke signals, semaphore flags and pigeon posts were not fully developed until the nineteenth century. Other forms such as lighted beacons conveyed only one message: for example, that an invasion had occurred.

Sound was a rapid and potentially sophisticated means of communication. For example, the sound of bells communicated significant events, marked time, and provided a focus of communal or even national identity. Due to the need for bronze to make armaments, King Frederick I of Denmark issued a decree in 1528 calling for the confiscation of church bells, the first of several such confiscations between then and 1602. However, removing bells could also have a powerful political and religious impact. Lutherans were not opposed to bell ringing, but Calvinist iconoclasts of the sixteenth century and Jacobins of the 1790s smashed bells because they recognised their importance to French Catholic worship and community identity (Fouilheron 1976). Bells had their own language and were important for practical and symbolic reasons in a rich world of sound.

Sound played an important role in early modern culture. Towards the middle of the seventeenth century, Franciscans in Bosnia and Herzegovina set up a seminary to compose folk songs so that spiritual messages could be propagated. Songs used simple images such as that of the holy family or stories about saints to popularise their activities (Hsia 1989: 101). Across the confessional divide, 'the hymn became an indispensable form of personal piety, the hymnal and hymn singing symbols of Lutheran confessional identity' (Hsia 1989: 107; Robinson-Hammerstein 1989: 141–71). The psalms were an evocative and expressive way of transmitting Calvinist ideas in mid-sixteenth-century France, and their singing became a symbol of what it meant to belong to the Reformed faith. Each psalm had a different tune, the sound of which was as stirring as its words. During the Wars of Religion (1562–98), Calvinist armies singing psalms struck fear into their Catholic opponents and singing hymns was regarded as clear evidence of Calvinist heresy by the Catholic authorities. Song was seen as so powerful that heretics condemned to die generally had their tongues cut out prior to execution.

The sung word has left tangible traces of its importance for the historian. A hymnbook, the *Graduale*, was to be found in seven out of ten Icelandic households in the mid-eighteenth century while Denmark's authorised hymn-book, produced in 1699 by Thomas Kingo, had been reprinted 90 times by 1771 (Guttormsson 1990: 14). All faiths recognised the power of song. Jewish communities in Venice, Amsterdam and Hamburg all (controversially) introduced choirs into their formal worship around 1600. Yet, because of their reverence for the spoken and printed word, and their rejection of drama as a means of conveying religious messages, Protestants placed particular emphasis on the ear (Crockett 1993). Calvin himself recognised that while his exegetical works would work well in print, his sermons (prolix and full of local references) relied far more on delivery and setting for their effect (Gilmont 1995).

Slow as a means of transmitting ideas – at least by modern standards – word of mouth was by no means inferior to the written or printed word where public opinion was concerned. The power of rumour and innuendo was considerable in small communities where an individual's reputation was vital to his or her social and economic welfare. It could also create vigorous climates of opinion on more momentous events. Oral transmission was at least as fast as written, and in the form of rumour and gossip it could be faster and more influential. Public opinion was formulated by discussion among people as they tried to make sense of conflicting accounts and interpretations of events.

The printed or written word might be more permanent than the spoken. For some purposes it might be more discreet, as in the case of anonymous denouncements of allegedly corrupt civic officials encouraged by the provision of letter drops in the shape of lion's heads in towns like Venice and Verona. What writing and print lacked was the speed of penetration and therefore the immediate impact of oral communication. Climates of opinion on current affairs were created locally, dependent on personal contact, attendance at sermons or participation in acts of protest such as religious iconoclasm or riots about over-taxation or grain shortages (Scribner 1984: 247). Formally trained discussants came from a tradition marked by 'literacy, learning, patronage and authority', whereas casual conversers were grounded in 'gossip, proverbial wisdom, dependency and subordination'. Gossip can be 'private communication of information' or 'dissemination of judgmental opinion', perhaps shading into malice: what in Hebrew is known as *lashon hara* – the tongue of the wicked.

Competing political, religious and military camps recognised the power of the pulpit in forming opinion. Indeed, in winning mass support for a cause, the voice of the clergy was often more powerful than the weight of printed propaganda. This was certainly the case in mid-seventeenth-century Scotland. The 'Scottish Revolution', a reaction to the religious changes proposed by Charles I's unpopular archbishop Laud, began in 1637. Between then and 1648 the Covenanters, as the reformers were called, presented a united front. In 1648 a more moderate, Royalist group called the Engagers broke away from the Presbyterian, pro-Parliamentary Covenanters embodied in the Kirk and its General Assembly. The Covenanters retained control of the pulpit and used it to deadly effect against the Engagers, whose only propaganda weapon was the pamphlet and the newspaper, which proved inadequate to win over the hearts and minds of the majority of Scots. Realising that they were losing the propaganda battle, the Engagers set up a committee to investigate 'the fittest way how the publict conditioun of the affaires of the kingdome and of our Armie may be weiklie represented to the kingdome'. Unfortunately for the Engagers, there was no better method than the weekly sermon and they were defeated soon after (Stevenson 1981).

Spoken communication was quick and economical, conveying meaning in a few words by the use of inflection, intonation, gestures and facial expressions. Collating and printing was time-consuming and most transactions of information in great centres of exchange like Amsterdam or Venice took place in personal conversations. Strangers and travellers must have played a vital part in disseminating information and ideas. This helps to explain ambivalent attitudes towards travellers. Village and town authorities adopted a suspicious and censorious attitude towards people who spread ideas which might foment fear and unrest. Individuals or communities might be apprehensive of a passing stranger as a potential robber, beggar or carrier of disease, but they might equally be eager for the news which a traveller could bring. Certain innkeepers made a business of collecting stories from travellers and selling them to publishers (Scribner 1984). In eighteenth-century Germany,

> if a stranger comes travelling through, he will generally show up at the *Spinnstube* in order to share his store of novelties, and if a newspaper reader came from the village into the room, he was hardly allowed to catch his breath. Even if he did not bring the newspaper with him to read out loud, he had to describe the latest events in exact details (Medick 1984: 334).

Speaking could be accompanied by other means of communication. Gesture can be any movement or state of the body or its parts, and can be voluntary (as in a bow) or involuntary (as in a blush). Gesture can substitute for speech. Generally it complemented (confirming or undermining) the spoken word. It symbolised and protected the dignity of the participants.

Some gestures, like looking down to indicate submission, seem timeless. More often, gesture was a subtle and changing language which varied considerably over both time and space, and between social groups and sexes. Samuel Johnson observed in the mid-eighteenth century that English etiquette books required updating every couple of generations. The existence of such guides is a reminder that learning the silent literacy of bodily gesture could be achieved through the equally silent products of written and printed literacy. During the early modern period a gulf developed between the relatively disciplined gestural culture of northern Europe and the more flamboyant south. Kissing on greeting went out of fashion in England during the sixteenth century. The shaking of hands probably did not come into general use until the eighteenth century (the gap was filled by bowing and hat doffing). At prayer or in social and business interactions, the importance of postures, attitudes, bearings, salutes and bows was great and increased during the Baroque period. Pupils at Jesuit schools in eighteenth-century Poland received training in posture and gesture (Bremmer and Roddenburg, 1991; Muir 1997).

The language of gesture (including facial expression) could be highly ·sophisticated. Even something as simple as a bow may have many components. Does one stand close to or far away from the person greeted; should the action be performed before, after, or simultaneously with the person greeted; how low does one bow; are the eyes averted or raised; in which position are the feet to be placed; what happens to the hands? It was not just the movement or posture which mattered, but when it was used and with whom which indicated politeness or rudeness, civility or its lack. At the other end of the spectrum, unstructured use of bodily movement – gesticulation – was a sign of mental derangement.

Other apparently mundane actions or artefacts need to be seen as part of the rich language of symbolism which characterised early modern communication. People did not dress simply to stay warm or decent. How they wore their hair (or wigs at certain periods) could make a statement about their social status and political affiliations. Similarly shop and house signs cannot be seen simply as advertising or navigation aids for the pre-literate. Instead they must be understood as a form of communication within an intimate communal referencing system, conveying symbolically information on status and politico-religious allegiances (Garrioch 1994). Sign and symbol complemented rather than substituted for literacy.

Gesture was the sole means of communication for some groups. A sixteenth-century Spanish Benedictine called Pedro Ponce de Leon was one of the first to attempt the education of the mute in lip-reading and talking.

Signing was not well regarded because verbal communication was seen as the highest form of achievement. It gave unique expression to the soul – God's gift to mankind. The French priest and educator Claude François Deschamps was one of those who argued that speech provided the only means of equipping the human soul with the abstract ideas essential to religion and morality. The deaf were often discouraged from using sign-language because gesture, which appeared to those unacquainted with its meaning to be gesticulation, was regarded as at best uncivilised and at worst sub-human. However, from the seventeenth century the use of manual gestures by deaf-mutes began to have its advocates. Intellectual fashions changed. Condillac and Diderot even argued that visible gesture was superior to speech because, far from being uniquely civilised, it was singularly natural and uncorrupted. Signing systems were in place by the early nineteenth century when a distinction could be made between 'natural' signs (*ad hoc*, individualised, and intuitive) and 'systems' which were codified and stan-dardised. Seen language could be as sophisticated as what was heard. The same came to be true of touch for the blind. Gall's Triangular Alphabet for the Blind competed in the early nineteenth century with the system of Louis Braille.

Chapter 10

＊ ～ ＊

CONCLUSION

Education was a medium through which social attitudes were conveyed and portrayed. Literacy for its part was at least as much an indicator of attitudes and opportunities created by social, economic, cultural and political factors as it was an independent force for change. The ways in which education and literacy developed in the early modern period were complex and contingent on a wide variety of circumstances. Certain features were common to all parts of Europe and bear witness to the superficial similarity between the social organisation of the continent's diverse regions. Elementary education came out of two traditions: one was clerical and religious, concerned with the transmission of norms through reading; the other was commercial and focused on recording and transmitting in writing (Hébrard 1988). Men were everywhere more literate than women, the upper classes more literate than the lower, and towns generally enjoyed less illiteracy than the deeply rural environment in which most people lived. Educational provision improved across Europe between 1500 and 1800 and, partly as a result, so too did levels of literacy. A much larger proportion of the population could read and write in 1800 than had been the case three centuries before. Mass literacy existed in parts of north-western Europe. The uses to which literacy could be put had increased greatly. After the middle of the sixteenth century printed books became much more widely available in languages which ordinary men and women could understand, and literate ways of thinking and acting became more common. The control of secular authorities over education was growing and the presence of increasingly powerful states made demand for education and literacy more insistent, its organisation more uniform and structured. The fortunes of higher education were less clear-cut after *c.*1650. In some parts of Europe universities flourished, elsewhere they marked time or declined. Everywhere, their relationship with society changed, notably in providing certification for national populations rather than education for an international republic of letters. Books were the products and producers of their culture rather than simply literary documents, economic commodities, or technical artefacts.

Patterns there may be, but generalisations from them have to be made with caution. There is, for example, no simple and universal explanation of why men and women became more literate between the end of the fifteenth century and the start of the nineteenth. Schools were important to developments in France, England and part of the Netherlands. They were marginal to the advances made in some Scandinavian countries during the eighteenth century. Becoming literate was a complex process of schooling, self-learning and vocational training. Funding too made a difference to the availability of education to ordinary children. In Scotland and Baden in Germany, where taxation of landowners or the use of communal funds reduced the net cost of education to parents, literacy tended to be high. Yet comparable levels of signing can also be found in England where fees paid for most schooling. Protestants were usually more literate than Catholics in the sixteenth century, though the drive to christianise the masses and the competition generated by the great religious conflicts of the period were important in raising levels of basic reading and religious knowledge for all denominations. High levels of economic development seem to have created resources to spend on education in areas like Holland or the towns of northern Italy, alongside a demand for learning among the commercial and artisan classes. On the other hand, there were valleys in the Alpine parts of south-east France or northern Italy which, even by contemporary standards, were economically backward, but which had exceptionally high levels of literacy. A desire to improve their social and economic position through migration might explain this. Yet not all upland zones adjacent to more developed lowland ones were so blessed: Highland Scotland and the Pyrenees are examples. Illiterate zones generally had few schools, low demand for literacy, dialect or language differences, a dispersed or sparse population and limited economic development. Yet, trends in literacy cannot simply be attributed to schools, prosperity, environment or religion.

Just as the reasons for literacy differed between social groups and regions, so too did the implications of rising literacy for society and culture. Writing helped to objectify speech, fix it and extend communication over time and space, giving rise to more complex administrative forms which in turn help to integrate societies and further religious evangelism. By increasing the number of contacts an individual could have, writing and reading hastened the pace of life (Goody 1968: 1–2). Print and writing further aided the growing distinction between the natural, divine and human orders, enlarged the choice of literature and furthered both the intellectual and physical 'division of labour' in early modern Europe. Some communities were already at home with these implications by the Renaissance (Goody and Watt 1968: 62). In the cities of northern Italy, a 'literate mentality' was already present in the fifteenth century. In the rural south of Italy, Hungary and the Russian empire verbal communication remained dominant until the nineteenth or twentieth century. An extension of the ability to read and write sometimes helped slowly to replace oral forms as the culture of the masses, as in England, while in southern France it reinforced and enriched those forms.

Print could divide as well as unify European culture. When books were printed in Latin educated élites anywhere in Europe could read them, thus unifying intellectual life. Vernacular printing reached a wider audience, provided it was in a type-face they could decipher and a version of their own everyday tongue they could recognise. More languages were needed to gain access to what, in Latin, had been common intellectual property. Yet even in the eighteenth century, when vernacular publication expanded enormously, full understanding and enjoyment of scientific literature or the novel depended on high-quality education that was still restricted principally to men from the middling and upper classes. Basic literacy could provide a start for approaching such culture, but elementary reading and writing did not give automatic access to all the products of literacy. At the same time, the penetration of print and writing into everyday life could enrich experience. Arguably, oral culture allowed wider participation by individuals in forming the total cultural tradition. However, context and intention are as important to the extent of participation as they are with literate forms. For those interested in preserving arcane lore such as poetry, oral transmission had immense archaic value because its teaching could be confined to a few initiates.

Using literacy was as complex a process as getting it. The interaction between oral and literate forms, and the rich variety of oral culture does not mean that it had the same value as the culture of the book and the pen. Similarly, many people could afford literature, but one had to be a fluent reader with access to print culture to keep up with fashions in appreciation. Whatever the validity of oral culture, it was potentially different from literate culture and, from the eighteenth century onwards, that attribution of difference also became one of worth as oral forms were increasingly devalued in the west. 'Those who could not read lacked a crucial link in the chain of communication that connected public exhibition and performance to the printed column and the written manuscript, and both to the spoken realm of drawing-room conversation' (Brewer 1997: 94).

Literacy did not necessarily involve a change of attitudes since printing, reading and writing might simply fix existing ideas rather than offering new ones – even if the potential for innovation was considerable. Printing developed in phases and its influence was neither immediate nor continuous. Its huge potential took perhaps a century to be realised and it was arguably not fully developed until the eighteenth century. Printing created a vast reservoir of potential intellectual stimuli whose development depended on the social, intellectual and political circumstances. Its influence, like that of education, was slow, contingent and selective. In England there was no major shift from communal to individual forms of economic and social organisation between the fourteenth and seventeenth centuries. The spread of literacy merely offered a different medium of transactions. Contrast this with the Burgundy region of France where the power of the *seigneur* and communal life in the village and fields, previously determined by custom and memory, became fixed in written contracts and court records. Writing could fix dependency as well as creating possibilities for independence. Basic literacy conferred few material benefits to ambitious individuals and, in any case, inequalities of wealth and status were extensive enough in early modern societies to limit the advantages which modern societies expect to accrue to the literate. By itself, literacy does nothing. Just as literacy and individuality are commonly linked, so too are literacy and rationality, since the ability to read and write is said to break the mental mould of irrational custom. Printed texts offered a new view of the world during the seventeenth century, but they also provided a rationalisation and intellectualisation of witchcraft beliefs in the form of texts like Jean Bodin's *De la Démonomanie des Sorciers* (1586).

If literacy was used to strengthen and extend existing beliefs and attitudes, then its value as a liberator of minds should not be exaggerated. Education was designed to transmit set information and approved viewpoints. It could open up the possibility of transmitting new ideas, for example between members of religious or secular groups who questioned the existing structures of power and authority. The very act of individual choice of what was read was potentially subversive. Nevertheless it is hard to escape the conclusion that new ways of thinking and acting came about despite rather than because of education. Literacy might create new possibilities for thought and action, but that was not the direct aim of most forms of education. There were numerous theorists who wrote about education and there were developments in pedagogic practice. Yet those like the Piarists who tried to break away from the models established by groups like the Jesuits found themselves drawn back to existing methods.

For all the scholarly writing about education and literacy, there are still subjects requiring further research. For example, it might be more productive to analyse higher education as a whole rather than focusing on specific (élite) institutions, chartered as universities, which were in apparent competition with inferiors and pretenders. Student life is imperfectly understood. What made young men decide to study; what did they do outside the classroom (including involvement with riot and prostitution); how did they spend vacations or more prolonged intermissions in their studies; and what were their early years in the world of work like? Harvey Graff (1987: 5) has written that 'literacy was *formed*, *shaped*, and *conditioned* by the oral world that it penetrated', but interactions between oral, aural, visual and literate culture are still not fully appreciated. Both the timing and the process by which oral forms were superseded by written or printed ones remains to be identified and explained rather than simply asserted. Similarly, the relationship between minority languages and literacy needs to be charted more fully. In Provence and north-west Spain, it was literacy itself as much as the language of literacy which was devalued. Why did some social groups, communities or regions apparently value education more than others? The ways literate media were read and understood are still shadowy.

General texts are designed to make material accessible to non-specialist audiences in a straightforward way. This volume has hopefully succeeded in that task. The general features of education and literacy in the early modern period have lessons for understanding those aspects of modern life. Yet they also highlight the need to appreciate the complexity of historical experience. Patterns and trends there were, but also discontinuities, anomalies and contradictions. Ultimately, an awareness of the reasons why cultural characteristics differ from one country to another may prove more fruitful to an understanding of the present than a search for grand theories and interpretative frameworks which distort by simplifying. The study of education and literacy in early modern Europe shows how different meanings and understandings fit together to produce cultural characteristics, and it is that sense of context which history so perfectly provides.

BIBLIOGRAPHY

Adams, J. R. R., 1980, 'Reading societies in Ulster', *Ulster Folklife*, **26**: 55–64.

Addy, G. M., 1977, 'The first generation of academic reform in Spanish universities, 1760–1789', in Leith (ed.), 1977.

Adler, P. J., 1974, 'Habsburg school reform among the Orthodox minorities, 1770–1780', *Slavic Review*, **33**: 23–45.

Ajzensztejn, A., 1994, 'Jüdische Studenten an der Königsberger Universität zur Zeit Kants', *Nordost-Archiv*, **3**: 357–74.

Åkerman, S. *et al.*, 1979, 'Splitting background variables: AID analysis applied to migration and literacy research', *Journal of European Economic History*, **8**: 157–92.

Alexander, D. and Strauss, W. L., 1977, *The German single-leaf woodcut, 1600–1700*. 2 vols. New York.

Allen, E. J. B., 1972, *Post and courier service in the diplomacy of early modern Europe*. The Hague.

Alston, P., 1969, *Education and the state in Tsarist Russia*. Stanford.

Arnove, R. and Graff, H. J. (eds), 1987, *National literacy campaigns*. New York.

Art, J., 1980, 'Volksonderwijs in de Zuidelijke Nederlanden', *Algemene Geschiedenis der Nederlanden*, vol. 7. Haarlem.

Aston, T. H. (ed.), 1983, *Social relations and ideas. Essays in honour of R. H. Hilton*. Cambridge.

Astoul, G., 1992, 'L'alphabétisation en Haut-Languedoc au XVIIIe siècle: les aléas de la méthode Maggiolo dans le diocèse de Montauban', *Annales du Midi*, **104**: 175–194.

Astoul, G., 1994, 'Les protestants et leurs écoles dans le colloque de Bas-Quercy aux XVIIe et XVIIIe siècles', *Bulletin de la Société de l'Histoire du Protestantisme Français*, **140**: 183–207.

Astoul, G., 1996, 'L'instruction des enfants protestants et catholiques en pays Aquitains du milieu du XVIe siècle à la révocation de l'Edit de Nantes', *Histoire de l'Education*, **69**: 37–61.

Auty, R., 1977a, 'The Russian language', in Auty and Obolensky (eds), 1977.

Auty, R., 1977b, 'Russian writing', in Auty and Obolensky (eds), 1977.

Auty, R. and Obolensky, D. (eds), 1977, *An introduction to Russian language and literature*. Cambridge.

Bailey, C. R., 1977, 'Attempts to institute a "system" of secular secondary education in France, 1762–1789', in Leith (ed.), 1977.

Bainton, R. H., 1980, 'Learned women in the Europe of the sixteenth century', in Labalme (ed.), 1980.

Bajkó, M., 1977, 'The development of Hungarian formal education in the eighteenth century', in Leith (ed.), 1977.

Baker, D. N. and Harrigan, P. J. (eds), 1980, *The making of Frenchmen: current directions in the history of education in France, 1679–1979*. Waterloo, Canada.

Baldo, V., 1977, *Alunni, maestri e scuole in Venezia alla fine del xvi secolo.* Como.

Bárány, G., 1966, 'The awakening of Magyar nationalism before 1848', *Austrian History Yearbook,* **2**: 19–50.

Barber, G., 1981, 'Who were the booksellers of the Enlightenment?', in Barber and Fabian (eds), 1981.

Barber, G. and Fabian, B. (eds), 1981, *Buch und Buchhandel in Europa im achtzehnten Jahrhundert.* Hamburg.

Barker, H., 2000, *Newspapers, politics and English society, 1695–1855.* Harlow.

Bartnicka, K., 1973, 'Les activités de propaganda de la commission d'éducation nationale', *Przeglad Historyczny,* **54**: 518.

Barton, H. A., 1977, 'Popular education in Sweden: theory and practice', in Leith (ed.), 1977.

Baumann, G. (ed.), 1986, *The written word. Literacy in transition.* Oxford.

Becker, P. J., 1980, 'Bibliotheksreisen in Deutschland im 18. Jahrhundert', *Archiv für Geschichte des Buchwesens,* **21**: 1361–1534.

Becker-Cantarino, B., 1977, 'Joseph von Sonnenfels and the development of secular education in eighteenth-century Austria', in Leith (ed.), 1977.

Beckett, J. C., 1986, 'Literature in English, 1691–1800', in Moody and Vaughan (eds), 1986.

Benítez, M. P., 1997, 'Literacy in Spain: research approaches and recent publications', *Paedagogica Historica* **33**: 483–508.

Bennassar, B., 1982, *Un siècle d'or Espagnol, 1525–1648.* Paris.

Bennett, H. S., 1952, *English books and readers, 1475–1557.* Cambridge.

Bercé, Y-M., 1976, *Fête et révolte. Des mentalités populaires du XVIe au XVIII siècle.* Paris.

Bernard, L., 1970, *The emerging city. Paris in the age of Louis XIV.* Durham, NC.

Beutler, C., 1973, 'Un chapitre de la sensibilité collective: la littérature agricole en Europe continentale au XVIe siècle', *Annales E.S.C.,* **28**: 1280–1301.

Bieńkowski, T., 1981, 'Wiedza o przyrodzie w Polsce XVI–XVIII wieku', *Rozprawy z Dziejów Oświaty,* **14**: 15–31.

Biller, P. and Hudson, A. (eds), 1993, *Heresy and literacy, c.1100–c.1530.* Cambridge.

Birn, R., 1981, 'La contrabande et la saisie de livres à l'aube du siècle des lumières', *Revue d'Histoire Moderne et Contemporaine,* **28**: 158–73.

Black, J., 1994, 'Continuity and change in the British press, 1750–1833', *Publishing History,* **36**: 39–85.

Black, J., 1997, *Maps and history: constructing images of the past.* London.

Black, J. L., 1977, 'Citizenship training and moral regeneration as the mainstay of Russian schools', in Leith (ed.), 1977.

Black, J. L., 1979, *Citizens for the fatherland. Education, educators and pedagogical ideals in eighteenth-century Russia.* New York.

Blanc, D., 1988, 'Les saisonniers de l'écriture: regents de villages en Languedoc au XVIIIe siècle', *Annales E.S.C.,* **43**: 867–895.

Bliss, A., 1976, 'The development of the English language in early modern Ireland', in Moody, Martin and Byrne (eds), 1976.

Blühm, E., 1985, 'Die ältesten Zeitungen und das Volk', in Brückner *et al.* (eds), 1985, 741–52.

Bödeker, H. E. and Hinrichs, E. (eds), 1999, *Alphabetisierung und Literalisierung in Deutschland in der Frühen Neuzeit.* Tübingen.

Bollème, G., 1965, 'Littérature populaire et littérature de colportage au 18e siècle', in Bollème, G., (ed.), *Livre et société dans la France du XVIIIe siècle, tome 1.* Paris.

Bollème, G., 1969, *Les almanachs populaires aux XVIIe et XVIIIe siècles.* Paris.

Bollème, G., 1971, *La bibliothèque bleue.* Paris.

de Booy, E. P., 1977, *De weldaet der scholen.* Haarlem.

de Booy, E. P., 1980a, 'Volksonderwijs in de Noordelijke Nederlanden', *Algemene Geschiedenis der Nederlanden,* vol. 7. Haarlem.

de Booy, E. P., 1980b, *Kweekhoven der wijsheid.* Zutphen.

Bordes, M., 1979, 'La réforme scolaire Sarde de 1729 dans le comté de Nice', *Annales du Midi,* **91**: 415–22.

Bottigheimer, R. B., 1993, 'Bible reading, "bibles" and the bible for children in early modern Germany', *Past and Present,* **139**: 66–89.

Bouyssy, M. T. (ed.), 1970, *Livre et société dans la France du XVIIIe siècle,* vol. 2. Paris.

Braida, L., 1990, 'Metamorfosi ed evoluzione di un genere letterario: l'almanacco Piemontese nel '700', *Mélanges de l'Ecole Française de Rome. Italie et Méditerranée,* **102**: 321–51.

Brancolini, J. and Bouyssy, M. T., 1970, 'La vie provinciale du livre à la fin de l'ancien régime', in Bouyssy (ed.), 1970.

Bremmer, J. and Roodenburg, H. (eds), 1991, *A cultural history of gesture from antiquity to the present day.* Cambridge.

Brewer, J., 1997, *The pleasures of the imagination. English culture in the eighteenth century.* London.

Bridgman, A., 1977, 'Aspects of education in eighteenth-century utopias', in Leith (ed.), 1977.

Brockliss, L. W. B., 1978, 'Patterns of attendance at the university of Paris, 1400–1800', *Historical Journal,* **21**: 503–44.

Brockliss, L. W. B., 1987, *French higher education in the seventeenth and eighteenth centuries.* Oxford.

Brooks, J., 1985, *When Russia learned to read. Literacy and popular culture, 1861–1917.* Princeton.

Brown, J. C., 1982, *In the shadow of Florence. Provincial society in Renaissance Pescia.* Oxford.

Brückner, W., Blickle, P. and Breuer, D. (eds), 1985, *Literatur und Volk im 17. Jahrhundert. Probleme populärer Kultur in Deutschland,* vol. 2. Wiesbaden.

Brüggemann, S., 1988, *Landschullehrer in Ostfriesland und Harlingerland Während der ersten Preussischen Zeit (1744–1806).* Cologne.

Burian, P., 1970–71, 'The state language problem in old Austria (1848–1918)', *Austrian History Yearbook,* **6–7**: 81–103.

Burke, P., 1978, *Popular culture in early modern Europe.* London.

Burke, P., 1987, *The historical anthropology of early modern Italy.* Cambridge.

Burke, P. and Porter, R. (eds), 1987, *The social history of language.* Cambridge.

Butel, P., 1976, 'L'instruction populaire en Aquitaine au XVIIIe siècle: l'exemple de l'Agenais', *Revue d'Histoire Economique et Sociale,* **54**: 5–28.

Bylebyl, J. L., 1979, 'The school of Padua: humanistic medicine in the sixteenth century', in Webster (ed.), 1979.

Camic, C., 1985, *Experience and enlightenment. Socialization for cultural change in eighteenth-century Scotland.* Edinburgh.

Capp, B., 1979, *Astrology and the popular press. English almanacs, 1500–1800.* London.

Capp, B., 1985, 'Popular literature', in Reay (ed.), 1985.

Caravolas, J. A., 1995, 'Apprendre à parler une langue étrangère à la renaissance', *Historiographia Linguistica,* **22**: 275–309.

Carlino, A., 1994, 'Corpi di carta: fogli volanti e diffusione delle conoscenze anatomiche nell'Europa moderna', *Physis,* **31**: 731–69.

Carnie, R. H., 1965, 'Scottish printers and booksellers, 1668–1775: a study of source-material', *Bibliotheck,* **4**: 213–27.

Carrato, J. F., 1977, 'The enlightenment in Portugal and the educational reforms of the marquis of Pombal', in Leith (ed.), 1977.

Caspard, P., 1996, 'Pourquoi on a envie d'apprendre: l'autodidaxie ordinaire à Neuchâtel (XVIIe siècle)', *Histoire de l'Education,* **70**: 65–110.

Chartier, R., (ed.), 1989, *The culture of print. Power and the uses of print in early-modern Europe,* translated by L. G. Cochrane. Oxford.

Chartier, R., 1994, *The order of books: readers, authors, and libraries in Europe between the four-teenth and eighteenth centuries,* translated by L. G. Cochrane. Cambridge.

Chartier, R., 1995, *Forms and meanings: text, performance, and audience from codex to computer.* Philadelphia.

Chartier, R., Julia, D. and Compère, M-M., 1976, *Education en France du XVIe au XVIIIe siècle.* Paris.

Chevalier, M., 1976, *Lectura y lectores en España de los siglos XVI y XVII.* Madrid.

Chisick, H., 1981, *The limits of reform in the Enlightenment: attitudes towards the education of the lower classes in eighteenth-century France.* Princeton.

Chojnacki, S., 1974, 'Continuity and discontinuity in Italian culture, 1300–1800', *History of Education Quarterly,* **14**: 533–41.

Cholvy, G., 1980, 'Une école des pauvres au debut du 19e siècle: "pieuses filles", béates ou soeurs des campagnes', in Baker and Harrigan (eds), 1980.

Choppin, A., 1980, 'L'histoire des manuels scolaires: une approche globale', *Histoire de l'Education,* **9**: 1–25.

Chrisman, M. U., 1982, *Lay culture, learned culture. Books and social change in Strasbourg, 1480–1599.* New Haven.

Cipolla, C. M., 1969, *Literacy and development in the west.* Harmondsworth.

Cipolla, C. M., 1972, 'The diffusion of innovations in early modern Europe', *Comparative Studies in Society and History,* **14**: 46–52.

Claeyssen, M., 1980, 'L'enseignement de la lecture au 18e siècle', in Baker and Harrigan (eds), 1980.

Clark, P., 1983, 'Visions of the urban community: antiquarians and the English city before 1800', in Fraser, D. and Sutcliffe, A. (eds), 1983, *The pursuit of urban history.* London.

Cohen, P. C., 1999, *A calculating people. The spread of numeracy in early America.* London (first edition 1982).

Compère, M-M., 1995, *L'histoire de l'éducation en Europe. Essai comparatif sur la façon dont elle s'écrit.* Paris.

Compère, M-M. and Pralon-Julia, D., 1990, 'Les exercices latins au collège Louis-le-Grand vers 1720,' *Histoire de l'Education*, **46**: 5–51.

Corvisier, A., 1979, *Armies and societies in Europe, 1494–1789*. Bloomington.

Craig, J. E., 1981, 'The expansion of education', *Review of Research in Education*, **9**: 151–213.

Cranfield, G. A., 1978, *The press and society: from Caxton to Northcliffe*. London.

Cressy, D., 1980, *Literacy and the social order*. Cambridge.

Cressy, D., 1986, 'Books as totems in seventeenth-century England and New England', *Journal of Library History*, **21**: 92–106.

Crockett, B., 1993, '"Holy cozenage" and the Renaissance cult of the ear', *Sixteenth Century Journal*, **24**: 47–65.

Croix, A., 1981, *La Bretagne aux 16e et 17e siècle*, vol. 2. Paris.

Csáky, M., 1978, 'Von der Ratio Educationis zur educatio nationalis', in Klingenstein *et al.* (eds), 1978.

Cullen, L. M., 1980, 'The social and cultural modernisation of Ireland, 1600–1900', in Cullen, L. M. and Furet, F. (eds), 1980, *Ireland and France, 17th–20th centuries. Towards a comparative study of rural history*. Paris.

Dahl, S., 1959, 'Travelling pedlars in nineteenth century Sweden', *Scandinavian Economic History Review*, **7**: 167–78.

de Dainville, F., 1957, 'Collèges et frequentation scolaire au XVIIe siècle', *Population*, **12**: 467–94.

Daly, M. and Dickson, D. (eds), 1990, *The origins of popular literacy in Ireland: language change and educational development, 1700–1920*. Dublin.

Darnton, R., 1971, 'Reading, writing and publishing in eighteenth-century France', *Daedalus*, **100**: 214–56.

Darnton, R., 1976, 'Trade in the taboo: the life of a clandestine book dealer in pre-revolutionary France', in Korshin (ed.), 1976.

Darnton, R., 1984, 'The great cat massacre, 1730', *History Today*, **34**: 7–15.

Darnton, R., 1985, *The great cat massacre and other episodes in French cultural history*. Harmondsworth.

Darnton, R., 1986, 'First steps towards a history of reading', *Australian Journal of French Studies*, **23**: 5–30.

Darnton, R., 1989, 'Toward a history of reading', *Wilson Quarterly*, **13**: 86–102.

Daston, L. J., 1988, *Classical probability in the Enlightenment*. Princeton.

Daston, L. J., 1994, 'Enlightenment calculations', *Critical Inquiry*, **21**: 182–202.

Daumas, M., 1993, 'Manuels épistolaires et identité sociale (XVIe–XVIIIe siècles)', *Revue d'Histoire Moderne et Contemporaine*, **40**: 529–66.

Davies, J., 1983, 'A student library in sixteenth-century Toulouse', *History of Universities*, **3**: 61–86.

Davis, N. Z., 1975, *Society and culture in early modern France*. London.

Davis, N. Z., 1983, 'Beyond the market: books as gifts in sixteenth-century France', *Transactions of the Royal Historical Society*, 5th series, **33**: 69–88.

Dedieu, J-P., 1979, '"Christianisation" en Nouvelle Castille. Catéchisme, communion, messe et confirmation dans l'archevêché de Tolède, 1540–1650', *Mélanges de la Casa de Velazquez*, **15**: 261–94.

van Deursen, A. Th., 1978, *Het kopergeld van de gouden eeuw. Volkskultur.* Amsterdam.

Dixon, W., 1958, *Education in Denmark.* London.

Ducreux, M-E., 1989, 'Reading unto death: books and readers in eighteenth-century Bohemia', in Chartier (ed.), 1989.

Duggan, L. G., 1989, 'Was art really the "book of the illiterate"?', *Word and Image*, **5**: 227–51.

Duglio, M. R., 1971, 'Alfabetismo e società a Torino nel seculo XVIII', *Quaderni Storici*, **17**: 485–509.

Dunn, P. P., 1976, ' "That enemy is the baby": childhood in imperial Russia', in de Mause (ed.), 1976.

Durkacz, V. E., 1983, *The decline of the Celtic languages.* Edinburgh.

Eeckaute, D., 1970, 'A propos de la pédagogie en Russie au début du XIXe siècle', *Cahiers du Monde Russe et Soviétique*, **11**: 244–58.

Eisenstein, E. L., 1968, 'Some conjectures about the impact of printing on western society', *Journal of Modern History*, **40**: 1–56.

Eisenstein, E. L., 1979, *The printing press as an agent of change.* Cambridge.

Eisenstein, E. L., 1983, *The printing revolution in early modern Europe.* Cambridge.

Eisenstein, E. L., 1992, *Grub Street abroad: aspects of the French cosmopolitan press from the age of Louis XIV to the French Revolution.* Oxford.

Engelsing, R., 1973, *Analphabetentum und Lektüre.* Stuttgart.

Engelsing, R., 1974, *Der Bürger als Leser. Lesergeschichte in Deutschland, 1500–1800.* Stuttgart.

Ettinghausen, H., 1984, 'The news in Spain: *Relaciones de Sucesos* in the reigns of Philip III and IV', *European History Quarterly*, **14**: 1–20.

Evans, R. J. W., 1974, 'Humanism and counter-reformation at the central European universities', *History of Education*, **3**: 1–15.

Evans, R. J. W., 1979, *The making of the Habsburg monarchy, 1550–1700.* Oxford.

Evans, R. J. W., 1981, 'German universities after the thirty years war', *History of Universities*, **1**: 169–90.

Faber, J., 1980, 'Inhabitants of Amsterdam and their possessions, 1701–1710', in van der Woude, A. and Schuurman, A. (eds), 1980, *Probate inventories.* Utrecht.

Fabian, B., 1976, 'English books and their eighteenth-century German readers', in Korshin (ed.), 1976.

Fairchilds, C. C., 1976, *Poverty and charity in Aix-en-Provence, 1640–1789.* London.

Faragó, T., 1994, 'Seasonality of marriages in Hungary from the eighteenth to the twentieth centuries', *Journal of Family History*, **19**: 333–50.

Febvre, L. and Martin, H-J., 1976, *The coming of the book.* London.

Féliciangéli, D., 1980, 'Substrat éducatif dans le comté de Nice à l'arrivée des français en 1792', in Baker and Harrigan (eds), 1980.

Ferté, P., 1980, 'La géographie statistique du recruitment des anciennes universités', in Baker and Harrigan (eds), 1980.

Fienberg, S. E., 1991, 'A brief history of statistics in three and one-half chapters', *Historical Methods*, **24**: 124–35.

Fletcher, J. M., 1981, 'Change and resistance to change: a consideration of the development of English and German universities during the sixteenth century', *History of Universities*, **1**: 1–36.

Fouilheron, J., 1976, 'Légendaire et histoire: les cloches-monstres dans la psychologie collective à Mende et à Saint-Flour', *Revue d'Histoire Moderne et Contemporaine*, **23**: 321–53.

Fournel-Guerin, J., 1979, 'Le livre et la civilisation écrite dans la communauté morisque aragonaise', *Mélanges de la Casa de Velazquez*, **15**: 241–59.

Fox, A., 1989, 'Custom, memory and the authority of writing', in Griffiths, P., Fox, A. and Hindle, S. (eds), *The experience of authority in early modern England*. London.

Fox, A., 2000, *Oral and literate culture in England, 1500–1700*. Oxford.

Foxon, D., 1964, *Libertine literature in England, 1660–1745*. London.

François, E., 1977, 'Die Volksbildung am Mittelrhein im ausgehenden 18. Jahrhundert: eine Untersuchung über den vermeintlichen "Bildungsrückstand" der katholischen Bevölkerung Deutschlands im Ancien Régime', *Jahrbuch für westdeutsche Landesgeschichte*, **3**: 277–304.

François, E., 1982, 'Livre, confession et société urbaine en Allemagne au XVIIIe siècle: l'exemple de Spire', *Revue d'Histoire Moderne et Contemporaine*, **29**: 353–375.

François, E., 1986, 'Les Protestants allemands et la Bible: diffusion et pratiques', in Belaval, Y. and Bourel, D. (eds), *La siècle des lumières et la Bible*. Paris.

François, E., 1987, 'Publications récentes sur l'histoire de l'éducation en Allemagne de la fin du moyen age à la fin du XIXe siècle', *Histoire de l'Education*, **33**: 3–20.

Franklin, S., 1985, 'Literacy and documentation in early medieval Russia', *Speculum*, **60**: 1–38.

Freeze, G. L., 1974, 'Social mobility and the Russian parish clergy in the eighteenth century', *Slavic Review*, **33**: 641–62.

Friedrichs, C. R., 1979, *Urban society in an age of war: Nördlingen, 1580–1720*. Princeton.

Friedrichs, C. R., 1982, 'Whose house of learning? Some thoughts on German schools in post-Reformation Germany', *History of Education Quarterly*, **22**: 371–7.

Frijhoff, W., 1979, 'Surplus ou déficit? Hypothèses sur le nombre réel des étudiants en Allemagne à l'époque moderne (1576–1815)', *Francia*, **7**: 173–218.

Frijhoff, W., 1981, *La société néerlandaise et ses gradués, 1575–1815: une recherche sérielle sur le statut des intellectuels*. Amsterdam.

Frijhoff, W., 1995, *Wegen van Evert Willemsz., 1607–1647: Een Hollands weeskind op zoek naar zichzelf*. Nijmegen.

Frijhoff, W., 1996, 'Autodidaxies, XVIe–XIXe siècles: jalons pur la construction d'un objet historique', *Histoire de l'Education*. **70**: 5–27.

Frijhoff, W. and Julia, D., 1976, 'L'éducation des riches. Deux pensionnats: Belley et Grenoble', *Cahiers d'Histoire*, **21**: 105–31.

Furet, F. and Ozouf, J., 1982, *Reading and writing. Literacy in France from Calvin to Jules Ferry*. Cambridge.

Fussell, G. E., 1932, 'Early farming journals', *Economic History Review*, **3**: 417–22.

Gadd, F., 1981, 'Læse- og skrivekyndigheden indtil 1814, belyst ved det grønlandske materiale', *Ur Nordisk Kulturhistoria. Studia Historica Jyväskyläensiä*, **22**: 73–86.

Gadd, F., 1985, 'Læse- og skrivekyndigheden i 1700- og 1800- tallet indtil 1880. Grønland', in Skovgaard-Petersen (ed.), 1985.

Galenson, D., 1979, 'Literacy and the social origins of some early Americans', *Historical Journal*, **22**: 75–91.

Galenson, D., 1981, 'Literacy and age in pre-industrial England: quantitative evidence and implications', *Economic Development and Cultural Change*, **29**: 813–29.

Garden, M., 1976, 'Ecoles et maîtres: Lyon au XVIIIe siècle', *Cahiers d'Histoire*, **21**: 133–56.

Garrioch, D., 1994, 'House names, shop signs and social organization in western European cities, 1500–1900', *Urban History*, **21**: 20–48.

Gawthrop, R. and Strauss, G., 1984, 'Protestantism and literacy in early modern Germany', *Past and Present*, **104**: 31–55.

Georgelin, J., 1978, *Venise au siècle des lumières*. Paris.

Gibbs, C. G., 1971, 'The role of the Dutch republic as the intellectual entrepot of Europe in the seventeenth and eighteenth centuries', *Bijdragen en Mededelingen . . . der Nederlanden*, **86**: 323–49.

Gilmont, J-F., 1995, 'Les sermons de Calvin: de l'oral à l'imprimé', *Bulletin de la Société de l'Histoire du Protestantisme Français*, **141**: 145–162.

Ginzburg, C., 1980, *The cheese and the worms*. London.

Gold, C., 1977, 'Educational reform in Denmark, 1784–1814', in Leith (ed.), 1977.

Goldthwaite, R., 1972, 'Schools and teachers of commercial arithmetic in Renaissance Florence', *Journal of European Economic History*, **1**: 418–33.

Goldthwaite, R., 1980, *The building of Renaissance Florence*. Baltimore and London.

Goody, J. (ed.), 1968, *Literacy in traditional societies*. Cambridge.

Goody, J. and Watt, I., 1968, 'The consequences of literacy', in Goody (ed.), 1968.

Goulemot, J. M., 1994, *Forbidden texts: erotic literature and its readers in eighteenth-century France*, translated by J. Simpson. Philadelphia.

Graff, H. J. (ed.), 1981, *Literacy and social development in the west: a reader*. Cambridge.

Graff, H. J. 1987, *Legacies of literacy. Continuities and contradictions in western culture and society*. Bloomington.

Grafton, A. and Jardine, L., 1986, *From humanism to the humanities. Education and the liberal arts in fifteenth- and sixteenth-century Europe*. London.

Grambo, R., 1977, 'Folkloristic research in Norway, 1945–76', *Norveg*, **20**: 221–86.

Grambo, R., 1983, 'Folkloristic research in Norway, 1977–1982', *Norveg*, **26**: 107–55.

Granet-Abisset, A-M., 1996, 'Entre autodidaxie et scolarisation: les Alpes briançon-naise', *Histoire de l'Education*, **70**: 111–41.

Green, I., 1996, *The Christian's ABC. Catechisms and catechizing in England c.1530–1740*. Oxford.

Green, L., 1979, 'The education of women in the Reformation', *History of Education Quarterly*, **19**: 93–116.

Grendler, P. F., 1975, 'The Roman inquisition and the Venetian press, 1540–1605', *Journal of Modern History*, **47**: 48–65.

Grendler, P. F., 1977, *The Roman inquisition and the Venetian press, 1540–1605*. Princeton.

Grendler, P. F., 1989, *Schooling in Renaissance Italy: literacy and learning, 1300–1600*. Baltimore.

Grendler, P. F., 1990, 'Schooling in western Europe', *Renaissance Quarterly*, **43**: 775–787.

Grevet, R., 1985, 'L'alphabétisation urbaine sous l'ancien régime: l'exemple de Saint-Omer (fin XVIIe début XIXe siècle)', *Revue du Nord*, **67**: 609–32.

Grobelak, L., 1979, 'Les premises de l'enseignement du français en Pologne aux XVIe–XVIIe siècles', *Acta Poloniae Historica*, **40**: 175–82.

Groenveld, S., 1987, 'The Mecca of authors? State assemblies and censorship in the seventeenth-century Dutch republic', in Duke, A. A. and Tamse, C. A., (eds), *Too mighty to be free: censorship and the press in Britain and the Netherlands*. The Hague.

Grosperrin, B., 1976, 'Faut-il instruire le peuple? La réponse des physiocrates', *Cahiers d'Histoire*, **21**: 157–69.

Gutton, J-P., 1970, *La société et les pauvres. L'exemple de la généralité de Lyon, 1534–1789*. Paris.

Guttormsson, L., 1981, 'Læsfærdighed og folkeuddannelse, 1540–1800', *Ur Nordisk Kulturhistoria. Studia Historica Jyväskyläensiä*, **22**: 123–92.

Gutturmsson, L., 1985, 'Skrivefærdighed i et skoleløst samfund (*ca*.1800–1880)', in Skovgaard-Petersen (ed.), 1985.

Guttormsson, L., 1990, 'The development of popular religious literacy in the seventeenth and eighteenth centuries', *Scandinavian Journal of History*, **15**: 7–35.

Hallgrímsson, H., 1925, *Íslensk Alþýðumentum á 18.öld*. Reykjavík.

Hanebutt-Benz, E-M., 1983, 'Studien zum deutschen Holzstich im 19. Jahrhundert', *Archiv für Geschichte des Buchwesens*, **14**: 581–1266.

Hansson, S., 1986, '1600-Talsalmanackan: Allemansbiblioteket?', *Lychnos*: 29–53.

Harris, J. R., 1985, 'Industrial espionage in the eighteenth century', *Industrial Archaeology Review*, **7**: 127–38.

Hébrard, J., 1988, 'La scolarisation des savoirs élémentaires à l'époque moderne', *Histoire de l'Education*, **38**: 7–58.

Heiss, G., 1978, 'Konfession, Politik und Erziehung', in Klingenstein *et al.* (eds), 1978.

Hermannsson, H. (ed.), 1914, 'The story of Griselda in Iceland', *Islandica*, **7**: 1–48.

Hermannsson, H., 1918, 'The periodical literature of Iceland down to the year 1874: an historical sketch', *Islandica*, **11**: 1–100.

Hermannsson, H., 1929, 'Icelandic manuscripts', *Islandica*, **19**: 1–80.

Hermannsson, H., 1958, 'The Hólar Cato. An Icelandic schoolbook of the seventeenth century', *Islandica*, **39**: 1–91.

Higonnet, P. L-R., 1980, 'The politics of linguistic terrorism and grammatical hegemony during the French revolution', *Social History*, **5**: 41–69.

Hills, H., 1996, 'Mapping the early modern city', *Urban History*, **23**: 145–70.

Hinrichs, E., 1982, 'Zum Alphabetisierungsstand in Norddeutschland um 1800: Erhebungen zur Signierfähigkeit in zwölf oldenburgerischen ländlichen Gemeinden', in Hinrichs, E. and Wiegelmann, G. (eds), *Sozialer und kultureller Wandel in der ländlichen Welt des 18. Jahrhunderts*. Wolfenbüttel.

Hofmeister, A., Prass, R. and Winnige, N., 1998, 'Elementary education, schools, and the demands of everyday life: Northwest Germany in 1800', *Central European History*, **31**: 329–84.

Horn, P., 1981, 'The contribution of the propagandist to eighteenth-century agricultural improvement', *Historical Journal*, **25**: 313–29.

Houdaille, J., 1977, 'Les signatures au mariage de 1740 à 1829', *Population*, **32**: 65–90.

Houston, R. A., 1985, *Scottish literacy and the Scottish identity*. Cambridge.

Houston, R. A., 1994, *Social change in the age of Enlightenment. Edinburgh, 1660–1760*. Oxford.

Houston, R. A., 2000, *Madness and society in eighteenth century Scotland*. Oxford.

Houston, R. A. and van der Heijden, M. P. C., 1997, 'Hands across the water: the making and breaking of marriage between Dutch and Scots in the mid-eighteenth century', *Law and History Review*, **15**: 215–42.

Houston, R. A. and Frith, U., 2000, *Autism in history. The case of Hugh Blair of Borgue*. Oxford.

Høyer, S., 1982, 'Recent research on the press in Norway', *Scandinavian Journal of History*, **7**: 15–30.

Hsia, R. Pó-Chia, 1989, *Social discipline in the reformation: central Europe, 1550–1750*. London.

Hufton, O., 1974, *The poor of eighteenth-century France*. Oxford.

Huppert, G., 1984, *Public schools in Renaissance France*. Urbana.

Hyde, J. K., 1979, 'Some uses of literacy in Venice and Florence in the thirteenth and fourteenth centuries', *Transactions of the Royal Historical Society*, 5th series, **29**: 109–28.

Isaievych, I., 1993, 'The book trade in eastern Europe in the seventeenth and early eighteenth centuries', in Brewer, J. and Porter, R. (eds), *Consumption and the world of goods*. London.

Jahns, S., 1995, 'Juristenkarrieren in der Frühen Neuzeit', *Blätter für Deutsche Landesgeschichte*, **131**: 113–34.

Jakobson, R., 1955, 'Ivan Fedorov's primer', *Harvard Library Bulletin*, **9**: 5–39.

Jenkins, G. H. (ed.), 1997, *The Welsh language before the industrial revolution*. Cardiff.

Johansson, E., 1981, 'The history of literacy in Sweden', in Graff (ed.), 1981.

Julia, D., 1970, 'L'enseignement primaire dans la diocèse de Reims à la fin de l'ancien régime', *Annales Historiques de la Révolution Française*, **200**: 233–86.

Julia, D., 1980, 'Les professeurs, l'église et l'état après l'expulsion des Jesuites, 1762–1789', in Baker and Harrigan (eds), 1980.

Julia, D., 1989, 'Selection des élites et egalité des citoyens. Les procédures d'examen et de concours de l'ancien régime à l'empire', *Mélanges de l'Ecole Française de Rome: Italie et Méditerranée*, **101**: 339–81.

Julia, D., Revel, J. and Chartier, R. (eds), 1986, *Les universités européenes du XVIe au XVIIIe siècle. Histoire sociale des populations étudiantes. Tome 1*. Paris.

Kaestle, C. F., 1976, '"Between the Scylla of brutal ignorance and the Charybdis of a literary education": elite attitudes towards mass schooling in early industrial England and America', in Stone (ed.), 1976.

Kagan, R., 1974, *Students and society in early modern Spain*. London.

Kagan, R., 1975, 'Law students and legal careers in eighteenth-century France', *Past and Present*, **68**: 38–72.

Kagan, R., 1986, 'Universities in Italy, 1500–1700', in Julia *et al.* (eds), 1986.

Kahan, A., 1985, *The plow, the hammer and the knout. An economic history of eighteenth-century Russia*. London.

Kaiser, T. E., 1983, 'The abbé de Saint-Pierre, public opinion and the reconstitution of the French monarchy', *Journal of Modern History*, **55**: 618–43.

Kamber, P., 1991, 'Enlightenment, revolution, and the libraries in Lucerne, 1787–1812', *Libraries and Culture*, **26**: 199–218.

Kamen, H., 1965, *The Spanish inquisition*. London.

Kamen, H., 1984, *European society, 1500–1700*. London.

Kaniewska, I., 1986a, 'Les étudiants de l'université de Cracovie aux XVe et XVIe siècles (1433–1560)', in Julia *et al.* (eds), 1986.

Kaniewska, I., 1986b, 'La conjuncture étudiante de l'université de Cracovie aux XVIIe et XVIIIe siècles', in Julia *et al.* (eds), 1986.

Karant-Nunn, S. C., 1990, 'The reality of early Lutheran education: the electoral district of Saxony', *Lutherjahrbuch*, **57**: 128–46.

Kaspar, J., 1972, 'Skolní Písmo v Cechách Letech, 1774–1932', *Sborník Národního Muzea v Praze. Rada C: Literárni Historie*, **17**: 57–86.

Keep, J. L. H., 1985, *Soldiers of the Tsar*. Oxford.

Kessler, W., 1976, 'Buchproduction und Lektüre in Zivilkroatien und -Slawonien zwischen Aufklärung und "nationaler Weidergeburt" (1767–1848)', *Archiv für Geschichte des Buchwesens*, **26**: 339–790.

Kintzinger, M., 1990, *Das Bildungswesen in der Stadt Braunschweig im hohen und späten Mittelalter*. Cologne.

von Klarwill, V., 1970, *The Fugger news letters*. Freeport, NY. (Reprints of 1924 and 1926 volumes.)

Klepikov, S., 1971, 'Russian block books of the seventeenth and eighteenth centuries', *The Papers of the Bibliographical Society of America*, **65**: 213–24.

Klingenstein, G., Lutz, H. and Stourzh, G. (eds), 1978, *Bildung, Politik und Gesellschaft*. Vienna.

Knight, K. G., 1985, 'Populärliteratur und Literaturgeschmack in den achtziger Jahren des 17. Jahrhundert', in Brückner (ed.), 1985.

Kohler, A., 1978, 'Bildung und Konfession', in Klingenstein *et al.* (eds), 1978.

Korshin, P. (ed.), 1976, *The widening circle. Essays on the circulation of literature in eighteenth-century Europe*. Pennsylvania.

Krukowski, J., 1979, 'Szkoły pokatne w Krakowie w okresie komisji edukacji narodowej', *Rozprawy z Dziejów Oświaty*, **22**: 69–82.

Krupa, M., 1981, 'Szkoła ludowa w Galicji w latach 1772–1790', *Rozprawy z Dziejów Oświaty*, **14**: 57–82.

Kuijpers, E., 1997, 'Lezen en schrijven: onderzoek naar het alfabetiseringsniveau in zeventiende-eeuws Amsterdam', *Tijdschrift voor Sociale Geschiedenis*, **23**: 490–522.

Kukk, H., 1982, 'Tartu university library through three centuries', *Journal of Baltic Studies*, **13**: 349–63.

van der Laan, H., 1977, 'Influences on education and instruction in the Netherlands, especially 1750 to 1815', in Leith (ed.), 1977.

Labalme, P. H. (ed.), 1980, *Beyond their sex. Learned women of the European past*. London.

Labarre, A., 1971, *La livre dans la vie Amiénoise du seizième siècle*. Paris.

Laget, M., 1971, 'Petites écoles en Languedoc au XVIIIe siècle', *Annales E.S.C.*, **26**: 1398–1418.

Langeli, A. B. and Toscani, X. (eds), 1991, *Istruzione, alfabetismo, scrittura. Saggi di storia dell'alfabetizzazione in Italia (secolo XV–XIX)*. Milano.

Langer, H., 1978, *The thirty years war*. Poole.

Laqueur, T. W., 1976, 'The cultural origins of popular literacy in England, 1500–1850', *Oxford Review of Education*. **2**: 255–75.

Larquié, C., 1981, 'L'alphabétisation à Madrid en 1650', *Revue D'Histoire Moderne et Contemporaine*, **28**: 132–57.

La Vopa, A. J., 1980, *Prussian schoolteachers. Profession and office, 1763–1848*. Chapel Hill, NC.

Lebrun, F., 1984, 'Le contenu idéologique de la littérature "populaire" du XVIe au XIX siècle d'après "L'enfant sage à trois ans"', in Croix, A., Jacquiart, J. and Lebrun, F. (eds), 1984, *La France d'ancien régime*, vol. 1. Toulouse.

Lehmann, H., 1985, 'Die Kometenflugschriften des 17. Jahrhundert abs historische Quelle', in Brückner *et al.* (eds), 1985.

Leith, J. A. (ed.), 1977, *Facets of education in the eighteenth century. Studies on Voltaire and the eighteenth century*, **167**. Oxford.

Le Roy Ladurie, E., 1974, *The peasants of Languedoc*. Urbana.

Lewin, P., 1977, 'The Ukrainian popular religious stage of the seventeenth and eighteenth centuries on the territory of the Polish commonwealth', *Harvard Ukrainian Studies*, **1**: 308–29.

Liebreich, A. K., 1985, 'Piarist education in the seventeenth century', *Studi Secenteschi*, **26**: 225–78.

Liebreich, A. K., 1986, 'Piarist education in the seventeenth century', *Studi Secenteschi*, **27**: 57–89.

Lindberg, S. G., 1981, 'The Scandinavian book trade in the eighteenth century', in Barber and Fabian (eds), 1981.

Lisboa, J. L., 1991, *Ciência e política*. Lisbon.

Litak, S., 1973, 'The parochial school network in Poland prior to the establishment of the Commission of National Education', *Acta Poloniae Historica*, **27**: 45–65.

Litak, S., 1978, 'Das Schulwesen der Jesuiten in Polen', in Klingenstein *et al.* (eds), 1978.

Litak, S., 1983, 'Z działalności szkolnej Michała Jerzego Poniatowskiego na Mazowszu', *Rozprawy z Dziejów Oświaty*, **25**: 15–36.

Longuet, Y., 1978, 'L'alphabétisation à Falaise de 1670 à 1789', *Annales de Normandie*, **28**: 207–23.

Lottin, A. *et al.*, 1983, *Etudes sur les villes en Europe occidentale. Milieu du XVIIe siècle à la veille de la révolution française. Tome 2. Angleterre, Pays-Bas et Provinces Unies, Allemagne Rhénane*. Paris.

Lottin, A. and Soly, H., 1983, 'Aspects de l'histoire des villes des Pays-Bas méridionaux et de la principauté de Liege', in Lottin *et al.* (eds), 1983.

Loubès, G., 1983, 'Ecoles en Gascogne centrale au XVe siècle', *Annales du Midi*, **95**: 309–20.

Lucchi, P., 1978, 'La Santacroce, il Salterio e il Babuino: libri per imparare a leggere nel primo secolo della stampa', *Quaderni Storici*, **38**: 593–630.

Lukasiewicz, D., 1996, 'Pruska szkola na Pomorzu Zachodnim w XVII–XVII W.: programy nauczania nauczyciele', *Przeglad Historyczny*, **87**: 1–31.

Luppov, S. P., 1981, 'Die Nachfrage nach Büchern der Akademie der Wissenschaften und nach auslandischen Veröffentlichungen in Petersburg und Moskau in der mitte des XVIII. Jahrhundert', *Archiv für Geschichte des Buchwesens*, **22**: 257–300.

Luttinen, R., 1985, 'Skrivkunnigheten i Finland fram till början av 1900– talet', in Skovgaard-Petersen (ed.), 1985.

McClelland, C. E., 1977, 'German universities in the eighteenth century: crisis and renewal', in Leith (ed.), 1977.

McClelland, C. E., 1980, *State, society and university in Germany, 1700–1914*. Cambridge.

MacInnes, J., 1950, 'Gaelic religious poetry, 1650–1850', *Records of the Scottish Church History Society*, **10**: 31–53.

MacKenney, R., 1987, *Tradesmen and traders. The world of the guilds in Venice and Europe, c.1250–c.1650*. London.

McLuhan, M., 1973, *Understanding media*. London.

MacLysaght, E., 1969, *Irish life in the seventeenth century*. Dublin, 3rd edition.

McMullen, N., 1977, 'The education of English gentlewomen, 1540–1640', *History of Education*, **6**: 87–101.

Macedo, J. Borges de, 1975, 'Livros impressos em Portugal no século XVI: interesses e formas de mentalidade', in *Arquivos do Centro Cultural Portugues*: 183–221.

Magalhães, J. P. de, 2000, 'Lire et écrire dans le Portugal d'ancien régime', *Paedagogica Historica*, **36**: 1–23.

Mah, H., 1991, 'Suppressing the text: the metaphysics of ethnographic history in Darnton's *Great Cat Massacre*', *History Workshop*, **31**: 1–20.

Majorek, C., 1973, 'Podręczniki komisji edukacji narodowej w aspekcie rozwiązań dydaktycznych', *Rozprawy z Dziejów Oświaty*, **16**: 69–140.

Malcolmson, R. W., 1981, *Life and labour in England, 1700–1780*. London.

Mamontowicz-Łojek, B., 1968, 'Szkoła artystyczno-teatralna Antoniego Tyzenhauza, 1774–1785', *Rozprawy z Dziejów Oświaty*, **11**: 36–98.

Mandrou, R., 1975, *De la culture populaire aux 17e et 18e siècles*. Paris, 2nd edition.

Marchesini, D., 1985, 'La fatica di scrivere. Alfabetismo e sottoscrizioni matrimoniali in Emilia tra settecento e ottocento', in Brizzi, G. P. (ed.), '*Il catechismo e la grammatica*', I: *istruzione e controllo sociale nell'area emiliana e romagnola nel settecento*. Bologna.

Marchesini, M., 1992, *Il bisogno di scrivere. Usi della scrittura nell'Italia moderna*. Bari.

Marco, J., 1977, *Literatura popular en España en los siglos XVIII y XIX. Una aproximación a los pliegos de cordel*. Madrid.

Marker, G., 1982, 'Russia and the "printing revolution": notes and observations', *Slavic Review*, **41**: 26–83.

Marker, G., 1990, 'Literacy and literacy texts in Muscovy: a reconsideration', *Slavic Review*, **49**: 74–89.

Markoff, J., 1986, 'Some effects of literacy in eighteenth-century France', *Journal of Interdisciplinary History*, **17**: 311–33.

Markussen, I., 1993, 'Kunne Jeppe påberget laese og skrive: laese- og skrivefaerdighed i Dansk og internationalt historisk perspektiv', *Jyske Historiker*, **62–63**: 24–42.

Markussen, I. and Skovgaard-Petersen, V., 1981, 'Læseindlærning og læsebehov i Danmark, ca1550–ca1850', *Ur Nordisk Kulturhistoria. Studia Historica Jyväskyläensiä*, **22**: 13–72.

Marques, A. H. de Oliveira, 1972, *History of Portugal*, vol. 1. New York and London.

Márquez, A., 1980, *Literatura e inquisición en España, 1478–1834*. Madrid.

Martel, A., 1938, *La langue polonaise dans les pays ruthènes, ukraine et russie blanche, 1569–1667*. Lille.

Martin, H-J., 1969, *Livre, pouvoirs et société à Paris*. Geneva.

Martin, H-J., 1978, 'The *bibliothèque bleue*', *Publishing History*, **3**: 70–103.

Martin, H-J., 1981, 'Livre et lumières en France. A propos de travaux récents', in Barber and Fabian (eds), 1981.

Marvick, E. W., 1976, 'Nature versus nurture: patterns and trends in seventeenth-century French child-rearing', in de Mause (ed.), 1976.

Maternicki, J., 1974, 'L'enseignement de l'histoire en Pologne au XVIIIe siècle', *Acta Poloniae Historica*, **29**: 161–79.

Mathias, P., 1975, 'Skills and the diffusion of innovations from Britain in the eighteenth-century', *Transactions of the Royal Historical Society*, 5th series, **25**: 93–114.

de Mause, L. (ed.), 1976, *The history of childhood*. London.

Maynes, M. J., 1979, 'The virtues of archaism: the political economy of schooling in Europe, 1750–1850', *Comparative Studies in Society and History*, **21**: 611–25.

Maynes, M. J., 1980, 'Work or schools? Youth and the family in the Midi in the early nineteenth century', in Baker and Harrigan (eds), 1980.

Medick, H., 1984, 'Village spinning bees: sexual culture and free time among rural youth in early modern Germany', in Medick, H. and Sabean, D. W. (eds), *Interest and emotion. Essays on the study of family and kinship*. Cambridge.

Medick, H., 1991, 'Buchkultur auf dem Lande: Laichingen, 1748–1820. Ein Beitrag zur Geschichte der protestantischen Volksfrömmigkeit in Altwürttemberg', in Bödeker, H. E., Chaix, G. and Veit, P. (eds), *Der Umgang mit dem religiösen Buch*. Göttingen.

Melton, J. H., 1988, *Absolutism and the eighteenth-century origins of compulsory schooling in Prussia and Austria*. Cambridge.

le Menn, G., 1985, 'Une "bibliothèque bleue" en langue Bretonne', *Annales de Bretagne et des Pays de l'Ouest*, **92**: 229–40.

Métayer, C., 1990, 'De l'école au Palais de Justice: l'itineraire singulier des mâitres écrivains de Paris (XVIe–XVIIIe siècles)', *Annales E.S.C.*, **45**: 1217–1237.

Meyer, J., 1974, 'Alphabétisation, lecture et écriture. Essai sur l'instruction populaire en Bretagne du XVIe au XIXe siècle', in *Actes du 95e congrès national des sociétés savantes. Histoire de l'enseignement de 1610 à nos jours*, vol. 1. Paris.

Millett, B., 1976, 'Irish literature in Latin, 1550–1700', in Moody, Martin and Byrne (eds), 1976.

Montanari, A. P., 1988, 'Gli almanacchi lombardi del XVIII secolo', *Annali della Fondazione Luigi Einaudi*, **22**: 43–95.

Moody, T. W., Martin, F. X. and Byrne, F. J. (eds), 1976, *A new history of Ireland, vol. 3. Early Modern Ireland, 1534–1691*. Oxford.

Moody, T. W. and Vaughan, W. E. (eds), 1986, *A new history of Ireland, vol. 4. Eighteenth-century Ireland*. Oxford.

Moore, C. N., 1985, 'Mädchenlektüre im 17. Jahrhundert', in Brückner *et al.* (eds), 1985.

Moore, C. N., 1988, *The maiden's mirror. Reading material for German girls in the sixteenth and seventeenth centuries*. Wiesbaden.

Moran, G. T., 1981, 'Conception of time in early modern France: an approach to the history of collective mentalities', *Sixteenth Century Journal*, **12**: 3–20.

Morgan, V., 1978, 'Approaches to the history of the English universities in the sixteenth and seventeenth centuries', in Klingenstein *et al.* (eds), 1978.

Muchembled, R., 1985, *Popular culture and elite culture in France, 1400–1750*. London.

Muir, E., 1997, *Ritual in early modern Europe*. Cambridge.

Muldrew, C., 1997, *The economy of obligation*. London.

Nalle, S. T., 1989, 'Literacy and culture in early modern Castile', *Past and Present*, **125**: 65–96.

Nalle, S. T., 1992, *God in La Mancha: religious reform and the people of Cuenca, 1500–1650*. Baltimore.

Nash, C. S., 1981, 'Educating new mothers: women and the enlightenment in Russia', *History of Education Quarterly*, **21**: 301–16.

Neugebauer, W., 1985, *Absolutistischer Staat und Schulwirklichkeit in Brandenburg-Prussen*. Berlin.

Nicholson, E. E. R., 1996, 'Consumers and spectators: the public of the political print in eighteenth-century England', *History*, **81**: 5–21.

Norberg, K., 1985, *Rich and poor in Grenoble, 1600–1814*. Berkeley.

Norden, W., 1980, 'Die Alphabetisierung in der oldenburgischen Küstenmarsch im 17. und 18. Jahrhundert', in Hinrichs, E. and Norden, W. (eds), *Regionalgeschichte – Probleme und Beispiele*. Hildesheim.

Norton, F. J., 1958, *Italian printers, 1501–20*. London.

Norton, F. J., 1966, *Printing in Spain, 1501–20*. Cambridge.

Novák, J., 1992, 'Prícny vylucnosti pouzívania obrazovych pecatí v starsej diplomatickej praxi', *Acta Universitatis Carolinae Philosophica et Historica*, **1**: 113–16.

O'Brien, G. M., 1970, 'Maria Theresa's attempt to educate an empire', *Paedagogica Historica*, **10**: 542–65.

Ó Ciosáin, N., 1997, *Print and popular culture in Ireland, 1750–1850*. London.

Ó Cuív, B., 1976, 'The Irish language in the early modern period', in Moody, Martin and Byrne (eds), 1976.

O'Day, R., 1982, *Education and society, 1500–1800*. London.

Ó Tuathaigh, M. A. G., 1980, ' "Early modern Ireland, 1534–1691": a reassessment', in Drudy, P. J. (ed.), 1980, *Irish studies, vol. 1*. Cambridge.

Ogilvie, S. C., 1986, 'Coming of age in a corporate society: capitalism, Pietism and family authority in rural Württemberg, 1590–1740', *Continuity and Change*, **1**: 279–331.

Okenfuss, M. J., 1973, 'Technical education in Russia under Peter the Great', *History of Education Quarterly*, **21**: 325–45.

Okenfuss, M., 1980, *The discovery of childhood in Russia. The evidence of the Slavic primer*. Newtonville, MA.

Ólason, V., 1982, *The traditional ballads of Iceland*. Reykjavík.

Olczak, S., 1974, 'Le réseau d'écoles paroissiales dans le diocèse de Poznan (première moitié du XVIIe siècle)', *Miscellanea Historiae Ecclesiasticae*, **5**: 323–6.

Olson, D. R. and Torrance, N. (eds), 1991, *Literacy and orality*. Cambridge.

Ong, W. J., 1986, 'Writing as a technology that restructures thought', in Baumann (ed.), 1986.

Overton, M., 1985, 'The diffusion of agricultural innovations in early modern England: turnips and clover in Norfolk and Suffolk, 1580–1740', *Transactions of the Institute of British Geographers*, new series **10**: 205–21.

Ovsyannikov, Y., 1968, *The lubok. 17th–18th century Russian broadsides*. Moscow.

Palmer, R. R., 1980, 'The central schools of the first French republic: a statistical survey', in Baker and Harrigan (eds), 1980.

Parker, D., 1996, 'Women in the book trade in Italy, 1475–1620', *Renaissance Quarterly*, **49**: 509–541.

Parker, G., 1979, *The Dutch revolt.* Harmondsworth.

Pelizzari, M. R. (ed.), 1989, *Sulle vie della scrittura. Alfabetizzazione, cultura scritta e istituzioni in età moderna.* Napoli.

Pelizzari, M. R., 2000, *La penna e la zappa. Alfabetizzazione culture e generi di vita nel Mezzogiorno moderno.* Salerno.

Perrel, J., 'Les écoles de filles dans la France d'ancien régime', in Baker and Harrigan (eds), 1980.

Perrot, J-C., 1981, 'Les dictionnaires de commerce au XVIIIe siècle', *Revue d'Histoire Moderne et Contemporaine*, **28**: 36–67.

Perry, M. E., 1980, *Crime and society in early modern Seville.* London.

Peset, M. and Mancebo, M. F., 1986, 'La population des universités espagnoles au XVIIIe siècle', in Julia *et al.* (eds), 1986.

Petrat, G., 1985, 'Der Kalender im Haus des Illiteraten und Analphabeten', in Brückner *et al.* (eds), 1985.

Petrucci, A., 1978, 'Scrittura, alfabetismo e educazione grafica nella Roma del primo cinquecento. Da un libretto di conti di Maddalena pizzicarola in Trastevere', *Scrittura e civiltà*, **2**: 163–207.

Petschauer, P., 1976, 'Improving educational opportunities for girls in eighteenth-century Germany', *Eighteenth Century Life*, **3**: 56–62.

Pettersson, L., 1996, 'Reading and writing skills and the agrarian revolution: Scanian peasants during the age of enclosure', *Scandinavian Economic History Review*, **44**: 207–221.

Phillips, C. R., 1977, 'Education in the service of the Spanish state', *History of Education Quarterly*, **17**: 345–51.

Pollock, L. A., 1983, *Forgotten children. Parent–child relations from 1500 to 1900.* Cambridge.

Popkin, J. D., 1989, *News and politics in the age of revolution: Jean Luzac's Gazette de Leyde.* Ithaca.

Popkin, J. D., 1990, *Revolutionary news: the press in France, 1789–1799.* Durham, NC.

Porter, R., 1982, *English society in the eighteenth century.* Harmondsworth.

Pośpiech, A. and Tygielski, W., 1981, 'The social role of magnates' courts in Poland (from the end of the 16th to the 18th century)', *Acta Poloniae Historica*, **43**: 75–100.

Potkowski, E., 1979, 'Écriture et société en Pologne du bas moyen age (XIVe–XVe siècles)', *Acta Poloniae Historica*, **39**: 47–100.

Poussou, J-P., 1993, 'La "méthode Maggiolo" et la mesure de l'alphabétisation du Sud-Ouest de la France à la fin du XVIIIe siècle', *Annales du Midi*, **105**: 209–223.

Poutet, Y., 1971, 'L'enseignement des pauvres dans la France du XVIIe siècle', *XVIIe Siècle*, **90–91**: 87–111.

Raine, J. (ed.), 1845, *Depositions and other ecclesiastical proceedings from the courts of Durham.* Durham.

Rappaport, S., 1983, 'Social structure and mobility in sixteenth century London, part 1', *London Journal*, **9**: 107–35.

Raun, T., 1979, 'The development of Estonian literacy in the 18th and 19th centuries', *Journal of Baltic Studies*, **10**: 115–26.

Raven, J., 1993, 'Selling books across Europe, *c.*1450–1800: an overview', *Publishing History*, **34**: 5–19.

Raven, J., Small, H. and Tadmor, N. (eds), 1996, *The practice and representation of reading in England.* Cambridge.

Reay, B., 1985, 'Introduction: popular culture in seventeenth-century England', in Reay (ed.), 1985.

Reay, B., 1985 (ed.), *Popular culture in seventeenth-century England.* New York.

Richardson, R. C. and James, T. B. (eds), 1983, *The urban experience: a sourcebook. English, Scottish and Welsh towns, 1450–1700.* Manchester.

De Ridder-Symoens, H. (ed.), 1996, *A history of the university in Europe. Volume II: universities in early modern Europe (1500–1800).* Cambridge.

Ries, P., 1982, 'Staat und Presse im 17. Jahrhundert in England', *Daphnis*, **11**: 351–75.

Ries, P., 1987, 'Der Inhalt der Wochenzeitungen von 1609 im Computer', in Blühm, E. and Gebhardt, H. (eds), *Presse und Geschichte, band II.* Munich.

Roberts, M., 1968, *The early Vasas. A history of Sweden, 1523–1611.* Cambridge.

Roche, D., 1998, *France in the enlightenment*, translated by A. Goldhammer. London.

Robinson-Hammerstein, H., 1989, 'Introduction: Luther and the laity', in Robinson-Hammerstein, H. (ed.), *The transmission of ideas in the Lutheran Reformation.* Dublin.

Rodriguez, M-C. and Bennassar, B., 1978, 'Signatures et niveau culturel des témoins et accusés dans les procès d'inquisition du ressort du tribunal de Tolède (1525–1817), et du ressort du tribunal de Cordoue (1595–1632)', *Cahiers du Monde Hispanique et Luso-Brésilien*, **31**: 17–46.

Rogers, P., 1972, 'Book subscriptions among the Augustans', *Times Literary Supplement*, 15 December 1972: 1539–40.

Rogers, P., 1985, *Literature and popular culture in the eighteenth century.* Brighton.

Roggero, M., 1992, *Insegnare lettere. Richerche di storia dell'istruzione in èta moderna.* Turin.

Roggero, M., 1994a, 'Le métier de maître d'école. Problèmes et transformations dans les états Italiens', *Paedagogica Historica*, **30**: 207–29.

Roggero, M., 1994b, 'Conti sulle dita, calcoli a penna: l'aritmetica elementare a fine settecento', *Studi Storici*, **35**: 1039–1060.

Roggero, M., 1996, 'Arithmétique populaire et arithmétique savante. Apprentissages et enseignement à la fin du XVIIIe siècle', *Paedagogica Historica*, **32**: 623–45.

Roggero, M., 1999, *L'alfabeto conquistato. Apprendere e insegnare nell'Italia tra sette e ottocento.* Bologna.

Ross, J. B., 1976, 'The middle-class child in urban Italy, fourteenth to early sixteenth century', in de Mause (ed.), 1976.

Rubio Franco, G. A., 1997, 'Educación femenina del Colegio de las Salesas Reales en el siglo XVIII', *Cuadernos de Historia Moderna*, **19**: 171–81.

Ruciński, H., 1974, 'La confrérie "litteraire" de Koprzywnica en tant qu'image de la structure sociale d'une petite ville dans les années 1694–1795', *Przeglad Historyczny*, **55**: 282–3.

Ruwet, J. and Wellemans, Y., 1978, *L'analphabétisme en Belgique (XVIIIe–XIXe siècles).* Louvain.

Saenger, P., 1989, 'Books of Hours and reading habits of the later middle ages', in Chartier (ed.), 1989.

Sallmann, J-M., 1989, 'Les niveaux d'alphabétisation en Italie au XIXe siècle', *Mélanges de l'Ecole Française de Rome: Italie et Méditerranée*, **101**: 183–337.

Saunders, D., 1985, *The Ukrainian impact on Russian culture, 1750–1850.* Edmonton.

Schenda, R., 1970, *Volk ohne Buch: Studien zur Sozialgeschichte der populären Lesestoffe 1770–1910.* Frankfurt.

Schenda, R., 1981, 'Alphabetisierung und Literarisierungsprozesse in Westeuropa im 18. und 19 Jahrhundert', in Herrmann, U. (ed.), *'Das pädagogische Jahrhundert': Volksaufklärung und Erziehung zur Armut im 18. Jahrhundert in Deutschland.* Weinheim.

Schenda, R., 1985, 'Orale und Literarische Kommunikationsformen im Bereich von Analphabeten und Gebildeten im 17. Jahrhundert', in Brückner *et al.* (eds), 1985.

Schilling, M., 1985, 'Das Flugblatt als Instrument gesellschaftlicher Anpassung', in Brückner *et al.* (eds), 1985.

Schmitt, C. B., 1974, 'The university of Pisa in the Renaissance', *History of Education*, **3**: 3–17.

Schofield, R. S., 1968, 'The measurement of literacy in pre-industrial England', in Goody (ed.), 1968.

Schubert, E., 1975, '"Bauerngeschrey". Zum problem der öffentichen Meinung im spätmittelalterlichen Franken', *Jährbuch für Fränkische Landesforschung*, **34/35**: 883–907.

Schulte, H. F., 1968, *The Spanish press, 1470–1966. Print, power, and politics.* Urbana.

Schutte, A. J., 1980, 'Printing, piety and the people in Italy: the first thirty years', *Archiv für Reformationsgeschichte*, **71**: 5–20.

Schutte, A. J., 1986, 'Teaching adults to read in 16th century Venice: Giovanni Antonio Tagliente's *Libro Maistrevolè*', *Sixteenth Century Journal*, **17**: 3–16.

Schutz, A. H., 1955, *Vernacular books in Parisian private libraries of the sixteenth century according to the notarial inventories.* Chapel Hill, NC.

Scribner, R. W., 1981, *For the sake of simple folk. Popular propaganda for the German Reformation.* Cambridge. Second edition, Oxford 1994.

Scribner, R. W., 1984, 'Oral culture and the diffusion of Reformation ideas', *History of European Ideas*, **5**: 237–56.

Seidler, G. L., 1977, 'The reform of the Polish school system in the era of the enlightenment', in Leith (ed.), 1977.

Shapiro, B. J., 1983, *Probability and certainty in seventeenth-century England.* Princeton.

Siddle, D. J., 1987, 'Cultural prejudice and the geography of ignorance: peasant illiteracy in south-eastern France, 1550–1790', *Transactions of the Institute of British Geographers*, new series **11**: 1–10.

Simmons, J. S. G., 1977, 'Russian printing', in Auty and Obolensky (eds), 1977.

Simone, R., 1978, 'Scrivere, leggere e capire', *Quaderni Storici*, **38**: 666–82.

Skovgaard-Petersen, V. (ed.), 1985, *Da menigmand i norden lærte at skrive – en sektionsrapport fra 19 nordiske historikerkongres, 1984.* Copenhagen.

Slack, P., 1979, 'Mirrors of health and treasures of poor men: the uses of vernacular medical literature in Tudor England', in Webster (ed.), 1979.

Šmahel, F., 1986, 'L'université de Prague de 1433 à 1622: recrutement géographique, carrières et mobilité sociale des étudiants gradués', in Julia *et al.* (eds), 1986.

Smith, A., 1979, *The newspaper. An international history.* London.

Smith, R. E. F., 1983, 'Time, space and use in early Russia', in Aston (ed.), 1983.

Smith, W. D., 1984, 'The function of commercial centers in the modernization of European capitalism: Amsterdam as an information exchange in the seventeenth century', *Journal of Economic History*, **44**: 985–1005.

Smout, T. C., 1982, 'Born again at Cambuslang: new evidence on popular religion and literacy in eighteenth-century Scotland', *Past and Present*, **97**: 114–127.

Soubeyroux, J., 1987, 'L'alphabétisation à Madrid aux XVIIIe et XIXe siècles', *Bulletin Hispanique*, **89**: 227–65.

Soubeyroux, J., 1998, 'L'alphabétisation dans l'Espagne moderne: bilan et perspectives de recherche', *Bulletin Hispanique*, **100**: 231–54.

Sporhan-Krempel, L., 1975, 'Das nürnberger Nachrichten- und Zeitungswesen', *Archiv für Geschichte des Buchwesens*, **25**: 999–1026.

Sprandel-Krafft, L., 1983, 'Über das Verhältnis von Autor und Druckherr in der Inkunabelzeit', *Archiv für Geschichte des Buchwesens*, **14**: 353–84.

Spufford, M., 1981, *Small books and pleasant histories. Popular fiction and its readership in seventeenth-century England*. London.

Steinberg, S. H., 1974, *Five hundred years of printing*. Harmondsworth edition.

Stephens, C. B., 1980, 'Belgorod: notes on literacy and language in the seventeenth-century Russian army', *Russian History*, **7**: 113–24.

Stevenson, D., 1981, 'Scotland's first newspaper, 1648', *The Bibliotheck*, **10**: 123–6.

Stone, L., 1964, 'The educational revolution in England, 1560–1640', *Past and Present*, **28**: 41–80.

Stone, L., 1969, 'Literacy and education in England, 1640–1900', *Past and Present*, **42**: 69–139.

Stone, L. (ed.), 1976, *Schooling and society*, Baltimore.

Stone, L., 1977, *The family, sex and marriage in England, 1500–1800*. London.

Strauss, G., 1978, *Luther's house of learning. Indoctrination of the young in the German Reformation*. London.

Strauss, G., 1980, 'The mental world of a German pastor', in Brooks, P. N. (ed.), 1980, *Reformation principle and practice. Essays in honour of A. G. Dickens*. London.

Sührig, H., 1979, 'Die Entwicklung der niedersächsischen Kalender im 17. Jahrhundert', *Archiv für Geschichte des Buchwesens*, **20**: 329–794.

Sührig, H., 1981, 'Kalender – zur Publizistik eines Massenkommunikations-mediums vom 18. bis 20. Jahrhundert', *Archiv für Geschichte des Buchwesens*, **22**: 207–56.

de Tapia, S. 1989, 'Nivel de alfabetizatión en una ciudad castellana del siglo XVI: sectores sociales y grupos éthnicos en Ávila', *Studia Historica: historia moderna. Homenage al profesor dr. Manuel Fernández Alvárez vol. 1*. Salamanca.

Tarkiainen, K., 1972, 'Rysstolkarna som yrkeskår, 1591–1661', *Historisk Tidskrift*, **92**: 490–522.

Thirsk, J., 1983, 'Plough and pen: agricultural writers in the seventeenth century', in Aston (ed.), 1983.

Thomas, D. M., 1979, 'Printing privileges in Spain', *Publishing History*, **5**: 105–26.

Thomas, K., 1986, 'The meaning of literacy in early modern England', in Baumann (ed.), 1986.

Thomas, K., 1987, 'Numeracy in early modern England', *Transactions of the Royal Historical Society*, 5th series **37**: 103–32.

Thomsen, N., 1982, 'Why study press history?', *Scandinavian Journal of History*, **7**: 1–13.

Tompson, R. S., 1977, 'English and English education in the eighteenth century', in Leith (ed.), 1977.

Toscani, X., 1993, *Scuole e alfabetismo nello stato di Milano da Carlo Borromeo all rivoluzione*. Brescia.

Tóth, I. G., 1989, 'L'alfabetizzazione in Ungheria (1600–1800)', in Pelizzari (ed.), 1989.

Tóth, I. G., 2000, *Literacy and written culture in early modern central Europe*. Budapest.

Trenard, L., 1977, 'Histoire des sciences de l'éducation (période moderne)', *Revue Historique*, **257**: 429–72.

Trenard, L., 1980, 'L'enseignement de la langue nationale: une réforme pédagogique, 1750–1790', in Baker and Harrigan (eds), 1980.

Trial, G. T., 1975, *History of education in Iceland*. Cambridge.

Tucker, M. J., 1976, 'The child as beginning and end: fifteenth and sixteenth century English childhood', in de Mause (ed.), 1976.

Tveit, K., 1981, 'Lesekunne og undervisning før folkeskolevesenet', *Ur Nordisk Kulturhistoria, Studia Historica Jyväskyläensiä*, **22**: 87–122.

Tveit, K., 1985, 'Skrivekyndighet i Norden i det 18. og 19. århundre. Norge', in Skovgaard-Petersen (ed.), 1985.

Urban, W., 1977, 'La connaissance de l'écriture en Petite Pologne dans la seconde moitié du XVIe siècle', *Przeglad Historyczny*, **68**: 257.

Urban, W., 1984, 'Sztuka pisania w województwie Krakowskim w XVII i XVIII wieku', *Przeglad Historyczny*, **75**: 39–80.

Van Roey, J., 1968, 'De correlate tussen het sociale-beroepsmilieu en de godsdienstkeuze te Antwerpen op het einde der XVIe eeuw', in *Sources de l'Histoire Religieuse de la Belgique*, Louvain.

Van Uytven, R., 1968, 'Invloeden van het sociale en professionele milieu op de godsdienstkeuze: Leuven en Edingen', in *Sources de l'Histoire Religieuse de la Belgique*, Louvain.

Van der Woude, A. M., 1980, 'De alfabetisering', in *Algemene Geschiedenis der Nederlanden*, vol. 7. Haarlem.

Vassberg, D. E., 1983, 'Juveniles in the rural work force of sixteenth-century Castile', *Journal of Peasant Studies*, **11**: 62–75.

Verberckmoes, J., 1999, *Laughter, jestbooks and society in the Spanish Netherlands*. London.

Viazzo, P. P., 1983, *Alagna Valsesia, una comunita walser*. Borgosesia.

Vierhaus, R., 1988, *Germany in the age of absolutism*, translated by J. B. Knudsen. Cambridge.

Vigo, G., 1972–73, 'Istruzione e società nel regno Italico. II caso di Vigevano (1806–1814)', *Bolletino della Societá Pavese di Storia Patria*, **22–3**: 125–39.

Vīksniņš, N., 1973, 'Some notes on the early histories of Latvian books and newspapers', *Journal of Baltic Studies*, **4**: 155–8.

Viñao, A., 1990, 'The history of literacy in Spain: evolution, traits, and questions', *History of Education Quarterly*, **30**: 573–99.

Viñao, A., 1993, 'La educación instituciónal', in Delgado Criado, B. (ed.), *Historia de la educación en España y América: la educación en la España moderna (siglos XVI–XVIII)*. Madrid.

Viñao, A., 1997, 'Aprender a leer en el antiguo régimen: cartillas, silabarios y catones', in Escolano Benito, A. (ed.), *Historia illustrada del libro escolar en Espana del antiguo régimen a la segunda rúpublica*. Madrid.

Viñao, A., 1998, 'Alfabetización e ilustración, diez años después (de las evidencias directas e las indirectas)', *Bulletin Hispanique*, **100**: 255–69.

Viñao, A., 1999, 'Alfabetización y primeras letras (siglos XVI–XVII)', in Castillo Gómez, A. (ed.), *Escribir y leer en el siglo de Cervantes*. Barcelona.

Vincent, D., 1981, *Bread, knowledge and freedom. A study of nineteenth-century working-class auto-biographers*. London.

Vogler, B., 1975, 'La politique scolaire entre Rhin et Moselle: l'exemple du duché de Deux Ponts (1556–1619)', *Francia*, **3**: 236–320.

Vogler, B., 1976, 'La politique scolaire entre Rhin et Moselle: l'exemple du duché de Deux Ponts (1556–1619)', *Francia*, **4**: 287–364.

Vogler, B., 1983, 'La Rhénanie', in Lottin *et al.* 1983.

Voss, V. B., 1980, 'Onderwijs en opvoeding: inleiding', *Algemene Geschiedenis der Nederlanden*, vol. 7. Haarlem.

Vovelle, M., 1975, 'Y a-t-il eu une révolution culturelle au XVIIIe siècle? A propos de l'éducation populaire en Provence', *Revue d'Histoire Moderne et Contemporaine*, **22**: 89–141.

Waquet, F., 1993, 'Au "pays de belles paroles". Premières recherches sur la voix en Italie aux XVIe et XVIIe siècles', *Rhetorica*, **11**: 275–92.

Ward, A., 1974, *Book production, fiction and the German reading public*. Oxford.

von Wartburg-Ambühl, M-L., 1981, *Alphabetisierung und Lektüre. Untersuchung am Beispiel einer ländlichen Region im 17. und 18. Jahrhundert*. Berne.

Watt, I., 1972, *The rise of the novel. Studies in Defoe, Richardson and Fielding*. Harmondsworth edition.

Watt, T., 1991, *Cheap print and popular piety, 1550–1640*. Cambridge.

Webster, C. (ed.), 1979, *Health, medicine and mortality in the sixteenth century*. Cambridge.

Weyrauch, E., 1985, 'Die Illiteraten und ihre Literatur', in Brückner *et al.* (eds), 1985.

Whittaker, D. J., 1984, *New schools for Finland. A study in educational transformation*. Reports from the institute for educational research, university of Jyväskylä, 352.

Wide, S. M. and Morris, J. A., 1967, 'The episcopal licensing of schoolmasters in the diocese of London, 1627–1685', *Guildhall Miscellany*, **2**: 392–406.

Wiles, R. M., 1976, 'The relish for reading in provincial England two centuries ago', in Korshin (ed.), 1976.

Williams, G., 1971, 'Language, literacy and nationality in Wales', *History*, **56**: 1–16.

Wiswe, M., 1975, 'Bücherbesitz und Leseinteresse Braunschweiger Bauern im 18. Jahrhundert', *ZAgrarGAgrarSoz*, **23**: 210–15.

Wiśniowski, E., 1973, 'The parochial school system in Poland towards the close of the middle ages', *Acta Poloniae Historica*, **27**: 29–43.

Wiśniowski, E. and Litak, S., 1974, 'L'enseignement paroissial en Pologne jusqu'au XVIIIe siècle à la lumière des plus récentes recherches', *Miscellanea Historiae Ecclesiasticae*, **5**: 320–23.

Wood, A., 1999, 'Custom and the social organisation of writing in early modern England', *Transactions of the Royal Historical Society*, 6th series **9**: 257–69.

Wood, M. W., 1981, 'Paltry peddlers or essential merchants? Women in the distributive trades in early modern Nuremberg', *Sixteenth-Century Journal*, **12**: 3–14.

Woolf, D. R., 1986, 'Speech, text, and time: the sense of hearing and the sense of the past in Renaissance England', *Albion*, **18**: 159–94.

Wrightson, K., 1982, *English society, 1580–1680*. London.

Wyczanski, A., 1974, 'L'alphabétisation et structure sociale en Pologne au XVIe siècle', *Annales E.S.C.*, **29**: 705–13.

INDEX

Lightning Source UK Ltd.
Milton Keynes UK
UKHW021104141019
351577UK00009B/2421/P